# Introduction to C++ for
# Financial Engineers

# Introduction to C++ for Financial Engineers

## An object-oriented approach

### Daniel J. Duffy

John Wiley & Sons, Ltd

Published by          John Wiley & Sons Ltd, The Atrium, Southern Gate, Chichester,
                      West Sussex PO19 8SQ, England

                      Telephone    (+44) 1243 779777

Email (for orders and customer service enquiries): cs-books@wiley.co.uk
Visit our Home Page on www.wiley.com

*Other Wiley Editorial Offices*

John Wiley & Sons Inc., 111 River Street, Hoboken, NJ 07030, USA

Jossey-Bass, 989 Market Street, San Francisco, CA 94103-1741, USA

Wiley-VCH Verlag GmbH, Boschstr. 12, D-69469 Weinheim, Germany

John Wiley & Sons Australia Ltd, 42 McDougall Street, Milton, Queensland 4064, Australia

John Wiley & Sons (Asia) Pte Ltd, 2 Clementi Loop #02-01, Jin Xing Distripark, Singapore 129809

John Wiley & Sons Canada Ltd, 6045 Freemont Blvd, Mississauga, ONT, L5R 4J3, Canada

Wiley also publishes its books in a variety of electronic formats. Some content that appears
in print may not be available in electronic books.

*Library of Congress Cataloging-in-Publication Data*

Duffy, Daniel J.
   Introduction to C++ for financial engineers : an object-oriented approach / Daniel J Duffy.
       p.   cm.—(Wiley finance series)
   Includes bibliographical references and index.
   ISBN-13: 978-0-470-01538-4 (cloth: alk. paper)
   ISBN-10: 0-470-01538-1 (cloth : alk. paper)
   1. Financial engineering—Computer programs.   2. C++ (Computer program
language)   I. Title.
HG176.7.D843 2006
005.13′3024332—dc22                                        2006020622

*British Library Cataloguing in Publication Data*

A catalogue record for this book is available from the British Library

ISBN 13 978-0-470-01538-4 (HB)
ISBN 10 0-470-01538-1 (HB)

Typeset in 10/12pt Times by TechBooks, New Delhi, India
Printed and bound in Great Britain by Antony Rowe Ltd, Chippenham, Wiltshire
This book is printed on acid-free paper responsibly manufactured from sustainable forestry
in which at least two trees are planted for each one used for paper production.

# Contents

# 0
## Goals of this Book and Global Overview

### 0.1 WHAT IS THIS BOOK?

The goal of this book is to introduce the reader to the C++ programming language and its applications to the field of Quantitative Finance. It is a self-contained introduction to the syntax of C++ in combination with its applications to current topics of interest. In particular, we develop libraries, frameworks and applications for a variety of derivatives models using numerical methods such as binomial and trinomial trees, finite difference methods (FDM) and the Monte Carlo (MC) method.

The book consists of three major parts. The first part concentrates on essential C++ syntax that must be learned before proceeding. The second part introduces generic programming and design pattern techniques and we show how to create libraries and data structures that we use in part three that deals with full applications. We also have written a number of chapters on topics related to the current book, for example a review of the C language, interfacing with Excel and an introduction to the Component Object Model (COM).

This book is a thorough introduction to C++ and how to use it to write non-trivial and robust applications in Quantitative Finance. Some special features of the book are:

- A full discussion of C++ syntax (as described in Stroustrup, 1997)
- Advanced topics in C++: memory management, exceptions, templates and RTTI
- An introduction to data structures and Complexity Analysis
- The Standard Template Library (STL) and its applications to Quantitative Finance
- Introduction to Design Patterns and integration into Quantitative Finance applications
- Creating real applications for derivative pricing
- **Working** source code for all chapters and applications
- Exercises for every chapter

After having read this book, studied the code and done the exercises you will be in a position to appreciate how to use C++ for Quantitative Finance.

### 0.2 WHY HAS THIS BOOK BEEN WRITTEN?

We have written this book for a number of reasons. First, in our opinion there are very few books on C++ that teach the language and apply it to interesting and non-trivial problems in Quantitative Finance. This book assumes no knowledge of C++ nor do we assume that the reader is conversant with the C programming language. The first ten chapters of the book introduce the major syntax elements that you will need in order to write C++ applications.

The second reason was to show how to apply C++ to writing flexible and robust applications using an appropriate combination of the object, generic and functional programming models. Furthermore, we apply design patterns and established frameworks to help create extendible applications.

Finally, seeing that C++ is an important language in the financial world we have included exercises, questions and projects at the end of each chapter. We advise the reader to answer these questions and implement the exercises and projects because the best way to learn C++ is by doing it. It is our feeling (and hope) that you will then be able to face job interviews with confidence.

## 0.3   FOR WHOM IS THIS BOOK INTENDED?

We have written this book for quantitative analysts, designers and other professionals who are involved in developing front office and trading systems. The book is structured in such a way that both novice and experienced developers can use it to write applications in Quantitative Finance.

The book is also suitable for university students in finance, mathematics and other disciplines where C++ is used as the language for computation.

## 0.4   WHY SHOULD I READ THIS BOOK?

This is the first book (in our opinion) that attempts to give a complete overview of C++ and some of its applications to Quantitative Finance. We employ modern design and programming techniques to create flexible and robust software. Finally, we provide the reader with working source code in this book.

## 0.5   THE STRUCTURE OF THIS BOOK

The book is divided into four major sections with each section devoted to one major focus of attention. The sections are:

Part I: C++ Essential Skills
Part II: Data Structures, Templates and Patterns
Part III: Quantitative Finance Applications
Part IV: Background Information

Each part represents a level of C++ expertise. If you learn Part I you will receive a green belt, completing Part II entitles you to brown belt grade and if you learn the contents of Part III you may then call yourself a black belt.

An overview of the contents of this book is given in Chapter 21.

I would like to thank **Dr Joerg Kienitz** for his willingness to write a chapter in this book on the Monte Carlo method.

## 0.6   WHAT THIS BOOK DOES NOT COVER

This book is about C++ syntax and its applications to Quantitative Finance. It uses a number of concepts and techniques that are discussed elsewhere in more detail. Thus, this book is not:

- an introduction to Quantitative Finance (see Hull, 2006)
- an introduction to numerical methods (see Duffy, 2006)
- advanced C++ programming and Excel AddIn interfacing (see Duffy, 2004)

The source code on the CD is Datasim copyrighted and you may use it for your own applications provided you keep the copyright notice in the source. It may not be sold on to third parties.

## 0.7 MORE INFORMATION AND SUPPORT

We will continue to support this book (as well as my other books) on the web sites www.datasim.nl and www.datasim-component.com. We also give both in-company and courses in this area.

The author can be contacted at dduffy@datasim.nl. I welcome your feedback and suggestions for improvement.

Good luck with C++ and Finance.

# Part I
# C++ Essential Skills

# 1
## Introduction to C++ and
## Quantitative Finance

## 1.1 INTRODUCTION AND OBJECTIVES

In this chapter we give an overview of the C++ programming language, its relationship with Quantitative Finance (QF) and why C++ is suitable for complex applications in this domain. In particular, we discuss the various programming paradigms and how each paradigm is suited to software projects in QF. Furthermore, we shall describe how these paradigms can be dovetailed to help us build efficient and robust code. Last, but not least, our objective is to create software that is also easy to understand and to maintain. This is an extremely important requirement because a large C++ application consisting of a network of tightly coupled objects can be difficult to maintain at best, and a nightmare at worst. In this day and age the focus is on developing flexible frameworks that can be easily and quickly customised to changing requirements in the market place. To this end, we are convinced that C++ can realise these requirements if and only if we design our software systems in a correct and proper way.

You can skip this chapter if you wish to start as soon as possible on this C++ journey. Then you should go immediately to chapter two. Before doing so, however, we would strongly advise you to read section 1.3 (Programming Paradigms). This book complements my book on C++ for financial instrument pricing (Duffy, 2004) because the latter book assumes previous C++ knowledge and the current book takes a more leisurely pace by discussing each topic in detail.

If we compare this book to an opera, then this chapter would correspond to the overture. It sets the tone by providing some background information on C++ and its relevance and applicability to Quantitative Finance.

## 1.2 A SHORT HISTORY OF C++

The object-oriented way of thinking and programming (we call this a *paradigm*) is almost fifty years old and it has its origins in the programming language Simula that was developed in Norway. Simula was the first language to support the concept of a class as we know it in its current form.

C++ has its origins in the early 1980's when its inventor, Dr Bjarne Stroustrup (Stroustrup, 1997) was working at AT&T. The original name for the language was 'C with classes' because the language was developed as an object-oriented extension to the programming language C while still remaining compatible with it. This very fact may be a reason why C++ has weathered the storm: the legacy C code that organisations maintained could be upgraded to C++. C++ is compatible with C and was called a 'better C' in those early days.

The late 1980's can be seen as the period when C++ came out of the laboratories and began to manifest itself in mainstream applications. The first C++ compiler (actually, precompiler because C++ code was compiled to C code) was from a company called Glockenspiel in Dublin in 1988 and it was in this period that the current author started to work with C++.

The early 1990's saw a remarkable growth in interest in the object-oriented (OO) paradigm in general and in C++ in particular. As with many new technologies promises were made that were not met. For example, it was believed in some circles that OO would solve all software ails and that a new industry would emerge in which application builders would purchase reusable class libraries from companies that could be described as 'class library builders'. The most important applications in this period were in the following domains: simulation (Computer Aided Design (CAD), Computer Graphics), telecommunications and real-time applications (for example, medical devices and process control). It was during this period that the current author worked on an early version of a pricing and risk management system in C++.

At the moment of writing we can conclude that the object-oriented paradigm is (justifiably) accepted as a necessary precondition for success in software development. However, it is not sufficient in the sense that blind adherence to it will not automatically lead to good results. First, there are other software paradigms that complement and even compete with the object-oriented paradigm and second the paradigm can be taken to extremes, as we have seen in the past. We discuss these problems and risks in this chapter and we provide some guidelines on how to turn our object-oriented projects into success stories.

## 1.3    C++, A MULTI-PARADIGM LANGUAGE

One of the features of C++ is that it supports many kinds of programming paradigms, unlike some languages that are 'pure' object-oriented languages (in the sense that every piece of software must be an object or a class). Instead, we can write applications that are a mixture of different programming styles. Whether this is a wise thing to do is debatable but that is not the issue at the moment. In general, the author does not believe that a single paradigm is flexible enough to encompass every possible kind of application and in general some parts of an application can be written in an object-oriented fashion while other parts can and should be written using a modular approach, reminiscent of Fortran, C and Cobol.

### 1.3.1    Object-oriented paradigm

This paradigm is based on the concept of a class. Classes have their origins in philosophy, logic and cognitive psychology (Eysenck and Keane, 2000). In particular, the theory of concepts has been an important influence on the development of the object paradigm. There are a number of theories, one of which is the *defining attribute view*. This view was developed and elaborated by the German logician Frege (Frege, 1952). Frege maintained that a concept can be characterised by a set of defining attributes or semantic features. He distinguishes between a concept's intension and extension. The *intension* of a concept consists of the set of attributes that determine what it is to be a member of the concept. This idea is similar to a class in *class-based object-oriented languages*. The *extension* of a concept is the set of entities that are members of the concept. This idea corresponds to class instances or objects. Some features of the defining attribute view are:

- The meaning of a concept is captured by its defining attributes
- Attributes are atomic building blocks for concepts
- Attributes are necessary and sufficient for defining members of a concept
- There is no doubt about whether an entity is in the concept; there are clear-cut boundaries between members and non-members of the concept

- All members of the concept are equally representative of the concept; we cannot say that one member is more typical of the concept than another member
- When concepts are organised in a hierarchy the defining attributes of the more specific concept (for example, a sparrow) include all the attributes of the superordinate concept (in this case, bird).

These features are implemented in many class-based object-oriented languages such as C++, Java and C#. In this case we first define a class consisting of data and functions and we then create objects or so-called instances of the class by initialising the data in the class. Looking back in hindsight (which is always easy), the author concludes that these assumptions are too restrictive for certain types of applications. There are other object-oriented languages where there is no class concept. Instead, if we wish to create an object we must clone or copy it from an existing *prototypical* object. The Self language is one example of a so-called classless object-oriented language.

Let us take a simple example. In this case we wish to model one-factor plain options (in other words we can only exercise at the maturity date T). An option can be a call option or a put option. When we model this as a class we must discover its attributes and the messages to which instances (objects) of the class respond to. The attributes are:

- The risk-free interest rate: r
- The volatility of the relative price change: $\sigma$
- The strike price: K
- The time to expiration (in years): T
- The cost-of-carry: b

These attributes are just names and when we create instances of the class we must assign values to them, for example (Haug, 1998):

- Volatility $\sigma = 0.15$
- Strike Price $K = 490$
- Time to expiry $T = 0.25$ (3 months)
- Risk-free interest rate $r = 0.08$
- Cost-of-carry $b = 0.03$

We thus see that the object is concrete while its corresponding class is abstract. Having defined the object's data we may speculate on the kinds of information we wish to extract from the object. Since this is a context-sensitive question we would expect different answers from various stakeholder groups such as:

- Traders
- Quantitative analysts
- Risk managers
- IT personnel

Each group has its own requirements and features that they would like to have. For example, a common set of requirements might be:

- Calculate the option price
- Calculate an option's sensitivities (for hedging applications)
- The ability to support constant, time-dependent and stochastic volatility models
- Export option-related information to a spreadsheet, for example Excel

These features will be implemented by one or more so-called member functions. In order to reduce the scope we concentrate on the pricing and hedging functionality. For example, the price for a one-factor plain call or put option is known analytically:

```
double CallPrice()
{
        double tmp = sig * sqrt(T);
        double d1 = ( log(U/K) + (b+ (sig*sig)*0.5 ) * T )/ tmp;
        double d2 = d1 - tmp;

        return (U * exp((b-r)*T) * N(d1)) - (K * exp(-r * T)* N(d2));
}
```

and

```
double PutPrice()
{
        double tmp = sig * sqrt(T);

        double d1 = ( log(U/K) + (b+ (sig*sig)*0.5 ) * T )/ tmp;
        double d2 = d1 - tmp;
        return (K * exp(-r * T)* N(-d2)) - (U * exp((b-r)*T) * N(-d1));
}
```

In this code we use the variable U to denote the underlying variable.


### 1.3.2   Generic programming

This is a paradigm that can be a competitor of the object-oriented paradigm and it can also be used in conjunction with the latter paradigm.

When we design a software entity using the generic paradigm we try to stop thinking about hard-wired data types and so on. We then design the software using generic underlying types. When we wish to work with specific data types we *instantiate* or clone the software entity by replacing the generic types by these specific types. The compiler takes care of these replacement issues and it checks that the specific data types satisfy the interface requirements demanded by the generic type.

Let us take a simple example. Suppose that we wish to define a function that calculates the maximum of two numbers. In C++ we realise this using a *template function*:

```
template <class Numeric>
        Numeric Max(const Numeric& x, const Numeric& y);
```

This template function in C++ accepts two parameters of a generic type and then calculates their maximum. The code for the function is easy to read if you have programmed in any high-level language:

```
template <class Numeric>
Numeric Max(const Numeric& x, const Numeric& y)
{
```

```
        if (x > y)
                return x;
        return y;
}
```

The only difference with normal programming practice in this case is that we need to give the compiler a hint that we are working with generic data types and not with specific ones. An example of use is:

```
long dA = 12334; long dB = 2;
cout << "\n\nMax and min of two numbers: " << endl;
cout << "Max value is: " << Max<long>(dA, dB) << endl;
```

Concluding, when we work in this way we write the software once and reuse it many times. We have applied the generic paradigm to quantitative finance applications in Duffy (2004).

### 1.3.3 Procedural, modular and functional programming

The programming language Fortran (Formula Translation) has been the most successful language of all time for scientific, mathematical and engineering applications. It is ideally suited to problems involving data structures such as vectors and matrices and the corresponding algorithms that use these data structures. Hundreds of libraries have been built to help Fortran programmers, for example:

- Numerical linear algebra
- Initial value problems
- Ordinary and partial differential equations
- And many more . . .

Fortran achieves this level of reusability by the use of subroutines and modules. A module is a function that produces output from input. It is not a member function of a class and hence we do not need to create an object in order to use it. Object-oriented purists may frown on this approach but my answer would be: not everything is, or needs to be, an object.

We have applied the modular paradigm to quantitative finance applications in Duffy (2004).

## 1.4   C++ AND QUANTITATIVE FINANCE: WHAT'S THE RELATIONSHIP?

C++ has become very popular in Quantitative Finance and its importance will grow rather than diminish in the coming years (in my humble opinion). It may not be the most elegant and usable language out there but – all things being equal – it is the most flexible and adaptable language. It is an ISO standard, which means your C++ code will also work in 20 years time!

I could say much more, but for good or bad there is no way we can ignore C++. An important point is that potential employers wish to see employees with C++ experience. Accepting this fact, and the fact that so many people wish to learn the language (and learn it well) I have decided to write this book. I hope that it will help you in your career.

## 1.5   WHAT IS SOFTWARE QUALITY?

The ISO 9126 standard (see Kitchenham and Pfleeger, 1996) is a description of a set of characteristics that measures the quality of software products. It consists of six orthogonal quality characteristics that describe how good a product is. We discuss them because they are very useful in all phases of the software development lifecycle (in particular, business modelling) and not just in the more solution-dependent stages such as design, coding and maintenance. In fact, many managers think in term of these characteristics, albeit implicitly. Furthermore, each characteristic has several sub-characteristics.

The six characteristics are:

- Functionality
- Reliability
- Usability
- Efficiency
- Maintainability
- Portability

*Functionality* refers to the capability of a system (in fact, the software that implements the system) to satisfy user needs. These needs may be explicitly stated but they can also be implicit. This characteristic has five sub-characteristics:

- *Suitability*: this has to do with functions for specified tasks and their appropriateness for their tasks
- *Accuracy*: this has to do with the problem of producing correct and agreed results or the agreed effect
- *Interoperability*: this has to do with the ability to interact with other systems. An important precondition is that the systems are predefined
- *Compliance*: this sub-characteristic refers to whether the system adheres to standards and conventions such as regulations, domain-related standards and the law
- *Security*: this has to do with the ability of the system to prevent unauthorised access, whether it be deliberate or accidental

*Reliability* is concerned with how a system maintains a given level of performance over some given period of time. We must also state the conditions under which the system performs

This characteristic has three sub-characteristics:

- *Maturity*: has to do with the frequency of failure in the system. Most failures are caused by so-called faults
- *Fault tolerance*: refers to the ability of the system to maintain a specified level of performance. We must specify the duration of time in which that level is to be maintained. Disturbances compromise this level of performance. These disturbances are caused by software faults and bad interfaces, for example
- *Recoverability*: this refers to the capability to re-establish previous levels of performance. For example, we could consider the time and effort it takes to recover information and data after a system crash

*Usability* refers to the effort that is needed in order to 'use' an application or system. Of course, there are many kinds of users of a system and each one has a definition of usability. For example, there are both direct and indirect users of the system. It is important to define what developers, managers and users of the software mean by usability.

This characteristic has three sub-characteristics:

- *Understandability*: the effort needed to recognize logical concepts and their applicability
- *Learnability*: the effort needed to learn the application, for example how often the user manual is consulted
- *Operability*: the effort for operation and operational control, for example backup and file management

*Efficiency* refers to the level of performance and the amount of resources needed to achieve the performance.

This characteristic has two sub-characteristics:

- *Time behaviour*: this is related to response and processing times
- *Resource behaviour*: has to do with the amount of resources needed to perform functions. This sub-characteristic is also concerned with how long the resources are held while performing the functions

*Maintainability* refers to the effort needed to make specified modifications. These modifications may include corrections, improvements or adaptation. In general, modifications are caused by changes in the environment and by changes to requirements and functionality.

This characteristic has four sub-characteristics:

- *Analysability*: the effort needed for diagnosis or deficiency detection. We wish to detect the causes of failure in this case and to identify parts of the system requiring modification
- *Changeability*: this is related to the effort that is needed for modification, fault removal or environmental change
- *Stability*: the risk of unexpected effect of modification. This is the sub-characteristic that gives managers and project leaders nightmares. Traditional object-oriented software projects tend to suffer from this problem because of their inherent bottom-up approach, aggravated by overuse of the C++ inheritance mechanism. The end-result is a tightly coupled set of object networks that *can* (and usually) does lead to huge maintenance problems
- *Testability*: the effort that is needed to validate the modified software or the effort that is needed to test it

*Portability* refers to the ability of software in a system to be transferred from one environment to another environment. This includes organisational, hardware and software environments.

This characteristic has four sub-characteristics:

- *Adaptability*: the opportunity for adaptation of software to different specified environments. This implies that no other actions should be applied or changes made
- *Installability*: the effort needed to install software in a specified environment
- *Conformance*: does software adhere to standards or conventions?
- *Replaceability*: the opportunity and effort of using software in place of other software in the same environment. This sub-characteristic may also include attributes of both installability and adaptability

## 1.6   SUMMARY AND CONCLUSIONS

In this chapter we have given an overview of a number of programming *paradigms* and how they are supported in C++. Furthermore, we gave a short history of C++ and its applications during the last 25 years. Finally, we gave an introduction to the ISO 9126 standard that describes the quality of *software products*. Just like my car or washing machine, we wish to create software applications that are extendible and easy to maintain and of course, fast. We realise the first two requirements by improving design and programming skills while the third requirement can be realised by a clever synergy between software and hardware.

## 1.7   EXERCISES

1. Which programming language(s) are you using at the moment? In how far does it support the following paradigms:
   - Object oriented programming
   - Generic programming (as is seen with C++ templates)
   - Procedural and modular programming
   
   Are there things you would like to do with the language that are not possible?

2. In how far do the following languages support the above three paradigms: Java, VBA, C#, C, Cobol, Fortran, APL, PL/I, Maple, Matlab, Smalltalk, VB.NET?

3. Which ISO 9126 characteristics are important for the following kinds of software projects:
   (a) A throwaway prototype application to test if a new pricing model is accurate
   (b) A COM Addin (written in C++) that will be used on the trading floor
   (c) A large system using the finite difference method that will be updated, extended and improvement over a period of years

4. What are the three most important ISO 9126 characteristics in general in your opinion?

# 2

# The Mechanics of C++: from Source Code to a Running Program

*Tús maith leath na hoibre (a good start is half the work)*

## 2.1 INTRODUCTION AND OBJECTIVES

In this chapter we introduce the C++ language by defining just enough syntax to allow us to create and run simple programs. We concentrate on the steps that you need to carry out in order to create an executable file. Of course, we need to introduce some C++ syntax so that we are in a position to understand what is being presented. In this chapter both the code and the examples are simple enough to be understood by a reader with some knowledge of programming. In particular, we discuss three major examples:

Problem 1: Procedures for calculating the maximum and minimum of some numbers
Problem 2: A simple C++ class
Problem 3: A simple template class and template function

The objective is thus to understand the full process of creating C++ code, compiling it and linking with the other code and libraries in the system. Only when all compiler and linker errors have been resolved can we run our program.

The main objectives in this chapter are:

- Discuss what is actually needed when creating a C++ program
- A short introduction to the compilation and linking processes
- How C++ works with header and code files
- Integration: the structure of a typical C++ program

This chapter is special in the sense that it does not introduce C++ syntax in any great detail but it provides a working framework that supports the development process in later chapters.

The program structure in later chapters will be the same as the structure in this chapter except that we shall have more include and code files residing in various directory locations.

You may skip this chapter if you already know how to set up projects in C or C++.

## 2.2 THE COMPILATION PROCESS

C++ is a programming language and it is possible to write code in this language using some kind of text editor. The sentences in the language must conform to rules as described by the specification of the language. The C++ language is discussed in Stroustrup (1997).

A compiler is an executable program that accepts a text file containing C++ code. It translates this code (in a series of steps) to a form that can eventually be executed in a computer. Basically, it translates human-readable text into machine-readable code. This is a very simplistic explanation but it is reasonably accurate.

## 2.3   HEADER FILES AND SOURCE FILES

When writing programs we try to split the problem into independent pieces or modules. Each module will be implemented by valid C++ code, for example:

- A C/C++ function
- A C++ class

In general we create two files, one containing the declaration of all relevant functions and data while the other file contains the actual code body of each function. These two files are called the header and code files.

Summarising:

- *Header file*: contains declarations of all functions (sometimes called *function prototypes*) and data
- *Code file*: the file containing the actual body of all functions and the initialised data from the header file

There are variations on, and exceptions to this basic strategy but these will be discussed later. We do not wish to address these issues yet.

In general the header file contains the declaration of all functions and data that we are going to use. In the case of functions we define the signature of a function as consisting of:

- Its name
- Its return type
- Its input arguments (also called input parameters)

In the case of data we need:

- The name of the data (called the variable name)
- The type of the data (this could be a built-in type or a user-defined type)

Let us take an example. In this case we wish to find the maximum or minimum of two or three numbers. These functions are useful when we define payoff functions for one-factor and two-factor options. To this end, we create two files called:

- Inequalities.hpp   (contains function declarations)
- Inequalities.cpp   (contains function code)

The header file is given by:

```
// Inequalities.hpp
// Header file containing declarations of functions
// (C) Datasim Education BV 2006
//
// Preprocessor directives; ensures that we do not include a file twice
// (gives compiler error if you do so)
#ifndef Inequalities_HPP
#define Inequalities_HPP

////////// Useful functions ////////////////
// Max and Min of two numbers
double Max(double x, double y);
double Min(double x, double y);
```

```
// Max and Min of three numbers
double Max(double x, double y, double z);
double Min(double x, double y, double z);
/////////////////////////////////////////////////
#endif
```

We thus see that only the function prototypes are given here and hence no source code. This code is found in the code file and is given by:

```
// Inequalities.cpp
// Code file containing bodies of functions
//
// Last Modification Dates:
// 2006-2-17 DD kick-off code
//
// (C) Datasim Education BV 2006
//
#include "Inequalities.hpp"
////////// Useful functions //////////////////

// Max and Min of two numbers
double Max(double x, double y)
{
    if (x > y)
        return x;
    return y;
}
double Min(double x, double y)
{
    if (x < y)
        return x;
    return y;
}

// Max and Min of three numbers
double Max(double x, double y, double z)
{
    return Max(Max(x,y), z);
}
double Min(double x, double y, double z)
{
    return Min(Min(x,y), z);
}
```

Here we see that the header file is included by use of a special preprocessor command:

```
#include "Inequalities.hpp"
```

In this case the above command is replaced by the contents of the file. If the filename is quoted (that is, using ") searching for the file typically begins where the source .cpp file resides; if it is not in the same directory then searching follows an implementation-defined rule to find the file. **This is a major source of confusion for C++ novices.** You need to learn how each specific compiler vendor defines how to search for include files.

We now discuss how to use these functions in an application. To this end, we create a program that uses these functions. Of course we must include the header file `Inequalities.hpp` otherwise the compiler will not know the signature of these functions. Second, the file `Inequalities.cpp` must be visible to the linker because the source code is needed. How to do this is implementation-dependent.

The source code for the program with file name `TestInequalities.cpp` is given by:

```cpp
// TestInequalities.cpp
//
// Main program (Console-based) to test Max and Min functions.
//
// (C) Datasim Education BV 2006
//

#include <iostream>          // Console input and output
using namespace std;         // I'll talk about this later

#include "Inequalities.hpp"

int main()
{
    // Prompt the user for input. Console output (cout)
    // and input (cin)
    double d1, d2;
    cout << "Give the first number: ";
    cin >> d1;
    cout << "Give the second number: ";
    cin >> d2;

    char c;      // Character type
    cout << "Which function a) Max() or b) Min()? ";
    cin >> c;
    if (c == "a")
    {
        cout << "Max value is: " << Max(d1, d2) << endl;
    }
    else
    {
        cout << "Min value is: " << Min(d1, d2) << endl;
    }
    double dA = 1.0; double dB = 2.0; double dC = 3.0;
    cout << "\ n\ nMax and min of three numbers: " << endl;
```

```
        cout << "Max value is: " << Max(dA, dB, dC) << endl;
        cout << "Min value is: " << Min(dA, dB, dC) << endl;

        return 0;
}
```

The output from this program is:

```
Give the first number: 12
Give the second number: 1
Which function a) Max() or b) Min()? a
Min value is: 1

Max and min of three numbers:
Max value is: 3
Min value is: 1
```

This concludes our first example.

## 2.4  CREATING CLASSES AND USING THEIR OBJECTS

We now discuss how to set up a program that uses C++ classes. This is not much more difficult than in the previous section and in this case we use three files:

- Header file describing the class members (data and functions)
- Code file containing the bodies of member functions
- File containing the test program

The situation is somewhat more complicated now because we have to use several header and code files from different sources, some of which may be from external vendors and directories. The situation is depicted in Figure 2.1. In order to 'integrate' (compile and link) all these files into a running program we have a number of all-or-nothing activities to address. We draw a distinction between three kinds of 'environments' where code is to be found:

D1: System directories
D2: Remote ('Other') directories
D3: Local directories

In D1 we find all code from the system and in principle you do not have to worry but you do have to include the correct libraries using the correct syntax, for example:

```
#include <string>            // Standard string class in C++
using namespace std;
```

We now turn to directories D2. This is the critical part of the process and the part that goes wrong for many novices. There are two main issues, namely including the header file for a remote file and second adding the .cpp file to the current project. Let us take an example. The include directives look like:

```
#include "datasimdate.hpp"    // Dates and other useful stuff
#include "Person.hpp"         // Interface functions for Person
```

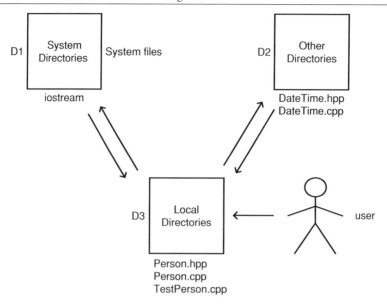

**Figure 2.1**   Directory structure for project

In the first case we include a date class but we have to tell the compiler where to look for this file. This is an implementation-dependent problems and under Visual Studio – for example – we must edit the project properties dialog box and add an entry in the 'additional include directories' box. Then the system will look there and find the file. Second, we have to open the code file for the date class and add it to the project. That's it.

The last part (directories D3) is easy because this is the current working directory and no additional include directories need be specified in the project properties. However, you do need to add the code file to the project.

Having done all this, you can build and run the project, assuming that you have not any compiler errors. Of course, you may get warnings and you should study them very carefully.

For completeness, we give the code for this problem; don't worry about the syntax details because they will be discussed in detail later in this book.

The header file for the person class is:

```
// Person.hpp
//
// "Hello World" class. Function declarations.
//
// (C) Datasim Education BV 2005-2006
//

#ifndef Person_HPP
#define Person_HPP

#include "datasimdate.hpp"     // My dates and other useful stuff
#include <string>              // Standard string class in C++
```

```
using namespace std;

class Person
{
public: // Everything public, for convenience only

            // Data
            string nam;                 // Name of person
            DatasimDate dob;            // Date of birth
            DatasimDate createdD;       // When object was created
public:
            Person (const string& name,
                const DatasimDate& DateofBirth);
            void print() const;
            int age() const;
};
#endif
```

The body of these functions is given in the .cpp file:

```
// Person.cpp
//
// "Hello World" class
//
// Last Modification Dates
//
// 2006-2-17 DD Kick-off
//
// (C) Datasim Education BV 2005-2006
//


#include "Person.hpp"

Person::Person (const string& name, const DatasimDate& DateofBirth)
{
                nam = name;
                dob = DateofBirth;
                createdD = DatasimDate();        // default, today
}
void Person::print() const
{ // Who am I?

    cout << "\ n** Person Data **\ n";
    cout << "Name: " << nam << ", Date of birth: " << dob
                                << ", Age: " << age() << endl;

}
int Person::age() const
{
```

```
            return int( double(DatasimDate() - dob) / 365.0);
}
```

The test program is defined in the current directory and is given by:

```
// TestPerson.cpp
//
// "Hello World" Testing the first C++ class
//
// (C) Datasim Education BV 2005-2006
//
#include "datasimdate.hpp" // Dates and other useful stuff
#include "Person.hpp"      // Interface functions for Person
#include <string>          // Standard string class in C++
using namespace std;

int main()
{
        DatasimDate myBirthday(29, 8, 1952);
        string myName ("Daniel J. Duffy");
        Person dd(myName, myBirthday);
        dd.print();

        DatasimDate bBirthday(06, 8, 1994);
        string bName ("Brendan Duffy");
        Person bd(bName, bBirthday);
        bd.print();
        return 0;
}
```

The output from this program is:

```
** Person Data **
Name: Daniel J. Duffy, Date of birth: 29/8/1952, Age: 53

** Person Data **
Name: Brendan Duffy, Date of birth: 6/8/1994, Age: 11
```

## 2.5   TEMPLATE CLASSES AND TEMPLATE FUNCTIONS

We now turn our attention to the last relevant topic, namely the facility in C++ to support generic classes and functions. Instead of having to work with specific and hard-wired entities we can create types. Of course, templates will be discussed later in this book but the focus here is on showing what needs to be done to compile, link and run programs that use template classes and functions.

Templates are trickier because we must include the file (whatever its name may be) that contains the bodies of the functions that we are calling. In order to motivate templates we wish to make the functions in section 2.3 more generic in the sense that we would like to use them with other data types such as C++ built-in types and even user-defined types. To this end, we copy the original header and code files and we add some new syntax to signal that the functions now depend on a generic type. The new header file is:

```
// GenericInequalities.hpp
//
// Header file containing declarations of functions
//
// This is the template/generic version.
//
// (C) Datasim Education BV 2006
//


// Preprocessor directives; ensures that we do not
// include a file twice (gives compiler error)
#ifndef GenericInequalities_HPP
#define GenericInequalities_HPP


////////// Useful functions /////////////////


// Max and Min of two numbers
template <class Numeric>
    Numeric Max(const Numeric& x, const Numeric& y);
template <class Numeric>
    Numeric Min(const Numeric& x, const Numeric& y);

// Max and Min of three numbers
template <class Numeric>
    Numeric Max(const Numeric& x,const Numeric& y,const Numeric& z);
template <class Numeric>
    Numeric Min(const Numeric& x,const Numeric& y,const Numeric& z);
#endif
```

The code file is now:

```
// GenericInequalities.cpp
//
// Code file containing bodies of functions
//
// (C) Datasim Education BV 2006
//


#ifndef GenericInequalities_CPP
#define GenericInequalities_CPP

#include "GenericInequalities.hpp"

////////// Useful functions /////////////////
```

```cpp
// Max and Min of two numbers
template <class Numeric>
Numeric Max(const Numeric& x, const Numeric& y)
{
    if (x > y)
        return x;

    return y;
}

template <class Numeric>
Numeric Min(const Numeric& x, const Numeric& y)
{
    if (x < y)
        return x;

    return y;
}

// Max and Min of three numbers
template <class Numeric>
Numeric Max(const Numeric& x, const Numeric& y, const Numeric& z)
{
    return Max<Numeric>(Max<Numeric>(x,y), z);
}

template <class Numeric>
Numeric Min(const Numeric& x, const Numeric& y, const Numeric& z)
{
    return Min<Numeric>(Min<Numeric>(x,y), z);
}
#endif
```

Because we are working with templates we must include the code file in the test program:

```cpp
#include <iostream>          // Console input and output
using namespace std;         // I'll talk about this later

#include "GenericInequalities.cpp" // Needed because it is templated

int main()
{
    // Prompt the user for input. Console output (cout)
    // and input (cin)
    int d1, d2;
    cout << "Give the first number: ";
    cin >> d1;
```

```
        cout << "Give the second number: ";
        cin >> d2;

        char c; // Character type
        cout << "Which function a) Max() or b) Min()? ";
        cin >> c;
        if (c == "a")
        {
                cout << "Max value is: " << Max<int>(d1, d2) << endl;
        }
        else
        {
                cout << "Min value is: " << Min<int>(d1, d2) << endl;
        }
        long dA = 12334; long dB = 2; long dC = -3;
        cout << "\ n\ nMax and min of three numbers: " << endl;
        cout << "Max value is: " << Max<long>(dA, dB, dC) << endl;
        cout << "Min value is: " << Min<long>(dA, dB, dC) << endl;

        return 0;
}
```

This completes (for the moment) our discussion of template functions in applications. It is possible to create and use template classes but we postpone this topic when we discuss genericity in detail.

## 2.6   KINDS OF ERRORS

One of the most annoying aspects of programming is getting a bunch of error messages on your console and wondering to yourself:

- Where did these messages come from?
- What do these messages mean?
- How do I resolve these messages?
- What am I going to do, it's driving me crazy?!

What we need to do is to remain calm and collected and think about what is really happening. Errors arise in different places and for different reasons. We attempt to categorise these errors and give some typical examples in the hope that you will be able to resolve them quickly and efficiently. It does not do any harm to actually read and try to understand compiler errors, no matter how cryptic they might be.

### 2.6.1   Compiler errors

These are the errors that arise when we compile a source file in an attempt to transform the text in the file to binary form. The two main sources of error are:

E1: Syntax errors
E2: Compiler unable to find a class definition, variable name or some other 'syntactical' entity

We do not concentrate on issue E1 because that is something that cannot be learned in a book. In this regard you need to plod on until you have no more syntax errors. The second category E2 produces errors for a number of reasons, some of which are:

E2.1 The objects and variables that you are using cannot be found
E2.2 Compiler complains that it cannot find a given include file

The solution to error E2.1 is to include the header file of the appropriate object and its class (and don't forget to add the .cpp file to the project). Problem E2.2 might be caused by the fact, that even though you have included the header file you have not told the compiler where to look (see Figure 2.1 again).

Finally, do not forget that many compiler errors are caused by typing errors.

### 2.6.2  Linker errors

In the linkage phase all the functions bodies are brought together as it were to produce an executable file. The modules comprising a program need not all be compiled at one time. Normally the source text is kept in separate files and precompiled routines may be loaded from libraries. So basically, in the linkage phase we need to associate all the identifiers originating from separately compiled translation units.

Linkage errors occur because the bodies of functions or the initialisation of data cannot be found. The root cause of these errors is usually:

E1: A typing error; for example, mismatch between the signature of a function as declared in a header file and its definition in the code file
E2: You forgot to add the relevant source file to your project

An example of E1 would be in the person class where one of its member functions is declared as:

```
int age(); // NO "const" in this declaration
```

while in the code file the function is defined as:

```
int Person::age() const
{
        return int( double(DatasimDate() - dob) / 365.0);
}
```

Summarising, linker errors arise because the linker cannot find the code for a function that has been used in some source file.

### 2.6.3  Run-time errors

These are the errors that occur when you run the executable file. Basically, when a run-time error occurs the program halts and you are left with a meaningless dialog box on your screen.

Run-time errors have many causes, some of which are:

E1: Memory management errors: the C++ program writes into a piece of memory that has not been reserved
E2: Overflow/underflow errors: very large or very small numbers arise in the program and cause the program to crash
E3: Logic errors: the user has entered a value that is not allowed

We resolve errors of type E1 by ensuring that we write correct code before we deliver it to the customer. In particular, in a later chapter we discuss the scary topic of heap memory. Then this problem should be resolved once and for all. The errors in category E2 need to be resolved by a combination of good coding and algorithmic precision. Finally, the errors in category E3 can be accommodated by using the exception mechanism in C++. We discuss this topic in a later chapter.

## 2.7   THE STRUCT CONCEPT

This is a book on C++ for Quantitative Finance and in this case the object-oriented paradigm is used to create classes and their instances. We shall of course pay much attention to this issue but at this stage of the game we mention that it is possible to use the struct mechanism because it has been used in C applications and it can be seen as a simpler version of a C++ class.

Some general remarks on structs are:

- They are useful as data containers
- All the members are public (accessibility by client code is not an issue)
- They can be used in conjunction with classes
- In some applications they are used as a building block in interface technology (for example, the Component Object Model (COM))

An introduction for structs is given in Chapter 23.

## 2.8   USEFUL DATA CONVERSION ROUTINES

In many applications we need to convert certain data types to strings (and vice versa). In this section we concentrate on converting built-in types to strings.

There is a standard library for these conversions. It is the so-called *string stream* library and you may find it useful in your applications, for example when you transfer data from your application to an external database system. Basically, in order to convert a data type to a string we carry out the following operations:

- Place the data type into a string stream object
- Convert the string stream object to a string
- Return the new string object to the client code

The actual code is:

```
// Hard-coded example for starters
double myDouble = 1.0;
stringstream s;
s << myDouble;
string result = s.str();
cout << "String value is: " << result << endl;
```

In general we wish to convert different kinds of data to string format. To this end, we have created a template function to do it for us:

```
template <typename T>
    string getString(const T& value)
```

```
    {
            stringstream s;
            s << value;
            return s.str();
    }
```

This is a highly reusable function (at least for built-in types). The following complete program shows how to use the function:

```
// TestConversions.cpp
//
// Simple stuff for converting built-in
// types to strings.
//
// (C) Datasim Education BV 2006
//

#include <sstream>
#include <string>
#include <iostream>

using namespace std;

int main()
{
    int i = 10;
    long j = 1234567890;
    float f = 3.14f;
    double d = 2.712222222223;

    string myString = getString<int>(i);
    cout << myString << endl;

    myString = getString<long>(j);
    cout << myString << endl;

    myString = getString<float>(f);
    cout << myString << endl;

    myString = getString<double>(d);
    cout << myString << endl;

    return 0;
}
```

For a user-defined type you can create similar functionality to convert its instances to string format.

We conclude this section by discussing data conversion based on C functions. You may skip this if you do not have to worry about legacy applications. The following conversion routines are simple but effective:

```
#include <string>
using namespace std;
#include <stddef.h>

std::string getString(long j)
{
        char str[200];
        sprintf(str, "%d", j);
        std::string result(str);
        return result;
}

std::string getString(int j)
{
        char str[200];
        sprintf(str, "%d", j);
        std::string result(str);
        return result;
}

std::string getString(size_t j)
{
        char str[200];
        sprintf(str, "%d", j);
        std::string result(str);
        return result;
}
```

Of course, the generic solution using template functions using the string stream object is preferable. The C++ code is on the CD.

## 2.9   SUMMARY AND CONCLUSIONS

We have given an overview of a number of important issues that you will need to master as soon as possible. In particular, we discuss how to set up a C++ project consisting of multiple header and code files.

The goal of this chapter was to show how to assemble related functionality in the form of files containing C++ code to form a running program. It is important that you understand how to compile, link and run simple programs as discussed in this chapter.

## 2.10   EXERCISES AND PROJECTS

1. This is a simple exercise that you can do in order to test the specific compiler that you are using. Carry out the following steps:
   (a) Create two directories called D1 and D2 (for convenience, of course you can choose more descriptive names). In D1 you place your test program and in D2 you place your potentially reusable code

(b) Based on the examples in this chapter create (simple) functions to calculate the sum of two and three double precision numbers. To this end, create a header file containing the two function declarations and a code file containing the implementation

(c) Create a program to test the new functionality. Make sure that you resolve any compiler and linker errors

(d) Generalise the new Sum() function so that it works with generic types. Employ the same approach as discussed in section 2.5

(e) Again, create a test program using the template function. Do not forget to include the file (usually a .cpp file) that contains the source of each function. Otherwise you will get a linker error.

# 3
# C++ Fundamentals and My First Option Class

## 3.1 INTRODUCTION AND OBJECTIVES

In this chapter we design and implement our first real working C++ code. Our goal is to model a European option by a C++ class. We know that a class has member data and member functions in general and in this case we model the following option attributes:

- Strike price
- Volatility
- Risk-free interest rate
- Expiry date

as member data. Furthermore, we are interested in designing call and put options as well as modelling some of their interesting properties, namely option price and option sensitivities, for example:

- Option delta
- Option gamma
- Other option sensitivities (for more options, see Haug, 1998)

We set up the basic infrastructure by implementing the software in two files. First, we define the EuropeanOption class in a so-called *header file*. This means that we declare the option's member data and member functions in this file. It can be seen as a specification of the class. Second, we implement the functions that were declared in the header file and this is done in a so-called *code file*. Together, these two files describe the class. It is possible to use just one file but we prefer using two files because the code is easier to maintain in this case.

We take a well-known example, in this case a European option. We implement it in C++ and in this way the reader will become familiar with C++ syntax and the object-oriented way of thinking as soon as possible. In later chapters we shall add more functionality to this class. This is the best way to learn, namely step-by-step.

The following topics will be discussed in this chapter:

- Creating my first C++ class: separating class design issues from class implementation
- Member data and member functions in C++; the different categories of member functions
- Determining accessibility levels in a class
- Using the EuropeanOption class in test programs and applications

After having studied this chapter you will have gained a good understanding of a basic C++ class. Having understood the topics in this chapter we then proceed to more advanced functionality in chapter four. In particular, we discuss a number of C++ features in more detail.

The C++ class that we introduce in this chapter implements the closed form solution for the Black Scholes equation and it will be used in later chapters to test the accuracy of approximate methods such as the binomial method and finite difference schemes.

## 3.2   CLASS == MEMBER DATA + MEMBER FUNCTIONS

In general, programming any class involves – *grosso modo* – determining its member functions and member data. We are working in Financial Engineering and in order to reduce the scope here we examine European options.

C++ is an example of a *class-based object-oriented language*. A class is a description of a group of related attributes and operations. In C++ we use the synonyms *member data* for attributes and *member functions* for operations. The member data and member functions are closely related. This feature is called *encapsulation*. In short, the class' functions know which attributes to use. Let us take an example of a class implementing European options for stocks. The defining parameters for the European option will be designed in C++ as the following member data:

- The risk-free interest rate: r
- The volatility of the relative price change: $\sigma$
- The strike price: K
- The time to expiration (in years): T
- The stock price: S (or U depending on the underlying)
- The cost-of-carry: b

The cost-of-carry for the Black-Scholes model has the same value as r but will have different values depending on the type of the underlying asset (for example, b = 0 for a futures option, see Haug, 1998). We must define the data types of the member data. In this case we usually design them as `double` precision numbers although C++ allows us to design classes with so-called *generic data types*. This means that the member data can be customized with different *specific data types* depending on the current requirements. Having defined the member data we now must decide what to do with the data. To this end, we introduce the concept of *object* (or *instance* of a class). A class is abstract in the sense that its member data have not been instantiated (they are just abstract descriptions of data) while an object is tangible and all its member data have been initialised. For example, the following assignments describe a European put option on an index (Haug, 1998, p. 15):

- Underlying value (stock price index) U = 500
- Volatility $\sigma = 0.15$
- Strike Price K = 490
- Time to expiry T = 0.25 (3 months)
- Risk-free interest rate r = 0.08
- Cost-of-carry b = 0.03

Having discussed member data we now describe the functionality of classes and objects. In general, a class has member functions that model the lifecycle of an object. The main categories in general are:

- Member functions (*constructors*) for creation of objects
- Member functions that modify the member data (*modifiers*)
- Member functions that perform calculations on the member data (*selectors*)
- A member function (*destructor*) that deletes an object when no longer needed

There are various ways to create an object using constructors. For example, it is possible to create an instance of a European option class by initialising its member data. Two other constructors deserve mention: first, the *default constructor* creates an object with default member data values while the *copy constructor* creates an object as a deep copy of some other object. The destructor is the other extreme; it removes the object from memory when the object is no longer needed. We note that the names of constructors and of the destructor are the same as the name of their corresponding class.

We now discuss the member functions that operate on an object after it has been constructed and before it is destructed. Again, we concentrate on the class for European options.

C++ is based on the *message-passing paradigm*. This means that client code sends a message to an object by calling its member functions. For example, here is a piece of code that calculates the price of the index put option that we introduced earlier (we assume that the member data have been initialised):

```
ExactEuropeanOption myobject ("P", "Index Option");

// ...

double d = myObject.Price();
```

The variable d will now contain the price of the put on the index option. Notice that there was no need to include parameters in the function `Price()` because of the tight binding between data and functions in C++. This is in contrast to procedural languages (such as Visual Basic and Cobol) where the coupling between data and functions is looser.

## 3.3   THE HEADER FILE (FUNCTION PROTOTYPES)

In general, the code that is needed for a complete description of a class in C++ is contained in two files: first, the header file (this section) and this contains the formal descriptions of the member data and member functions in the class. Second, the code file contains the body of each declared member function. In other words, each member function declaration in the header file must have a corresponding entry in the code file.

We now discuss the details of the header file. First, there are two regions or parts called *private* and *public*, respectively. Both parts may contain member data and member functions. Members that are declared in the private part are not accessible from outside the class and may only be accessed by members in the class itself while public members may be accessed by any C++ code. In general, all data should be declared in the private part because this tends to change; however, in this chapter we place the data that represents the structure of an option in the public area. This is for convenience only.

The public member functions in the options class can be categorised as follows (see the code below):

- Constructors: the different ways of creating instances of the option class
- Destructor: deleting an object when it is no longer needed (automatically taken care of by the runtime system)
- Assignment operator: the ability to assign one object to another object (this is a 'deep' copy)
- 'Core business' functions: these are the functions that calculate the price and the delta for the option, for example
- Other functions: for example, it is possible to switch a call option to a put option (and vice versa). Of course, the price and delta will be different!

The full interface for the option class is now given:

```cpp
// EurpeanOption.hpp
class EuropeanOption
{
private:

        void init();        // Initialise all default values
        void copy(const EuropeanOption& o2);
        // "Kernel" functions for option calculations
        double CallPrice() const;
        double PutPrice() const;
        double CallDelta() const;
        double PutDelta() const;

public:
        // Public member data for convenience only
        double r;        // Interest rate
        double sig;      // Volatility
        double K;        // Strike price
        double T;        // Expiry date
        double U;        // Current underlying price
        double b;        // Cost of carry

        string optType; // Option name (call, put)

public:
// Constructors
EuropeanOption(); // Default call option
EuropeanOption(const EuropeanOption& option2); // Copy constructor
EuropeanOption (const string& optionType);    // Create option type

// Destructor
virtual ~EuropeanOption();

// Assignment operator
EuropeanOption& operator = (const EuropeanOption& option2);

// Functions that calculate option price and (some) sensitivities
double Price() const;
double Delta() const;

// Modifier functions
void toggle();                  // Change option type (C/P, P/C)

};
```

## 3.4   THE CLASS BODY (CODE FILE)

Having discussed the function prototypes for the option class, we need to describe how to fill in the body of the code for these functions. To this end, there are two major issues to be addressed. First, we must include the header file and other headers of libraries that are needed by the code. In this case, this leads to:

```cpp
#include "EuropeanOption.hpp"// Declarations of functions
#include <math.h>              // For mathematical functions, e.g. exp()
```

Second, each function body must be implemented. This is where C++ differs somewhat from non-object-oriented languages, namely the concept of *function overloading*. This means that it is possible to define several functions having the same name and return type but differing only in the number and type of arguments. Furthermore, each function is 'scoped' or attached to its class by use of the so-called *scope resolution operator* '::' as shown in the following typical code:

```cpp
double EuropeanOption::PutPrice() const
{

        double tmp = sig * sqrt(T);

        double d1 = ( log(U/K) + (b+ (sig*sig)*0.5 ) * T )/ tmp;
        double d2 = d1 - tmp;

        return (K * exp(-r * T)* N(-d2)) - (U * exp((b-r)*T) * N(-d1));

}
```

This function calculates the price of a put option. Note that that the function returns a `double` value (the price of the put option) while all needed parameters (such as the volatility, interest rate and so on) are none other than the member data of the object that have already been initialised in the constructor!

The full source code now follows:

```cpp
// EurpeanOption.cpp
//
// Author: Daniel Duffy
//
// (C) Datasim Education BV 2003
//

#include "EuropeanOption.hpp" // Declarations of functions
#include <math.h>             // For mathematical functions, e.g. exp()

// Kernel Functions
double EuropeanOption::CallPrice() const
```

```
{

     double tmp = sig * sqrt(T);

     double d1 = ( log(U/K) + (b+ (sig*sig)*0.5 ) * T )/ tmp;
     double d2 = d1 - tmp;

     return (U * exp((b-r)*T) * N(d1)) - (K * exp(-r * T)* N(d2));

}

double EuropeanOption::PutPrice() const
{

     double tmp = sig * sqrt(T);

     double d1 = ( log(U/K) + (b+ (sig*sig)*0.5 ) * T )/ tmp;
     double d2 = d1 - tmp;

     return (K * exp(-r * T)* N(-d2)) - (U * exp((b-r)*T) * N(-d1));
}

double EuropeanOption::CallDelta() const
{

     double tmp = sig * sqrt(T);

     double d1 = ( log(U/K) + (b+ (sig*sig)*0.5 ) * T )/ tmp;

     return exp((b-r)*T) * N(d1);
}

double EuropeanOption::PutDelta() const
{
     double tmp = sig * sqrt(T);

     double d1 = ( log(U/K) + (b+ (sig*sig)*0.5 ) * T )/ tmp;

     return exp((b-r)*T) * (N(d1) - 1.0);
}

void EuropeanOption::init()
{ // Initialise all default values

     // Default values
     r = 0.08;
     sig = 0.30;
```

```
        K = 65.0;
        T = 0.25;
        U = 60.0;        // U == stock in this case
        b = r;           // Black and Scholes stock option model (1973)
        optType = "C";   // European Call Option (the default type)


}
void EuropeanOption::copy(const EuropeanOption& o2)
{

        r = o2.r;
        sig = o2.sig;
        K = o2.K;
        T = o2.T;
        U = o2.U;
        b = o2.b;

        optType = o2.optType;

}


EuropeanOption::EuropeanOption()
{ // Default call option

        init();
}

EuropeanOption::EuropeanOption(const EuropeanOption& o2)
{ // Copy constructor

        copy(o2);
}

EuropeanOption::EuropeanOption (const string& optionType)
{ // Create option type

        init();
        optType = optionType;

        if (optType == "c")
                optType = "C";


}
EuropeanOption::~EuropeanOption()
{ // Destructor

}
```

```
EuropeanOption& EuropeanOption::operator = (const EuropeanOption& opt2)
{ // Assignment operator (deep copy)

        if (this == &opt2) return *this;

        copy (opt2);

        return *this;
}

// Functions that calculate option price and sensitivities
double EuropeanOption::Price() const
{
    if (optType == "C")
    {
        return CallPrice();
    }
    else
        return PutPrice();
}

double EuropeanOption::Delta() const
{
    if (optType == "C")
        return CallDelta();
    else
        return PutDelta();
}

// Modifier functions
void EuropeanOption::toggle()
{ // Change option type (C/P, P/C)

        if (optType == "C")
                optType = "P";
        else
                optType = "C";
}
```

## 3.5   USING THE CLASS

The code file is compiled and syntax errors should be resolved. We then need to write a program to test the class. The corresponding file is then compiled and linked with the other code to form an executable unit.

In this section we give an example of a test program. The object-oriented paradigm is based on the *message-passing metaphor*. Here we mean that client software sends messages to an object (by means of member function calls) by using the so-called *dot notation*. For example, to calculate the price of an existing option instance we code as follows:

```
double option_price = myOption.Price();
```

Here `myOption` is an object and `Price()` is one of its member functions.

The following code is an example of how to use the option class.

```
// TestEuropeanOption.cpp
//
// Test program for the solutions of European option pricing
// problems.
//
// (C) Datasim Education Technology BV 2003
//

#include "EuropeanOption.hpp"
#include <iostream>
int main()
{ // All options are European

    // Call option on a stock
    EuropeanOption callOption;
    cout << "Call option on a stock: " << callOption.Price() << endl;

    // Put option on a stock index
    EuropeanOption indexOption;
    indexOption.optType = "P";
    indexOption.U = 100.0;
    indexOption.K = 95.0;
    indexOption.T = 0.5;
    indexOption.r = 0.10;
    indexOption.sig = 0.20;
    double q = 0.05;          // Dividend yield
    indexOption.b = indexOption.r - q;

    cout << "Put option on index: " << indexOption.Price() << endl;

    // Call and put options on a future
    EuropeanOption futureOption;
    futureOption.optType = "P";
    futureOption.U = 19.0;
    futureOption.K = 19.0;
    futureOption.T = 0.75;
    futureOption.r = 0.10;
    futureOption.sig = 0.28;
    futureOption.b = 0.0;
```

```
        cout << "Put option on future: " << futureOption.Price() << endl;

        // Now change over to a call on the option
        futureOption.toggle();
        cout << "Call on future: " << futureOption.Price() << endl;

        return 0;
}
```

The output from this program is:

```
Call option on a stock: 2.13293
Put option on an index: 2.4648
Put option on a future: 1.70118
Call option on a future: 1.70118
```

These numbers are the same as found in the benchmark examples in Haug (1998).

## 3.6   EXAMINING THE CLASS IN DETAIL

The code that implements the class for a plain one-factor option has been discussed in some detail in the previous section. We have not done justice to all the details but our objective was to create 'working' code as soon as possible in the book. Furthermore, we shall discuss the syntax in greater detail in later chapters, especially Chapter 4.

Nonetheless, it is advisable at this stage to say something about the syntax that we use here. In this sense we avoid forward references.

### 3.6.1   Accessibility issues

A class consists of members in general. A member is either a member data or a member function. All members in a class are accessible from any other members of the class. However, a class can decide to 'expose' certain members to outside clients just as it can decide to keep some members 'hidden' from the outside world. To this end, we can define *private* and *public* member areas:

• Public member: any client can access it
• Private member: not accessible to clients, only to member of the class

In general, data and functions are tightly coupled and this principle is called encapsulation. In general, it is advisable to define data to be private because this feature seems to be the most volatile part of a class interface. **In this chapter the member data are public but this is for convenience only**.

### 3.6.2   Using standard libraries

In later chapters we shall introduce the Standard Template Library (STL), a library of template classes or containers, algorithms that operate on those containers and so-called iterators that allow us to navigate in the containers.

Some important data containers are:

- Vectors
- Lists
- Maps (or dictionaries)

It is important to note at this stage that it is not necessary to create your own data containers and corresponding algorithms.

### 3.6.3   The scope resolution operator ':::'

Contrary to C and other procedural languages, C++ allows us to define member functions as elements of a class. To make this relationship explicit we use the so-called scope resolution operator ':::', for example:

```
double EuropeanOption::Price() const
{
      if (optType == "C")
      {
            return CallPrice();
      }
      else
            return PutPrice();
}
```

In this case the pricing function belongs to the given option class.

### 3.6.4   Virtual destructor: better safe than sorry

We start with the conclusion:

*Declare all destructors to be virtual*

The reason why this is so will be discussed in a later chapter. Failing to declare a destructor to be virtual *may* result in memory problems, so we play safe.

## 3.7   OTHER PARADIGMS

The first example in this chapter was a C++ class that models plain one-factor options. This is a good application of the object-oriented paradigm: we encapsulate tightly-coupled data representing an option's parameters and we then create member functions that act on that data. Before we go overboard by thinking that everything in sight *must* be a class or object we mention that there are other paradigms that are just as effective and that can be used in conjunction with, or as a competitor to, the object-oriented paradigm. To this end, we show how modular programming techniques can be used in Quantitative Finance by taking some simple examples of interest rate calculations (see Fabozzi, 1993; Hull, 2006). The examples are not difficult but we use them because they elaborate on a number of coding issues that will be needed in this book.

We have created a number of functions for the following kinds of calculations:

- Calculating the future value of a sum of money (paid once per year, m times a year and continuous compounding)
- Future value of an ordinary annuity
- Simple present value calculations
- Present value of a series of future values
- Present value of an ordinary annuity

As usual, we create two files, one (the header) containing function declarations and the other one containing code. The header file is given by:

```cpp
// SimpleBondPricing.hpp
//
// Simple functions for interest rate calcuations.
//
// (C) Datasim Education BV 2006
//


#ifndef SimpleBondPricing_HPP
#define SimpleBondPricing_HPP

#include <vector>
using namespace std;

namespace Chapter3CPPBook // Logical grouping of functions and others
{


        // Handy shorthand synonyms
        typedef vector<double> Vector;
        // Recursive function to calculate power of a number. This
        // function calls itself, either directly or indirectly
        double power(double d, long n);

        // Future value of a sum of money invested today
        double FutureValue(double P0, long nPeriods, double r);

        // Future value of a sum of money invested today, m periods
        // per year. r is annual interest rate
        double FutureValue(double P0, long nPeriods, double r, long m);

        // Continuous compounding, i.e. limit as m -> INFINITY
        double FutureValueContinuous(double P0, long nPeriods, double r);

        // Future value of an ordinary annuity
        double OrdinaryAnnuity(double A, long nPeriods, double r);

        // Present Value
        double PresentValue(double Pn, long nPeriods, double r);
```

```
// Present Value of a series of future values
double PresentValue(const Vector& prices,long nPeriods,double r);

// Present Value of an ordinary annuity
double PresentValueOrdinaryAnnuity(double A,long nPer,double r);

}
```

```
#endif
```

This is just a set of functions that are *logically related* by the use of the keyword 'namespace' (we shall discuss namespaces in more detail in a later chapter). For the moment, we use a namespace to scope a function, class, variable or some other C++ construct. If you wish to access a function in a namespace, for example you must use the namespace name, either explicitly as follows:

```
double fv2 = Chapter3CPPBook::FutureValue(P, nPeriods, r, freq);
```

or, as in a kind of state declaration, as follows:

```
using namespace Chapter3CPPBook;

cout << "**Future with " << m << " periods: "
                << FutureValue(P0, nPeriods, r, m) << endl;
```

The main advantage of using namespaces is that there is little chance of name collisions with code in other parts of your application. But as already noted, we shall discuss this topic in another chapter.

We continue with a discussion of the code that actually realises the above function declarations. We take several representative examples (the full source code is on the CD).

The first example is the code to calculate the future value of money:

```
// Future value of a sum of money invested today
double FutureValue(double P0, long nPeriods, double r)
{

        double factor = 1.0 + r;
        return P0 * power(factor, nPeriods);
}
```

where we have written our own function to calculate the power of a number (this is for pedagogical reasons):

```
// Non-recursive function to calculate power of a number.
double power(double d, long n)
{
        if (n == 0) return 1.0;
        if (n == 1) return d;
```

```
        double result = d;
        for (long j = 1; j < n; j++)
        {
                result *= d;
        }
        return result;
}
```

The second example is less trivial because we work with a container class from the Standard Template Library (STL). This is a template class for vectors and in the current case we use double as the underlying data type. Furthermore, it is convenient to create a synonym or short-hand syntax for the special vector class we are going to use:

```
// Handy shorthand synonyms
typedef vector<double> Vector;
```

Incidentally, we define this within the scope of the namespace declaration. We note that the typedef declaration does not create a new type in any sense (Kernighan & Ritchie, 1988). Its function is to add a new name for an existing type and it is particularly useful when used with template classes, as in the above example. Actually, it is much the same as a #define and hence no new semantics are introduced. Finally, it does not reserve storage and it is called a storage class specifier.

Having discussed typedef we now show how it can be applied in a function, in this case to calculate the present value of a series of future prices:

```
// Present Value of a series of future values
double PresentValue(const Vector& prices,long nPeriods, double r)
{
        // Number of periods MUST == size of the vector
        assert (nPeriods == prices.size());

        double factor = 1.0 + r;

        double PV = 0.0;

        for (long t = 0; t < nPeriods; t++)
        {
                PV += prices[t] / power(factor, t+1);
        }

        return PV;
}
```

In this code we have a vector of future prices, the number of periods and the interest rate. The size of the vector must be the same as the number of periods, otherwise the assert() function will be called and the program terminates immediately. This is a rather drastic measure but we must realise that this is a program to help us learn C++ and we do not – at least not yet – have intentions of creating production software. In a later chapter we shall show how this run-time error can be caught and resolved without having to stop the program. This is called the *exception handling mechanism.*

We now give an example of how to use the functions.

```
// Present Value of a series of future values
Vector futureValues(5); // For five years, calls constructor
for (long j = 0; j < 4; j++)
{ // The first 4 years
      futureValues[j] = 100.0; // Vector has indexing []
}
futureValues[4] = 1100.0;

int nPeriods = 5;
double r = 0.0625;
cout << "**Present value, series: "
          << PresentValue(futureValues, nPeriods, r) << endl;
```

This concludes our first encounter with non-member functions in C++.

## 3.8   SUMMARY AND CONCLUSIONS

In this chapter we have created our first class and first set of basic functions. You should experiment with them, test them and even extend them with the objective of getting to know your new C++ development environment, whether that be Windows-based or Linux-based. It might be an idea to glance at Chapter 2 every now and then; it may be of use if and when you stumble across compiler and linker errors. You may even get runtime errors.

## 3.9   QUESTIONS, EXERCISES AND PROJECTS

In section 3.7 we have created a number of functions that perform calculations related to interest rate modelling:

Calculating the future value of a sum of money

$$P_n = P_0(1 + r)^n$$

$$n = \text{number of periods}$$

$$P_n = \text{future value } n \text{ periods from now}$$

$$P_0 = \text{original principal}$$

$$r = \text{interest rate per period (decimal form)} \tag{3.1}$$

Future value of an ordinary annuity

$$P_n = A\left[\frac{(1+r)^n - 1}{r}\right]$$

$$A = \text{annuity amount}$$

$$r = \text{interest rate}$$

$$n = \text{number of periods} \tag{3.2}$$

Simple present value calculations

$$PV = P_0 = P_n \left[ \frac{1}{(1+r)^n} \right]$$

$P_n$ = future value $n$ periods from now

$r$ = interest rate

$PV$ = present value                                  (3.3)

Present value of a series of future values

$$PV = \sum_{t=1}^{n} \frac{P_t}{(1+r)^t}$$

$P_t$ = value at period $t$ from now

$r$ = interest rate                                   (3.4)

Present value of an ordinary annuity

$$PV = A \left\{ \frac{1 - \dfrac{1}{(1+r)^n}}{r} \right\}$$

$A$ = amount of the annuity                           (3.5)

Continuous Compounding

$$P_n = P_0 e^{rn}$$

$r$ = interest rate

$P_0$ = original principal

$n$ = number of years                                 (3.6)

m-Period Compounding

$$P_n = P_0 \left( 1 + \frac{r}{m} \right)^{mn} \tag{3.7}$$

Answer the following questions:

(a) Check that the code on the CD which implements the above maths works as it should (I am only human)
(b) Test the functions with your own test data
(c) Add a number of new functions to the namespace (see for example, Hull, 2006, p. 79). The first function converts the rate of interest with continuous compounding to the equivalent rate with compounding m times per year. The second function is an implementation in the opposite direction as it were. The corresponding mathematical formulae are:

$$r_c = mlog \left( 1 + \frac{r_m}{m} \right) \tag{3.8}$$

and

$$r_m = m(e^{r_c/m} - 1) \tag{3.9}$$

where

$r_c$ = continuous compounding interest rate
$r_m$ = $m$ times per year compounding rate

# 4

# Creating Robust Classes

## 4.1 INTRODUCTION AND OBJECTIVES

In chapter three we coded a simple class in C++ using the syntax that we had introduced in that chapter. Of course, it was not possible (or even desirable) to discuss all possible 'syntax avenues' because doing so would be confusing. In this chapter we wish to create more robust and efficient classes and we realise this goal by using some of the syntax that C++ offers. In particular, we address a number of issues that have to do with data and object security, such as:

Issue 1: Ensuring that objects and their data are created in a safe way
Issue 2: Accessing and using objects in a safe way; avoiding side-effects
Issue 3: Working with object references rather than copies of objects
Issue 4: Optimization: static objects and static member data

This is quite a lot of territory to cover and the results in this chapter will be used again and again throughout this book. Thus, this chapter is a vital link to future chapters.

The most important topics are:

- Passing parameters to functions by value or by reference
- Function overloading: ability to define several functions having the same name
- More on constructors
- Not all functions need be member functions: non-member functions
- The 'const' keyword and its consequences for C++ applications

After having understood these topics and having implemented them in simple classes the reader will have reached a level of expertise approaching yellow belt. We discuss these topics not only because they are supported in C++ but because they help us become good C++ developers. They also promote the reliability and efficiency of our code.

## 4.2 CALL BY REFERENCE AND CALL BY VALUE

In C++ one can create functions taking zero or more arguments in their parameter list. To this end, we need to discuss in what forms these arguments are created and used in a function. We take a simple example to motivate what we mean. Let us consider a function that calculates the larger of two numbers:

```
double Max(double x, double y)
{
        if (x > y)
                return x;

        return y;
}
```

This is a very simple function of course and in this case we say that the input parameters x and y are used in a *call-by-value* manner; this means that copies of these variables are made on the stack when the function is called:

```
double d1 = 1.0;
double d2 = - 34536.00;

// Copies of d1 and d2 offered to the function Max()
double result = Max(d1, d2);
cout << "Maxvalue is " << result << endl;
```

In this case we work with copies of d1 and d2 in the body of Max() and not d1 and d2 themselves. This process is taken care of automatically and you do not have to worry about this as programmer.

The call-by-value technique is also applicable, not only to built-in types as we have just seen but also to class instances (objects). This means that objects (even 'big' ones) will be copied if they are used in this call-by-value way. Let us take an example of a class having an embedded fixed-size array as member data:

```
class SampleClass
{
public:     // For convenience only

        // This data created at compile time
        double contents[1000];

public:
        SampleClass(double d)
        {
                for (int i = 0; i < 1000; i++)
                {
                        contents[i] = d;
                }
        }

        virtual ~SampleClass()
        {
                cout << "SampleClass instance being deleted\ n";
        }
};
```

We now define a global function that adds up the elements of an instance of this class. Again, we employ call-by-value:

```
double Sum(SampleClass myClass)
{
        double result = myClass.contents[0];
        for (int i = 1; i < 1000; i++)
```

```
        {
            result += myClass.contents[i];
        }
        return result;
};
```

We call this function in a program as follows:

```
SampleClass sc(1.0);
double sum = Sum(sc);
```

What is happening here is that a copy of sc will be created and this is the object the function will work on. The code works correctly but it is not efficient. We circumvent this problem by using object addresses and the *call-by-reference* technique. First, we declare an object to be a reference as follows:

```
double Sum2(SampleClass& myClass)
{
        double result = myClass.contents[0];
        for (int i = 1; i < 1000; i++)
        {
            result += myClass.contents[i];
        }
        return result;
};
```

In this case we work directly with the address of the input parameter and not a copy of it. We are, in fact working with the 'live' object and it is in fact possible to modify it in the body of the function that it is being used in. For example, after having called the function Sum2() we could assign all of its values to zero! This is a side-effect and we shall see how to resolve this problem in the next section.

Some remarks on this section are:

- You can use call-by-value or call-by-reference for any type or class but in general I use the former for built-in types while I use the latter for objects and class instances
- I try to avoid using pointers as input parameters to functions and we shall discuss why in a later chapter. By this statement we mean a function prototype having the following signature:

```
double Sum2(SampleClass* myClass);
```

This is the style reminiscent of bygone days and we advise against its use. We use modern C++ syntax and in this sense it is a 'better C'.
- When using call-by-reference it is only necessary to declare an object once as an address while in a main program you can use it as a 'normal' object (that is, without having to use '&')
- An introduction to references, the stack and other topics relevant to the current context can be found in Chapters 22 and 23

## 4.3   CONSTANT OBJECTS EVERYWHERE

One of the disadvantages of using references in argument lists is that the function is able to modify the input arguments. What we would ideally like to use is the address of an object while at the same time not be able to change the object in any way. To this end, we define the object to be a constant reference by introducing a new keyword as follows:

```
double Sum3(const SampleClass&  myClass)
{
        // N.B. not possible to modify myClass
};
```

The body of this function can no longer modify the input argument and thus we avoid any side effects; the client code that delivered the object to the function can rest assured that the object will not be modified. In fact, if you try to modify the object you will receive a compiler error.

   The above conclusions are valid for member functions as well as global functions and we shall give some examples in the coming section. But we first wish to discuss another aspect of 'constantness'.

### 4.3.1   Read-only (const) member functions

After having creating an object (by calling a constructor of its class) we would like to access its data by defining public member functions. To this end, we wish either to (a) give a copy of the data or (b) a reference to the data itself. We discuss the first case here and to this end we look at an example of a class that models two-dimensional points in Cartesian space. Having created a point we would like to access its x and y coordinates in a read-only manner as it were:

```
class Point
{
private:
        void init(double xs, double ys);

        // Properties for x- and y-coordinates
        double x;
        double y;

public:

        // Constructors and destructor
        Point();                        // Default constructor
        Point(double xs, double ys);  // Construct with coordinates
        Point(const Point& source);  // Copy constructor
        virtual ~Point();               // Destructor

        // Selectors
        double X() const;               // Return x
```

```
      double Y() const;                 // Return y

      // ...
};
```

Here we see that the functions X() and Y() are declared as being constant member functions and this means (in this case) that their bodies cannot modify the private member data of the point. This is like an insurance policy because client code can use these functions and be sure that its objects will not be modified. The body of the two selector functions above is given by:

```
double Point::X() const
{// Return x
      return x;
}

double Point::Y() const
{// Return y
      return y;
}
```

In this case we state that copies of the member data are returned to the client, not the member data itself. This needs to be known and in other cases we may need to define functions that actually give the address of the member data as return types. This is an issue for a later chapter.

On the other hand, functions that modify the member data in general cannot be const for obvious reasons; they are, by definition functions that change the member data in some way. In this case the function prototypes are:

```
// Modifiers
void X(double NewX);      // Set x
void Y(double NewY);      // Set y
```

while the body of these functions is given by:

```
// Modifiers
void Point::X(double NewX)
{// Set x
      x = NewX;
}

void Point::Y(double NewY)
{// Set y
      y = NewY;
}
```

Here is an example:

```
Point p1(1.0, 3.14);

// Read the coordinate onto the Console
cout << "First coordinate: " << p1.X() << endl;
cout << "Second coordinate: " << p1.Y() << endl;
```

```
// Modify coordinates
p1.X(2.0);
p1.Y(5.0);
```

```
// Read the coordinate onto the Console
cout << "First coordinate: " << p1.X() << endl;
cout << "Second coordinate: " << p1.Y() << endl;
```

Thus, we need to determine in our code if a function does or does not modify the member data in a class. Functions that do not modify the member data should be const. Please note that the specifier 'const' must be placed in both the header and code files, otherwise the compiler will think there are two different functions.

We have now discussed enough in order to allow us to proceed. This was a very important section in a very important chapter.

## 4.4   CONSTRUCTORS IN DETAIL

We know at this stage that a constructor is a special member function that is responsible for initialising the member data in a class in order to create an instance of that class. A class may have many constructors. For example, the constructors for class Point above have the following body:

```
Point::Point()
{ // Default constructor

    init(0.0, 0.0);
}
```

```
Point::Point(double xs, double ys)
{ // Normal constructor with coordinates

    init(xs, ys);
}
```

```
Point::Point(const Point &source)
{ // Copy constructor

    init(source.x, source.y);
}
```

where each constructor calls the (private) *helper function*:

```
void Point::init(double xs, double ys)
{ // Initialize the point

    x = xs;
    y = ys;
}
```

There are two special kinds of constructor, namely:

- Default constructor
- Copy constructor

By definition, the default constructor has no parameters while the copy constructor takes a constant reference of an object of the same class:

```
Point();                    // Default constructor
Point(const Point& source); // Copy constructor
```

The body for these functions has been given above.

We use these constructors as follows:

```
Point p1(1.0, 3.14);
Point p2(p1);
Point p3;
```

You can create as many constructors as you wish in a class.

### 4.4.1   Member initialisation

Up until now we have defined code for constructors in a class by assignment of its member data to some other data. This is not the only way (see Stroustrup, 1997, p. 248) and in some cases it is not even possible to do the assignment, for example for:

- Instances of classes that have no default constructors
- const member data
- reference member data

Of course, in most cases we can choose between an assignment and the *initializer*. Furthermore, the latter technique is more efficient than using the assignment statement. For example, compare the two valid ways of defining a constructor:

```
Point::Point(double newx, double newy)
{// Initialize using newx and newy
     init(newx, newy);
}

Point::Point(double newx, double newy) : x(newx), y(newy)
{// Initialize using newx and newy

     // init(newx, newy); NOT NEEDED
}
```

We shall need and use this '*colon syntax*' when we introduce the concept of inheritance in a later chapter.

## 4.5   STATIC MEMBER DATA AND STATIC MEMBER FUNCTIONS

There are three basic ways of using memory in C++:

- Static memory
- Automatic memory
- Free store (discussed in Chapter 6)

An introduction to these topics is given in Chapters 22 and 23 and furthermore, we shall deal with free store issues in great detail in chapter six when we discuss heap-based memory allocation using the new and delete operators. Automatic memory has to do with the allocation of function arguments and local variables. Each entry into a function block gets its own copy. This kind of memory is thus automatically created and destroyed. This memory is said to be on the stack (Stroustrup, 1997) and we shall discuss this issues in Chapters 22 and 23.

In this section we discuss *static memory*. This memory is allocated by the linker and it exists for the duration of a program. The following entities are stored in static memory:

S1 Global and namespace variables
S2 Static class member functions
S3 Static member data
S4 Static variables in functions

An object that is allocated in static memory is constructed just once and it persists until the program ends. It always has the same address.

We give an example of using cases S2 and S3 above (cases S1 and S4 are probably not needed in applications especially if the application is object-oriented). Let's say we wish to create a global instance of class Point  and that this instance is unique (incidentally, this is a simple variant of the *Singleton* pattern). The steps are:

(1) Declare the static object (usually a private member data in the .hpp file)

```
class Point: public Shape
{
private:

        // Properties for x- and y-coordinates
        double x;
        double y;

        static Point OriginPoint;

public:

        // Other members
};
```

(2) Initialise the static object (usually at the start of the .cpp file)

```
Point Point::OriginPoint = Point(0.0, 0.0);
```

(3) Provide a member function that allows you to access the static object (this will be a so-called static member function). In the .hpp file we have:

```
// Accessing the "global" object
static Point& GetOriginPoint();
```

while in the .cpp file we have:

```
Point& Point::GetOriginPoint()
{
        return OriginPoint;
}
```

We are finished and we can then use this Singleton in applications. We notice that:

- The static function must be called in a special way. Normally we send messages to objects in the form of member functions but in the current case we send a message to the class itself rather than to any individual object
- The return type of the static member function is a reference and hence the address of the private static variable is returned and not some copy thereof. Furthermore, this function can be used on the left-hand side of an assignment statement to allow us to modify the contents of the static object, as the following code shows:

```
// Work with the unique Origin Point
cout << "Origin point: " << Point::GetOriginPoint() << endl;

// Now choose new coordinates for the new origin
Point::GetOriginPoint() = Point(1.0, 2.0);
cout << "Origin point: " << Point::GetOriginPoint() << endl;
```

The technique used in this section is a viable and reliable competitor for the famous/infamous Singleton pattern (see GOF, 1995). On the other hand, a singleton is initialised only when needed and can be deleted at any moment while a static object persists in memory for the duration of the program. It's a trade-off between resource and time efficiency.

You can use the techniques in this section to create your own static and global objects.

## 4.6  FUNCTION OVERLOADING

One of the nice things about C++ is that it is possible to define more than one member function in a class having the same name and return type but only differing in the numbers and types of the arguments. It is possible to apply this technique to all member (and even non-member) functions, including constructors. Of course, you cannot overload a class' destructor because there is only one way to delete an object. For example, let us examine the Point class again and its constructors:

```
Point();                        // Default constructor
Point(double xs, double ys);    // Construct with coordinates
Point(const Point& source);     // Copy constructor
```

Of course, we can define many more constructors depending on our motivation and knowledge of Cartesian geometry!

In much the same way we can overload other member functions. Let us take an example of a function that calculates the distance between points:

- The distance between the current point and the global origin from section 4.5
- The distance between two arbitrary points

We refer the reader to the source code on the CD for these examples.

## 4.7  NON-MEMBER FUNCTIONS

A non-member function is by definition, one that is not a member function of some class. In other words, it is not defined in the scope of a class. This means that by default it cannot access the private members of the class (unless the class gives it a special dispensation by declaring it to be a *friend*, a topic we discuss in Chapter 5). There are two main kinds of non-member function:

- Functions that are declared within the class scope
- Global functions

We shall discuss these functions in more detail in later chapters. We thus see how flexible C++ is: you can mix functions using the object and procedural paradigms and we do not have to work in a 'one size fits all' environment.

## 4.8  PERFORMANCE TIPS AND GUIDELINES

We discuss some topics that may help you to produce more robust and efficient code.

### 4.8.1  The 'inline' keyword

In general we draw a distinction between the declaration of a function (the so-called *function prototype*) and its definition (the code that actually implements the function). There are several ways of realising this, three of which are:

- Declaration in the header .hpp file and code in the code .cpp file (this is the usual and advisable route to take)
- *Default inline functions*: these are functions that we declare and define in a single file (usually the .hpp file)
- Using the keyword 'inline' as an optimisation trick

We have already discussed the first scenario in previous chapters. The second scenario is when the function is declared and defined in one sweep as it were, for example:

```
double X() const{return x;}
double Y() const {return y;}
```

The third option means that we can define a function to be inline, for example:

```
inline double X() const{return x;}
inline double Y() const {return y;}
```

This new specifier is a hint to the compiler that it should attempt to generate code when the above member functions are called instead of laying down the code for the function once and then calling through the usual *function call mechanism* (Stroustrup, 1997). This may improve performance but this is not guaranteed.

Inlining may be useful for short, typically one-line functions that are often called, for example in loops. We have seen cases where its use results in a 20 % boost in performance (for example using vectors and matrices in numerical calculation) while in other cases (for example, inlining Set() and Get() functions) we have not seen any improvement. A possible explanation for this is that the compiler has optimised these short 'one-liners' already!

The use of inline is only a hint to the compiler.

### 4.8.2   Anonymous objects in function code

Some member functions produce an object of some class as return type. For example, we examine class `Point` and let us now suppose that we wish to find the point midway between the current point and a second point. The member function declaration is given by:

```
Point MidPoint(const Point& p2) const;
```

The code for this entails creating a new point on the stack, initialising its member data appropriately and returning it. The code for doing this is:

```
Point Point::MidPoint(const Point& p2) const
{ // Calculate the point between the two points

        Point result((x+p2.x)*0.5 , (y+p2.y)*0.5 );
        return result;
}
```

In this case we explicitly create a *named object* by calling a constructor in `Point`. Instead of using an explicit name we can call the appropriate constructor and let the compiler create the name for us. In fact, as programmer we create an *anonymous object* as the following code shows:

```
Point Point::MidPoint(const Point& p2) const
{ // Calculate the point between the two points

        // Create "any old" point
        return Point( (x+p2.x)*0.5 , (y+p2.y)*0.5 );
}
```

As client, we can use this function as follows:

```
Point pL(0.0, 0.0);
Point pU(1.0, 1.0);

Point pM = pL.MidPoint(pU);
cout << "Midpoint: " << pM << endl;
```

The use of anonymous objects may not improve the run-time performance of your program (because the compiler optimises a lot for you anyway) but it is a useful trick to employ because it allows us to realise the same result in less lines of code.

As a last example, we rewrite the above piece of code and instead of creating a point explicitly we use an anonymous object instead:

```
Point pM2 = pL.MidPoint(Point(1.0, 1.0));
cout << "Midpoint: " << pM2 << endl;
```

The output is exactly the same as before except that our code is more compact and in this case easier to read, possibly.

### 4.8.3 Loop optimisation

Many applications in Quantitative Finance have a core that consists essentially of one or more loops. What typically goes on within a loop is an update of a data container such as a vector, matrix or higher-dimensional structure. If we wish to pay attention to performance, both in the data containers and the client code that use them we must take a number of issues into consideration (Stroustrup, 1997, p. 675):

(1) Minimise the number of temporary objects. For example, when multiplying a matrix and a vector we may sometimes create temporary objects to store data that is then copied into the result. It would be better to work with references directly
(2) The copying of vectors and matrices must be minimised
(3) Optimisation of the use of composite operator expressions (for example, $U = M*V + W$) in multiple loops

We shall return to this important issue in a later chapter. Optimisation of code should take place when the basic C++ structure is in place and when the results are correct. In the words of Michael Jackson, the software guru (not the singer) there are two basic rules:

Rule 1: Don't optimise
Rule 2: Don't optimise yet

Our goal in general is to get it working, then get it right, then get it optimised.

## 4.9   SUMMARY AND CONCLUSIONS

You don't have to learn all the syntax of C++ in order to write useful programs. In fact, the 80–20 rule applies in this context, by which we meant that 80 % of programmer productivity is achieved by 20 % of the features in the language. To this end, we have introduced a number of essential features that certainly add to the reliability and efficiency of your C++ applications.

## 4.10   QUESTIONS, EXERCISES AND PROJECTS

1. State, in your own words how the use of the const keyword in function argument lists and const member functions promotes the reliability and performance of C++ code.

2. What is wrong when we return a local (automatic) object from a function that expects a reference as return type? For example, have a look at the following code:

```
// Incorrect example
int& FlunkyFunc()
{
    int result = 1;
    cout << "Funny";
    return result;
}
```

What happens when you compile this function? Do you get a compiler error or a warning? Furthermore, what happens when you call the function in the following ways:

```
FlunkyFunc() = 12;
cout << FlunkyFunc() << "eee";
```

We now examine the same highly dangerous situation in a class. Consider the inline function in class Point:

```
double& WrongFunction()
{
    double d = 3.1415; return d;
}
```

and its use in a program:

```
Point pt; cout << "wrong" << pt.WrongFunction() << endl;
```

Explain what is going on here.

3. Create the bodies of the member functions of the following class whose interface is given by:

```
#ifndef LineSegment_HPP
#define LineSegment_HPP

#include "Point.hpp"

class LineSegment
{ // A Line segment consisting of two points

private:
        Point e1;    // End Point of line
        Point e2;    // End Point of line

public:
        // Constructors
        LineSegment();    // Line with both end Points at the origin
        LineSegment(const Point& p1, const Point& p2);
        LineSegment(const LineSegment& l);      // Copy constructor
        virtual ~LineSegment();                 // Destructor

        // Accesssing functions
        Point start() const;                    // Synonym for e1
        Point end() const;                      // Synonym for e2

        // Modifiers
        void start(const Point& pt);            // Set Point pt1
        void end(const Point& pt);              // Set Point pt2

        // Arithmetic
        double length() const;                  // Length of line

        // Interaction with Points
        Point midPoint() const;                 // MidPoint of line
```

```
         // Print a line, the code is "default" inline
         void print () { cout << e1 << "," << e2 << endl; }
};
```

```
#endif
```

Use the syntax you have learned in Chapters four, three and two to write the code for this class. Furthermore, create a test program and in particular:

- Create some linesegments
- Calculate their lengths and midpoints
- When you have done this exercise properly you can say that you have your yellow belt.

# 5

# Operator Overloading in C++

## 5.1 INTRODUCTION AND OBJECTIVES

In this chapter we introduce a useful mechanism called *operator overloading*. This allows us to define standard mathematical operators, such as $+$, $-$, $*$ and $/$ as special member functions (and even non-member functions). We can then use these operators in expressions that mimic what we see in mathematics and physics. For example, let us examine a class that represents complex numbers (recall that a complex number has a real part and an imaginary part, see Rudin, 1970, Spiegel, 1999, Volkovyskii *et al.*, 1965). In Complex Analysis we can carry out many operations on complex numbers and it would be nice if we could 'mirror' these operations in C++. In fact, it is possible to use almost the same notation in C++ as what we use in mathematics. Here is a prelude; we create a number of complex numbers using appropriate constructors and we define some operators on them:

```
Complex z1(-23.0, 5.3);
Complex z2(2.0, 3.0);
Complex z3 = z1 * z2;
Complex z4 = 2.0 * z4;
Complex z5 = - z3;
```

In this piece of C++ code we create complex numbers and carry out operations on them in much the same way as we would in mathematics. In other words, we have created a class called `Complex` and have imbued it with functionality that mirrors that in mathematics. This facility offers many advantages because it makes it easy to write and read code written in this way.

The process of actually defining operators in a class is a simple extension of the process of creating normal member function. However, we have to use a special keyword in conjunction with the specific operator that we wish to define.

In this chapter we introduce most of the syntax that is needed in order to understand operator overloading and how it can be applied to financial engineering applications.

In order to focus on the essentials of operator overloading we shall implement a class in C++ that models the complex number system and we pay particular attention to how the most important mathematical operations are realised in the class. We shall also give several other practical examples that show the power of operator overloading and its application to a wide range of problems.

## 5.2 WHAT IS OPERATOR OVERLOADING AND WHAT ARE THE POSSIBILITIES?

Operator overloading in C++ allows the developer to define functionality by the use of a number of operators. The following operators can be used in C++:

| + | – | * | / | % | ^ | & | \| | ~ |
|---|---|---|---|---|---|---|---|---|
| ! | = | < | > | <= | >= | == | += | -= |
| /= | ++ | -- | != | && | >> | << | &= | <<= |
| >>= | ^= | () | [] | new | delete | | | |

In this chapter we shall show how to define these operators in C++ classes and in particular how to apply them in the class `Complex`. In later chapters we shall introduce more examples of where the feature is used.

There are two kinds of operator, namely *binary* and *unary* operators. A binary operator has so-called left and right operands and some examples of use are:

```
x + y
os << "help"; // Using the operator <<
a % b
```

We note that the operands do not necessarily have to belong to the same class, for example:

```
Complex z6 = z2 * 2.0;
Complex z7 = 2.0 * z2;
Complex z8 = z6* z7;
```

In this case we pre- and post-multiply a complex number by a double and we multiply two complex numbers. This has been made possible because we have implemented the corresponding functionality in class `Complex`. Actually, the assignment operator '=' in the above code is another example of operator overloading. In this case we assign the contents of one object to the contents of another object. We call this a *deep copy* and we shall discuss this operator in this and later chapters in more detail. Again, the assignment operator is binary because it has two operands, namely the right-hand operand and the left-hand operand. Some other examples are:

```
Matrix m1(100, 50);     // A matrix with 100 rows and 50 columns
Matrix m2 = m1;         // A new matrix of same size as m1
```

Thus, the code that implements the assignment operator must allocate memory for m2 and then copy all the values from m1 to m2. This is also true in the general case, that is for any C++ class.

The second kind of operator is the so-called unary operator. This has one operand only and there are situations where we can use it, for example:

```
b= - a; // b is the negative of a
b++;     // Postfix increment
++a;     // Prefix increment
```

With the exception of the negation operator we do use unary operators in C++.

What is the most effective way to use operators in C++ classes? As a first guideline the operator overloading mechanism was sometimes taken to extremes in the past. This resulted in a backlash as can be seen in Java where operator overloading is not supported. It can lead to very cryptic code and we advise using operators only when it is appropriate. We give a list of situations where we think it is useful to apply operator overloading:

- The category of mathematical operators such as $+$, $-$ and $*$. In general you can define your own notation for specific applications
- Using the indexing operators [] and () to access elements of vectors and matrices, respectively
- Overloading the operators `new` (allocate memory) and `delete` (deallocate memory) for heap memory management. Thus, it is possible to overload default memory management in C++
- Overloading the operators `<<` and `>>` in classes to allow us to perform console I/O in conjunction with the standard I/O stream
- The assignment operator that assigns an instance of a class to another instance of the same class

These cases are possibly the most important applications of operator overloading. Again, we use this mechanism when the situation warrants it and when it leads to code that is easy to understand.

## 5.3   WHY USE OPERATOR OVERLOADING? THE ADVANTAGES

In general, using operators makes code easier to read than code that uses member functions with alphanumeric names. For example, let us suppose that we wish to multiply two matrices. Here are the two possibilities:

```
Matrix m3 = m1 * m2;
Matrix m4 = m1.Add(m2);
```

Although each of these options is perfectly legitimate the first solution is better because first it is easier to read and second, and perhaps more importantly it mirrors the notation that we use in matrix algebra. In other words, the cognitive distance between the problem domain (in this case matrix algebra) and the C++ code is quite small and can be comprehended.

In Financial Engineering applications we use the operator overloading mechanism sparingly and only in those cases where it is appropriate to do so. Its use should not be an objective in itself and overuse can lead to code that is very difficult to understand. In fact, some object-oriented languages do not support operator overloading.

A good rule-of-thumb is to use operator overloading in your applications when:

- Everyone agrees on what the semantics of the operator are
- Your problem has a mathematical or well-defined structure
- When you wish to create compact code
- Creating specialised 'languages', for example Boolean algebra

There are several applications of operator overloading that can be used in Financial Engineering:

- Operations on `Date`, `Time` and `TimeStamp` objects (Duffy, 2004)
- Defining classes for algebraic data structures (Landin, 1969)
- Matrix algebra in C++ (Duffy, 2004)
- Computer graphics (Foley *et al.*, 1990)
- Expressions and expression parsers, for example composing mathematical equations at run-time

We give short examples from some of the above areas to show how operator overloading can be used. In later sections and chapters we shall elaborate more on these.

Time as a concept is very important in Financial Engineering applications. For example, in fixed-income applications we wish to carry out several kinds of operations on dates, for example:

- What is the date 100 days from now?
- Compare two dates (is a date before another date?)
- How many days are there between two dates?
- Increment/decrement a date by one day
- Add a part of a year to a date, for example what is the date 6 months from now?

To this end, we have created a class DatasimDate that encapsulates this functionality. For example, here is code that creates 12 dates with offsets of 30 days from a given fixed date:

```
DatasimDate fixed(1, 1, 94);
DatasimDate current(1, 1, 94);
int interval = 30;

for (int j = 0; j < 12; j++)
{
        current = fixed - (j*interval);
        cout << current << endl;
}
```

The output from this code gives the following dates (in the format dd/mm/yy; other formats are also possible):

```
1/1/94, 2/12/93, 2/11/93, 3/10/93, 3/9/93, 4/8/93
5/7/93, 5/6/93, 6/5/93, 6/4/93, 7/3/93, 5/2/93
```

We thus see that it is very easy to generate dates for cash-flows, for example. Our last example is to show how we can add and subtract periods of three and six months (I ran this program on Sunday February 13, 2005):

```
// Offsets; quarters + half years
cout << "Offset stuff\ n";
DatasimDate today;
DatasimDate d3 = today.add_quarter();
DatasimDate d4 = today.add_halfyear();

cout << d3 << endl;
cout << d4 << endl;

d3 = d3.sub_quarter();
d4 = d4.sub_halfyear();

cout << d3 << endl;
cout << d4 << endl;
```

The output from this code is:

```
Offset stuff
13/5/2005
13/8/2005
13/2/2005
13/2/2005
```

Another good example where operator overloading is useful is three-dimensional computer graphics. In particular, we are interested in modelling vectors and their interactions. For example, it is possible to form so-called dot (scalar) and cross products of two vectors and to this end we create a class `Vector` that consists of two `Point` instances. We implement dot and cross products using specially chosen operators:

```
Vector cross(const Vector& vec) const;        // Cross product
Vector operator ^  (const Vector& vec) const;  // Cross product

double dot(const Vector& vec) const;          // Dot product
double operator % (const Vector& vec) const;   // Dot product
```

We have included two variants for each kind of product; if you prefer not to use operator overloading you can use the more readable version. Having coded these functions we can then create more complicated functions:

```
Vector Vector::vtproduct(const Vector& B, const Vector& C) const
{ // Vector triple product A X (B X C)

      // Schaum Vectors page 17

      Vector tmp = B ^  C;
      return (*this) ^  tmp;
}

double Vector::stproduct(const Vector& B, const Vector& C) const
{ // Scalar triple product A . (B X C)

      // Schaum Vectors, page 17
      Vector tmp = B ^ C; // Cross
      return (*this) % tmp; // Dot
}
```

We can use vectors in other classes. For example, we model a plane in three dimensions by a point on the plane and its direction that we model as a vector:

```
class Plane
{ // A class for a plane in three dimensions
private:

      Vector n;    // Normal unit vector to plane
      Point p;     // Point on plane
};
```

Then the member functions in `Plane` *delegate* to `Vector`. This is important because we hide or encapsulate difficult code behind these appealing operators. For example, here is code that calculates the point in the plane that is closest to a given point:

```
Point Plane::closest(const Point& pt) const
{ // The point on plane closest to the point pt

    // GEMS IV page 154
    double d = n % (p - pt);
    Point result = pt + (n.components() * d);
    return result;
}
```

Having given some examples of operator overloading we now discuss how to actually realise this technique in your classes.

## 5.4   OPERATOR OVERLOADING: THE STEPS

Operator overloading may look strange at first sight but it is a variation of using member functions in a class. Let us take an example, in this case we wish to add two complex numbers. We can achieve this end by defining a member function 'add' that takes a complex number as argument. The declaration is given by:

```
Complex add (const Complex& c2) const;
```

In this case the real and imaginary parts of the 'current' object are added to the corresponding parts of c2 to produce a new complex number. The code body is:

```
Complex Complex::add(const Complex& c2) const
{ // Add two complex numbers

    Complex result;
    result.x = x + c2.x;
    result.y = y + c2.y;

    return result;
}
```

In this code we define a new complex number, initialise it accordingly and then return it as the return type. We can now use this member function in applications:

```
Complex z3 = z1.add(z2);
```

The use of member functions becomes cumbersome in more complex cases and we would prefer to use operators. Syntactically, this is a minor variation. The declaration now becomes:

```
Complex operator + (const Complex& c2) const;
```

while the code for the declaration is:

```
Complex Complex::operator + (const Complex& c2) const
{ // Add two complex numbers
```

```
        Complex result;
        result.x = x + c2.x;
        result.y = y + c2.y;

        return result;
}
```

In general, we optimise the code in the above example. Instead of explicitly defining a named complex number result we use a so-called *anonymous object* that we initialise using a constructor and we return this anonymous object. The new code is more compact and will possibly perform better than before:

```
Complex Complex::operator + (const Complex& c2) const
{ // Add two complex numbers

        return Complex(x + c2.x, y + c2.y);
}
```

Similarly, we define the code for the other operators in exactly the same way as described above:

```
Complex operator - (const Complex& c2) const;
Complex operator * (const Complex& c2) const;
Complex operator / (const Complex& c2) const;
```

It is important to note in these cases that three objects are involved; first, the current object that plays the role of the left operand, the argument c2 that is the right operand and a new object that is the return type of the member function. Furthermore, neither the current object nor c2 are modified by the operation (note the presence of const).

Until now, we discussed binary operators in which both operands were instances of the same class. It is possible to define operators where the operands are of different types. For example, we might wish to multiply complex numbers and scalars (in this case double precision numbers) and since multiplication is commutative both of the following operations should be possible:

```
Complex z2(2.0, 3.0);

Complex z7 = 2.0 * z2;
Complex z8 = z2 * 2.0;
```

If we wish to support this kind of functionality we state that it is now not possible to achieve this end with member functions. To this end, we must define *non-members*, that is, they are not members of the class. In practice however, we declare them in the class declaration and furthermore we usually declare them as being a *friend*. Thus means that the body of the operator is able to access the private member data of Complex. By default, a non-member function cannot access the private member data of a class unless the class explicitly states that that function is allowed to do so. Thus, in the case of scalar multiplication of a complex number by a scalar, we declare the operators as follows:

```
friend Complex operator * (const Complex& c, double d);
friend Complex operator * (double d, const Complex& c);
```

The first declaration allows us to create expressions of the form `Complex*double` while the second operator allows us to create expressions of the form `double*Complex`. The code for these operators is given by:

```
Complex operator * (const Complex& c, double d)
{ // Scaling by a double

        return Complex(c.x * d, c.y * d);
}

Complex operator * (double d, const Complex& c)
{ // Scaling by a double
        // Reuse already made operator
        return c * d;
}
```

Notice the absence of the scope resolution operator here because the functions are not members of class `Complex`. Furthermore, these functions have been granted access to the private member data of `Complex` because they are friends.

### 5.4.1   A special case: the assignment operator

There is one operator that deserves a full section on its own. This is the assignment operator as well-known in most programming languages. With C++, assignment means *deep copy* and this implies that when we write something like:

```
Complex z7 = z2;
```

that the object z7 is created and its values are initialised from the member data in z2. In this case the left-hand operand is modified (think about it) and hence the body of this operator must return the address of the current object. The declaration is:

```
Complex& operator = (const Complex& c);
```

and the code body is:

```
Complex& Complex::operator = (const Complex& c)
{
        // Avoid doing assign to myself
        if (this == &c)
                return *this;

        x = p.x;
        y = p.y;

        return *this;
}
```

With this specification we can carry out a *chain of assignments* such as

```
Complex z0(1.0, 2.0);
Complex z1, z2, z3, z4;
z4 = z3 = z1 = z0;
cout << "Chain: " << z0 << z1 << z3 << z4;
```

All the complex numbers will now have the same value as $z0$, as we would expect.

We now come to the following issue; it is possible to define 'combined' or 'shortcut' operators:

```
+=, *=, -=, /=
```

The syntax is the same as the normal assignment operator and of course the object returned is the address of the current object. Let us take an example. Suppose we wish to do the following in C++:

```
z4 += z1;      // Multiply z4 by z1 and modify it
```

In this case we have a very compact and efficient means of multiplying a complex number by another one. How do we do this? First, the declaration is:

```
Complex& operator += (const Complex& c);
```

and the code that does the implementation is given by:

```
Complex& Complex::operator += (const Complex& c)
{
        x += c.x;
        y += c.y;

        return *this;
}
```

Implementing the assignment operator for classes whose member data are defined on the stack is relatively easy because it is a matter of copying the member-data. For classes where the member-data is defined on the heap the situation is different because we then have to explicitly allocate and deallocate memory. This topic will be discussed in Chapter 6.

## 5.5  USING OPERATOR OVERLOADING FOR SIMPLE I/O

C++ has facilities for console input and output. At this stage all we wish to say is that it supports the `iostream` library for input and output operations. For built-in types you can use the library as-is. It uses operator overloading with two special operators, namely << (for output) and >> (for input). There are two special objects called `cin` and `cout` that we use for input and output, respectively. In order to use these you should include the following in your code:

```
#include <iostream>
using namespace std;
```

For the moment let us accept that this works. We discuss namespaces in a later chapter.

Our first example is to ask the user to enter two numbers and then to use these as data to create a complex number:

```
double real;
double imaginary;
cout << "Creating a complex number" << endl;
cout << "Give real part: ";
cin >> real;
cout << "Give imaginary part: ";
cin >> imaginary;

// User-defined class and output for its objects
Complex c(real, imaginary);
cout << c;
```

What's going on here? Well, we use the I/O library to prompt the user for input and we create a complex number c based on that input. Then we print the complex number. However, this latter facility is not in any I/O library but we must implement the code ourselves in class Complex. It is an application of operator overloading and we choose for the non-member variant because the first operand is an ostream object and the second operator is an instance of Complex:

```
friend ostream& operator << (ostream& os, const Complex& cmp);
```

We note that this function returns an address of an ostream object. The body of the function is:

```
ostream& operator << (ostream& os, const Complex& cmp)
{ // Print the complex number

    os << "(" << cmp.x << ", " << cmp.y << ")\ n";
    return os;
}
```

We note that this function is able to access the private member data of Complex because it is a friend. Finally, we can insert a number of objects in an output expression for ease of use. For, example, here is a code snippet that prints some complex numbers interspersed with text:

```
cout << "First: " << z1 << "Second: " << z2 << endl;
```

This concludes our introduction to the I/O stream library. It is useful when you write a class and you wish to print its instances. It is also useful for testing and debugging purposes. For extended testing we prefer to use more advanced graphics output devices such as Excel, for example.

## 5.6   FRIEND FUNCTIONS IN GENERAL

While we are on the subject of friends, it is possible to define friend functions for a class where the situation warrants it or it is appropriate. We take some examples again from class Complex and we wish to define common functions for instances of this class, for example, exponential, trigonometric and hyperbolic functions. The declarations are:

```
friend Complex exp(const Complex& c);      // Exponential
friend Complex cos(const Complex& c);      // Cosine function
friend Complex sin(const Complex& c);      // Sine function
friend Complex cosh(const Complex& c);     // Hyperbolic cosine
friend Complex sinh(const Complex& c);     // Hyperbolic sine
```

We now proceed to defining the bodies of these functions. The code is in fact a mapping to C++ of the mathematical definition of these functions. For example, the exponential function is defined by:

```
Complex exp(const Complex& c)
{ // Exponential function
      double ex = exp(c.x);
      return Complex(ex * cos(c.y), ex * sin(c.y));
}
```

Similarly, the code for some trigonometric hyperbolic functions is:

```
Complex cosh(const Complex& z)
{ // Hyperbolic cosine function

      return (exp(z) + exp(- (z))) * 0.5;

}


Complex cotanh(const Complex& z)
{ // Hyperbolc cotangent

      return cosh(z) / sinh(z);
}
```

To show how easy it is to use these functions in applications we give some examples:

```
Complex za = exp(Complex(0.0, 0.0));
cout << za;

Complex zs = sinh(za);
Complex zc = cosh(za);

cout << zs << zc;
Complex c2(0.0, 0.0);
cout << sinh(c2) << cosh(c2);
```

We use non-member functions when it is appropriate to do so. It simplifies the code as the example shows. Not everything is an object.

### 5.6.1  Friend classes

A less common example of a friend is the so-called friend class. A given class A declares a class B as a friend and this means that all of B's member functions can access the private member data of A. This feature can be useful for tightly coupled or highly dependent classes and is used when performance is important, for example in matrix algebra where we wish to have a tight coupling between vectors and matrices.

If class A wishes to say that class B is a friend, the syntax is:

```
class A
{
private: // Don't tell others who my friends are
friend class B; // Hi B class, you my friend

// ...
};
```

Some remarks on friend classes are:

- It is not possible for B to claim that it is a friend of A. A class grants friendship on another class and not the other way around
- The friend relationship is *reflexive* because it is a friend of itself. Of course, all member functions in a class can access all member data
- The friend relationship is not *symmetric* because saying that B is a friend of A does not mean that A is a friend of B. Unfortunately, you cannot choose your friends, they choose you
- The friend relationship is not *transitive* because the relationships 'A is a friend of B' and 'B is a friend of C' does not imply that 'A is a friend of C'. In other words, a friend of a friend is not a friend
- Friends are not inherited (we discuss inheritance in Chapter 8)

For me personally, using friend classes is a last resort. If I have to use it I suspect that my design is a bit shaky in the first place.

## 5.7   SUMMARY AND CONCLUSIONS

We have given a detailed introduction to the operator overloading mechanism in C++. This allows us to mimic operations from mathematics and Financial Engineering. The cognitive distance between problem and solution is reduced and it makes the resulting code easier to understand.

Operator overloading has some good applications in applied mathematics and to this end we have developed a C++ class that models complex numbers. We can create complex numbers, add, multiply and subtract them and carry out other operations on them, all with the help of operator overloading. We shall use this class in later chapters once we have developed some more supporting C++ functionality. There are several applications of complex numbers in Financial Engineering, for example numerical integration of functions of complex variables (Heston, 1993) and option pricing using Fourier transforms (Carr and Madan, 1999).

## 5.8   EXERCISE

1. Operating overloading is important for problems involving mathematical structures. The objective of this exercise is to familiarise yourself with the Vector and NumericMatrix classes that are provided on the CD. Read the following text and then investigate how we

have applied operator overloading in this context. But you should first read the following section on Vector and Matrix classes.

# APPENDIX: USEFUL DATA STRUCTURES IN C++

We concentrate on one-dimensional and two-dimensional data structures. To this end, we introduce basic *foundation* classes, namely:

- Array: sequential, indexible container containing arbitrary data types
- Vector: array class that contains numeric data
- Matrix: sequential, indexible container containing arbitrary data types
- NumericMatrix: matrix class that contains numeric data

The code for these classes is on the accompanying CD. The classes Array and Vector are one-dimensional containers whose elements we access using a single index while Matrix and NumericMatrix are two-dimensional containers whose elements we access using two indices.

We now discuss each of these classes in more detail.

We start with the class Array. This is the most fundamental class in the library and it represents a sequential collection of values. This template class that we denote by Array<V, I, S> has three generic parameters:

- V: the data type of the underlying values in the array
- I: the data type used for indexing the values in the array (integral)
- S: the so-called storage class for the array

The *storage class* is in fact an encapsulation of the STL vector class and it is here that the data in the array is actually initialised. At the moment there are specific storage classes, namely FullArray<V> and BandArray<V> that store a full array and a banded array of values, respectively.

Please note that it is **not** possible to change the size of an Array instance once it has been constructed. This is in contrast to the STL vector class where it is possible to let it grow.

The declaration of the class Array is given by:

```
template <class V, class I=int, class S=FullArray<V> >
class Array
{
private:
        S m_structure; // The array structure
        I m_start; // The start index
};
```

We see that Array has an embedded storage object of type S and a start index. The default storage is FullArray<V> and the default index type is int. This means that if we work with these types on a regular basis that we do not have to include them in the template declaration. Thus, the following three declarations are the same:

```
Array<double, int, FullArray<double> > arr1;
Array<double, int> arr1;
Array<double> arr1;
```

You may choose whichever data types that are most suitable for your needs.

The constructors in `Array` allow us to create instances based on size of the array, start index and so on. The constructors are:

```
Array();                              // Default constructor
Array(size_t size);                   // Give length start index ==1
Array(size_t size, I start);          // Length and start index
Array(size_t size, I start, const V& value);// Size, start, value
Array(const Array<V, I, S>& source);  // Copy constructor
```

Once we have created an array, we may wish to navigate in the array, access the elements in the array and to modify these elements. The member functions to help you in this case are:

```
// Selectors
I MinIndex() const;                   // Return the minimum index
I MaxIndex() const;                   // Return the maximum index
size_t Size() const;                  // The size of the array
const V& Element(I index) const;      // Element at position

// Modifiers
void Element(I index, const V& val);  // Change element at position
void StartIndex(I index);             // Change the start index

// Operators
virtual V& operator [] (I index);     // Subscripting operator
virtual const V& operator [] (I index) const;
```

This completes the description of the `Array` class. We do not describe the class that actually stores the data in the array. The reader can find the source code on the accompanying media kit.

We now discuss the `Vector` and `NumericMatrix` classes in detail. These classes are derived from `Array` and `Matrix`, respectively. Furthermore, we have created constructors for `Vector` and `NumericMatrix` classes as well. So what have these classes got that their base classes do not have? The general answer is that `Vector` and `NumericMatrix` assume that their underlying types are numeric. We thus model these classes as implementations of the corresponding mathematical structures, namely *vector space* and, *inner product spaces.*

We have implemented `Vector` and `NumericMatrix` as approximations to a vector space. In some cases we have added functionality to suit our needs. However, we have simplified things a little because we assume that the data types in a vector space are of the same types as the underlying field. This is for convenience only and it satisfies our needs for most applications in financial engineering.

Class `Vector` is derived from `Array`. Its definition in C++ is:

```
template <class V, class I=int, class S=FullArray<V> >
class Vector: public Array<V, I, S>
{
private:

        // No member data
};
```

We give the prototypes for some of the mathematical operations in Vector. The first is a straight implementation of a vector space; notice that we have applied operator overloading in C++:

```
Vector<V, I, S> operator - () const;
Vector<V, I, S> operator + (const Vector<V, I, S>& v) const;
Vector<V, I, S> operator - (const Vector<V, I, S>& v) const;
```

The second group of functions is useful because it provides functionality for *offsetting* the values in a vector:

```
Vector<V, I, S> operator + (const V& v) const;
Vector<V, I, S> operator - (const V& v) const;
Vector<V, I, S> operator * (const V& v) const;
```

The first function adds an element to each element in the vector and returns a new vector. The second and third functions are similar except that we apply subtraction and multiplication operators.

Class NumericMatrix is derived from Matrix. Its definition in C++ is:

```
template <class V, class I=int, class S=FullMatrix<V> >
class NumericMatrix: public Matrix<V, I, S>
{
private:

        // No member data
};
```

The constructors in NumericMatrix are the same as for Matrix. We may also wish to manipulate the rows and columns of matrices to this end to provide 'set/get' functionality. Notice that we return vectors for selectors but that modifiers accept Array instances (and instances of any derived class!):

```
// Selectors
Vector<V, I> Row(I row) const;
Vector<V, I> Column(I column) const;

// Modifiers
void Row(I row, const Array<V, I>& val);
void Column(I column, const Array<V, I>& val);
```

Since we will be solving linear systems of equations in later chapters we must provide functionality for multiplying matrices with vectors and with other matrices:

- Multiply a matrix and a vector
- Multiply a (transpose of a) vector and a matrix
- Multiply two matrices

Notice that the last two functions are not member of NumericMatrix but are non-member friends. This ploy allows us to multiply a matrix by a vector or vice versa.

We give some simple examples showing how to create vectors and how to perform some mathematical operations on the vectors.

```
// Create some vectors
Vector<double, int> vec1(10, 1, 2.0);// Start = 1, value 2.0
Vector<double, int> vec2(10, 1, 3.0);// Start = 1, value 3.0

Vector<double, int> vec3 = vec1 + vec2;
Vector<double, int> vec4 = vec1 - vec2;

Vector<double, int> vec5 = vec1 - 3.14;
```

We give an example to show how to use numeric matrices. The code is:

```
int rowstart = 1;
int colstart = 1;
NumericMatrix<double, int> m3(3, 3, rowstart, colstart);
for (int i = m3.MinRowIndex(); i <= m3.MaxRowIndex(); i++)
{

        for (int j = m3.MinColumnIndex(); j <= m3.MaxColumnIndex(); j++)
        {
            m3(i, j) = 1.0 /(i + j -1.0);
        }
}

print (m3);
```

The output from this code is:

```
MinRowIndex: 1 , MaxRowIndex: 3
MinColumnIndex: 1 , MaxColumnIndex: 3

MAT:[
Row 1 (1,0.5,0.333333,)
Row 2 (0.5,0.333333,0.25,)
Row 3 (0.333333,0.25,0.2,)]
```

# 6

# Memory Management in C++

## 6.1  INTRODUCTION AND OBJECTIVES

In this chapter we introduce the important and thorny issue of memory management in C++. Many developers have difficulty understanding how objects are created, how memory is allocated for these objects and when the objects are removed from memory. Before reading this chapter you must have a good understanding of the topics in Chapters 22 and 23 in this book, especially the following issues:

- Pointers and references (**vitally important**)
- Fixed-size and variable-sized arrays
- The essentials of memory allocation and deallocation

Whereas in these chapters we concentrated on built-in data type here we will now be interested in instances of user-defined C++ classes. In particular, we address the following topics:

- Creating 'single' objects on the stack and on the heap (also called the *free store*)
- Creating fixed-size and variable-sized arrays of objects
- Using the operators 'new' and 'delete'
- Creating classes whose member data are pointers to other objects: how does it work and what do we have to do?
- Some do's and don'ts with memory management

This is our first encounter with heap-based memory management. We shall elaborate on this subject in chapter 8 when we introduce inheritance. Our motto at this stage is to advance slowly in order to learn essential fundamentals. There is also time later to put the icing on the cake as it were. Thus we should:

- First get it working
- Then get it right
- And only then get it optimised

After having studied this chapter you should have a firm grasp of memory management features in C++.

## 6.2  SINGLE OBJECTS AND ARRAYS OF OBJECTS ON THE STACK

There are two ways to allocate memory, namely via the stack and via the heap. We discuss stack-based memory in this section and we then move on to heap-based memory management in the next section.

The advantage of defining objects on the stack is that memory management is taken care of for you. You do not have to worry about cleaning up because this is done automatically. A variable is defined in a scope and once it leaves the scope it is not longer accessible. For example, let us look at the code:

```
int main()
{

    { // Define a scope

        int j = 2;
        cout << j << endl;

    }

    cout << j;

    return 0;
}
```

This code will give a compiler error because the variable j does not exist outside the scope of the block in which it is defined.

We now discuss how to define a static array in C++. This means that the size of the array is known at compile time and it is not possible to extend its size at run-time. Let us take an example of defining an array of int of length 10:

```
int myArr[10];

// Initialise the array
for (int j = 0; j < 10; j++)
{
    myArr[j] = j + 1;
    cout << myArr[j] << ",";
}
```

Notice that the first index is 0 (this is standard C agreement) and the last index is 9. One of the dangers of writing this kind of code is that no range checking is carried out. Thus, the inclusion of the following code will produce erroneous answers (or worse):

```
cout << endl << myArr[-1];
cout << endl << myArr[1000];
```

This is serious state of affairs because random values will be read from memory. Some compilers have debug facilities for checking these *range errors* but we wish to ensure at the code level that such errors are caught and resolved. We shall come back to this problem in a later chapter when we discuss exception handling. In general, we wish to write code that catches these range errors and then lets us gracefully recover if and when these errors occur.

In this section we have discussed the creation of built-in types (both single variables and arrays) on the stack. The same conclusions hold for user-defined types. To this end, we define a very simple class as follows:

```
class SimpleOption
{
public:
        double T;
        double K;
        // ...

        SimpleOption () { T = 1.0; K = 100.0; }

        void print() const
        { // Read contents of option

                cout << "Expiry: "<< T << ", " << "Strike: " << K;
        }

};
```

We now create an instance (object) of this class by calling the default constructor:

```
{ // Define a scope

        SimpleOption opt1;
        opt1.print();
}
```

Trying to access the object outside the scope will result in a compile error.

Now, we define instances and arrays of instances of this class as follows:

```
SimpleOption myPortfolio[10];

// Initialise the array
for (int j = 0; j < 10; j++)
{
        myPortfolio[j].print();
}
```

This code creates an array of instances of class SimpleOption by calling the default constructor ten times. As before, indexing begins at zero.

Finally, accessing elements outside the array ranges will give unpredictable results, for example:

```
myPortfolio[-1].print();
myPortfolio[1000].print();
```

Creating single variables and objects on the stack is quite common in C++. In general, I do not like creating fixed arrays in my code because they use *magic numbers* and these will need to be changed when requirements change. In general, we should define arrays using dynamic memory allocation or even by using the C++ template mechanism to define compile-time parametric arrays (we shall discuss this topic in a later chapter). Finding the source of these 'magic' numbers may be difficult. One exception to this rule is to declare a fixed-sized array in our `main()` program because this place is highly visible to all and sundry.

## 6.3    SPECIAL OPERATORS: 'new' AND 'delete'

In this section we discuss how it is possible, as programmer to gain more control over how memory is managed in C++. To this end, we discuss how to work with the heap. Please note that we have given a short introduction to this topic in Chapter 22 (it might be an idea to have a quick read of it again just to refresh your memory).

In general, as programmer you have the power to do the following in C++:

- Explicit allocation of memory for single objects and arrays of objects
- Navigating in an array of objects
- Removing the memory that an object points to
- Forcing object pointers to go out of scope

Having understood these important issues you will be in a position to say that you know how memory management works in C++.

There are four basic activities in the current context:

A1: Declaring a pointer data type (no definition, no memory allocated)
A2: Allocating memory for the data type
A3: Accessing the values in the object
A4: Removing the data type and its data from memory (explicitly)

We now give some examples in the coming sections.

### 6.3.1   Single objects

C++, like C, supports pointer types. In the following snippet we declare two pointer types and initialise them using the operator 'new' (a reserved keyword); finally we clean up the memory. First, we define the pointer types as follows:

```
SimpleOption* opt;
SimpleOption* opt2;
```

The values that these point to are undefined. To this end, we initialise these with values by calling the appropriate constructors, as follows:

```
// Call default constructor
opt = new SimpleOption;
opt -> print();
```

or equivalently in deferenced form

```
(*opt).print();
```

```
// Call constructor with 2 parameters
opt2 = new SimpleOption(0.25, 90.0);
opt2 -> print();
```

We note that we can call a member function by using the operator '->' or dereferencing the pointer to get the object itself using the operator '*'.

Finally, the memory that you create must be cleaned up at some stage and to this end we use the operator 'delete':

```
delete opt;
delete opt2;
```

An important point to note is that the pointer types still exist (they have not gone out of scope, remember pointer types are defined on the stack); thus, we can allocate memory again:

```
opt = new SimpleOption;
(*opt).print();
delete opt;
```

Finally, once the pointer goes out of scope you cannot access it any more (it does not exist).

### 6.3.2  Arrays of objects

Our concern in this subsection is to create a *dynamic array* of objects. The steps are similar to those to create a single object on the heap, with one major difference, namely we create an array of objects on the heap. We show how the process works by taking an example. Suppose we wish to create an array of objects. First, we declare the pointer to the object:

```
// Now create an array of options
SimpleOption* optArray;
```

Now we define the array of options. Notice that the default constructor will be called ten times:

```
const int N = 10;
optArray = new SimpleOption[N]; // Default constructor called
```

We now modify each option in the array:

```
for (int j = 0; j < N; j++)
{ // Member data public for convenience only

    optArray[j].T = 1.0; // 1 year expiry

    optArray[j].K = 100.0; // Strike price

    optArray[j].print();
}
```

Finally, we clean up the memory as follows (**the square brackets are essential**):

```
delete [] optArray;
```

The above prototypical example shows how to create arrays of objects on the heap. You can and should apply the same ideas in other code and classes. In later chapters we shall show how this kind of code is used in C++ data structures.

## 6.4  SMALL APPLICATION: WORKING WITH COMPLEX NUMBERS

In chapter five we created C++ classes that models complex numbers. Recall that a complex number has a real part and an imaginary part. In this section we give some examples of where arrays of complex numbers can be used.

There are many applications of complex number theory to financial engineering, for example:

- Numerical integration of complex-valued functions on a line
- Functions of several complex variables
- Divided differences and numerical differentiation of complex-valued functions

The main objective of this section is to apply our new knowledge to a compact problem in mathematics.

The first example is to define a function that accepts a complex number as input and produces a complex number as output:

```
Complex myFunc(const Complex& z)
{ // Single valued function of a complex variable

        return z * z;
}
```

The objective now is to calculate the values of this function for a given array of complex numbers. We first create a bunch of complex numbers and insert them in a dynamic array:

```
Complex z1(1.0, 1.0);
Complex z2(2.0, 3.0);

Complex z3 = z1 * z2;
Complex z4 = 2.0 * z3;
Complex z5 = - z3;

// Create a dynamic list of Complex numbers
int Size = 5;
Complex* cpArray = new Complex[Size];
cpArray[0] = z1;
cpArray[1] = z2;
cpArray[2] = z3;
cpArray[3] = z4;
cpArray[4] = z5;
```

We now wish to print the values in this array and then remove the array from memory:

```
// Call function and print values for each z
for (int j = 0; j < Size; j++)
{
     cout << myFunc(cpArray[j]) << ", ";

}

delete [] cpArray;
```

We could use these function values in applications for complex numerical integration, for example.

The second example has to do with functions of several complex variables. In this case we wish to find the product and sum of an array of complex numbers. These functions are defined as follows:

```
Complex ComplexProduct(Complex* carr, int n)
{ // Complex function of several complex variables

    Complex product = carr[0];

    for (int j = 1; j < n; j++)
    {
        product *= carr[j];
    }

    return product;

}

Complex ComplexSum(Complex* carr, int n)
{ // Complex function of several complex variables

        Complex sum = carr[0];

        for (int j = 1; j < n; j++)
        {
            sum += carr[j];
        }

        return sum;

}
```

We see that the input consists of the start of an array and its size. It is the responsibility of the main program to supply 'real' arrays to these functions. In this case we use a fixed-sized array just to show that it is not always necessary to have dynamic arrays:

```
const int N = 5;
Complex fixedArray[5]; // The constant "5" is mandatory
for (int i = 0; i < Size; i++)
{
        fixedArray[i] = Complex ((double) i, 0.0);

}
```

The call to the functions for product and sum now reads:

```
Complex product = ComplexProduct(fixedArray, Size);
cout << "Product: " << product << endl;

Complex sum = ComplexSum(fixedArray, Size);
cout << "Sum: " << sum << endl;
```

This ends our short discussion on complex numbers and arrays of complex numbers. You can experiment with the source code on the CD to improve your knowledge of dynamic array allocation and deallocation.

There is quite a bit of administration involved with the above code, for example we must not forget to clean up memory. In the next section we shall create a new class that represents arrays of complex numbers and where much of the previous 'housekeeping' code is hidden from the user. This will improve the reliability and robustness of client code.

## 6.5   CREATING AN ARRAY CLASS

We now propose and develop a C++ class that models complex arrays. In particular, we encapsulate much of the nitty-gritty details in easy-to-use member functions. These functions hide how the code is actually realised, thus making life easier for the programmer. The ability to hide data and code details is one of the main advantages of the object-oriented paradigm.

We now discuss how we have implemented this C++ class.

### 6.5.1   Memory allocation and deallocation

In the first place we need to create arrays. This is done using constructors. We have defined the default constructor in the private region and this means that it cannot be used by client code. We create an array of a given size and we also can create an array as a copy of another one (the copy constructor).

The member data is given as follows:

```
private:
      Complex* arr;
      int size;
```

The declaration for the public constructors are:

```
ComplexArray(int size);
ComplexArray(const ComplexArray& source);
```

The body of these constructors is given by:

```
// Constructor with size
ComplexArray::ComplexArray(int Size)
{
     arr=new Complex[size];
     size=Size;
}

// Copy constructor
ComplexArray::ComplexArray(const ComplexArray& source)
{
     // Deep copy source
     size=source.size;
     arr=new Complex[size];
     for (int i=0; i<size; i++) arr[i]=source.arr[i];
}
```

The destructor for this class has a non-zero body. It must be declared using the virtual specifier (we shall explain why in a later chapter):

```
virtual ~ComplexArray();
```

The body of the destructor is given by:

```
ComplexArray::~ComplexArray()
{
    delete[] arr;
}
```

Please note that the `virtual` specifier should only be used once, namely in the header file, otherwise you will get a compiler error.

### 6.5.2    Accessing functions

Once we have created an array we now need some way of accessing and modifying its elements. To this end, we use the overloaded indexing operator `[]`. Furthermore, in order to avoid range errors, we have created two member functions that return the smallest and largest indices in the array:

```
int MinIndex() const; // Smallest index in array
int MaxIndex() const; // Largest index in array
```

The indexing operator is defined by:

```
const Complex& operator[](int index) const;
Complex& operator[](int index);
```

Here is a good example on how to use the indexing operator and ensuring that the arrays in your code remain within their legitimate bounds:

```
Complex ComplexSum(const ComplexArray& carr, int n)
{ // Complex function of several complex variables

    Complex sum = carr[carr.MinIndex()];

    for(int j = carr.MinIndex() + 1; j <= carr.MaxIndex(); j++)
    {
        sum += carr[j];
    }
    return sum;

}
```

Note that we have not included code for exception handling. That's the stuff of another chapter. The advice at this stage is to use the two member functions above for the smallest and largest indices in the array.

### 6.5.3  Examples

We now give a simple example on how to use the array. It is much easier than before, for example:

```
ComplexArray fixedArray(5);
for (int i=fixedArray.MinIndex();i<=fixedArray.MaxIndex(); i++)
{
      fixedArray[i] = Complex ((double) i, 0.0);

}
```

The difference now is that we state what we want to do and not how we want to do it. Furthermore, when the array object goes out of scope its destructor is called whereby the array's memory is cleaned up.

### 6.5.4  The full header file

We now assemble the declaration of member functions of the class ComplexArray for easy reference, on the one hand, and we give an example of what the author considers to be a good C++ style in terms of readability and reliability, on the other hand.

```
// ComplexArray.hpp
//
// Simple Complex Array class.
//
// (C) Datasim Education BV 1995-2006

#ifndef ComplexArray_hpp
#define ComplexArray_hpp

#include "Complex.hpp"

class ComplexArray
{
private:
      Complex* arr;
      int size;

public:

      // Constructors & destructor
      ComplexArray();
      ComplexArray(int size);
      ComplexArray(const ComplexArray& source);
      virtual ~ComplexArray();

      // Selectors
      int Size() const;
```

```
int MinIndex() const;      // Smallest index in array
int MaxIndex() const;      // Largest index in array

// Operators
const Complex& operator[](int index) const;
Complex& operator[](int index);

ComplexArray& operator = (const ComplexArray& source);
};

#endif // ComplexArray_hpp
```

## 6.6  SUMMARY AND CONCLUSIONS

We have introduced the vitally important topic of memory management. In particular, we discussed the problem of *explicitly* allocating and deallocating memory on the heap. This is a topic that tends to be glossed over. To this end, we hope that this chapter (and Chapter 22) will dispel the bogeyman of 'blue screen' and infamous memory leaks.

In order to promote relevance to the current reader group, we have taken an example (a C++ class that models arrays of complex numbers) that has a number of applications to financial engineering.

In later chapters we shall show how to hide low-level memory management details in easy-to-use classes. This is an example of the *Information Hiding principle*.

## 6.7  EXERCISES

1. In this exercise we create a two-dimensional matrix structure containing 10 rows and 20 columns (for example). You can create the matrix using static or dynamic memory or even by combining the two forms, for example:

```
// Compile-time
Complex matrix [10][20];

// Run-time (pointers to pointers)
Complex** matrix2;

// "Hybrid": pointers to fixed arrays
Complex* matrix3[10];
```

   Create code to initialise each of the above variables. Each element in the matrices should have the default value Complex (1.0, 0.0). Create code to print the contents of each of these matrices.

   Pay attention to allocation and deallocation of memory if you are using pointers!
2. Let us suppose that we wish to write a global function that we call MySwap that interchanges the values of two complex numbers. Consider the following alternatives by examining their

function prototypes:

```
void MySwap(Complex c1, Complex c2); // Call by value
void MySwap2(Complex& c1, Complex& c2); // Call by reference
void MySwap3(const Complex& c1, const Complex& c2); // const references
void MySwap4(Complex* c1, Complex* c2); // Using pointers
void MySwap5(const Complex* c1, const Complex* c2); // const pointers
```

Write the bodies of each of these functions and test the functions to see what happens. What happens? What goes wrong and what goes right? Which solution do you approve of most and why?

3. A C++ struct is similar to a class in C++ except that all members are public. In fact, they are used as a kind of data container although they also may have member functions. Consider the structure for a two-dimensional point:

```
struct Point
{
    double x;      // x coordinate
    double y;      // y coordinate
}
```

Now define an array of Point instances representing the unit rectangle (0,0), (1,0), (0,1) and (1,1). Consider using structs and dynamic arrays (for example, you like to create a Polyline at a later stage; a polyline is a dynamic array of points).

4. Modify and adapt the code in ComplexArray to create a data container representing a bounded stack of doubles. In general, it is possible to create a stack of a given size and then it is possible to push a double onto the stack and it is also possible to pop the most-recent value from the stack (we call stack a *LIFO == Last In First Out structure*). The interface is:

```
class Stack
{
private:

        // EXX What is the member data in this case?

        Stack(const Stack& source);        // Copy constructor
        // Operators
        Stack& operator = (const Stack& source);

public:
        // Constructors & destructor
        Stack();                           // Default constructor
        Stack(int NewSize);                // Initial size of the stack

        virtual ~Stack();                  // Destructor
```

```
        void Push(double NewItem);      // Push element onto stack
        double Pop();                   // Pop last pushed element


};

#endif // STACK_HPP
```

Write the body of each member function and write a test program. Again, take care of memory management (new in constructors and delete in the destructor).

5. Let us have a look at matrices with 10 rows and 20 columns again. To this end, examine the following code for motivation:

```
#include <iostream>
using namespace std;

int main()
{

        double m[10][20];

        m[0][1] = 2.0;

        // etc.

        cout << m[0][1] << endl;

        return 0;
}
```

Write global functions for:
(a) adding, subtracting and multiplying matrices
(b) multiplication of a matrix by a scalar
(c) the minimum, maximum and average values of a matrix
(d) sum of squares of the elements of a matrix
Create a test program and run it.

## 6.8   REVIEW QUESTIONS AND COMMENTS

1. There are two ways to declare variables and assign memory for them in C++: the stack and the heap (or free store). Discuss their differences as well as their similarities. When and how are variables created and deleted on the stack and heap and discuss how variables can be accessed and modified?

2. Define the following terms: pointer, references, dereferencing. What is a null pointer? Is this the same as an uninitialized pointer? How can you initialise a pointer?

3. Explain the difference between compile-time and run-time memory allocation.

4. In the following statement determine the rows and columns of the following two-dimensional matrix structure:

`double mat[10][20];`

Which index changes most rapidly in a for loop?

5. What is a `const` pointer? Why is it useful?

# 7
# Functions, Namespaces and Introduction to Inheritance

## 7.1 INTRODUCTION AND OBJECTIVES

We introduce three new C++ concepts in this chapter. First, we discuss how to model functions and we introduce the so-called *function pointer* mechanism. This feature is important in the current book because much of our work involves defining functions that implement algorithms. Second, we introduce the *namespace* mechanism. A namespace is used to group logically related C++ code. You can place almost anything in a namespace. Namespaces can be nested. Finally, we introduce the concept of inheritance. In particular, we discuss how to share common functionality between similar classes and we do this by defining a so-called *base class* that we can specialise by defining *derived classes*.

Having understood the C++ theory in this chapter you will be in a position to apply the knowledge to financial engineering applications. In order to keep the material relevant to your domain we have developed a number of examples and test cases:

- Defining function pointers and using them as class members. In this way we can create flexible code by allowing member functions to switch between different functionality
- Grouping related functions in namespaces and using namespaces in financial engineering applications
- Basic examples of inheritance: we avoid all examples that have to do with dogs, cats and other kinds of hierarchies. Instead, we give examples that are of direct relevance to the current domain. In this case, we introduce several non-linear solvers such as the Bisection method and the Newton-Raphson method. Each specific solver will be implemented as a C++ class
- We can use the above solvers to solve problems related to volatility estimation (Haug, 1998), fixed income problems (Fabozzi, 1993) and finding the roots of polynomials (Scheid, 1968)

To summarise, this chapter introduces a number of mechanisms that promote code reusability, understandability and reliability.

## 7.2 FUNCTIONS AND FUNCTION POINTERS

In this section we show how to work with functions and function pointers in C++. A function pointer is defined on the stack and it can be assigned to a real function at run-time. The advantage is clear: no hard-coded functions in client code but run-time switching ability.

We also discuss the applications of functions and function pointers to financial engineering in this section. A more detailed discussion can be found in Duffy (2004).

### 7.2.1   Functions in financial engineering

A significant part of financial engineering involves defining functions that do something of relevance in this domain. One reason why writing C++ software for this domain is so difficult is that the functions must satisfy stringent requirements. For example, we can think of the following features that we would like to support:

- A function may have one, two and n-dimensional equivalents
- The number of input arguments to a function may be variable
- The return type of a function may be a scalar or a vector quantity
- The return types can be real-valued or complex-valued, for example
- It must be possible to replace the code that implements a function by another block of code (this is called a *Strategy* pattern)

These are not the only requirements that may be desired in an application but they do give an indication of the challenges that we must surmount in our applications. In this chapter we shall resolve some of these using 'standard' C++ while in later chapters we shall see how the Standard Template Library (STL) and Design Patterns enable us to define classes that realise the above requirements.

### 7.2.2   Function categories

We now discuss what functions are from a mathematical point of view.

A *function* (or *mapping*) $f$ between elements of a space $D$ (called the *domain* of $f$) and a space $R$ (called the *range* of $f$) is an association in which each value of a variable $x$ in $D$ is mapped to one and only one variable $y$ in $R$. A function is a particular kind of *relation* and we can then view the function as a set of ordered pairs $(x, y)$ with $x$ in $D$ and $y$ in $R$.

A common notation for a function $f$ from $D$ to $R$ is

$$f: D \rightarrow R \tag{7.1}$$

Functions can be composed. For example, suppose $f$ is a mapping from $D$ to $R1$ and $g$ is a mapping from $R1$ to $R2$ then the composition of $g$ and $f$ is defined by

$$(gf)(x) = g(f(x)) \text{ for all } x \text{ in } D \tag{7.2}$$

Notice that the range of the composed mapping $gf$ is $R2$.

In equation (7.1) we have not said anything about the structure or 'texture' of the spaces $D$ and $R$. For example, these spaces may be continuous or discrete, deterministic, fuzzy and so on. We concentrate in this chapter on deterministic functions only and the possible kinds of mappings are:

G1: Continuous to continuous
G2: Continuous to discrete
G3: Discrete to continuous
G4: Discrete to discrete

In order to reduce the scope even further we distinguish between the following kinds of functions:

- Scalar-valued function (maps a `double` to a `double`, for example)
- Vector function (maps a `double` into a vector)

- Real-valued function (maps a vector into a `double`)
- Vector-valued function (maps a vector into a vector)

A *scalar-valued function* takes a single scalar argument as input and produces a single scalar result as output. A *vector function* takes a scalar as input and produces a vector as output. Thus, a vector function can be seen as an array of scalar-valued functions. A *real-valued function* accepts a vector as input and produces a `double` as output. Finally, a *vector-valued function* accepts a vector as input and produces a vector result as output.

In this chapter we concentrate on scalar-valued and real-valued functions. Of course, it is not difficult to define the equivalent complex-valued functions.

### 7.2.3  Modelling functions in C++

In this section we discuss function pointers and we give an example to show how they work. In general, pointers to functions can be assigned, placed in arrays, passed to functions, returned by functions, and so on.

We declare a function pointer by defining its input arguments, return type and its name by using pointer arithmetic. We now give an example of a function declaration with an embedded function pointer:

```
void genericFunction (double myX, double myY,
                            double (*f) (double x, double y))
{
        // Call the function f with arguments myX and myY
        double result = (*f)(myX, myY);

        cout << "Result is: " << result << endl;
}
```

This is the declaration of a function called `genericFunction`. It is a specific function (that is, it is not a function pointer) and it accepts arguments `myX` and `myY` that will be passed to the function pointer `f`. You can then call `genericFunction` by giving any two arguments and a specific function that has two arguments of type `double` and whose return type is a `double`, for example the following:

```
double add(double x, double y)
{
    cout << "** Adding two numbers: " << x << ", " << y << endl;
    return x + y;
}
double multiply(double x, double y)
{
    cout << "** Multiplying two numbers: " << x << ", " << y << endl;
    return x * y;
}
double subtract(double x, double y)
{
    cout << "** Subtracting two numbers: " << x << ", " << y << endl;
    return x - y;
}
```

The advantage of using function pointers is that functions using them are not hard-wired into specific functions but a primitive form of *polymorphism* is offered. We shall introduce this topic when we discuss the C++ inheritance mechanism in detail.

Continuing with the above example, we define the basic operations for addition, multiplication and subtraction and these functions will be called from `genericFunction`. We now show how this is done by giving the source code. We call `genericFunction` three times from the `main()` program:

```
int main()
{
    double x = 3.0;
    double y = 2.0;
    genericFunction(x, y, add);
    genericFunction(x, y, multiply);
    genericFunction(x, y, subtract);
    return 0;
}
```

### 7.2.4   Application areas for function pointers, part I

We give a short discussion of where function pointers can be of use in numerical analysis and financial engineering. Later chapters will elaborate on these issues:

- As members of classes: we can declare a function pointer as a (private or public) member of a class. We can then call this function from the member functions of the class
- Any function `func()` can contain a function pointer as formal parameter. Client code can then call function `func()` with the function pointer assigned to a specific function, as the code in section 7.2.3 has shown
- It is possible to define 'global' functions (here we mean non-member functions) that contain function pointers as formal arguments and can be used by function pointers in an assignment statement. This is an example of procedural programming and it can be useful because it is not mandatory to define classes to achieve a similar effect. In short, they reduce cognitive overload

We shall elaborate on these issues in the coming chapters.

## 7.3   AN INTRODUCTION TO NAMESPACES IN C++

A namespace is a mechanism for expressing logical grouping (Stroustrup, 1997). This mechanism allows us to group code that belongs together into a common package as it were. The concept is not just restricted to C++ and its use is found in languages such as C# and Extensible Markup Language (XML).

Let us take an example. Suppose we wish to model a Stochastic Differential Equation (SDE) (Kloeden *et al.*, 1994). Each SDE has a diffusion term and a drift term, each of which is modelled as a simple function (in this case). There are many implementations of the diffusion and drift functions and we wish to replace one set (or logical grouping) by another one. To this end, we define a namespace for each set of functions and we use the keyword 'namespace' as follows:

```
namespace MyFunctions
{
    double diffusion (double x) { return x; }
    double convection (double x) { return x*x; }
}
namespace YourFunctions
{
    double diffusion (double x) { return 2.0; }
    double convection (double x) { return 1.0; }
}
```

In a sense these namespaces represent mutually exclusive functionality. The next question is how to access functionality in a given namespace. The two main ways of doing this are:

- By means of *qualified names*
- The 'using' declaration
- The 'using' directive

We discuss the first option now. Since a namespace is a scope it is possible to access its members using explicit qualification, for example as in the code snippet:

```
cout << YourFunctions::convection (10.0) << endl;
```

This way of programming can become a bit tedious especially if the above function is the one that we use on a regular basis. We resolve this small problem by a *using-declaration* to state in one place that the function convection() has the scope YourFunctions:

```
using YourFunctions::convection;
cout << convection (10.0) << endl;
```

Finally, a *using directive* is a global command that gives us 'default' access to all the members of a namespace, for example:

```
using namespace MyFunctions;
cout << "Directive: \ n";
cout << convection (10.0) << endl;
cout << diffusion (2.0) << endl;
```

In this way we define a common standard set of interface functions and then each specific namespace can implement the functionality differently. For example, choosing another namespace produces a new set of results:

```
using namespace YourFunctions;
cout << convection (10.0) << endl;
cout << diffusion (2.0) << endl;
```

### 7.3.1 Some extra functionality

We now give a brief discussion of some other useful features associated with namespaces. In general, it is a good idea to create names that will not 'collide' with other code in your application; for example, it is better to choose a name 'DatasimArrayContainerNS' than

'`Array`'. On the other hand, it is laborious to have to type in such long names and furthermore it clutters our code and tends to make it unreadable. C++ has a solution to this problem and to this end it is possible to define an *alias* (synonym) for the namespace. Referring to the above example, we can now see how useful the alias is:

```
namespace YA = YourFunctions; // Define alias NS called YA
cout << YA::diffusion (2.0) << endl;
```

Finally, we can combine function pointers and namespaces to help us create flexible and interchangeable software. For example, let us suppose that we have a namespace containing two function pointers:

```
namespace StandardInterface
{
    // Namespace consisting of function pointers
    double (*func1) (double x);
    double (*func2) (double x, double y);
}
```

In general, different developers may have various implementations of these functions, for example:

```
namespace Implementation1
{
    double F1 (double x) { return x; }
    double F2 (double x, double y) { return x*y; }
}


namespace Implementation2
{
    double G1 (double x) { return -x; }
    double G2 (double x, double y) { return -x*y; }
}
```

Then we can switch (at compile time) between the different implementations just by assigning each function pointer:

```
// Assign the function pointers from NS
StandardInterface::func1 = Implementation1::F1;
StandardInterface::func2 = Implementation1::F2;
```

We then can use the functions in a transparent way by using an alias:

```
using namespace StandardInterface;
cout << func1(2.0) << ", " << func2(3.0, -4.0) << endl;
```

Then, if we wish to use a different implementation of the namespace, we just assign the function pointers:

```
func1 = Implementation2::G1;
func2 = Implementation2::G2;
cout << func1(2.0) << ", " << func2(3.0, -4.0) << endl;
```

We thus see that we can keep our code reasonably portable by using namespaces. But be careful; too many namespaces and/or deeply nested namespaces may not always be a good idea in C++.

## 7.4   AN INTRODUCTION TO THE INHERITANCE MECHANISM IN C++

In this section we give a short introduction to inheritance in C++. We discuss enough theory so that we can apply it to a simple problem in financial engineering.

In general, a class (call it B for base class) has member data and member functions. Some of these members are `public`, meaning that any class can access them while other members are `private`, which means that they cannot be accessed by classes outside the class B itself (there is another level of accessibility called `protected` but this is outside the scope of the current discussion). It is now possible to inherit a new class (call it D for derived class) from B. This means that all the public member function in B can be used by instances of D without having to rewrite the functions again in D! Thus, inheritance in C++ is the realisation of the Gen/Spec relationship between two classes, that is:

**Rule: An instance of D is also an instance of B**

It is possible to append new functionality to D that the base class B does not have. For example, D could have extra member data or new member functions. Furthermore, it is possible to override functions in B because D implements them differently. We examine each of these scenarios in the following sub-sections. To this end, we take a 'hello world example' of person and employee classes but of course the ideas carry over to problems in any domain. We discuss these issues in later chapters.

### 7.4.1   Basic inheritance structure

We commence with a base class representing a person entity. This is a time-dependent class because it contains date and timestamp information as well as string information concerning the name of the person, for example. We use the Datasim classes for dates and time that you can find on the accompanying medium. The declaration and member data are:

```
class Person
{
public: // Everything public, for convenience only
          // Data
          string nam;                        // Name of person
          DatasimDate dob;                   // Date of birth
          DatasimDate createdD;              // Internal, date created
          DatasimDateTime createdT;          // Internal, time created
public:
          // Public functions
};
```

We see that the class contains member data to tell when the object was created. This is useful for administration later.

The only constructor in this class is defined inline and is given by:

```
Person (const string& name, const DatasimDate& DateofBirth)
{
    nam = name;
    dob = DateofBirth;
    createdD = DatasimDate();        // default, today REALLY!
    createdT = DatasimDateTime();    // default, now REALLY!
}
```

We see that the default constructors for date and time classes give us today's date and the time now (based on the computer clock).

We have defined a number of member functions in this class:

```
void print() const
{
 // Who am I?
        cout << "\ n** Person Data **\ n";
        cout << "Name: " << nam << "Date of birth: " << dob
                        << ", Age: " << age() << endl;
        cout << "Object created: " << createdD
                        << " "; createdT.print(); cout << endl;
}
int age() const
{
        return int( double(DatasimDate() - dob) / 365.0);
}
```

We now construct some instances of the class Person and we print them on the screen console:

```
DatasimDate myBirthday(29, 8, 1952);
string myName ("Daniel J. Duffy");
Person dd(myName, myBirthday);
dd.print();

DatasimDate bBirthday(06, 8, 1994);
string bName ("Brendan Duffy");
Person bd(bName, bBirthday);
bd.print();
```

The output from this program is given by:

```
** Person Data **
Name: Daniel J. Duffy, Date of birth: 29/8/1952, Age: 52
Object created: 15/4/2005 19:11:32
** Person Data **
Name: Brendan Duffy, Date of birth: 6/8/1994, Age: 10
Object created: 15/4/2005 19:11:32
```

Having defined the base class for the person entity, we now wish to create a class that models an employee abstraction. An employee is in all respects a person, in other words it inherits all the members of the latter. But it can also define new members such as salary, function in a company and retirement age. Furthermore, we must define a function that prints employee instances. The declaration of the employee class reads:

```
class Employee : public Person
{
public: // For convenience only
        string fun; // Function
        double sal; // Salary
        int rAge; // Retirement age
        // other functions
};
```

We say that Employee is publicly derived from Person and this means that all public functions in Person are accessible from Employee.

Of course, we now have to create employee instances, but the question is how? Before we answer this question we must realise that in general, an instance of a derived class D has data corresponding to its own class declaration as well as the data that it inherits from the base class B. This is true even if the data in B is private; the data is inherited even though it is not directly accessible. Thus, the derived class *delegates* responsibility for the initialisation of appropriate member data to the base class. This is a recommended way to do this because the derived class does not need to know all the *irrelevant* details of how the data in the base class was initialised. This is one example of what is called *information hiding*.

### 7.4.2 Adding new functionality

We now add new member functions to Employee. In particular, we wish to print employees and we wish to calculate other things, for example how many years left to retirement. First, to print an employee instance we print its person-relation data and then we print the employee-related data. Again, we use a form of delegation to the base class:

```
void print() const
{ // Who am I and what do I do?

// Print Base class data
cout << "\ n** Employee Data **\ n";
Person::print(); // Call print() in the base class

// Now print data from current derived class
cout << "\ nFunction: " << fun << ", Salary: " << sal
        << ", Retires at: " << rAge << endl
        << YearsToRetirement() << " years to retirement.\ n";
}
```

We thus call the print function in the base class by using the scope resolution operator. The second added functionality is to calculate the number of years to retirement:

```
int YearsToRetirement() const
{ // How many more years slogging away at C++?
      return rAge - age();
}
```

Here we see that we call the member function age() that is derived from Person; you do not have to recode it in Employee. The following code creates an employee instance:

```
Employee dde (myName, myBirthday, string("Cuchulainn Chief")
                          , 0.01, 65);
dde.print();
```

The output when we run this code is:

```
** Employee Data **
** Person Data **
Name: Daniel J. Duffy, Date of birth: 29/8/1952, Age: 52
Object created: 15/4/2005 19:11:32
Function: Cuchulainn Chief, Salary: 0.01, Retires at: 65
13 years to retirement.
```

### 7.4.3   Overriding functionality: polymorphic and non-polymorphic behaviour

We now come to an important topic in C++. This is the virtual keyword and it has applications in object-oriented programming. Let us begin with a simple counter-example. In general, a pointer to any base class can always be assigned to the address of a derived class. You, as programmer do not have to do any coding in order to realise that functionality, for example:

```
Employee dde (myName, myBirthday, string("Cuchulainn")
               , 0.01, 65);
Person* p = &dde;
p -> print();
```

The output is:

```
** Person Data **
Name: Daniel J. Duffy, Date of birth: 29/8/1952, Age: 52
Object created: 15/4/2005 19:11:32
Working with pointers II
```

Something is wrong! The pointer to the base class Person really contains the address of an Employee instance but unfortunately the wrong print() function is called. What we really want is to call Employee::print(). In order to achieve this we must use the virtual keyword. To this end, we define the function in Person:

```
virtual void DeepPrint() const
{
        print(); // Calls Person::print()
}
```

Then the overridden function in Employee is now:

```
void DeepPrint() const
{
    print(); // Calls Employee::print()
}
```

Finally, we can now define a pointer and print the employee data:

```
Employee dde (myName, myBirthday, string("Cuchulainn Chief")
        , 0.01, 65);
Person* p = &dde;
p -> DeepPrint();
```

The output is now:

```
** Employee Data **
** Person Data **
Name: Daniel J. Duffy, Date of birth: 29/8/1952, Age: 52
Object created: 15/4/2005 19:11:32
Function: Cuchulainn, Salary: 0.01, Retires at: 65
13 years to retirement.
```

The use of the virtual keyword in C++ allows us to implement *polymorphism*. In other words, we have a pointer to a base class and we do not know or even care which derived class address it points to. We do not have to implement checks to determine what the type of the derived class is. The compiler calls the correct DeepPrint() function in this case. For example, we could have different derived classes such as TaxPayer, Shareholder and so on, each one with its own DeepPrint() function. For example, the following pseudo code shows the power of polymorphism:

```
Person* parr[3]; // Array of pointers
parr[0] = new Employee(...);
parr[1] = new TaxPayer(...);
parr[2] = new ShareHolder(...);
// Now print the array
for (int j = 0; j < 3; j++)
{
    parr[j] -> DeepPrint();
}
```

In this loop we do not have to concern ourselves about the underlying types; the correct function is called depending on which derived class is being pointed to. Of course, we must clean up the above array.

Summarising: The rules when calling a member function in a derived class D are:

- If the member function is in D's interface, then this function is called
- If the member function is not in D's interface, then the base class B's interface is searched. If found in B then the function is called. This process is recursive because D may have direct and indirect parents
- If the function is not found in D or in any parent classes, a compile error occurs

## 7.5  MULTIPLE INHERITANCE

In the examples to date, we have derived a class from one base class. It is possible to derive a class from two or more base classes. This phenomenon is called multiple inheritance:

```
class D: public Base1, public Base2
{
        // Members of D here
};
```

In this case D inherits all the functionality of both Base1 and Base2. A full discussion of this topic is given in Stroustrup (1997).

We can avoid multiple inheritance by using a combination of (single) inheritance and composition:

```
class D : public Base1
{
private:
      Base2* base2;
public:
      // Members here
};
```

We shall discuss this topic in more detail in Chapter 25.

## 7.6  SOLUTION OF NONLINEAR EQUATIONS

In this and the following two sections we discuss an application of function pointers, namespaces and inheritance to a specific problem in financial engineering, namely calculating volatility and yields in fixed income applications (Haug, 1998). First, in this section we introduce a number of nonlinear solvers for real-valued functions of a single real variable. We introduce the mathematical background in this section and in section 7.7 we show how to 'map' the mathematics to C++ classes. Finally, in section 7.8 we apply the new C++ classes to solving a number of problems relating to volatility estimation.

The theory of nonlinear equations is very old and many techniques have been developed (Dahlquist and Björck, 1974; Press *et al.*, 2002). In this section we discus the problem of finding real values x that satisfy the equation

$$f(x) = 0$$

where $f$ is a real-valued function. The methods to be discussed are:

- Bisection Method
- Newton's method
- Secant method
- Steffensen iteration

The *Bisection method* assume that the function $f(x)$ has a zero in the interval $(a, b)$ and we assume that the signs are opposite at the end points, that is $f(a)f(b) < 0$. The essence of the method is to divide the interval into equal parts until we arrive at an interval that is so small that contains the zero of the function and is small enough to satisfy the given tolerance. The basic algorithm is defined using a sequence of intervals of ever-diminishing size:

$$(a, b) \supset (a_1, b_2) \supset (a_2, b_2) \supset (a_3, b_3) \supset \ldots$$

where

$$(a_k, b_k) = \begin{cases} (m_k, b_{k-1}) & \text{if } f(m_k) < 0 \\ (a_{k-1}, m_k) & \text{if } f(m_k) > 0 \end{cases} \qquad (7.1)$$

and

$$m_k = \tfrac{1}{2}(a_{k-1} + b_{k-1})$$
$$\text{(midpoint of interval)}$$

After n steps the root is in an interval having a length given by

$$b_n - a_n = 2^{-1}(b_{n-1} - a_{n-1}) = 2^{-n}(b - a) \qquad (7.2)$$
$$m_{n+1} \qquad\qquad \text{(root)} \qquad\qquad (7.3)$$

Thus the deviation from the exact root $\alpha$ is given by

$$\alpha = m_{n+1} \pm d_n, \quad d_n = 2^{-n-1}(b - a) \qquad (7.4)$$

In general, we are interested in locating the zero of the function to within a given tolerance TOL. This means that we wish to calculate the number of subdivisions of the original interval (a,b). To this end, some arithmetic based on the equation (7.4) gives us the following estimate:

$$n > \frac{\log\left(\dfrac{b-a}{TOL}\right)}{\log 2} - 1 \qquad (7.5)$$

The advantage of the Bisection method is that we always can define an interval of arbitrary size in which the zero is located. The disadvantage is that convergence is slow. In fact, at each step we gain one binary digit in accuracy. We note also that the rate of convergence is independent of the given function $f(x)$. The method may be used to give us good initial approximations to more sophisticated nonlinear solvers.

Newton's method (or the *Newton-Raphson* method as it is also called) is probably one of the most famous iterative schemes in Numerical Analysis.

The main advantage of the Newton-Raphson method is that it converges quickly. We say that its order of convergence is two by which we mean that the error at each iteration decreases quadratically:

$$x_{n+1} = x_n + h_n, \quad h_n = -\frac{f(x_n)}{f'(x_n)} \tag{7.6}$$

The disadvantage is that the choice of the initial approximation is vitally important. If this is not chosen carefully the method may not converge at all or it may even converge to the wrong solution. Furthermore, we must have an analytical expression for the derivative of $f$ and this may not always be available.

The *Secant method* can be derived from the Newton-Raphson method by approximating the derivative by a divided difference. The resulting iterative scheme now becomes:

$$x_{n+1} = x_n + h_n, \quad h_n = -f_n \frac{x_n - x_{n-1}}{f_n - f_{n-1}}, \quad f_n \neq f_{n-1} \tag{7.7}$$

We note that the Secant needs two initial approximations in contrast to Newton-Raphson, that only needs one initial approximation. In general, we must be careful when programming the Secant method when the function values are close and/or the solutions at levels n and n + 1 are close; in such cases we calculate terms that are effectively 0/0!

A disadvantage of the Secant method is that it is only first-order accurate. In order to achieve second-order accuracy without having to evaluate derivatives we propose *Steffensen's method*, given by the scheme:

$$x_{n+1} = x_n - \frac{f(x_n)}{g(x_n)}$$

$$g(x_n) = \frac{f(x_n + f(x_n)) - f(x_n)}{f(x_n)} \tag{7.8}$$

This scheme requires two function evaluations but no computation of a derivative.

With the exception of the Bisection method, the choice of the initial approximation is vital and it must be 'close' to the exact solution, otherwise the iterative scheme may not converge. There are iterative methods based on the continuation (or homotopy) methods that converge to the true solution even when the initial guess is not good, but a discussion of these techniques is outside the scope of this book.

## 7.7   NONLINEAR SOLVERS IN C++: DESIGN AND IMPLEMENTATION

We now discuss a C++ hierarchy for the different nonlinear solvers that we have just introduced. In particular, we create an extendible class hierarchy of nonlinear solvers for real-valued functions of a single variable. In general, we remark:

- The base class contains common data and default functionality while derived classes have extra data and functionality
- The base class may declare a pure virtual member function that specifies functionality for all its derived classes. These derived classes must implement this abstract functionality

The interface for the abstract base class is given as:

```
class NonlinearSolver
{
```

```
public:
            double (*myF)(double x);// Function whose root we want
            double tol;                 // Desired accuracy
public:
            NonlinearSolver(double (*function)(double)) { }
            virtual double solve() = 0;
};
```

Each of the above solvers is implemented as a derived class. For example, Steffensen's method
is:

```
class SteffensensSolver : public NonlinearSolver
{ // One-step nonlinear solver
private:
            double x0;                  // Initial guess
            double xPrevious, xCurrent;
            long n;                     // Number of iterations taken
public:
            SteffensensSolver(double guess, double (*myFunc)(double x))
            {
                x0 = guess; xPrevious = x0;
                myF = myFunc;
            }

            double solve()
            {
                    double tmp; double hn; n = 1; xPrevious = x0;
L1:
                    tmp = myF(xPrevious);
                    hn = (myF(xPrevious + tmp) - tmp)/ tmp;
                    hn = tmp/hn;
                    xCurrent = xPrevious - hn;
                    xPrevious = xCurrent;

                    n++;
                    if (::fabs(hn) <= tol)
                    {
                            return xCurrent;

                    }
                    goto L1;
            }

            void printStatistics() const
            {

                cout << "\ nData pertaining to Steffensen's method\ n";
```

```
                    cout << "Value: " << xCurrent << endl;
                    cout << "Number of iterations (actual): "
                                << n << endl;
              }
};
```

We have provided the full code on the CD.

## 7.8   APPLYING NONLINEAR SOLVERS: CALCULATING VOLATILITY

In previous chapters we gave some formulae for call and put options based on (known) parameters such as the strike price and the volatility, for example. But we now have the 'inverse'
problem: given that we know the price of the option and all its parameters except the volatility,
how do we calculate the volatility? We have an equation with one unknown, namely the
volatility. It is a scalar nonlinear equation and we solve using one of the above nonlinear
solvers. In general it is difficult to measure volatility directly and the objective in general is to
use that volatility that is compatible with the market price. We call this the *implied volatility*. In
general we estimate the volatility using call prices. There is no closed formula for the implied
volatility. In general we could calculate it for a set of strike prices and expiry dates on a single
underlying. This results in an array of values and hence we conclude that implied volatility is
not constant.

We have taken the test case from Haug (1998) and the code that calculates the price of a
call option (see the CD again):

```cpp
double CallPrice(double sig)
{

        // Test case Haug p. 172; student exercise to extend it
        double S = 59.0;
        double K = 60.0;
        double r = 0.067;
        double marketPrice = 2.82;     // The call price
        double b = r;
        double T = 0.25;                        // Three months

        double tmp = sig * sqrt(T);
        double d1 = ( log(S/K) + (b+ (sig*sig)*0.5 ) * T )/ tmp;
        double d2 = d1 - tmp;

        double calculatedValue =
                (S * exp((b-r)*T) * N(d1)) - (K * exp(-r * T)* N(d2));

        // Function in the form f(x) = 0
        return marketPrice - calculatedValue;
}
```

We have found the same results as in Haug (1998) for both the Secant Method and Steffensen's method but the Bisection method does not seem to converge to the correct solution for some reason.

Some code is now given:

```
// Steffensen's method
double guess = 0.2;

SteffensensSolver steff(guess, CallPrice);
steff.tol = 0.0001;

double resultST= steff.solve();
cout << "Steffensen's Method: " << resultST << endl;

steff.printStatistics();
```

## 7.9   SUMMARY AND CONCLUSIONS

We gave an introduction to a number of important topics in C++, namely function pointers, namespaces and an introduction to inheritance. We also gave some examples of how to use them and also how to write nonlinear solvers that calculate the implied volatility.

We continue in the next chapter with advanced issues related to inheritance.

## 7.10   EXERCISES AND PROJECTS

1. We wish to define a variable called MAX_ITERATIONS that represents the maximum number of iterations allowed during the execution of a nonlinear solver. This is a variable that is common to all instances of the classes in the hierarchy and we model this as a static variable. You should also define a 'running counter' variable that is incremented at each leg of the iterative scheme. If it becomes greater than MAX_ITERATIONS we know that the scheme has not converged and we should stop.

   Answer the following questions:
   (a) Set up the code to declare, define, initialise and integrate MAX_ITERATIONS into the class hierarchy
   (b) Use assert() or the Datasim Exception class in conjunction with the exception handling mechanism to throw an exception when the running counter exceeds MAX_ITERATIONS and then catch the exception in the client code (you may need to read the sections in Chapter 9 pertaining to exception handling first and examine the code on the CD that implements a class for exception handling)

2. We test the Bisection and Newton methods on a problem from a fixed income application (Fabozzi, 1993). In this case we calculate the yield measure of a bond and hence its relative attractiveness. The yield in this case is the interest rate that will make the present value of the cash flows from the investment equal to the price (or cost) of the investment. The yield y satisfies the equation:

$$P = \sum_{t=1}^{n} \frac{CF_t}{(1+y)^t} \tag{7.9}$$

where

$P$ = present value
$CF_t$ = Cash flow in year $t$
$n$ = number of years

We write this in the form that is suitable for computation:

$$f(y) = P - \sum_{t=1}^{n} \frac{CF_t}{(1 + y)^t} = 0 \qquad (7.10)$$

We now have a function of the unknown variable y and in fact we wish to find a root of this equation.

You have to pay attention to the following issues:

(a) The interval (a, b) in which the solution is to be found must be known
(b) In the case of the Bisection method we must have $f(a)f(b) < 0$; the values a = 0 (zero interest rate) and b = .25 (25 % interest rate) might be good choices but you may have to experiment with some sample values
(c) In the case of Newton's method we need to calculate the derivative of $f$ with respect to y, that is:

$$\frac{df}{dy} = -\sum_{t=1}^{n} \frac{tCF_t}{(1 + y)^{t+1}} \qquad (7.11)$$

(d) Now compare your results by applying the Secant and Steffensen's method. Examine speed of convergence and dependency of closeness of the initial guess to the exact solution.

3. Generalise the results and code from section 7.8 to allow us to calculate implied volatility for a number of strike prices. The output will now be a vector containing implied volatility data.

4. Use any of the nonlinear solvers to find a value for the square root of 2. The function to use is:

```
double SquareRoot(double x)
{
    return ::sqrt(2.0) - x;
}
```

Generalise the code to find a root of any power of x.

5. Implement the ancient method *Regula Falsi* (*method of false positions*). This is a method that uses linear interpolation by using two previous approximations. See Figure 7.1. Here we see that a and b are two estimates and that the new estimate c is given by the linear interpolation formula:

$$y = f(a) + \frac{f(a) - f(b)}{a - b}(x - a) \qquad (7.12)$$

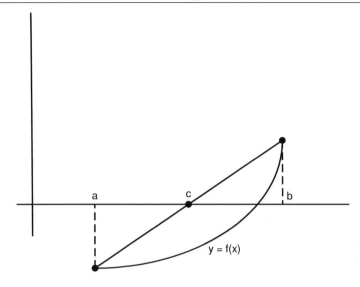

**Figure 7.1**    Regula falsi

giving the estimate for c:

$$c = a - \frac{(a - b)f(a)}{f(a) - f(b)}$$

(7.13)

This all translates to the algorithm:

$$x_n = x_{n-1} - \frac{(x_{n-1} - x_{n-2})f(x_{n-1})}{f(x_{n-1}) - f(x_{n-2})}$$

(7.14)

We have produced the code for this algorithm in the directory relating to Chapter 7.
   Answer the following questions:
(a)  Check the code against the algorithm (this is what is called a *code review*)
(b)  Test the code against the examples that we discussed in this chapter

6.  (Inheritance scenarios)
    Discuss the merits (or otherwise) of the following examples of deriving a class from a given
    base class:
    • Stack derived from a list (and vice versa)
    • Circle derived from an ellipse (and vice versa)
    • Call Option and Put Option derived from Option
    • What about Chooser Option?
    • SortedArray is derived from Array

7.  (Research)
    What is an *anonymous namespace* and in which circumstances would you use it? What are
    the advantages and disadvantages? Find out what the idea behind the keyword 'protected'
    is. When would it be useful to use it?

# 8
## Advanced Inheritance and Payoff Class Hierarchies

## 8.1 INTRODUCTION AND OBJECTIVES

In this chapter we introduce some advanced features of the inheritance mechanism in C++. This is an implementation of the *generalisation/specialisation relationship*. We show how to create new specialised classes by deriving them from more general classes. For ease of communication, we shall give generic examples to show how a given mechanism works. To this end, we denote base classes as B, B1 and B2 while we denote derived classes as D, D11, D12 and so on. We give some relevant examples from financial engineering but very simple examples are good motivators as well.

Using inheritance in the correct way allows us to create highly reusable and flexible software. In general, we write common or *invariant code* just once and place it in a so-called *base class*. Then we derive a class from this base class and it receives the invariant code for free as it were. This is called *implementation inheritance*. Another form, called *interface inheritance* is when a base class declares a function but provides no implementation; it is up to derived classes to implement this function. In fact, this is a kind of abstract function and we will implement this feature as *pure virtual member functions*.

In this chapter we also give some health warnings when employing the inheritance mechanism. Many novice and even experienced programmers tend to use the mechanism to excess. In general, using inheritance results in a tightly coupled network of classes and it becomes difficult to maintain the code. We discuss these problems and show how they can be avoided.

As a practical example, we create a class hierarchy of one-factor option payoffs. The ideas can be generalised to multi-factor option models and this will be done in a later chapter. We have three design techniques in C++ for modelling payoff functions. First, we create an abstract payoff class and we derive each specific class from it; for example, we have defined classes for calls, bull spreads and other one-factor options. The second approach uses composition by defining a generic payoff class that contains a link to the algorithm that actually implements the payoff function. The last design is to implement a payoff class that contains a function pointer as member data. This function pointer implements the specific payoff functionality. In short, we can choose the most appropriate design to suit our needs. In this sense we can offer 'heavyweight', 'lightweight' and 'super-lightweight' functionality for modelling both one-factor and two-factor payoff functions.

## 8.2 THE virtual SPECIFIER AND MEMORY DEALLOCATION

We have already introduced the virtual keyword in Chapter 7. In this section we discuss its use in a particular context, namely when an object goes out of scope. To this end, let us take a counterexample. In this case we examine a base class B whose member data is defined on the heap:

```
class B
{ // Class with non-virtual destructor
private:
        double* d;
public:
        B() { d = new double (1.0); }
        ~B() { cout << "Base destructor\ n"; delete d; }
};
```

We now derive a class D from this base class as follows:

```
class D : public B
{ // Derived class
private:
        int* iarr;
public:
        D(int N) { iarr = new int[N]; }
        ~D() { cout << "Derived destructor\ n"; delete [] iarr; }
};
```

Now for the interesting part: we define a B pointer and assign it to the address of D:

```
int main()
{
        {
                B* b = new D(10);
                delete b;
        }

        return 0;
}
```

The problem now is that the destructor of the base class is called but not that of the derived class even though the pointer is really pointing to an instance of the derived class! In other words, the destructor of the derived class never gets called. This problem constitutes a *memory leak* and it is resolved by declaring the destructor in the base class to be virtual, as follows:

```
virtual ~B() { cout << "Base destructor\ n"; delete d; }
```

Having done this the code in the main program will run properly in the sense that the memory will be deallocated as follows (and as it should be done):

```
Derived destructor
Base destructor
```

In general, one may declare all destructors in all classes to be virtual and then we will have one less problem to worry about. You should view virtual destructors as a kind of insurance policy. Your code may work without its use but things can go wrong sometimes and usually at the wrong moments. It's always the wrong moment.

Summarising, memory is allocated (via constructors) starting from the base class through its derived classes while memory is deallocated (via destructors) starting from the current derived class and traversing the inheritance hierarchy in an upward direction.

## 8.3    ABSTRACT AND CONCRETE CLASSES

By definition, an *abstract class* is one that cannot have any instances, that is one from which no objects can be created. We can produce abstract classes by defining at least one function to be pure virtual. A *concrete class* on the other hand is one that is not abstract. In other words, we can create instances of concrete classes.

What is the relationship between concrete and abstract classes? Usually an abstract class will be a base class for many other derived classes (which may themselves be abstract or concrete). The nice feature of this setup is that derived classes (if they wish to be concrete, that is) *must* implement the pure virtual member functions, otherwise they will also be abstract. The advantage should be obvious: *standardisation of interfaces*.

An example of an abstract class is one that models one-factor option payoffs. In fact, we create an abstract base class called Payoff that implements a pure virtual member function to calculate the payoff value for a given stock price. The header file is given by:

```
class Payoff
{
public:
        // Constructors and destructor
        Payoff();                              // Default constructor
        Payoff(const Payoff& source);          // Copy constructor
        virtual ~Payoff();                     // Destructor

        // Operator overloading
        Payoff& operator = (const Payoff& source);

        // Pure virtual payoff function
        virtual double payoff(double S) const = 0; // Spot price S
};
```

We notice that this class has no member data and this is advantageous because derived classes will not inherit possible unwanted members. Specific payoff classes can be defined by deriving them from Payoff and implementing the payoff() function. We look at a call option in detail. The header file is given by:

```
class CallPayoff: public Payoff
{
private:

        double K;    // Strike price

public:

        // Constructors and destructor
        CallPayoff();
        CallPayoff(double strike);
```

```
        CallPayoff(const CallPayoff& source);
        virtual ~CallPayoff();

        // Selectors
        double Strike() const;                  // Return strike price

        // Modifiers
        void Strike(double NewStrike);          // Set strike price

        CallPayoff& operator = (const CallPayoff& source);

        // Implement the pure virtual payoff function from base class
        double payoff(double S) const; // For a given spot price

};
```

We see that this class has private member data representing the strike price of the call option as well as public set/get member functions for this data. Furthermore, we have coded all essential functions in this class:

- Default constructor
- Copy constructor
- Virtual destructor
- Assignment operator

We call this the *canonical header file*. Finally, we must implement the payoff() function, otherwise CallPayoff will itself be an abstract class.

 We now examine the bodies of the member functions of CallPayoff. In general, a constructor in a derived class must initialise the local data as well as the data in the class that it is derived from. For the former case we use normal assignment but we can also use the so-called colon syntax to initialise the data in a base class. For example, the copy constructor in CallPayoff is given by:

```
CallPayoff::CallPayoff(const CallPayoff& source): Payoff(source)
{ // Copy constructor

        K = source.K;
}
```

In this case we initialise the data in Payoff by using the colon syntax (of course there is no data in the base class at the moment but this is irrelevant). This is something subtle happening here, namely the fact that the compiler knows what Payoff (source) is. The reason that the code is acceptable is due to the *Principle of Substitutability*; this means that a function that accepts a reference to a base class (in this case the copy constructor in Payoff) can be called by giving an instance of a derived class. This is of course related to the fact that an instance of a derived class is also an instance of its base class.

 We now discuss how to implement the assignment operator in the derived class. In general, the steps are:

1. Check that we are not assigning an object to itself
2. Assign the base class data (by calling '=' of the base class)
3. Assign the local data in the derived class
4. Return the 'current' object

The code that performs these steps is given by:

```
CallPayoff& CallPayoff::operator = (const CallPayoff &source)
{ // Assignment operator

        // Exit if same object
        if (this==&source) return *this;

        // Call base class assignment
        Payoff::operator = (source);

        // Copy state
        K = source.K;

        return *this;
}
```

This is an important piece of code because you can use the same construction for any base class and derived class relationships. Of course, the names and data will be different.

Derived classes may have private member data and it is usual to provide public member functions for returning this data and modifying it:

```
double CallPayoff::Strike() const
{
// Return K

        return K;
}

void CallPayoff::Strike(double NewStrike)
{// Set K

        K = NewStrike;
}
```

Finally, each derived class must implement the payoff function and in the case of an option class this is given by the following code:

```
double CallPayoff::payoff(double S) const
{ // For a given spot price

        if (S > K)
                return (S - K);
```

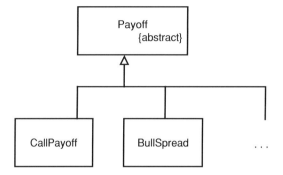

**Figure 8.1**　Payoff hierarchy: version 1

```
    return 0.0;

    // remark; possible to say max (S - K, 0)if you prefer
}
```

We can define other kinds of payoff classes as derived classes of `Payoff`; see Figure 8.1. For example, we can define payoff functions for trading strategies involving options (see for example, Hull, 2006). Examples are:

- *Spreads*: we take a position on two options of the same kind. A bull spread entails we buy a call option on a stock with strike K1 and sell a call on the same stock at a higher price K2. A bear spread is similar to a bull spread except that K1 > K2.
  A butterfly spread involves positions in options with three different strike prices.
- *Straddles*: we buy a call option and a put option with the same strike price and expiration date.
- *Strangles*: we buy a put and a call with the same expiration dates and different strike prices.

We implement each of these strategies by a separate derived class of `Payoff` and then by implementing the payoff function. For example, for a bull spread the payoff function is:

```
double BullSpreadPayoff::payoff(double S) const
{ // Based on Hull's book

        if (S >= K2)
                return K2 - K1;
        if (S <= K1)
                return 0.0;

        // In the interval [K1, K2]
        return S - K1;
}
```

### 8.3.1　Using payoff classes

We now give some examples of using payoff classes. We first consider payoffs for a call option. To this end, we create a call payoff with strike $K = 20$ and we can query for a given stock value and then compute the payoff function:

```
CallPayoff call(20.0);

cout << "Give a stock price (plain Call): ";
double S;
cin >> S;

cout << "Call Payoff is: " << call.payoff(S) << endl;
```

We now create a bull spread payoff and we note that it has four member data, namely two strike prices and the cost to buy a call and the sell price for the second call. The code is:

```
double K1 = 30.0;        // Strike price of bought call
double K2 = 35.0;        // Strike price of sell call
double costBuy = 3.0;    // Cost to buy a call
double sellPrice = 1.0;  // Sell price for call
BullSpreadPayoff bs(K1, K2, costBuy, sellPrice);
cout << "Give a stock price (BullSpread): ";
cin >> S;

cout << "Bull Spread Payoff is: " << bs.payoff(S) << endl;
cout << "Bull Spread Profit is: " << bs.profit(S) << endl;
```

Incidentally, the C++ code for the profit() function is given by:

```
double BullSpreadPayoff::profit(double S) const
{ // Profit

    return payoff(S) - (buyValue - sellValue);

}
```

The techniques developed in this section can be used in other applications in which we need to create derived classes in C++.

## 8.4 LIGHTWEIGHT PAYOFF CLASSES

In this section we discuss another design for payoff functions. The process of defining a pure virtual function in a base class and then implementing this function in the derived classes is acceptable in practice but it does have a number of disadvantages:

- We create a 'heavyweight' derived class for each kind of new payoff function.
- Once we create an instance of a payoff class in Figure 8.1 it is then not possible to change it to an instance of another class. For example, this approach might be difficult when we model chooser options in C++ (recall that a chooser is one where the holder can choose whether to receive a call or a put).

In order to resolve these and possible future problems, we adopt another approach. The UML class diagram is shown in Figure 8.2. In this case we create a single payoff class that has a

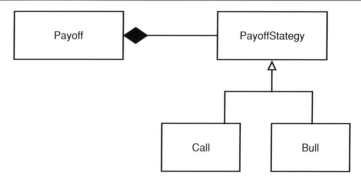

**Figure 8.2**   Payoff hierarchy: version 2

pointer to what is essentially an encapsulation of a payoff function. The pattern in Figure 8.2 is called the *Strategy* pattern (GOF, 1995). This pattern allows us to define interchangeable algorithms that can be used by many clients as we can see in Figure 8.2; each instance of Payoff has a pointer to a payoff strategy and this pointer can be changed at run-time. The header file for Payoff is:

```
class Payoff
{
private:
      PayoffStrategy* ps;
public:
      // Constructors and destructor
      Payoff(PayoffStrategy& pstrat);

      // Other member functions
};
```

We see that we must give a reference to a payoff strategy. We have programmed the strategy classes in Figure 8.2 in one file as follows:

```
class PayoffStrategy
{
public:
            virtual double payoff(double S) const = 0;
};
```

A specific derived class is given by:

```
class CallStrategy : public PayoffStrategy
{
private:
            double K;
public:
            CallStrategy(double strike) { K = strike;}
            double payoff(double S) const
```

```
            {
                if (S > K)
                    return (S - K);

                return 0.0;
            }
};
```

We have also created a simple strategy for a bull spread. An example of using the new configuration is now given where we create a payoff and we can choose its strategy type:

```
// Create a strategy and couple it with a payoff
CallStrategy call(20.0);
Payoff pay1(call);
```

This approach allows our software to be more efficient and flexible than the use of class inheritance in section 8.3. We discuss the Strategy pattern in other contexts in later chapters.

## 8.5   SUPER LIGHTWEIGHT PAYOFF FUNCTIONS

We now discuss the last design technique for creating payoff functions and classes. It is less object-oriented than the first two approaches (by the way, this does not necessarily make it bad) because we create a class with a function pointer as member data. This function pointer will be assigned to a 'real' function representing some payoff function. For convenience we look at special one-factor payoffs and in fact we create a class as follows:

```
class OneFactorPayoff
{
private:
      double K;
      double (*payoffFN)(double K, double S);

public:
      // Constructors and destructor
      OneFactorPayoff(double strike,
                double(*payoff)(double K,double S));
      // More ...

      double payoff(double S) const; // For a given spot price

};
```

The bodies of these member functions are given by:

```
OneFactorPayoff::OneFactorPayoff(double strike,
                    double (*pay)(double K, double S))
```

```cpp
{

    K = strike;
    payoffFN = pay;
}

double OneFactorPayoff::payoff(double S) const
{ // For a given spot price

    return payoffFN(K, S); // Call function
}
```

How do we use this class? The answer is that we carry out the following steps:

1. Write the payoff functions you would like to use
2. Create an instance of OneFactorPayoff with the payoff function of your choice
3. Test and use the payoff class.

An example of specific payoff functions is:

```cpp
double CallPayoffFN(double K, double S)
{
            if (S > K)
                    return (S - K);

            return 0.0;
}

double PutPayoffFN(double K, double S)
{
            // max (K-S, 0)
            if (K > S)
                    return (K - S);

            return 0.0;
}
```

An example of the code is:

```cpp
int main()
{

        OneFactorPayoff pay1(20.0, CallPayoffFN);
        cout << "Give a stock price (plain Call): ";
        double S;
        cin >> S;

        cout << "Call Payoff is: " << pay1.payoff(S) << endl;

        OneFactorPayoff pay2(20.0, PutPayoffFN);
```

```
        cout << "Give a stock price (plain Put): ";
        cin >> S;

        cout << "Put Payoff is: " << pay2.payoff(S) << endl;

        return 0;
}
```

This option can be quite effective; you do not have to create classes, just 'flat' C functions that you use as function pointers in existing classes. We do not have to worry about pointers to objects and this improves the reliability of our code.

## 8.6   THE DANGERS OF INHERITANCE: A COUNTEREXAMPLE

We now discuss some of the issues to look out for when creating a C++ class hierarchy. In general, deriving a class D from a class B introduces dependencies between B and D; in other words changes to B may result to changes in D.

Even though the inheritance mechanism is very powerful and useful it can be misused and its capabilities stretched to unacceptable limits. We now give an example to show how subtle errors can enter your code by the incorrect use of the inheritance mechanism. We shall then show how to resolve the corresponding problems induced by using the mechanism. The example that we take is unambiguous and there is little chance of it being misinterpreted. To this end, we create two-dimensional shapes, namely rectangles and squares. Of course, we would like to create code that is as reusable as possible. The first solution that might spring to mind is to say that a square is a specialisation of a rectangle. This sounds reasonable. We investigate the consequences of this decision. The interface for the rectangle class is:

```
class Rectangle : public Shape
{
protected: // Derived classes can access this data directly

        Point bp; // Base point, Point class given
        double h; // height
        double w; // width

public:
        Rectangle()
        {

                bp = Point();
                h = 1.0;
                w = 2.0;
        }
        Rectangle(const Point& basePoint, double height, double width)
        {
                bp = basePoint;
                h = height;
                w = width;
        }
```

```
     void setHeight(double newHeight)
     {
          h = newHeight;
     }

     void setWidth(double newWidth)
     {
          w = newWidth;
     }

     void print() const
     {
          cout << bp;
          cout << "Dimensions (H, W): " << h << ", "
                          << w <<endl;
     }
};
```

Thus, we can create rectangles and change its dimensions. We now derive a square class from it as follows (see Figure 8.3 for the corresponding UML diagram):

```
class BadSquare : public Rectangle
{ // Version 1, a Square is a Rectangle
private:

          // No member data, inherited from Rectangle
public:
     BadSquare() : Rectangle (Point(), 1.0, 1.0)
     {
          // We must implement this, otherwise this
               // default constructor inherits a default rectangle
     }

     BadSquare (const Point& basePoint, double size)
     {
          bp = basePoint;
          h = w = size;          // Starts off well
     }

};
```

This class has no member data because it is derived from Rectangle. In this case we defined the data in Rectangle as being protected (this means that it is directly available to derived classes) for convenience only. Furthermore, we need to say something about default constructors. Some rules are:

- A default constructor will be generated if you do not provide one
- The default constructor in the derived class will automatically call the default constructor in the base class

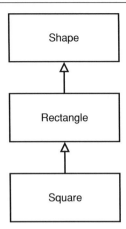

**Figure 8.3**   Incorrect inheritance

In general, we prefer to write default constructors in all classes because we control what default behaviour will be. Secondly, a default constructor in class `BadSquare` is not necessarily a default `Rectangle`! For this reason we must do things differently as can be seen in the above code.

We now come to the next attention point. Since squares are publicly derived from rectangles we can call all the latter's member function for instances of `BadSquare`. Let us take an example:

```
BadSquare bs;
bs.print();
```

This code creates a square at the origin with a side of 1. Now we call a member function that is inherited from the base class:

```
// Now change the size
bs.setHeight(2.0);
bs.print();
```

When we print the square we see that the height and width are different. So we do not have a square anymore!

What is the problem? At a superficial level the square inherits functionality that destroys its consistency. At a deeper level, a square is not a specialisation of a rectangle. We resolve this problem by using a slightly different design technique that is well documented in the literature but is not as well known as inheritance (for more information, see GOF (1995) for a discussion of the *Adapter* pattern). In general terms, we implement a new class that *uses* a rectangle as a private member data and we develop the member functions in the new square while we suppress those functions that are not relevant. The UML diagram is shown in Figure 8.4 and here we use the *Composition* technique: a square is composed from a rectangle. Furthermore, square delegates needed functionality to rectangle. The source code is given by:

```
class GoodSquare : public Shape
{ // Version 2, adapts a Rectangle's interface
private:
      Rectangle r;
public:
      GoodSquare ()
```

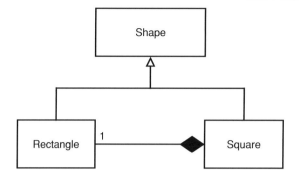

**Figure 8.4**  Combining inheritance and composition

```
        {

            double size = 1.0;
            r = Rectangle (Point(), size, size); // Unit square
        }
        GoodSquare (const Point& basePoint, double size)
        {
            r = Rectangle (basePoint, size, size);

        }

        void setSize(double newSize)
        { // An adaptor function, this ensures that constraints
          // on the square are always satisfied

            r.setHeight(newSize);
            r.setWidth(newSize);
        }

        void print() const
        {
            // Delegate to the embedded rectangle's output

            r.print();
        }
};
```

Not much can go wrong now; the square publishes its member functions to client code that have no idea that the square is implemented as a rectangle. The following source code shows how to use the new functionality:

```
GoodSquare gs;
gs.print();

// Now change the size
gs.setSize(2.0);
gs.print();
```

Concluding, we have given an example to show that inheritance is not always the best way to extend the functionality of a class. The above discussion has relevance to many situations in object-orient design. In particular, the same warnings apply when developing C++ class hierarchies in financial engineering applications.

## 8.7 IMPLEMENTATION INHERITANCE AND FRAGILE BASE CLASS PROBLEM

We know that a derived class D can use the public and protected members in a class B that it is derived from. In general, when a member (data or functions) is changed in B then it may be necessary to change the code in D. Of course, a change in D may trigger other changes in *its* derived classes. This particular situation is called the *Fragile Base Class Problem.*

There are some possible solutions to this problem, depending on the context:

- Instead of using inheritance we could consider using Composition and adapting the interface of B
- Try to create base classes with as few member data as possible
- Avoid deep inheritance hierarchies

### 8.7.1 Deep hierarchies

This is a problem that we, as C++ community have inherited (no pun intended) from the 1990's. In the past we had seen inheritance hierarchies with the 'most deep' derived class having up to six indirect base classes. Some of the disadvantages are:

- It has been proven that the human brain can hold approximately seven pieces of information in short-term memory at any one moment in time; this number is much less than the amount of information that we need to understand when working with deep C++ class hierarchies
- The chances that the structural relationships between the classes are correct decreases as the hierarchy grows.

### 8.7.2 Multiple inheritance problems

We have discussed multiple inheritance in Chapter 7. I do not use it for three main reasons:

- Its use leads to unmaintainable software systems
- It is a flawed way of thinking about relationships between entities in general and C++ classes in particular (in the author's opinion)
- In some cases we can use single inheritance for base class B1 and composition with class B2 instead of deriving class D from both B1 and B2

In the last case we see that D inherits all of the functionality from B1 and it *adapts* the interface functions in B2 to suit its own needs.

## 8.8 TWO-FACTOR PAYOFF FUNCTIONS AND CLASSES

In this section we give an overview of some kinds of options that depend on two or more underlying assets. These are called *correlation options* in general (see Zhang, 1998 for a comprehensive introduction). Our interest in these options is to cast them in PDE form. In particular, we must define the payoff function, boundary conditions and the coefficients of the

PDE and we focus on the following specific types:

- Exchange options
- Rainbow options
- Basket options
- Best/worst options
- Quotient options
- Foreign exchange options
- Spread options
- Dual-strike options
- Out-performance options

We have discussed the financial and mathematical background to these option types in detail in Duffy (2006). In particular we solved the partial differential equations associated with these option types by the finite difference method. In this book we concentrate on the C++ implementation for the payoff functions for these types and to this end we create a C++ class hierarchy consisting of a base class and derived classes, with one derived class for each payoff function. The abstract base class (note, it has no member data) is defined as:

```cpp
class MultiAssetPayoffStrategy
{ // Interface specification

public:
         virtual double payoff(double S1, double S2) const = 0;
};
```

There is no default structure or behaviour defined here, only a pure virtual function specification describing the pricing function based on two underlyings. Each derived class must implement this function. For example, for a basket option class we have the specification:

```cpp
class BasketStrategy : public MultiAssetPayoffStrategy
{ // 2-asset basket option payoff
private:
         double K;      // Strike
         double w;      // +1 call, -1 put
         double w1, w2; // w1 + w2 = 1
public:
         // All classes need default constructor
         BasketStrategy(): MultiAssetPayoffStrategy()
         { K = 95.0; w = +1; w1 = 0.5; w2 = 0.5;
         }
         BasketStrategy(double strike, double cp,double weight1,
                     double weight2) : MultiAssetPayoffStrategy()
         { K = strike; w = cp; w1 = weight1; w2 = weight2;
         }
         double payoff(double S1, double S2) const
```

```
            {
                    double sum = w1*S1 + w2*S2;
                    return DMax(w* (sum - K), 0.0);

            }
};
```

Please note that we use the colon syntax ':' to call the constructor of the base class from the derived class. This ensures that the member data in the base class will be initialised. Of course, the base class in this case has no member data (at the moment) but it might have in a future version of the software.

We have used two-factor payoff classes in conjunction with the finite difference method (see Duffy, 2006). The actual data and the relationship with the payoff function can be seen in the following classes (note that we have taken a basket option payoff for readability but it is easy to extend to the more general case):

```
class TwoFactorInstrument
{ // Empty class
public:

};
class TwoFactorOptionData : public TwoFactorInstrument
{
//private:
public: // For convenience only
        // An option uses a polymorphic payoff object
        BasketStrategy pay;
public:
        // PUBLIC, PURE FOR PEDAGOGICAL REASONS, 13 parameters
        double r;                       // Interest rate
        double D1, D2;                  // Dividends
        double sig1, sig2;              // Volatility
        double rho;                     // Cross correlation
        double K;                       // Strike price, now place in IC
        double T;                       // Expiry date
        double SMax1, SMax2;    // Far field condition
        double w1, w2;
        int type;                       // Call +1 or put -1

        TwoFactorOptionData()
        {
                // Initialise all data and the payoff
                // Use Topper's data as the default, Table 7.1
                r = 0.01;
                D1 = D2 = 0.0;
                sig1 = 0.1; sig2 = 0.2;
                rho = 0.5;
                K = 40.0;
```

```
                T = 0.5;
                w1 = 1.0;
                w2 = 20.0;

                type = -1;
                // Now create the payoff Strategy object
                BasketStrategy(double strike, double cp,
                                            double weight1, double weight2)
                { K = strike; w = cp; w1 = weight1; w2 = weight2;}

                pay = BasketStrategy(K, type, w1, w2);

                // In general 1) we need a Factory object as we have done
                // in the one-dimensional case and 2) work with pointers to
                // base classes
        }

        double payoff(double x, double y) const
        {
                return pay.payoff(x, y);
        }
};
```

We hope that this example gives an idea of using the inheritance mechanism in quantitative finance. To be honest, inheritance has its uses but the generic programming model is also useful. We discuss this topic later, beginning with Chapter 10 where we introduce template programming in C++.

The source code for two-factor payoff classes is to be found on the CD.

## 8.9   CONCLUSIONS AND SUMMARY

We have given a detailed discussion of using inheritance in applications. In particular, we showed how to derive a class from another, more general base class. We applied this knowledge to creating a hierarchy of option payoff functions. Finally, we have included several sections on the potential problems when using inheritance, why they occur and how they can be mitigated.

## 8.10   EXERCISES AND PROJECTS

1. We wish to create a hierarchy of classes for the (non-adaptive) numerical integration of real-valued functions on a bounded interval. The base class should contain the following members:
   - A function pointer that models the function to be integrated
   - The end points of the interval
   - The number of subdivisions of the interval
   - The function that computes the approximate integral

Create a derived class that models your favourite numerical integration scheme (for example, the midpoint rule). Pay attention to the following issues:
- Using the colon syntax
- Virtual destructor
- Implementing the pure virtual member function (what happens if you don't implement it?)

Create a program to test your scheme.

2. Identify potential C++ class hierarchies in quantitative finance and the corresponding pure virtual functions. Take the payoff classes in this chapter as your cue.

3. How would you generalise the two-factor classes to N dimensions ('big baskets')? In other words, we need to create a specification with N input parameters:

```
class MultiAssetPayoffStrategy
{ // Interface specification

public:
virtual double payoff(/* N params */) const = 0;
};
```

# 9

---

## Run-Time Behaviour in C++

---

### 9.1 INTRODUCTION AND OBJECTIVES

In this chapter we introduce C++ functionality that allows us to query objects at run-time, for example:

- Determining the class that an object pointer 'points to' (*dynamic type checking*)
- Casting an object pointer to an object pointer of another class (*dynamic casting*)
- Navigating in class hierarchies
- *Static casting*
- Modelling run-time errors with the exception handling mechanism

We have included the above functionality in this chapter for three main reasons. First, it is an essential part of the language and we would like to be as complete as possible. Second, we need to use this functionality in specific (and sometimes very esoteric) applications. In fact, you may need to use it because of a design flaw that you wish to have a workaround for. Thus, it is for this reason good to know the essentials of run-time behaviour in C++.

### 9.2 AN INTRODUCTION TO REFLECTION AND SELF-AWARE OBJECTS

Most of the examples up until now dealt with the creation of classes and the instantiation of these classes to form objects. Having created an object we can then call its member functions. But we now want to view classes themselves as objects in the sense that we wish to find out certain things about their structural and behavioural properties, for example:

- What are the member data of a given class?
- What are the names (as strings) of the member functions of a class?
- Execute a member function by 'invoking' it

It should be obvious that these questions have to do with a high level of abstraction. This feature is called *Reflection* and its added value is that it allows the programmer to query the characteristics of classes, objects and other software entities at run-time. In a sense we can create *self-aware objects* that know about their data and methods. We speak of *metadata*, or data that describes other data. A number of programming environments have extensive support for Reflection (for example, Microsoft's .NET framework) and support for the following features is not unusual:

- Reading metadata of types, classes, interfaces, methods and other software entities
- Dynamic object creation
- Dynamic method invocation
- Code generation

C++ has some support for these kinds of features. In the following sections we discuss these specific features in detail.

In order to show how run-time functionality works we examine two model examples. The first example is generic and minimal and the second example discusses run-time behaviour associated with classes in a class hierarchy.

## 9.3   RUN-TIME TYPE INFORMATION (RTTI)

In this section we begin our discussion of the run-time behaviour of objects. To this end, we introduce two features in C++:

- The typeid() operator
- The type_info class

First, by using type_info we can get the name of any object or built-in type in C++. Second, we use the typeid() operator on some object or built-in type to give a const reference to type_info. The interface functions in type_info are:

```
class type_info {

public:
        virtual ~type_info();
        int operator==(const type_info& rhs) const;
        int operator!=(const type_info& rhs) const;
        int before(const type_info& rhs) const;
        const char* name() const;
        const char* raw_name() const;
};
```

We see from this interface that we can:

- Compare two objects (operators == and !=)
- Find the human-readable name of an object

We do not discuss the other interface functions in this chapter as we think that they are too esoteric for most applications.

We must take note of the fact that this RTTI feature only works for polymorphic classes, that is classes with at least one virtual function. Furthermore, some compilers (for example, Microsoft C++ compiler) demand that you define certain compiler settings, otherwise a run-time error will occur. In the Microsoft environment, for example the RTTI option must be enabled. See the relevant on-line help for that environment.

We now take a simple generic example. To this end, we create a class hierarchy with two derived classes. The base class is defined as:

```
class Base
{

public:
        Base() {}
        virtual ~Base() {}

        virtual void print() const { cout << "I'm base\ n"; }
        virtual double calculate(double d) const = 0;

};
```

and the derived classes are:

```
class D1: public Base
{

public:
    D1() {}
    virtual ~D1() {}

    virtual void print() const { cout << "I'm a D1\ n"; }
    virtual double calculate(double d) const { return 1.0 * d; }
};

class D2: public Base
{
public:
    D2() {}
    virtual ~D2() {}

    virtual void print() const { cout << "I'm a D2\ n"; }
    virtual double calculate(double d) const { return 2.0 * d; }
};
```

The first example creates instances of the derived classes and examines their run-time properties:

```
D1 d1, d11;
D2 d2;

// Define a reference to type
const type_info& myRef = typeid(d1);

cout << "Human-readable name: " << myRef.name() << endl;

// Test if two objects have same type or not
if (typeid(d1) == typeid(d11))
{
    cout << "Types are the same\ n";
}

if (typeid(d1) != typeid(d2))
{
    cout << "Types are NOT the same\ n";
}
```

In this code we get the answers that we expect; first, the human-readable form of the class name is displayed on the console and second the classes corresponding to objects d1, d11 and d2 are compared. You can run this code to see how it works.

We now note that RTTI can be applied to base classes pointers. Let us take a simple example. As already discussed in this book, we can assign base class pointers to addresses of derived classes. What is of interest now is that RTTI knows that the dereferenced pointer is actually a derived class object:

```
Base* b = &d1;
const type_info& myRef2 = typeid(*b);
cout << "Human-readable name: " << myRef2.name() << endl;
```

This is quite a useful feature because in some applications we might have an array of base class pointers and we may wish to know what the 'real' underlying types are. Here is an example in which we create an array of pointers to D1 and D2 instances. Then we iterate in the array to determine what the actual type is that is 'hiding' behind the pointer:

```
// Create an array of Base class pointers
int size = 10;
Base* myArr[10]; // An array of pointers!

for (int j = 0; j < 6; j++)
{
      myArr[j] = &d1;
}

for (int k = 6; k < size; k++)
{
      myArr[k] = &d2;
}

// Now "filter" the real types. We have D1 and D2 types!
int counterD1 = 0;
int counterD2 = 0;

for (int i = 0; i < size; i++)
{
      if (typeid(*myArr[i]) == typeid(D1))
      {
            cout << "We have a D1\ n"; counterD1++;
      }

      if (typeid(*myArr[i]) == typeid(D2))
      {
            cout << "We have a D2\ n"; counterD2++;
      }
}
// Print final counts
cout << "Number of D1s: " << counterD1 << endl;
cout << "Number of D2s: " << counterD2 << endl;
```

We thus keep a count of the different types in the collection. This example could be modified to work in a financial engineering application. For example, let us suppose that we can have a class hierarchy of financial instruments with derived classes for options, bonds, futures and other specific derivatives products. We could then use RTTI to perform the following kinds of operations:

• Select all options in the portfolio
• Select all derivatives except futures in the portfolio
• Remove all futures from the portfolio
• Update some member data in options in the portfolio

In fact, we could create a simple query and manipulation language that allows us to access specific information in a portfolio. We could then use it in a pricing engine.

One final remark; when working with pointers to base classes, it is in general not possible to determine what the 'real' object (of a derived class) without using the RTTI functionality.

## 9.4   CASTING BETWEEN TYPES

Casting is the process of converting an object pointer of one class to an object pointer of another class. In general we must distinguish between *static casting* (for non-polymorphic classes) and *dynamic casting* (for polymorphic classes, that is classes with at least one virtual function). To this end, C++ has several operators that allow us to perform casting:

• dynamic_cast operator
• static_cast operator

The first casting operator takes two operands:

dynamic_cast<T*> (p)

In this case we attempt to cast the pointer p to one of class T, that is a pointer T*. We can use this operator when casting between base and derived class. An example is:

```
D1 d1A;
Base* base2 = &d1A;

D1* d1Cast = dynamic_cast<D1*> (base2);

if (d1Cast == 0)
{
      cout << "Cast not possible:\ n";
      // Should ideally throw an exception here
}
else
{ // This function gets called

      cout << "Cast is possible: ";
      d1Cast -> print();
}
```

In this case we have a pointer that points to a D1 instance and we can convert it to a pointer of the same class because the return type is not zero. We now give an example in which we attempt to convert a D1 pointer to a D2 pointer and of course this is not possible because they are completely different classes:

```
// Now cast a D1 to a D2 (not possible)
D2* d2Cast = dynamic_cast<D2*> (base2);

if (d2Cast == 0)
{ // This function gets called

        cout << "Cast not possible:\ n";
}
else
{
        cout << "Cast is possible:\ n";
        d2Cast -> print();
}
```

The above examples use *downcasting* because we are moving the base class pointer to one of a derived class. It does not always give desired results as we can see. *Upcasting*, on the other hand allows us to cast a derived class pointer to a base class pointer (this is a consequence of the fact that we are implementing generalisation/specialisation relationships and in this case the operation will be successful). The casting to be done can be to a direct or indirect base class:

```
D1* dd = new D1;
Base* b3 = dynamic_cast<Base*> (dd);

if (b3 == 0)
{ // This function gets called

        cout << "Cast not possible:\ n";
}
else
{
        cout << "Cast is possible:\ n";
        b3 -> print();
        b3 -> doIt();
}
```

There is a small run-time cost associated with the use of the dynamic_cast operator. We now discuss static casting. We find it to be very esoteric and we do not use it at all. However, we include it for completeness. An example is:

```
// Static casting
Base* bA = &d1;
Base* bB = &d2;

D1* dA = static_cast<D1*> (bA);
```

```
// Unsafe static cast
cout << "Unsafe cast ...\ n";
D1* dB = static_cast<D1*> (bB);
dB -> print();
```

In the last case we are casting a D2 pointer to a D1 pointer! We advise against the use of this specific feature. A possible workaround is to redesign the problem or implement it in such a way that it does not have to use casting.

### 9.4.1   More esoteric casting

We discuss two more operators for casting between objects:

* The reinterpret_cast
* The const_cast

The reinterpret_cast is the crudest and potentially nastiest of the type conversion operations. It delivers a value with the same bit pattern as its argument with the type required (Stroustrup, 1997). It is used for implementation-dependent problems such as:

* Converting integer values to pointers
* Converting pointers to integer values

We give an example of this mechanism. Here we create an object and we assign it to a fixed memory location. Then we can convert the memory location by using reinterpret_cast:

```
D2 d2Any;
Base* bb = reinterpret_cast<Base*>(&d2Any);
bb -> print();
```

In this case we create a new object by giving it the same bit pattern as its argument. Finally, we now discuss a mechanism that allows us to convert a const pointer to a non-const pointer. Here is an example:

```
D1 dAny;
const Base* bConst = &dAny;
bConst -> print();
// Base* bNonConst = bConst; DOES NOT WORK
Base* bNonConst = const_cast<Base*> (bConst);
bNonConst -> print();
```

Please note that the following conversions on the const pointer will not work:

```
Base* bNonConst1 = static_cast<Base*> (bConst);
Base* bNonConst2 = dynamic_cast<Base*> (bConst);
Base* bNonConst3 = reinterpret_cast<Base*> (bConst);
```

The compiler error message you get is something like:

```
d:\ users\ daniel\ books\ cppfeintro\ code\ chap14\ example1.cpp(193) :
error C2440: "static_cast" : cannot convert from "const class Base *"
to "class Base *"
```

## 9.5   CLIENT-SERVER PROGRAMMING AND EXCEPTION HANDLING

In the following sections we introduce the reader to client-server programming in C++ and how this relates to the problem of run-time exceptions and errors that arise in a running program.

We first discuss some things that can go wrong when clients call functions. In order to reduce the scope, let us examine a simple example of finding the sum of reciprocals of a vector:

```cpp
template <class V> V sumReciprocals(const vector<V>& array)
{ // Sum of reciprocals

        V ans = V(0.0);
        for (int j = 0; j < array.size(); j++)
        {
                ans += 1.0/array[j];
        }

        return ans;
}
```

We see that if any one of the elements in the vector is zero we shall get a run-time error and your program will crash. To circumvent this problem we use the exception handling mechanism in C++ to provide the client of the software with a 'net' as it were which will save the client if it encounters an exception. For example, consider the following code:

```cpp
int size = 10;
double elementsValue = 3.1415;
vector<double> myArray (size, elementsValue);
myArray[5] = 0.0;

double answer = sumReciprocals(myArray);
```

In this case only one element in the vector has a zero value but the end-result will not be correct. In fact, we get a value that is not a number, for example *overflow*.

Another example is when we change a value in a vector based on a given index. A problem is when you enter an index value that is outside the range of the vector. The consequence in this case is that the value will not be changed at best and that some other part of the memory will be overwritten at worst. Consider the following code:

```cpp
cout << "Which index change value to new value? ";
int index;
cin >> index;
myArray[index] = 2.0;
print(myArray);
```

In both of the above cases we could argue that the client should provide good input values but this line of thought is too naïve. Instead, we provide both client and server with tools to resolve the problem themselves. We now discuss the fine details of this mechanism.

## 9.6  `try`, `throw` and `catch`: INGREDIENTS OF THE C++ EXCEPTION MECHANISM

In order to understand exception handling we must discuss the concept of a *contract* between *client code* (the calling function) and the *server code* (the function being called). Each party has its rights and responsibilities. The server states what the conditions and rules are and the client should abide by these rules. If not, then there is no guarantee that the results are correct (or indeed that a result is returned at all). So, the client defines a block of code that captures any run-time errors, should they occur. The client calls a server function in this block. If the server discovers an error it will throw a newly created exception object back to the client.

In general, the steps to be taken by the developer are:

1. Client calls a server function from a client *try block*
2. Server checks if contract has been honoured (the *preconditions*)
3. If contract has been honoured, the server's *postconditions* are executed and control is returned to the client
4. If the contract has not been honoured, the server code throws an exception object back to the client which then catches it in its *catch block* (there may be several such blocks)

The main challenges for the developer are:

- Determining what is and what is not an exception
- Where to place *precondition* code that checks for break of contract in the server
- What data should we place in the exception object in order to help the client figure out what it did wrong?

In general, we design exception classes so that they contain enough state to help the client code make decisions on what to do if an exception does occur at run-time. Essential information includes the following:

- The type of exception thrown (e.g. `ZeroDivide`, `OutOfBounds`)
- The message text in the exception (this can be displayed on the client screen, for example)
- The source of the exception (in which server function did the exception occur?)

It is important to realise that software should be as reliable as possible and steps should be taken to ensure that code recovers from abnormal situations.

## 9.7  C++ IMPLEMENTATION

We propose developing a C++ class hierarchy that models exceptions pertaining to vectors and numerical problems. To this end, we design a simple hierarchy as shown in Figure 9.1. The design rationale is to design each class with enough information to help clients determine what the cause of the error is. In particular, we can support the features:

- A message name
- The method that threw the exception

Furthermore, derived classes can give extra information, for example the offending index for an `OutOfBounds` exception. We concentrate on `ZeroDivide` exceptions in this section and it is the hope that the ideas can be applied to other classes and applications (for example, in

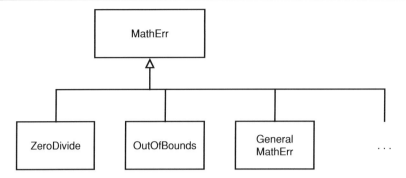

**Figure 9.1**   Exception class hierarchy

quantitative finance). The interfaces are:

```
class MathErr
{ // Base class for my current exceptions
private:
        string mess;      // The error message
        string meth;      // The method that threw the exception
public:
        MathErr()
        {
            mess = meth = string();
        }

        MathErr (const string& message, const string& method)
        {
            mess = message;
            meth = method;
        }

        string Message() const { return mess; }
        string Method() const { return meth; }

        virtual vector<string> MessageDump() const = 0;

        virtual void print() const
        {
            // This uses a Template method pattern

            // Variant part
            vector<string> r = MessageDump();

            // Invariant part
            for (int j = 0; j < r.size(); j++)
```

```
                      {
                              cout << r[j] << endl;
                      }
              }
};
```

and the interface for zero divide exceptions is given by:

```
class ZeroDivide : public MathErr
{
private:

              string mess;          // Extra information

public:
              ZeroDivide() : MathErr()
              {
                      mess = string();
              }

              ZeroDivide(const string& message,const string& method,
                                  const string& annotation )
                  : MathErr (message, method)
              {
                  mess = annotation;
              }

              vector<string> MessageDump() const
              { // Full message

                      vector<string> result(3);
                      result[0] = Message();
                      result[1] = Method();
                      result[2] = mess;
                      return result;

              }
};
```

We wish to use these exceptions in server code. In this case we extend the function sumReciprocals so that it checks for zero divide:

```
template <class V> V sumReciprocals(const vector<V>& array)
{ // Sum of reciprocals

      V ans = V(0.0);
      for (int j = 0; j < array.size(); j++)
      {
              if (fabs(array[j] < 0.001)) // Magic number!
```

```
                {
                        throw ZeroDivide("divide by zero",
                                "sumReciprocals", string());
                }

                ans += 1.0/array[j];
        }

        return ans;
}
```

Here we see that the code checks for zero divide conditions and if such an event occurs it will create an exception object of the appropriate type and throw it back to the client. It is then the client's responsibility to catch the exception and then determine what to do with it. Our first try/catch block is:

```
int size = 10;
double elementsValue = 3.1415;
vector<double> myArray (size, elementsValue);
myArray[5] = 0.0;
print(myArray);

// Now create a try/catch block
try
{
        double answer = sumReciprocals(myArray);
        cout << "Sum of reciprocals: " << answer << endl;
}
catch (ZeroDivide& exception)
{
        exception.print();
}
```

In this case the exception will be 'catched' in the *catch block* and the program continues. Incidentally, if a server code throws an exception and no try/catch block has been defined in the client code a run-time error will occur and the program will terminate abnormally.

We now investigate the case where the client can decide to repair the situation by giving itself the chance to give a new value for the offending value (namely myArray[5] = 0.0;) or allowing it to exit the try block. To this end, the following code allows the client to give a new value ad infinitum or it can exit by giving the magic number 999:

```
Lab1: try
{
        cout << "\ nGive a new value for index number 5:";
        double val;
        cin >> val;
        myArray[5] = val;
        if (val == 999.0)
```

```
        {
                return 1; // Exit the program
        }

        double answer = sumReciprocals(myArray);
        cout << "Sum of reciprocals: " << answer << endl;
}
catch (ZeroDivide& exception)
{
        exception.print();
        goto Lab1;
}
```

This completes our first example of the exception handling mechanism in C++. In later chapters we shall use the mechanism in financial engineering applications and test cases. Summarising, we have introduced the essentials of exception handling in C++ and we have shown how to use it. The knowledge can be applied in your applications.

We have not discussed the following topics (see Stroustrup, 1997 for the details):

- The throw specification (a function can declare the exceptions that it throws to the outside world)
- Nested try blocks and rethrow of exceptions
- Alternative ways of implementing exception handling
- Exceptions with constructors and destructors
- Exceptions and efficiency

## 9.8   PRAGMATIC EXCEPTION MECHANISMS

Instead of creating a hierarchy of exception classes (which involves having to create and maintain these) we take a somewhat more pragmatic approach by creating a single class that we use in all applications. Typical information could be:

- The error message
- The method that threw the exception
- More informational message

All this information is implemented as strings. The complete interface is given by:

```
#ifndef DatasimExceptions_HPP
#define DatasimExceptions_HPP

#include <string>
#include <vector>
using namespace std;
#include <iostream>

class DatasimException
{ // Base class for my current exceptions
```

```
private:
        string mess;          // The error message
        string meth;          // The method that threw the exception
        string why;           // More info on message

        // Redundant data
        vector<string> result;
public:
        DatasimException();

        DatasimException (const string& message,
                const string& method, const string& extraInfo);

        string Message() const;   // The message itself
        string rationale() const;             // Extra information
        string Method() const;                // In which method?

        // All information in one packet
        vector<string> MessageDump() const;

        // Print the full packet
        virtual void print() const;

};
#endif
```

The code file is:

```
#include "DatasimException.hpp"

DatasimException::DatasimException()
{
                mess = meth = why = string();
                result = vector<string>(3);
                result[0] = mess;
                result[1] = meth;
                result[2] = why;
}

DatasimException::DatasimException (const string& message,
                const string& method, const string& extraInfo)
{
                mess = message;
                meth = method;
                why = extraInfo;
                result = vector<string>(3);
```

```
                result[0] = mess;
                result[1] = meth;
                result[2] = why;
}
string DatasimException::Message() const
{

                return mess;
}
string DatasimException::rationale() const
{

                return why;
}

string DatasimException::Method() const
{

                return meth;
}

vector<string> DatasimException::MessageDump() const
{ // Full message

        return result;
}

void DatasimException::print() const
{

                // Variant part
                vector<string> r = MessageDump();

                cout << endl << r[0] << endl;
                // Invariant part
                for (int j = 1; j < r.size(); j++)
                {

                        cout << "\ t" << r[j] << endl;

                }

}
```

Please note the use of the Standard Template Library (STL) vector data container. This is a forward reference and we shall discuss it in a later chapter.

At some stage we could employ a single instance of the class DatasimException so that performance is improved because we create this object at program start and it is removed from memory when the program ends. In this sense, we can apply the *Singleton* pattern to this problem. In fact, the Singleton is reminiscent of the Err object in early versions of the Visual Basic programming language.

### 9.8.1  An example of use

We give an example. In this case we take the trivial problem of dividing a number x by another number y. The answer is undefined if y is zero and in this case a run-time error will occur if no provisions are taken for dealing with the problem. Thus, we use exception handling as follows:

```cpp
double Divide(double x, double y)
{
        // Precondition: y is not zero
        if (y == 0.0)
        {
                throw DatasimException(string("\ tDivide by zero"),
                string("In function Divide"),
                string("Try with non-zero value"));
        }
        return x/y;
}
```

This is the server code. The client code resides in a main program:

```cpp
#include "StringConversions.hpp"
#include "DatasimException.hpp"

#include <string>
using namespace std;

int main()
{

        try
        {
                cout << "Give a number to divide by: " << endl;
                double y; cin >> y;

                cout << Divide(2.0, y);
        }
        catch(DatasimException& e)
        {
                e.print();
                return 0;
        }
                return 0;
}
```

If we run this program and enter 0.0 for y we shall get the following output:

```
Give a number to divide by: 0.0

Divide by zero
In function Divide
Try with non-zero value
```

In later chapters we shall encounter more applications of this exception class when we discuss a visualization package in Excel.

## 9.9  CONCLUSIONS AND SUMMARY

We have given an introduction to a number of advanced and somewhat esoteric techniques that allow the programmer to investigate run-time behaviour in C++ programs. In particular, we discussed:

- Determining the class of an object at run-time
- Casting pointers
- Designing and implementing exceptions in C++

We have included these topics for completeness. We shall use them here and there in future chapters.

## 9.10  EXERCISES AND RESEARCH

1. What are the most common exceptions that you encounter in your daily work? What are they caused by? How would you like to resolve them?

   And finally, how would you implement the corresponding exception classes in C++ for these problems?

2. In Chapter 7 we created a hierarchy of C++ classes for solving nonlinear real-valued equations in a single variable. But there is no provision for exception handling. Typical problems include:
   - At some stage during the execution of the iterative algorithm we may try to divide by zero
   - The algorithm may not converge to the exact solution; in fact it just goes 'on and on'; you will need to build a counter that represents the total number of allowed iterations before the algorithm 'gives up'

   Answer the following questions:
   (a) Determine how you are going to redesign the class hierarchy to accommodate these new requirements
   (b) Implement the requirements in C++ and use the class `DatasimException`
   (c) Test the program again

3. We consider the class hierarchy in section 9.3 again and the code that creates an array of base class pointers to Base. This array is populated by a 'mix' of instances of classes D1 and D2.

   The objective of this exercise is to create a 'Bill of Materials' that tells us how many instances of each class there are.

4. Make an inventory of the most common run-time errors and exceptions that can occur in your applications. For example, errors occur for various reasons:
   - Bad input/output
   - Range and out-of-bounds errors
   - Memory problems (how does `auto_ptr` help?)
   - Others

Determine how you will model these exceptions in C++ and how to integrate them into your code.

5. (Research and Investigation)
   There are some more issues that we would like to discuss and the reader can pursue them further by referring to the reference manuals and specifications:
   - The *exception specification*; a function declaration can list those exceptions that it can throw by using an exception specification as a suffix of its declarator, for example:

```
void getValue(int j) throw (MathErr, DataSimException, int)
{
      if (j == 0) throw 123;
      if (j > 100) throw MatErr();
      if (j < 0) throw DatasimException();
      throw BoundsError();      // Throws unexpected
}
```

   This is a useful feature because it is an explicit statement of the contract between clients and servers
   - The exception handling mechanism relies on two functions for coping with errors; first, `terminate()` gets called when exception handling is abandoned for less subtle error handling techniques and second, `unexpected()` is called when a function with an exception specification throws an exception that is not listed in that specification. See the example above to see the circumstances under which this function is called. The function `unexpected()` calls `terminate()`
   - It might be a good idea to investigate the question of exception handling in constructors and destructors.
   - The '*catch every exception*' syntax; this is a degenerate catch and throw mechanism because it is a catch-all and is used to 'catch any exception'. It is like an insurance policy. Here is an example:

```
class BoundsError
{ // Empty exception class
public:
};

void getValue(int j) throw (int, string)
{
      if (j == 0) throw int(123);
      if (j > 100) throw string("out of bounds");
      throw BoundsError();   // Throws unexpected if no catch(...)
}

int main()
{
      try
      {
            cout << "Value: ";
```

```
            int val; cin >> val;
            getValue(val);
    }

    catch (int& e)
    {
            cout << "integer " << e << endl;
    }

    catch (string& e)
    {
            cout << e << endl;
    }
    catch (...)
    {
            cout << "No idea, really\ n:";
    }
    return 0;
}
```

- The *re-throw mechanism*: we have seen how to catch an exception but in the examples it was handled in the corresponding catch block. In some cases the handler cannot completely handle the error. In that case the handler can then throw the exception again. In this case a re-throw is indicated by a throw without an operand. But be careful; if a re-throw is attempted when there is no exception to re-throw then the terminate() function will be called:

```
void getValueVersionTwo(int j) throw (int, string)
{
        if (j == 0) throw int(123);
        if (j > 100) throw string("out of bounds");
        // Re-throw
        throw;
}
```

- The memory that is allocated for the thrown exception object persists as long as there is a handler being executed for that exception

6. (Exceptions and STL)
   We shall discuss the Standard Template Library (STL) in Chapter 11. This library has support for exception handling and we discuss this topic here. In C++ all exceptions in the language and the STL are derived from the base class called exception. There are three main categories (Josuttis, 1999):
   - Exceptions for language support: these are part of the core language and comprise the following specific exceptions:
     - bad_alloc: thrown when the global operator new fails
     - bad_cast: when things go wrong in dynamic_cast<T>

  – bad_typeid: thrown by the typeid operator
  – bad_exception: used to handle unexpected exceptions
- Exception classes for STL: all exceptions are derived from the base class logic_error. This has specific exception classes:
  – invalid_argument: this is for functions where arguments of the wrong type are used
  – length_error: doing something that exceeds some maximum allowable size
  – out_of_range: an argument is not in the expected range, for example an index in an array structure
  – domain_error: used to report a domain error.
- Exceptions for errors outside the scope of a program: the base class is called runtime_error and it has the following specialisations:
  – range_error: range error in some computation
  – overflow_error: arithmetic overflow exceptions
  – underflow_error: arithmetic underflow exceptions

Here is an example to motivate the above short discussion:

```
try
  {
    throw overflow_error(string("first"));
  }
    catch (const std::runtime_error& e)
    { // This gets caught
        cout << e.what() << endl;
    }
    catch (const std::exception& e)
    {
        cout << e.what() << endl;
    }
```

# 10

# An Introduction to C++ Templates

## 10.1 INTRODUCTION AND OBJECTIVES

C++ was the first mainstream object-oriented language to support the *generic programming paradigm*. In general terms this means that we can create classes that do not use a concrete underlying data type for their representation but rather use an unspecified data type that will later be replaced by a concrete type. The advantage of *generic classes* and *generic functions* is that we only have to write them once and they can subsequently be used again and again in many contexts. For example, a common data structure in financial engineering is one representing the data in the binomial method (Hull, 2006). We know that the binomial method has two dimensions, namely time t and asset price S. When investigating this lattice we may wish to keep the following components as flexible as possible:

- The index set (call it I) that describes the discrete time values
- The data type (call it V) that represents the values at the vertex points of the binomial mesh structure

In a sense, we would like to write classes in a kind of macro language, using the data structures I and V and then replacing these by concrete types in our application. This feature is possible in C++ and is called the C++ *template mechanism*. Going back to the above example we would declare the lattice class as depending on two generic parameters as follows:

```
template <class I, class V> class Lattice
{

        // private and public code here
        // Constructors, building a lattice, navigating
};
```

Different users will have their own specific data types for the data structures I and V. For example, a common example in the literature is when we work with integers for the values in the time direction and double to hold the values at the nodes:

```
Lattice<int, double> myBinomial(...);
```

In chapter 15, we shall use this generic data container as a storage medium for the binomial method. We shall also use it in chapter 19 when we discuss the trinomial method.

Some applications may demand a more complex structure, for example where the index set is a date and the node values is an array (containing various parameters such as jump probabilities, prices and sensitivities:

```
Lattice<DatasimDate, Array> myCallableBond(...);
```

Thus, we only have to write the generic code once and then instantiate it for many different kinds of concrete data types, as the two examples above show.

In this chapter we pay attention to the process of creating simple *template classes* and *template functions* as we think that this is one of the best ways to learn generic programming in C++. We learn by doing and by example. It is important to understand the corresponding syntax well because the compiler errors can be quite cryptic and difficult to understand. In most cases these errors are caused by typing errors or other silly mistakes. This may be the reason why generic programming techniques are not as popular as the more established object-oriented paradigm.

After having read and understood this chapter you will have crossed one hurdle, namely mastering the essential syntax of C++ templates.

We focus on syntax in this chapter. A good understanding of templates is a precondition for further progress.

## 10.2   MY FIRST TEMPLATE CLASS

In general it is our goal to deal with each topic in this chapter as concisely as possible. To this end, we introduce the template mechanism in C++ by first giving a representative example.

Templates in C++ are classes or functions that contain members or have parameters whose types are not yet specified but are generic. For example, we could create a class that represents complex numbers, but in contrast to the code in chapter five where the real and imaginary parts of a complex number are `double` precision numbers we now would like to create a more generic complex number class in which the real and imaginary parts can take on any types.

We now discuss the actual process of creating a template class. Our first remark is that creating template classes is not much more difficult than creating non-template classes. The main difference is that the template class depends on one or more generic parameters (generic type) and this has to be made known to the compiler. To this end, we need to introduce the keyword 'template' in combination with the names of the generic types. We shall create a generic class that represents a one-dimensional interval or range. The header file for this class declares the class, its member data and member function prototypes:

```
template <class Type = double> class Range
{ // Default underlying type is double

private:
    Type lo;
    Type hi;
    Range(); // Default constructor

public:
    // Constructors
    Range(const Type& low, const Type& high); // Low and high value
    Range(const Range<Type>& ran2);            // Copy constructor

    // Destructor
    virtual ~Range();

    // Modifier functions
```

```
        void low(const Type& t1);       // Sets low value of current range
        void high(const Type& t1);      // Sets high value of current range

        //Accessing functions
        Type low() const;                      // Lowest value in range
        Type high() const;                     // Highest value in the range

        Type length() const;                   // High - Low value

        // Boolean functions
        bool left(const Type& value) const; // Is value to the left?
        bool right(const Type& value) const;// Is value to the right?
        bool contains(const Type& value) const; // Range contains value?

        // Operator overloading
        Range<Type>& operator = (const Range<Type>& ran2);
};
```

Thus, this class models one-dimensional intervals and it has the appropriate functionality
for such entities, for example constructors, set-like operations and set/get functions. In this
declaration we see that 'Type' is generic (and not a 'real' class). Furthermore, the word
'Range' is not a class because, being a template we must use it in combination with the
underlying type 'Type'. For example, the copy constructor must be declared as:

```
Range(const Range<Type>& ran2);                    // Copy constructor
```

We now must know how to implement the above member functions. The syntax is similar to
the non-template case; however, there are two issues that we must pay attention to:

- The 'template' keyword must be used with each function
- The class name is Range<Type> and not Range

The compiler needs this information because the generic type will be replaced by a real type
in our applications, as we shall see.
    We give some examples. The following code represents some typical examples:

```
template <class Type> Range<Type>::Range()
{ // Default constructor.

        // Not defined since private
}

template <class Type> Range<Type>::Range(const Type& l, const Type& h)
{ //
        if (l < h)
        {
                lo = l;
                hi = h;
        }
```

```
        else
        {
                hi = l;
                lo = h;
        }
}
```

```
template <class Type> bool Range<Type>::contains(const Type& t) const
{// Does range contain t

        if((lo <= t) && (hi >= t))
                return true;

        return false;
}
```

Please note that constructors are called 'Range' and not 'Range<Type>'. This can be confusing but the constructors are just member functions.

### 10.2.1   Using template classes

A template class is a *type*. In contrast to non-templated classes, it has no instances as such. Instead, when you wish to use a template class in a program you need to *instantiate the template class*, that is we replace the generic underlying type (or types) by some concrete type. The result is a 'normal' C++ class. For example, we take the example of a range whose underlying data type is a date. This class is useful in many financial engineering applications, for example when defining cash flow dates in fixed-income modelling applications:

```
// Create interval between now and 1 year's time
DatasimDate now;
DatasimDate nextYear = now.add_years(1);
Range<DatasimDate> dateSchedule(now, nextYear);
```

This is very useful because we can now reuse all the generic code to work with dates. Some examples are:

```
DatasimDate datL = now - 1; // yesterday
DatasimDate datM = now.add_halfyear();
DatasimDate datR = nextYear + 1; // One year and a day from now

if (dateSchedule.left(datL) == true)
    cout << datL << " to left, OK\ n";

if (dateSchedule.contains(datM) == true)
    cout << datM << " in interval, OK\ n";

if (dateSchedule.right(datR) == true)
    cout << datR << " to right, OK\ n";
```

To take another example, we can instantiate the template class so that it works with integers, as the following code shows:

```
Range<int> range1 (0, 10);

int valL = -1;
int valM = 5;
int valR = 20;

if (range1.left(valL) == true)
      cout << valL << " to left, OK\ n";

if (range1.contains(valM) == true)
      cout << valM << " in interval, OK\ n";

if (range1.right(valR) == true)
      cout << valR << " to right, OK\ n";
```

Again, we did not have to write any extra code because we instantiated the template class again. On the other hand, the template class assumes that the underlying data type implements a number of functions and operators (for example, <, > , <= ). You must realise this fact.

We have used the following syntax in the declaration of the range class:

```
template <class Type = double> class Range
```

This means that when you instantiate the template class without a parameter the underlying type will be double! This saves you typing the data type each time (which can become quite tedious, especially when working with multiple data types). To this end, we can define synonyms by using typedef:

```
typedef Range<> DoubleRange;
DoubleRange d1(-1.0, 1.0);
print (d1);
```

When working with dates we can proceed as follows:

```
typedef Range<DatasimDate> DateRange;
DatasimDate today;
DatasimDate anotherDate = today + 365;
DateRange whatsAnotherYear(today, anotherDate);
print(whatsAnotherYear);
```

It is advisable to define all your synonyms in one place so that you can easily locate them later.

### 10.2.2   (Massive) reusability of the range template class

Let us pause for a moment to think about what we have done. We have created a template class that can be used in many kinds of applications. In the current book, there are many situations where we can use and reuse the range template class:

- Binomial, Trinomial and Finite Difference Methods
- Interval arithmetic and solution of linear and non-linear equations; interval arithmetic is based on achieving two-sided estimates for some (unknown) quantity (see Moore, 1966, 1979).
- Range as a building block in larger data structures as we shall see in Chapters 16 and 17

On the down side, if you are not satisfied with the functionality that a template class delivers you can always extend the functionality using any one of the three mechanisms:

- Inheritance
- Composition and delegation
- Defining non-member functions that accept an instance of a template class

## 10.3   TEMPLATE FUNCTIONS

In the previous section we have discussed how to create and instantiate a template class. It is perhaps worth mentioning that it is possible to create non-member (or C-style) template functions. This is a useful feature for several reasons. It is sometimes cumbersome or even wrong to be forced to embed functionality as a member function of some artificial class and second we wish to extend the functionality of a class without having to inherit from it. Let us take a simple example to show how to define a template function. To this end, we wish to write a function to swap two instances of the same class (incidentally, the Standard Template Library (STL) has a function to swap any two objects). The code for the swap function is given by:

```
template <class V> void mySwap(V& v1, V& v2)
{
      V tmp = v2;
      v2 = v1;
      v1 = tmp;
}
```

The code is very easy to understand. Of course, we see that the underlying type V should have a public assignment operator defined. If it is private, for example the code will not compile when we instantiate V with some concrete data type. Some examples of using the swap functions are:

```
int j = 10;
int k = 20;
mySwap(j, k);

Range<int> range1 (0, 10);
Range<int> range2 (20, 30);

mySwap (range1, range2);
```

We can write many kinds of related template functions and then group them into a namespace. This is the topic of the next section.

## 10.4   CONSOLIDATION: UNDERSTANDING TEMPLATES

It takes some time to master templates in C++ and most compiler errors are caused by invalid syntax, typing errors and forgetting to supply all the syntax that is needed. To make matters worse, the compiler can become confused and it then produces error messages that can be very difficult to understand.

In this and the following sections we give a complete example of a template class that you should read and understand. It models a point in two dimensions whose coordinates may belong to different data types. There are a number of issues to take care of:

- Declare that the class is a template class
- Define the class' member data
- Define the class constructors and destructor
- Define the other member and non-member functions

The full interface is now given. Please study it:

```cpp
// Point.hpp
//
// Generic point class. The first coordinate is of one
// type and the second coordinate is of the second type.
//
// (C) Datasim Education BV 2006

#ifndef Point_hpp
#define Point_hpp

#include <iostream>
using namespace std;

template <class TFirst, class TSecond>
class Point

{
private:
        // The two coordinates
        TFirst m_first;
        TSecond m_second;

public:
        // Constructors & destructor
        Point();
        // Default constructor
        Point(TFirst first, TSecond second);
        Point(const Point<TFirst, TSecond>& source);
        virtual ~ Point();    // Destructor

        // Selectors
```

```
      TFirst First() const;      // Get first coordinates
      TSecond Second() const;   // Get second coordinate

      // Modifiers
      void First(const TFirst& val);       // Set first coordinate
      void Second(const TSecond& val);     // Set second coordinate

      // Functions
      double Distance(const Point<TFirst, TSecond>& p) const;

      // Assignment operator
      Point<TFirst, TSecond>& operator =
                (const Point<TFirst, TSecond>& source);

      // Print
      template <class TFirst, class TSecond>
      friend ostream& operator << (ostream& os,
                      const Point<TFirst, TSecond>& p);
};
#endif
```

We note that that there is one non-member function defined here and newer versions of the C++ compiler demand that it declared the way it is, that is by using the `template` keyword and defining what the underlying types are.

We now discuss the code for each of the above functions. We have some remarks:

- Each member function must use the 'template' keyword
- The class name contains the underlying types

The complete code file is given as:

```
// Point.cpp
//
// Generic point class.
//
// Last modification dates:
//
// DD 2006-3-5 Kick off and << for print
//
// (C) Datasim Education BV 2006

#ifndef Point_cpp
#define Point_cpp

#include "Point.hpp"
#include <math.h>

// Default constructor
template <class TFirst, class TSecond>
```

```
Point<TFirst, TSecond>::Point()
{
    m_first=TFirst();
    m_second=TSecond();
}


// Constructor with coordinates
template <class TFirst, class TSecond>
Point<TFirst, TSecond>::Point(TFirst first, TSecond second)
{
    m_first=first;
    m_second=second;
}


// Copy constructor
template <class TFirst, class TSecond>
Point<TFirst, TSecond>::Point(const Point<TFirst, TSecond>& source)
{
    m_first=source.m_first;
    m_second=source.m_second;
}


// Destructortemplate <class TFirst, class TSecond>
template <class TFirst, class TSecond>
Point<TFirst, TSecond>::~Point()
{
}


// Get first coordinates
template <class TFirst, class TSecond>
TFirst Point<TFirst, TSecond>::First() const
{
    return m_first;
}


// Get second coordinate
template <class TFirst, class TSecond>
TSecond Point<TFirst, TSecond>::Second() const
{
    return m_second;
}


// Set first coordinate
template <class TFirst, class TSecond>
void Point<TFirst, TSecond>::First(const TFirst& val)
{
    m_first=val;
}
```

```
// Set second coordinates
template <class TFirst, class TSecond>
void Point<TFirst, TSecond>::Second(const TSecond& val)
{
    m_second=val;
}


// Calculate distance
template <class TFirst, class TSecond>
double Point<TFirst, TSecond>::Distance(const Point<TFirst, TSecond>&
p) const
{

    // Get the length of the sides
    TFirst a=p.m_first-m_first;
    TSecond b=p.m_second-m_second;

    // Use Pythagoras to calculate distance
    return ::sqrt(a*a + b*b);
}


// Assignment operator
template <class TFirst, class TSecond>
Point<TFirst, TSecond>& Point<TFirst, TSecond>::operator = (const
Point<TFirst, TSecond>& source)
{
    if (this == &source)
            return *this;

    m_first=source.m_first;
    m_second=source.m_second;

    return *this;
}


// Print
template <class TFirst, class TSecond>
ostream& operator << (ostream& os, const Point<TFirst, TSecond>& p)
{
    os << "(" << p.m_first << "," << p.m_second << ")\ n";
    return os;
}
#endif
```

### 10.4.1   A test program

We now show how to use the above template class in an application. First, it is mandatory to include the file that contains the source code of the member functions (in this case, Point.cpp) in client code. Any other construction will not work. Then we replace the generic data types by specific data types (this is called the *instantiation process*). To this end, consider the following code:

```
// TestGenericPoint.cpp
//
// Testing generic points
//
// (C) Datasim Education BV 2006
//

// The file that actually contains the code must be included
#include "point.cpp"
#include <iostream>
using namespace std;

int main()
{

        Point<double, double> p1(1.0, 1.0);
        Point<double, double> p2; // Default point

        cout << "p1: " << p1 << endl;
        cout << "p2: " << p2 << endl;

        cout << "Distance between points: " << p1.Distance(p2) << endl;
        return 0;
}
```

In this case we create points whose underlying types are double.

## 10.5   SUMMARY AND CONCLUSIONS

This chapter introduced the notion of generic programming as a programming paradigm and in particular we showed – by examples – how it is realised in C++ by the template mechanism. We focused on the syntax that we must learn if we are going to be successful in using template classes and functions in Quantitative Finance applications.

A template class is not much different from a non-template class except that we explicitly state that certain members are generic. Second, all functions that use the generic data types must state that it is using these types, for example:

```
template <class TFirst, class TSecond>
                        Point<TFirst, TSecond>::Point()
{
        m_first=TFirst();
        m_second=TSecond();
}
```

This chapter lays the foundation for the rest of this book in the sense that many of the specific instantiated classes and resulting applications make use of template classes and functions.

A good way to learn template programming is to take a working non-template class and then port it to a templated equivalent. A good example is the C++ class that models complex numbers. We have already discussed this class in Chapter 5.

## 10.6    EXERCISES AND PROJECTS

1. This exercise has to do with the class for a line segment in two dimensions that we discussed in Chapter 4. We give the class interface again for completeness:

```
// LineSegment.hpp
//
// (Finite) line segments in 2 dimensions. This class represents
// an undirected line segment. The functionality is basic. If you
// wish to get more functions then convert the line segment to a
// vector or to a line and use their respective member functions.
//
// This is a good example of Composition (a line segment consists of
// two points) and the Delegation principle. For example, the member
// function that calculates the length of a line is implemented as the
// distance function between the line's end points.
//
// (C) Datasim BV 1995-2006
//

#ifndef LineSegment_HPP
#define LineSegment_HPP

#include "Point.hpp"

class LineSegment
{
private:
    Point e1;    // End Point of line
    Point e2;    // End Point of line

public:
    // Constructors
    LineSegment();
    // Line with both end Points at the origin
    LineSegment(const Point& p1, const Point& p2);
    LineSegment(const LineSegment& l);         // Copy constructor
    virtual ~LineSegment();                    // Destructor

    // Accessing functions
    Point start() const;                       // Synonym for e1
    Point end() const;                         // Synonym for e2
```

```
        // Modifiers
        void start(const Point& pt);        // Set Point pt1
        void end(const Point& pt);          // Set Point pt2

        // Arithmetic
        double length() const;              // Length of line

        // Interaction with Points
        Point midPoint() const;             // MidPoint of line segment
};
```

```
#endif
```

The objective now is to model a new line class based on a generic point class. For convenience we assume that the first and second coordinates have the same underlying type:

```
template <class T>
        class LineSegment
        {
        private:
                // Points have the same kinds of coordinates
                Point<T,T> e1;
                Point<T,T> e2;
        public:

                // For you ☺
        };
```

Answer the following questions:
(a) Complete the header and code files for this class. Test the class by creating lines with specific underlying types, for example `double`. You need to test each member function because a template class that compiles and works for a given member function does not mean that it works for all member functions. In short, we have the same interface as before except that the all data is generic!
(b) We now wish to extend the functionality by producing code to calculate the 'taximan's' length for a line segment. This is the sum of the absolute value of the difference of the x coordinates and the absolute value of the difference of the y coordinates. `LineSegment` delegates to `Point` and this may necessitate two new useful functions in the point class:

```
double xExtent() const;
double yExtent() const;
```

2. Based on the C++ code for complex numbers in Chapter 5, the objective now is to create a generic version `Complex<T>`. Use the same programs as in chapter 5 to test this new template class.

# Part II
# Data Structures, Templates and Patterns

# 11

# Introduction to Generic Data Structures
# and Standard Template Library (STL)

## 11.1 INTRODUCTION AND OBJECTIVES

Chapter 10 introduced the template mechanism in C++ and we created a number of simple template classes to show how the syntax is used. In this chapter we give an overview of the Standard Template Library (STL). STL is a library of C++ template classes for commonly occurring data structures (such as lists and vectors), algorithms (for example, sorting, searching and extracting information) as well as functionality for navigating in data structures. It is part of the ISO C++ standard and is not specific to a particular vendor. Thus, code that you write and use with C++ compiler from vendor A will run using C++ compiler from vendor B. Furthermore, the *components* in STL have been designed and implemented with performance in mind. There is no point in trying to write your own components to compete with STL; a better idea would be to use and apply STL to create your own financial engineering applications.

STL components can be used as *foundation classes*. These are the data structures that one sees in computer science and algebra books, for example:

- Lists and vectors (linear sequences of data)
- Maps and multimaps (key-value pairs, like telephone books)
- Sets and multisets
- Specially adapted containers such as stacks and queues

You can use these containers in a myriad of ways in your applications. For example, you can use the above *containers* as follows:

- As member data in your classes
- To hold heterogenous data
- STL containers can be nested
- You can instantiate STL with your own specific data types and use them directly in applications

Furthermore, STL has many powerful *algorithms* that allow you to perform operations on containers and collections of data:

- Inserting data into a container
- Searching for data in a container
- Replacing data in a container
- Merging and combining containers
- Sorting a container
- Set-like operations (set union, intersection and difference)

Finally, STL *iterators* allow us to 'bind' containers and algorithms. Iterators are similar to traditional pointers in C but their added value is that they permit access to data in a container without having to know how the container is implemented. In this sense we view an iterator as a kind of *Mediator* (in the sense of Gamma et al., 1995).

In this chapter we give an overview of one subset of STL functionality. In particular, we discuss the list<T> container and how to use algorithms and iterators in conjunction with it.

After having read this chapter you will have gained an understanding of the following fundamental issues:

- Coming to terms with STL syntax
- Representative STL functionality and using it in simple applications
- Creating data structures that will be useful in options pricing applications

The following chapters expand on these issues. A more detailed discussion of template programming, STL and applications to QF can be found in Duffy (2004).

## 11.2  COMPLEXITY ANALYSIS

Before we discuss linear and nonlinear data structures in detail, we introduce a number of concepts that have to do with the efficiency of algorithms acting on data structures. This is a neglected topic in much of the modern literature but it is important to know what the time and space efficiency issues will be before we choose a certain data structure for use in an application. Conversely, assuming we know what our efficiency requirements are, how do we choose the 'optimal' data structure that fits the bill as it were?

We need to have some measure of the cost of an algorithm and we need an indication of what the total effort will be. To this end, we use so-called *logical units* that express a relationship between the size n of a data container and the amount of time t required to process the data. In general, it is difficult to find an exact, analytical formula for this relationship and we must then resort to other approximate techniques. But in many cases the approximate formula is sufficiently close to the exact formula, especially for an algorithm that processes large amounts of data, that is, when the size n becomes very large. This measure of efficiency is called *asymptotic complexity* and it is used when disregarding certain terms of a function that expresses the efficiency of an algorithm. For example, consider the function:

$$f(n) = n^2 + 100n + \log n + 1000 \tag{11.1}$$

For small values of n the fourth term is the largest. When n reaches the value 100, however the first and second terms are vying for first place. When n becomes even bigger we see that the first term in (11.1) predominates and we say that response time is quadratic.

We define a notation that specifies asymptotic complexity. To this end, we introduce the 'big-O' notation.

*Definition 1*: A function $f(n)$ is $O(g(n))$ (where $g(n)$ is a given function) if there exist positive numbers $c$ and $N$ such that:

$$f(n) \leq cg(n) \text{ for all } n \geq N \tag{11.2}$$

This inequality states that $g(n)$ is an upper bound for the value of $f(n)$; alternatively, we can say that $f$ grows at most as fast as $g$ in the long term. In general, inequality (11.2) is an existence result only and it does not tell us how to calculate $c$ and $N$.

The *logarithmic function* is one of the most important functions when evaluating the efficiency of algorithms. In general, an algorithm is considered to be good if its complexity is of the order of the logarithmic function for large $n$. Some other examples are given in Table 11.1.

**Table 11.1**  Classes of algorithms

|  | $n$ |
|---|---|
| Constant | $0\,(1)$ |
| Logarithmic | $0\,(\log n)$ |
| Linear | $0\,(n)$ |
| $0\,(n\log n)$ | $0\,(n\log n)$ |
| Quadratic | $0(n^2)$ |
| Cubic | $0\,(n^3)$ |
| Exponential | $0\,(2^n)$ |

We now discuss some more notation that refers to issues that give lower bounds for the complexity of an algorithm, in contrast where the big-O notation gave upper bounds for the complexity.

*Definition 2*: The function $f(n)$ is $\Omega(g(n))$ (where $g(n)$ is a given function) if there exist positive numbers $c$ and $N$ such that:

$$f(n) \geq cg(n) \text{ for all } n \geq N \tag{11.3}$$

The only difference between (11.2) and (11.3) is the sign of the inequality.

### 11.2.1  Examples of complexities

An algorithm is called *constant* if its execution time is independent of the number of elements in the data container and we usually use the notation O(1). Similarly, an algorithm is called *logarithmic* if the execution time is O(log n). In general, we would like to determine the number of milliseconds for a given value of n. This result is machine-dependent.

An example is displayed in Table 11.2 for the case of $n = 10,000$ and on a CPU that has an execution time of a million operations per second. Thus, if you are using an algorithm whose complexity you know then you can get a rough idea of how long the algorithm will take to execute.

This concludes our example. Actually finding the asymptotic complexity for an algorithm is outside the scope of this book and we content ourselves with giving the estimates that we use, in particular in conjunction with the STL.

**Table 11.2**  Execution times (1 second $= 10^6 \mu$ sec $= 10^3$ ms)

|  | $n = 10^4$ |  |
|---|---|---|
| Constant | 1 | $1\,\mu$ sec |
| Logarithmic | 13.3 | $13\,\mu$ sec |
| Linear | $10^4$ | 10 m sec |
| $0\,(n\log n)$ | $133{*}\,10^3$ | 133 m sec |
| Quadratic | $10^8$ | 1.7 min |
| Cubic | $10^{12}$ | 11.6 days |
| Exponential | $10^{3010}$ | 'long' (forever) |

Before we go on to the next section we finish with a couple of concepts that you come across when dealing with *complexity classes*. We define the class **P** to consist of those decision problems that can be solved on a deterministic sequential machine in the amount of time that is a polynomial function of the size of the input. The class **NP** (non-deterministic polynomial time) consists of all those decision problems whose positive solutions can be verified in polynomial time given the right information, or equivalently, whose solution can be found in polynomial time on a non-deterministic machine. In complexity theory, the **NP-complete** problems are the most difficult to solve in **NP** in the sense that they are the ones most likely not to be in **P**. An example of an **NP**-complete problem is the subset sum problem: given a finite set of integers, determine whether any non-empty subset of them sums to zero.

## 11.3    AN INTRODUCTION TO DATA STRUCTURES

Before we discuss the programming details of the STL we think that it is a good idea to introduce data structures from a Computer Science perspective. A good understanding of the theoretical underpinnings will help you find which STL functionality you need for your QF applications.

### 11.3.1    Lists

A list is an example of a *sequential container*. This means that the data is stored in a sequential fashion. We distinguish between several kinds of linked list:

- Singly linked list
- Doubly linked list (supported in STL)
- Circular list
- Skip list

In general, a list consists of nodes. A node contains a data value as well as pointers to other elements in the list. In the case of a *singly linked list* (Figure 11.1) each node points to a single other node, usually called it successor. A *doubly linked list*, on the other hand consists of nodes, each one of which points to a successor and to a predecessor, see Figure 11.2. With circular lists, the nodes form a ring; the list is finite and each node has a successor, see Figure 11.3. Finally, a *skip list* is a specialised list in which certain elements in a list can be skipped when searching for a given data element, in contrast to the already-mentioned lists where sequential scanning is needed in order to locate an element.

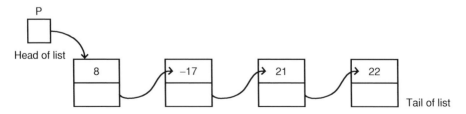

**Figure 11.1**    Singly linked list

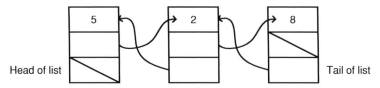

**Figure 11.2**    Doubly linked list

Doubly-linked lists are supported in STL. The following operations take constant time O(1):

- Insert an element at the beginning/end of the list
- Delete the first/last element
- Merge two lists
- Insert/delete an element at any position in the list

The following operations have O(n) complexity:

- Reverse the order of elements in the list
- Delete identical consecutive elements except the first one

Finally, a typical sorting algorithm for lists has a time complexity O(n log n).

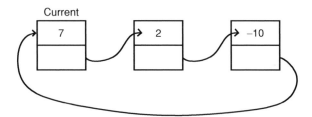

**Figure 11.3**    Circular list

## 11.3.2   Stacks and queues

These are data structures that we see in daily life. A stack is a linear data structure that can be accessed only at one of its ends. For example, imagine a stack of trays or plates in a restaurant. We put new trays on the top of the stack while we take trays off the stack one on by one, starting with the top-most tray. In this sense a stack is called a *LIFO* (*Last In, First Out structure*).

The operations on a stack are:

- Clear the stack
- Is the stack empty?
- Is the stack full?
- Put an element on the top of the stack (Push)
- Take the topmost element from the stack (Pop)

In programming terms, a C++ class for a stack is an *adapter class* because it uses the service of another data container, for example a double-ended queue. We shall address this

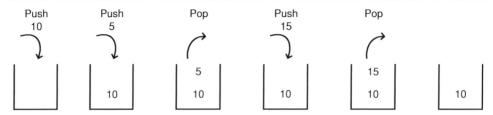

**Figure 11.4**   Series of operations on a stack

issue in a moment. Stacks are supported in STL. An example of using a stack is shown in Figure 11.4.

We now discuss queues. There are three main kinds and they are supported in STL:

- Double-ended queue (called deque)
- *FIFO (First In, First Out)* queue
- Priority queue

A *deque* is similar to a list because it allows insertions and deletions at the beginning and at the end in constant time, that is O(1). But insertions and deletions elsewhere in a deque are more costly, that is O(n) because a number of elements must be shifted.

A *queue* is a data structure where we can insert elements at one end and remove them from the opposite end. The elements at both ends can be read without being removed. We sometimes call a queue a *FIFO (First In, First out)* data structure. We thus see that the interface of a queue is more restricted than that of a deque. It can be modelled by adapting the interface of a deque.

In many applications we use simple queues because of the first in, first out scheduling regime they use. In some cases we would like to overrule this by using some priority criteria. For example, in a post office a handicapped person may have priority over other people. In operating system (OS) software, process B may need to execute before process A for the proper functioning of the system even though A was put on the queue of waiting processes before B. In these cases we need to define a modified queue or priority queue. In these queues the elements are dequeued (that is, taken off the queue) according to their priority and to their current position.

In STL, a *priority queue* always gives the element with the highest priority. We specify the *priority criteria* when creating the queue. This could be the greatest or smallest number in the queue, for example. In general, however we characterise the criterion by using a suitable *function object* for comparison. We have included some examples on the CD to show how this technique works.

Another example of a priority queue is a print spooler in which the elements of the queue store pairs consisting of references to print jobs and associated priorities.

### 11.3.3   Sets and multisets

A set is a collection of unique elements and is a fundamental data structure in Computer Science. Some examples of sets are:

- The set of natural numbers
- The set of dates before which I must pay the monthly mortgage

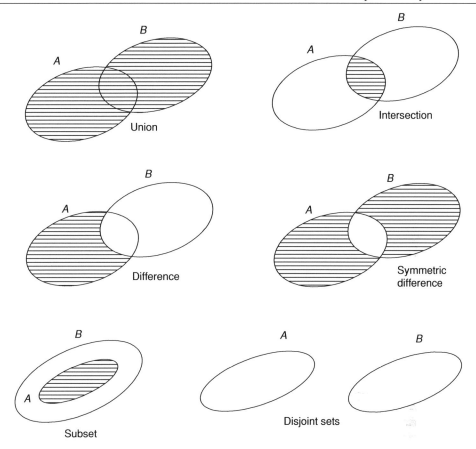

**Figure 11.5** Set operations

- Sets containing 'prototypical' instances of options, bonds and swaps classes
- Sets whose elements may also be sets ('nested' sets)

Sets can be used to configure applications. Some typical examples are:

- Creating member data (property sets) from sets of configuration data
- Pools of prototype objects
- Settings and global variables

STL supports sets and in particular it has functionality for the well-known set operations that we show in Figure 11.5. In Chapter 12 we shall create a class that hides much of the low-level details of the STL set<T> container.

A multiset is similar to a set but there is one difference; in the present case it is allowed to have more than one instance of an element. For example, the collection of positive integers $\{1,1,2,2,3,3, \ldots\}$ is a multiset. In some programming environments, such as Smalltalk-80, for example, multisets are called *bags*.

STL supports multisets. Sets and multisets make no distinction between keys and data: they are the same.

### 11.3.4   Maps and multimaps

A *map* is similar to a set except that the keys and associated data are different. A map is essentially a dictionary in which unique keys are associated with values. A good example of a map is a telephone book for a city; the name of the person represents the key while his or her unique telephone number is the value. Actually, the map<K,V> template class will prove to be very important for QF applications and we shall use it in many of the upcoming chapters. It has numerous applications, including:

- Creating large, sparse matrices
- Dynamic member data and property sets
- Using maps to administer and 'hold' objects together when using design patterns
- Associative arrays and matrices
- 'Dynamic' matrices

The last two examples are of relevance because we can create arrays and matrices containing elements that are accessed, not using integer types but by using generic types. Taking an associative matrix for example, we design it using three data types:

- The index type for rows, call it R
- The index type for columns, call it C
- The data type that represents the matrix values, call it V

Having created such an associative matrix class, we can then instantiate the different types to suit a particular application. For example, an 'Excel-like' matrix class could be declared as:

```
Matrix<string, string, double> myMatrix(100, 50);
```

There is a myriad of examples we could concoct but once the basic template class has been developed you can use it over and over again by just instantiating some (or all!) of the generic data types. For example, we could create a matrix whose elements are accessed using dates and doubles (for example, this could be some kind of volatility surface):

```
Matrix<DatasimDate, double, double> myMatrix(100, 50);
```

In short, maps are useful because we can access data safely and quickly.

A *multimap* is similar to a map in the same way that a multiset is similar to a set; keys do not necessarily have to be unique. We shall not discuss multimaps in this book. In general, they can be used to model many-to-many relationships.

## 11.4   ALGORITHMS

We have completed our discussion of data structures that we wish to apply in this book. But data structures do nothing by themselves and we would like to provide functions, modules and algorithms that manipulate the data in data structures. We can give some algorithm categories based on the lifetime of an instance of a data container:

A1: Creating instances (using various kinds of constructors)
A2: Finding information in a data structure
A3: Modifying information in a data structure
A4: Removing information from a data structure

These are very broad categories. In STL a more specialized classification is:

B1: Nonmutating sequence (read only)
B2: Mutating sequence operations (writable)
B3: Sorting and merging
B4: Set operations on sorted structures
B5: Heap algorithms

The specific algorithms in each category are documented in books that discuss STL. We content ourselves with a short inventory of some important algorithms:

B1

- `find`: locate an element in a container
- `count`: number of elements whose value equals a target value
- `search`: search for a subsequence within a sequence

B2

- `copy`: make a copy of a container
- `swap`: swap the contents of two sequences
- `transform`: modify a sequence and copy it into another container
- `replace`: replace a value by another value
- `unique`: delete identical consecutive elements
- `reverse`: 'first will be last and last will be first'
- `remove`: delete an element having a certain value

## 11.5   NAVIGATION IN DATA STRUCTURES: ITERATORS IN STL

We have now described the data structures and the algorithms that operate on those structures. But what is missing? We need a mechanism to allow the algorithms to access the individual elements of a data structure without actually having to know its internal workings. To this end, we define so-called *iterators* that we see as the glue between data and algorithms. In design patterns terms, an iterator is a *Mediator* between a data structure and an algorithm. It allows an algorithm to access the elements of a data structure. In STL each data structure has member functions that point to the beginning of the data structure and to just 'behind' the last element of the data structure as shown in Figure 11.6. There are different kinds of iterators:

- Forward and backward iterators
- Sequential and random access iterators
- Iterators that read from, and iterators that write to the data structure

A *forward iterator* is one that moves from the beginning of a data structure to its end while a *backward iterator* allows us to navigate from the end to the beginning. A *sequential iterator* moves from one element to its successor (or predecessor), that is one element at a time while *random iterators* allow us to jump to an element based on some index. Lists, for example, have sequential iterators only while vectors have random access iterators as well as sequential iterators.

An iterator can be seen as a sophisticated pointer and it is important to know that it points to one particular element in a data container at any one moment in time. Thus, we dereference the iterator to give the address of the element that it actually points to!

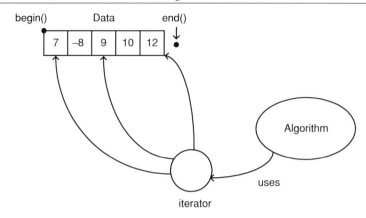

**Figure 11.6**   Container/iterator/alogrithm triad

Finally, we sometimes read the elements of a data structure without wishing to modify the element, or even being allowed to do so. In this case we employ read-only or `const` iterators. Conversely, we may wish to modify the elements in a data structure in some way and in this case we use a *non-constant iterator* that in this case allows us to write into the data structure.

STL provides support for the above-mentioned iterator types and we shall see examples of use in the following chapters. Finally, some object-oriented languages use so-called *Enumerators* to navigate in data structures but they are essentially the same as STL iterators.

## 11.6   STL BY EXAMPLE: MY FIRST EXAMPLE

We have given a bird's eye view of data structures and their realisation in STL. We did not give any code samples because we wished to give the reader an overview of the offerings before we jumped into the details of C++ and STL. However, it is a good idea to 'get our hands dirty' by examining a number of concrete STL data containers that are very important for QF applications. These containers are:

- `vector`: a sequence container that supports random access to elements, constant time insertion and removal of elements at the end, and linear time insertion and removal of elements at the beginning or in the middle. The number of elements in a vector is variable and memory management is automatic
- `valarray`: a vector that contains functionality for arithmetic operations such as +, -, multiplication by a scalar and so on

Please note that indexing starts at index 0 for both `vector` and `valarray`. This is in keeping with C in general but Fortran programmers are accustomed to defining the start index to be equal to 1.

We shall concentrate on `vector` first.

### 11.6.1  Constructors and memory allocation

There are different ways to create a vector. First, we can create a vector of a fixed size, second
we can create an empty vector and add elements as the need arises and finally we can reserve
a block of memory for a vector and then modify this memory using the indexing operator. In
this section we concentrate on the first option and to this end we shall create several vectors
of fixed size and containing various data types. The first example is straightforward:

```
size_t n = 10;
double val = 3.14;
vector<double> myVec(n, val); // Create n copies of val
print(myVec);
// Access elements of the vector by using indexing operator []
// Change some values here and there
myVec[0] = 2.0;
myVec[1] = 456.76;
int last_element= myVec.size() - 1;
myVec[last_element] = 55.66;
print(myVec);
```

We shall have need to use constructors later on in this chapter.

### 11.6.2  Iterators

We give an example of an iterator that navigates in a vector and prints each element on the
console display. Note that we are using a constant iterator because we do not change the
elements in the vector. To this end, we give the code for a template function that realises this
requirement:

```
template <class T>
     void print(const vector<T>& l, string s = string("data"))
{     // A generic print function for vectors
     cout << endl << s << ", size of vector is " << l.size() << "\ n[";
     // Use a const iterator here, otherwise we get a compiler error.
     vector<T>::const_iterator i;
     for (i = l.begin(); i != l.end(); i++)
     {
                cout << *i << ",";
     }
     cout << "]\ n";
}
```

An important remark: the iterator 'i' points to one specific element in the vector at any one
moment in time; hence, if we dereference it we get the element itself!

### 11.6.3  Algorithms

We now discuss how to apply some STL algorithms to vector<T>. These can also be applied
to many other container types as well.

The first algorithm is copy() and it copies the elements of a source range (that is bounded by two iterators written as a *closed-open interval* [first, last) ) into a target range:

```
vector<double> myVec2(myVec.size());
list<double> myList;
// Copy source range of type T1 into target range of type T2
copy(myVec.begin(), myVec.end(), myVec2.begin());
print(myVec2, string("copy to a vector"));
copy(myVec.begin(), myVec.end(), myList.begin());
```

In this case we have copied a vector into another vector and also into a list.

We now discuss the rotate() algorithm that shifts the elements of a sequence to the left in such a way that those elements that 'fall off' at the beginning as it were are inserted back at the end:

```
// Shift elements of vector to left; those that fall off
// are inserted at the end
int N = 6;
vector<double> myVec3(N);

for (int i = 0; i < myVec3.size(); i++)
{
            myVec3[i] = double (i);
}
int shiftFactor = 2;
rotate(myVec3.begin(), myVec3.begin() + shiftFactor,
                                           myVec3.end());
print(myVec3, string("Rotated vector by 2 units"));
```

The replace() algorithm replaces each and every occurrence of the value of an element by a new value:

```
// Now replace each occurrence of one value by a new value
double oldVal = 2;
double newVal = 999;
replace(myVec3.begin(), myVec3.end(), oldVal, newVal);
print(myVec3, string("Modified value of vec3"));
```

The remove() algorithm removes all elements from a sequence that equal to a given value (or that satisfy some predicate):

```
// Now remove this element
remove(myVec3.begin(), myVec3.end(), newVal);
print(myVec3, string("Removed element from vec3"));
```

It is possible to sort a vector. Of course, we must define how to compare two elements of a vector:

- By 'default' operator
- By defining our own comparison function

An example of the first option is:

```
// Sort the random access container vector<T> class
myVec3[myVec3.size() - 1] = 9999.0;
stable_sort(myVec3.begin(), myVec3.end());
print(myVec3, string("Sorted vec3 with "<" ASCENDING "));
```

We now wish to sort a vector in descending order and this is possible but we first must define a comparison function:

```
bool myGreater(double x, double y)
{
        return x > y;
}
```

We can now sort the elements in the vector by using this function as *comparitor*:

```
stable_sort(myVec3.begin(), myVec3.end(), myGreater);
print(myVec3,
        string("Sorted vec3 with DESCENDING comparitor function "));
```

An example of how to merge vectors is:

```
// Merge two sorted vectors
vector<double> myVec4(N, 2.41);
vector<double> myVec5(myVec3.size() + myVec4.size()); // Output
merge(myVec3.begin(), myVec3.end(), myVec4.begin(), myVec4.end(),
            myVec5.begin());
print(myVec5, string("Merged vector"));
```

Our final example is somewhat more advanced than a simple copy() algorithm, for example. In this case we copy elements while at the same time transforming them in some way. As an example, we create two vectors of strings, transforming the first vector to upper case and then joining the two vectors to form a new vector. First of all, here is the code to convert a string to upper case:

```
string UpperCase(string s)
{ // Convert a string to upper case
        for (int j = 0; j < s.length(); j++)
        {
                if (s[j] >= "a" && s[j] <= "z")
                {
                        s[j] -= "a" - "A";
                }
        }
        return s;
}
```

We now create two vectors whose elements are strings:

```
vector<string> First(3);
First[0] = "Bill";
```

```
First[1] = "Abbott";
First[2] = "Bassie";

vector<string> Second(3);
Second[0] = "Ben";
Second[1] = "Costello";
Second[2] = "Adriaan";
```

and we create another vector that will be their join in some sense:

```
vector<string> Couples(3);
```

We now transform the first vector's elements to upper case:

```
// Now convert the First names to upper case
transform (First.begin(), First.end(), First.begin(), UpperCase);
print(First, string("An upper case vector"));
```

In this case we say that the function is a *unary transformation*.

Finally, we define a *binary transformation* Join() that stores results in another container:

```
class Join
{
public:
        // Overloading of operator ()
        string operator () (const string& s1, const string& s2)
        {
                return s1 + " and " +s2;
        }
};
```

The transform is now: (use CD to check this output)

```
// Now join to make a team
transform (First.begin(), First.end(), Second.begin(),
                Couples.begin(), Join());
print(Couples, string("Joined couples"));
```

The output from **all** this code is:

```
data, size of vector is 10
[3.14,3.14,3.14,3.14,3.14,3.14,3.14,3.14,3.14,3.14,]
data, size of vector is 10
[2,456.76,3.14,3.14,3.14,3.14,3.14,3.14,3.14,55.66,]
copy to a vector, size of vector is 10
[2,456.76,3.14,3.14,3.14,3.14,3.14,3.14,3.14,55.66,]
An upper case vector, size of vector is 3
[BILL,ABBOTT,BASSIE,]
Joined couples, size of vector is 3
[BILL and Ben,ABBOTT and Costello,BASSIE and Adriaan,]
Rotated vector by 2 units, size of vector is 6
```

```
[2,3,4,5,0,1,]
Reversed vector vec3, size of vector is 6
[1,0,5,4,3,2,]
Modified value of vec3, size of vector is 6
[1,0,5,4,3,999,]
Removed element from vec3, size of vector is 6
[1,0,5,4,3,999,]
Sorted vec3 with "<" ASCENDING , size of vector is 6
[0,1,3,4,5,9999,]
Sorted vec3 with DESCENDING comparitor function , size of vector is 6
[9999,5,4,3,1,0,]
Merged vector, size of vector is 12
[2.41,2.41,2.41,2.41,2.41,2.41,9999,5,4,3,1,0,]
```

You can run the program from the code on the CD.

## 11.7   CONCLUSIONS AND SUMMARY

We have given an introduction to Complexity Analysis. We have introduced this topic for two main reasons; first, we wish to bring the material to the attention of the reader and second once we have given an overview of these topics we shall see that the transition to, and the understanding of STL will progress more easily than otherwise.

This is an important chapter and it is advisable to read it several times. It goes without saying that the best way to really learn the material is to code some examples in C++ in conjunction with STL.

## 11.8   EXERCISES AND PROJECTS

1. (Creating a Stack class) Even though STL has an implementation for a stack, we would like you to implement your own. It must contain the usual constructors, non-virtual destructor (why non-virtual?) and member functions for:
   - Clear the stack
   - Is the stack empty?
   - Is the stack full?
   - Put an element on the top of the stack ( Push() )
   - Take the topmost element from the stack ( Pop() )

   Implement the stack class using an embedded deque (using Composition). All new member functions that you create will delegate to the appropriate member functions in deque. You should define the Pop() function that returns the top-most element of the stack and removes it from the Stack<T> as well:

   ```
   T Pop();
   ```

   Why is this not declared as a const function?

   Now create a test program. Create a number of dates and push them onto the stack. Then pop them off the stack as you need them. This type of example can be used when you create a set of dates in the future, push them onto the stack and then pop each date off the stack as it is needed.

2. (Estimating volatility from historical data)

In this exercise we discuss a simple method for the estimation of the volatility based on historical data. The stock price is observed at fixed intervals of time, for example daily, weekly or monthly. Let us assume that we have $n + 1$ observation points:

$$S_j : \text{Stock price at end of } j^{th} \text{ interval, } j = 0, 1, \ldots, n$$
$$\tau : \text{Length of time interval in years}$$

Here $\tau$ is measured by using the number of trading days in a year. For example, if there are 250 trading days in a year, then $\tau = 1/250$. Now let:

$$u_j = log\left(\frac{S_j}{S_{j-1}}\right), \quad j = 1, \ldots, n$$

with standard deviation of the daily returns being:

$$s = \sqrt{\frac{1}{n-1}\sum_{j=1}^{n}(u_j - \bar{u})^2}$$

and

$$\bar{u} = \frac{1}{n}\sum_{j=1}^{n}u_j$$

In Hull (2006) the following estimate is given for the volatility:

$$\sigma = \frac{s}{\sqrt{\tau}}$$

and the standard error of this estimate is given by:

$$\frac{\sigma}{\sqrt{2n}}$$

You are going to solve this problem using `vector<T>`.

Answer the following questions:

(a) Ensure that you know what `vector<T>` has to offer in the way of member functions (hint: use on-line help and the examples on the CD)

(b) Create modules (non-member functions) for the following pieces of functionality based on the above formulae:
  • Calculating the array of logarithms
  • Calculating the standard deviation

(c) Develop an algorithm and implement the C++ code to estimate volatility from historical data. The input parameters are:
  • The number of observations
  • An array of stock prices at the observation dates
  • The length of time interval $\tau$ in years (or equivalently, the number of trading days per year)

  You may implement the algorithm as a module, that is a non-member function.

3. (A small Typo)

What's wrong with the following code? Do you get a compiler error or run-time error?

```
int N = 6;
vector<double> myVec3(N);
for (int i = 0; i <= myVec3.size(); i++)
{
            myVec3[i] = double (i);
}
```

What's the problem?

(Remark and hint: this code is an example of a common mistake in many applications where one works with vectors, matrices and other data structures with indexing operators; we run the risk of range errors)

4. Write a function to print a vector but use the indexing operator '[]' instead of an iterator as was used in section 11.6.2.

5. Write a function to print a list<T>. Implement all the code in section 11.6 for lists instead of vectors. Test the software and check that you get the same output as before.

6. (Small Research Project) Investigate the STL valarray<T> template class. In particular, answer the following questions:
   (a) What are the members of this class and where could you use them in QF applications?
   (b) Create an instance of valarray<double> of length 10. Fill it with some data. Investigate how to achieve the following functionality:
      • The sum of elements
      • The maximum and minimum elements
      • Shifting the array

# 12

# Creating Simpler Interfaces to STL
# for QF Applications

## 12.1  INTRODUCTION AND OBJECTIVES

In the previous chapter we gave an introduction to the theory of data structures and we gave some examples of sequential (or linear) data containers, such as list<T> and vector<T>. These need to be augmented by more advanced structures when we create non-trivial applications in QF. In particular, we examine two important data containers:

- set<T> a collection whose elements are unique in the collection
- map<K,V> a collection of Key/Value pairs, each key being unique

We shall discuss the members in these collections and we then progress to showing how to encapsulate them in more user-friendly classes. In particular, we create three interlinked classes that we use in spreadsheet and volatility surface modelling applications:

- Set<T> an extended and user-friendly version of set<T>
- AssocArray<V, AI> vectors whose elements V are accessed by an index AI
- AssocMatrix<V, AI1, AI2> associative matrix, similar to an Excel Range

The last two structures are called associative arrays and matrices, respectively because a non-integer index is associated with a value in the array or matrix structure. We use Set<T> as a 'control' in these classes because we wish to ensure that the set(s) of indices remain unique.

Having defined these classes we then proceed to show how they can be applied to QF applications. In order to reduce the scope we examine a mini-application, namely emulating spreadsheet functionality. In this case we can create modules and code that operate on the elements of the spreadsheet and in this way we can emulate Excel Automation AddIns and COM AddIns. Finally, we give a number of exercises and challenging projects that the reader should work on in order to consolidate understanding of STL and software design on the one hand, and financial engineering, on the other hand.

In Chapter 13 we shall develop some interesting classes based on the STL map<K, V>, namely properties and property sets that model the data in a derivatives product.

## 12.2  MAPS AND DICTIONARIES

A map or dictionary is a collection of key-value pairs. The keys are unique and it is thus not possible to have two records in a map having the same key. Each record is modelled as an STL pair<K,V> (this is a struct!) where the first element is the key and the second element is the value. A map has all the functionality we need to create instances, add data to the map, remove data from the map and iterate in the map.

This section is an exercise in learning by example. We first create a map and we give three different ways of adding records to the map; to this end, consider the following code:

```
map<char, double> map1;
// Different ways of adding values
// Using indexing
map1["A"] = 1.0;

// Inserting an "explicit" pair object
pair<char, double> myPair("B", 2.0);
map1.insert(myPair);

// Using make_pair template function
pair<char, double> tmp = make_pair("C", 4.0);
map1.insert(tmp);

// Using anonymous objects
map1.insert(pair<char, double>("F", 33.4));
```

We now have a map with four records. If we try to add a record that already exists nothing happens:

```
pair<char, double> tmp1 = make_pair("C", 55.0);
map1.insert(tmp1);
```

However, it is possible to change the value of an existing record in a map by using the assignment operator:

```
map1["A"] = 199.0; // Value will be changed however
```

### 12.2.1   Iterating in maps

We define iterators in much the same as with the examples in Chapter 11. We define `const` and non-`const` iterators and both kinds are needed in applications. First, we create a function to print a map by iterating over its elements:

```
void print (const map<char, double>& myMap)
{
      cout << "Number of elements in map: " << myMap.size() << endl;
      // Iterating in the map
      map<char, double>::const_iterator i = myMap.begin();
      while (i != myMap.end())
      {
            // NOTE THIS SYNTAX: IMPORTANT
            cout << (*i).first << ", " << ((*i).second) << endl;
            i++;
      }
      cout << endl;
}
```

In this code we notice that the iterator points to a record (pair) in the map. So when we dereference it we get a pair object having a first member data and a second member data.

We now give an example of a non-const iterator; in this case we modify the values in a map:

```
void modify(map<char, double>& myMap, double scaleFactor)
{ // Multiply each value by a double

        // Iterating in the map (non-const)
        map<char, double>::iterator i = myMap.begin();
        while (i != myMap.end())
        {
            ((*i).second) *= scaleFactor;
            i++;
        }
}
```

An example of use is:

```
// Change values
double scaleF = 0.5;
modify(map1, scaleF);
print(map1);
```

### 12.2.2  Erasing records in a map

Erasing or removing items from STL containers is an important issue and the code in this section shows how to do this for the case of a map. The ideas are applicable to other STL containers.

We can remove records in a map in a number of ways:

- On the basis of a key
- On the basis of an iterator
- On the basis of a closed-open iterator range [start, end)
- Remove all elements in the map

Some examples are now given; they are reasonably self-documenting:

```
// Now erasing things
// Erase a key
map1.erase("B");
print (map1);

// Erase one iterator, in this case
map1.erase(map1.begin());
print (map1);

// Erase between 2 iterators; same as map1.clear()
map1.erase(map1.begin(), map1.end());
print (map1);

map1.clear(); // Delete an empty map has no effect
```

## 12.3   APPLICATIONS OF MAPS

The map<K,V> container is extremely useful in QF applications, both as a standalone container and in combination with other containers. In particular, it can be used in applications in which we wish to create suitable data structures in areas such as:

- Matrix algebra
- Creating spreadsheet-like functionality (ranges, cells and matrices)
- Modelling three-dimensional surfaces
- Modelling volatility surfaces

In matrix algebra for example, we can create a wide range of efficient matrix data structures for many problems:

- Lower-triangular and upper triangular matrices
- Symmetric matrices
- Sparse matrices
- Band matrices that occur when modelling multi-dimensional partial differential equations using the finite difference method
- Property sets (we discuss this topic in Chapter 13)

It is possible to create robust and 'clever' data structures in a fraction of the time that it would if we did not use STL or if we decided to handcraft the data structure.

We take a simple example of a so-called 'sparse' matrix. This is a matrix many of whose elements are zero. We model it as a two-dimensional structure and there are many choices. In this case we use a vector of maps:

```cpp
// Specific data types, can be generalised
typedef map<int, double> SparseRow;
template <int N> struct SparseMatrix
{
      map<int, SparseRow> data;
};
```

Notice that we have used structs and typedefs. In the past it would have taken many hours of work to program this structure in C or even in C++. In the past, one would need a complete chapter in order to describe how to create such a structure. Now we can do it in two lines of code, thanks to STL.

We now take a special case of a sparse array, namely a tridiagonal matrix. This is a matrix all of whose elements are zero except on the main diagonal, super diagonal and sub diagonal. In other words it is an example of a *band matrix*. Let us now initialise its elements. The code is:

```cpp
const int N = 5;
SparseRow current;
current.insert(pair<int, double> (0, -2.0));
current.insert(pair<int, double> (1, 1.0));
SparseMatrix<N> sparseMat;
sparseMat.data[0] = current;
```

```
int currentIndex = 0;
for (int row = 1; row < N-1; row++)
{ // Insert 3 elements
      current.clear();
      current.insert(pair<int, double> (currentIndex, 1.0));
      current.insert(pair<int, double> (currentIndex+1, -2.0));
      current.insert(pair<int, double> (currentIndex+2, 1.0));

      sparseMat.data[row] = current;
      currentIndex++;
}
current.clear();
current.insert(pair<int, double> (N-2, 1.0));
current.insert(pair<int, double> (N-1, -2.0));
sparseMat.data[N-1] = current;
print(sparseMat);
```

The code for the function for printing the matrix is given by:

```
template <int N>
          void print(SparseMatrix<N>& sm)
{
      SparseRow sr;
      SparseRow::const_iterator it;

      for (int row = 0; row < N; row++)
      {
            SparseRow sr = sm.data[row];
            // Now iterate over row
            for (it = sm.data[row].begin(); it != sm.data[row].end();
                              it++)
            {
                  cout << (*it).second << ", ";
            }

            cout << endl;
      }
}
```

The code in this section can be generalised and the ideas can be applied to construct many kinds of data structures that we can subsequently use in QF applications. We give some exercises at the end of the chapter.

## 12.4   USER-FRIENDLY SETS

We have introduced sets in Chapter 11 and we have described their operations. STL has support for these operations. They are called *set-like operations* because they are applicable to various kinds of data structures.

### 12.4.1  STL sets

We introduce the set<T> container in STL. It is the data structure that we learn about in high school. We introduce the functionality by giving some examples. To this end, we create an empty set and add some elements; then we create a second set as a copy of the first set and we then add some extra elements to it. Notice the two (crucial) member function insert() for adding elements to, and the function remove() for removing elements from a set:

```
set<string> first;                           // Default constructor
// Only unique (new elements) added
first.insert("r");
first.insert("T");
first.insert("sigma");

set<string> second (first);    // Copy constructor
// Add extra elements to second set
second.insert("r");       // "Interest rate"
second.insert("K");       // "Strike price"
second.insert("S");       // "Current underlying price"
second.insert("b");       // "Cost of carry"

print(second, "Second set");
second.erase("K");
print(second, "Second set");
```

Where we have written a simple function to print the values in a set:

```
template <class T> void print(const set<T>& mySet, const string& name)
{ // Print the contents of a set.

        cout << endl << name << ", size of set is "
                        << mySet.size() << "\ n[";

        set<T>::const_iterator i;
        for (i = mySet.begin(); i != mySet.end(); ++i)
        {
                cout << (*i) << ",";
        }
        cout << "]\ n";
}
```

Continuing, we would like to apply set-like operations to sets, such as:

- Union
- Intersection
- Difference
- Symmetric Difference

We give one specific example of these operations, namely the union of two sets. To this end, we create a generic function that actually does this and whose body actually calls STL code:

```
template <class T>
          void UnionSet(const set<T>& s1, const set<T>& s2,
                                          set<T>& myunion)
{ // Union of two sets
     set<int>::iterator i = myunion.begin();
     insert_iterator<set<int> > insertiter(myunion, i);
     set_union(s1.begin(), s1.end(), s2.begin(), s2.end(), insertiter);
}
```

We thus encapsulate difficult-to-remember code in a more friendly generic function. Using the function is very easy:

```
set<int> first; // Default constructor
// Only unique (new elements) added
first.insert(1);
first.insert(2);
first.insert(3);

set<int> second (first);
second.insert(51);
second.insert(52);

// Now the union of two sets using Information Hiding
set<int> myunion2;
UnionSet(first, second, myunion2);
```

Finally, we include some user-defined code that implements *subset/superset relationships*. To this end, we wrap the code for the includes() algorithm in a more user-friendly function:

```
template <class T> bool subset(const set<T>& super, const set<T>& sub)
{ // Is one set a subset of another set?

     // sub is a subset of superset iff superset includes sub

     return includes(super.begin(), super.end(), sub.begin(),
                                          sub.end());
}

template <class T> bool superset(const set<T>& super, const set<T>& sub)
{ // Is one set a superset of another set?
     // Superset contains sub iff sub is s subset of superset
     return subset(super, sub);
}
```

An example of using these two functions with the above sets is:

```
// Checking for subsethood in a more user-friendly way
if (subset (first, second) == true)
     cout << "Second set is a subset of first, OK\ n";
```

```
if (superset(first, second) == true)
    cout << "First set is a superset of second, OK\ n";
if (superset (second, first) == false)
    cout << "Second set is a NOT a superset of first, OK\ n";
```

We could continue with even more examples but we stop now because we will now discuss an adapter class that encapsulates all the low-level details in logical functions.

### 12.4.2   User-defined and wrapper classes for STL sets

We have encapsulated the functionality of the STL set<T> container in an easy-to-use class called Set<T>. Its interface contains most (all?) the mathematical functionality that we need in applications and is given by:

```
template <class V> class SetThing {};

template <class V> class Set : public SetThing<V>
{

private:
    set<V> s;
public:
    // Iterator functions; Navigating in a set
    typedef typename set<V>::iterator iterator;
    typedef typename set<V>::const_iterator const_iterator;

public:
    // Constructors
    Set();                        // Empty set
    Set(const set<V>& stlSet); // Create a Set from STL set
    Set(const Set<V>& s2);      // Copy constructor
    // Construct a set from V that has STL-compatible iterators
    Set(const list<V>& con);    // From an STL list
    Set<V> operator = (const Set<V>& s2);
    virtual ~Set();

    // Standard set operations from High School
    friend Set<V> Intersection(const Set<V>& s1, const Set<V>& s2);
    Set<V> operator   (const Set<V>& s2);     // Intersection

    friend Set<V> Union(const Set<V>& s1, const Set<V>& s2);
    Set<V> operator + (const Set<V>& s2);     // Union

    friend Set<V> Difference(const Set<V>& s1, const Set<V>& s2);
    Set<V> operator - (const Set<V>& s2);     // Difference

    friend Set<V> SymmetricDifference(const Set<V>& s1,
                                      const Set<V>& s2);
```

```
Set<V> operator % (const Set<V>& s2);

template <class V2>
            Set<pair<V, V2> > operator * (const Set<V2>& s2);

iterator Begin();        // Return iterator at begin of set
const_iterator Begin() const; // const iterator at begin
iterator End();               // Iterator after end of set
const_iterator End() const;   // const iterator after end

// Operations on a single set
long Size() const;            // Number of elements
void Insert(const V& v);      // Insert an element
void Insert(const Set<V>& v); // Insert another set
void Remove(const V& v);            // Remove an element
void Replace(const V& Old, const V& New); // old by new
void Clear();                       // Remove all
bool Contains(const V& v) const;    // Is v in set?
bool Empty() const;                 // No elements?

// Using "clever" operators
void operator + (const V& v);    // Insert an element
void operator - (const V& v);    // Remove an element

// Relations between sets (s1 == *this)
bool Subset(const Set<V>& s2) const;// s1 a subset of s2?
bool Superset(const Set<V>& s2) const;// s1 superset of s2?
bool Intersects(const Set<V>& s2) const; // common els?
};
```

A simple example on how to use the set is:

```
Set<int> first;    // Default constructor
// Only unique (new elements) added
first.Insert(1);
first.Insert(2);
first.Insert(3);
print (first, "First set");
```

The code for displaying a user-defined set is given by:

```
template <class T> void print(const Set<T>& l, const string& name)
{ // Print the contents of a Set. Note presence of constant iterator.

    Set<T>::const_iterator i;

    for (i = l.Begin(); i != l.End(); ++i)
```

```
            {
                    cout << *i << " ";
            }
    }
}
```

## 12.5   ASSOCIATIVE ARRAYS AND ASSOCIATIVE MATRICES

In some applications we would like to create arrays and matrices where the elements are
accessed by strings, dates and other types, for example. In general, we have been accustomed
to using integral types but this is too restrictive. To this end, we create a class that represents
arrays (we call them *associative arrays*) and we use an STL map<K,V> to approximate them.
The class interface is:

```
template <class V, class AI = string> class AssocArray
{ // Note that the first index is the value and second index is
  // "associative" key

private:
      map<AI,V> str;      // The list of associative values,
      // Redundant information for performance
      Set<AI> keys;
public:
      // Constructors & destructor
      AssocArray();
      AssocArray(const AssocArray<V, AI>& arr2);
      // Construct the map from a list of names and values
      AssocArray(const Set<AI>& names, const V& val);

      AssocArray<V, AI>& operator = (const AssocArray<V, AI>& ass2);

      // New overloaded indexing operator
      virtual V& operator [] (const AI& index);

      typedef typename map<AI,V>::iterator iterator;
      typedef typename map<AI,V>::const_iterator const_iterator;

      // Iterator functions
      iterator Begin(); // Return iterator at begin of assoc array
      const_iterator Begin() const; // const iterator at begin
      iterator End();                // Return iterator after end
      const_iterator End() const;    // Return const iterator

      // Selectors
      long Size() const { return str.size(); }
      Set<AI> Keys() const { return keys; }          // Copy
};
```

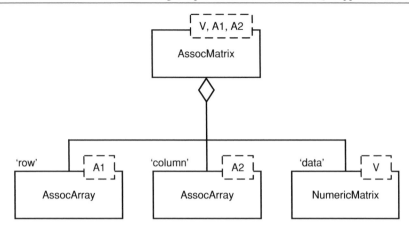

**Figure 12.1**   Structure of an associative matrix

This class is not much different from a 'normal' array class. We can construct an instance of this class by calling the constructor with a given set (this ensures uniqueness of the keys!). Having done that we can change the value in the array by using the provided index operator. Some code to show how this works is:

```
Set<string> names;
names.Insert("A1");
names.Insert("A2");
names.Insert("A3");
names.Insert("A4");

double defaultValue(0.0);
AssocArray<double, string> myAssocArray(names, defaultValue);
print(myAssocArray);
myAssocArray["A4"] = 99.99;
print(myAssocArray);
```

Having created the associative array class, we turn our attention to the construction of an association matrix. Its structure is shown in the UML diagram in Figure 12.1. We see that it is an aggregation of two associative arrays and a numeric matrix, the last of which holds the actual data or information.

The association matrix class has three template parameters:

- The row data type
- The column data type
- The 'values' data types

and the class interface is given by:

```
template <class V, class AI1 = string, class AI2 = string>
                class AssocMatrix
{ // Note that the first index is the value and second indices are
  // "associative" key
```

```
private:

        // The essential data
        NumericMatrix<V, long>* mat;// The real data
        AssocArray<long, AI1> r; // Rows
        AssocArray<long, AI2> c; // Columns

        // Redundant information for performance
        Set<AI1> keysRows;
        Set<AI2> keysColumns;
public:
        // Constructors & destructor
        AssocMatrix();
        AssocMatrix(const AssocMatrix<V, AI1, AI2>& arr2);
        // Construct the map from a list of names and values
        AssocMatrix(const Set<AI1>& Rnames, const Set<AI2>& Cnames,
                                NumericMatrix<V, long>& matrix);
        AssocMatrix<V, AI1, AI2>& operator = (
                                const AssocMatrix<V, AI1, AI2>& ass2);

        // New overloaded indexing operator
        virtual V& operator () (const AI1& index1, const AI2& index2);

        // Modifiers
        // Change values in some range
        void modify(const SpreadSheetRange<AI1, AI2>& range,
                                void (*f)(V& cellValue));
        // Selectors; inline for convenience and readability
        long Size() const { return str.size(); }
        NumericMatrix<V, long> extract(
                        const SpreadSheetRange<AI1, AI2>& range);

        // Return copies of keys
        Set<AI1> RowKeys() const { return keysRows; }
        Set<AI2> ColumnKeys() const { return keysColumns; }
        NumericMatrix<V, long>* Data() { return mat; }
};
```

The following code shows how to create an associative matrix by defining a set that will represent the associative arrays in the matrix and a numeric matrix that holds the data:

```
Set<string> names;
names.Insert("A1");
names.Insert("A2");
names.Insert("A3");
names.Insert("A4");

NumericMatrix<double, long> mat1(names.Size(), names.Size());
AssocMatrix<double, string, string> myMat2(names, names, mat1);
```

This data structure is very general and it can be customised to many different kinds of applications.

## 12.6   APPLICATIONS OF ASSOCIATIVE DATA STRUCTURES

We now give some examples of operations on the data in an associative matrix:

- Modify the elements in a 'range' in a matrix
- Extract a matrix from a range

To this end, we define some simple structures that emulate ranges in Excel:

```
// Spreadsheet-like stuff
template <class AI1, class AI2>
         struct SpreadSheetVertex
{

         AI1 first;
         AI2 second;
};
template <class AI1, class AI2>
         struct SpreadSheetRange
{


         SpreadSheetVertex<AI1, AI2> upperLeft;
         SpreadSheetVertex<AI1, AI2> lowerRight;
};
```

We wish to call the member functions that modify the cells in a range and that extract data from a range of cells, respectively:

```
void modify(const SpreadSheetRange<AI1, AI2>& range,
                         void (*f)(V& cellValue));
```

and

```
NumericMatrix<V, long> extract(
               const SpreadSheetRange<AI1, AI2>& range);
```

We thus have to create a range and call `modify()` with a specific function. Here is the code:

```
// Create column keys
Set<string> columns;
columns.Insert("A");
columns.Insert("B");
columns.Insert("C");
columns.Insert("D");

// Create row keys
Set<long> rows;
rows.Insert(1);
rows.Insert(2);
rows.Insert(3);
```

```
rows.Insert(4);

NumericMatrix<double, long> mat1(rows.Size(), columns.Size());
AssocMatrix<double, long, string> myMat2(rows, columns, mat1);
```

We now work with vertices and ranges in this associative matrix:

```
SpreadSheetVertex<long, string> ul; // Upper left
ul.first = 1;
ul.second = string("B");

SpreadSheetVertex<long, string> lr; // Lower right
lr.first = 3;
lr.second = string("D");

SpreadSheetRange<long, string> myRange;
myRange.upperLeft = ul;
myRange.lowerRight = lr;
```

Finally we wish to modify all the values in the range by calling `modify()` with the following function as parameter:

```
myMat2.modify(myRange, Modifier1);
print (*(myMat2.Data()));
```

and

```
print(myMat2.extract(myRange));
```

A final remark: we have not introduced exception handling in the associative array and matrix classes. In other words, no range checked or 'array alignment' has been implemented. The full source code is on the CD.

## 12.7   CONCLUSIONS AND SUMMARY

We have given a short introduction to a number of topics and techniques to help us get more out of STL. In particular, we have created adapter classes that shield clients from much of the low-level details of STL. These adapter classes are useful building blocks that we can use in QF applications as the Excel-like spreadsheet classes have shown.

You can apply the techniques in this chapter to create your own data structures for your specific applications.

## 12.8   EXERCISES AND PROJECTS

1. (Matrix Structures) Use the techniques in section 12.3 to create 'quick' data structures for the following kinds of matrices:
   - General *band matrices* of width $2K + 1$: A banded $n \times n$ matrix is a matrix whose elements are zero everywhere except on the main diagonal and on the K super and sub diagonals (we have seen a special case in section 12.3 in the case $K = 1$, namely a tridiagonal matrix)

- *Lower and upper triangular matrices*: a lower triangular matrix is one all of whose elements are zero above the main diagonal (these structures are useful for Cholesky decomposition when we express a symmetric, positive definite matrix A as the product of a lower triangular matrix L and its transpose U (which we call an upper triangular matrix)
- *Symmetric matrices* (note that we only have to store the lower triangular or upper triangular part of the matrix)
- *General sparse matrices*
- *Lattice structures* as needed by the binomial and trinomial methods, for example (this topic will be discussed in Chapter 15)

2. (Lots of Nesting)
   Where would the following data structures be useful in your applications?
   - `list<list<T> >`
   - `list<vector<T> >`
   - `vector<vector<T> >`
   - `vector<map<T> >`
   - `map<map<T> >`

   Experiment with these classes and create functions to print their instances.

3. (*Template Member Functions*)
   It is possible to define member functions having template parameters in addition to the template parameters that belong to the 'enclosing' class. An example is the *Cartesian product* of two sets containing different data types:

```
template <class V2>
      Set<pair<V, V2> > CartesianProduct(const Set<V2>& s2)
{
      Set<pair<V, V2> > result;
      // Iterate from begin to end of first set
      // At each level create a pair with second element from s2
      set<V>::const_iterator iOuter;
      set<V2>::const_iterator iInner;

      for (iOuter = (*this).s.begin(); iOuter != (*this).s.end();
                                                        iOuter++)
      {
            for (iInner = s2.Begin(); iInner != s2.End(); iInner++)
            {
                  result.Insert(pair<V,V2>(*iOuter, *iInner));
            }
      }
      return result;
}
```

4. (Volatility Surface)
   This exercise is concerned with defining a class and corresponding algorithms for a volatility matrix. The rows of the associative matrix correspond to the expiry dates, the columns are the

strike prices while the data is the (calculated implied volatility based on some algorithm, for example the nonlinear solvers in Chapter 7 where we discussed various non-linear solvers).

Design and implement this class.

5. Investigate the applicability of the exception handling mechanism to the associative array and associative matrix classes that we introduced in this chapter.

# 13
## Data Structures for Financial
## Engineering Applications

## 13.1 INTRODUCTION AND OBJECTIVES

In this chapter we introduce a number of data structures and data containers that we use in applications. Data structures are the life-blood of an application because the results of calculations and algorithmic processing are stored in them. To this end, we adopt the approach that is used in Fortran by creating classes and libraries in C++ that the reader can use in his or her applications. This approach improves programmer productivity and the general quality of applications because, on the one hand the developer can concentrate on the financial aspects of the application without getting bogged down in details while on the other hand he or she can use the tested and reliable libraries by using them directly in applications.

If we examine the quantitative financial literature we see that there are several categories of data structures:

- Lattice and other related structures (for example, implied trees)
- Properties, property sets and flexible 'member data' for financial instruments
- Vectors and matrices

In this chapter we shall discuss these topics while we give lattice methods an airing in Chapter 15 where we model one-factor problems using binomial trees.

These 'substrate' classes will be used in a number of examples and applications in this and future chapters, for example:

- Solving systems of linear equations (Numerical Linear Algebra)
- Interpolation of data (linear, cubic splines, rational interpolation)
- Yield curves and temporal data types

C++ is very flexible and it is possible to write multi-paradigm applications in this language. In particular, the dove-tailing of the 'run-time' object-oriented and 'compile-time' template paradigms leads to highly flexible and at the same time, robust software.

## 13.2 THE PROPERTY PATTERN

When creating a C++ class we need to declare and define member data and the corresponding member functions that operate on that data. In general, the member data is private so that client software cannot access the data directly but instead it must use get/set member functions. The main disadvantages of this approach are:

- We have to write a set/get function for each data member that we wish to expose to clients
- Hard-coded member data remain a compile-time phenomenon; it is not possible to query an object for its member data at run-time. In other words, the client software must know what the member data is in advance

- You cannot add member data at run-time. This feature may be needed for certain kinds of advanced applications.

In order to resolve these issues, we have constructed a template class that models named member data. We call this the *property pattern* or *idiom* and it is a simple form of Reflection, that is the ability of objects to query their own state at run time.

The interface for the Property Pattern is given by:

```
#ifndef PROPERTY_HPP
#define PROPERTY_HPP

#include "propertything.cpp"
#include <string>

template <class Name = string, class Value = double> class Property
                                : public PropertyThing<Name, Value>
{
private:

        // Name-value pairs
        Name nam;
        Value con;

public:
        // Constructors and destructor
        Property();
        Property(const Name& name);
        Property(const Name& name, const Value& t);
        Property(const Property<Name, Value>& source);

        virtual ~Property();

        // Accessing function operators
        // Get and set the value of the Property
        virtual Value operator()() const;
        virtual void operator()(const Value& t);

        // Get the name of the property
        virtual Name name() const;

        Property<Name, Value>& operator =
                    (const Property<Name, Value>& source);

        // Ability to create a deep copy (Prototype pattern)
        PropertyThing<Name, Value>* Copy() const;

        // True iff names(keys) are the same
        bool operator == (const Property<Name, Value>& prop2);
        bool operator != (const Property<Name, Value>& source);
```

```
      // For Visitor pattern (later)
      void accept(PropertyThingVisitor<Name, Value>& pv);
};
```

```
#endif // PROPERTY_HPP
```

We thus see that a property is an ordered pair; the first element is the name or key of the property while the second element is its value. The interface consists of the following kinds of member functions:

- Constructors
- Set and Get functions; in this case we have used operator overloading.
- Deep copy; we can create a copy of a property on the heap (this is the essence of the *Prototype* pattern)
- A function 'accept' that is used in conjunction with the *Visitor* pattern. In this way (Duffy, 2004) we can extend the functionality of the Property class by adding new visitor classes to the corresponding Visitor hierarchy.

Let us take a simple example. In this case we create a number of properties in which the key is of string type and the values are double:

```
Property<string, double> r;          // Interest rate
Property<string, double> sig;        // Volatility
Property<string, double> K;          // Strike price
```

In this case the default constructor is called in all cases. We can now initialise the values by calling another constructor as follows:

```
r = Property<string, double> ("Interest rate", 0.08);
sig= Property<string, double> ("Volatility",0.30);
K = Property<string, double>("Strike Price", 65.0);
```

Of course it is possible to declare and define a property in one statement; an example is:

```
DatasimDate today;
Property<string, DatasimDate> divInfo(string("divdate"), today);
cout << "Dividend: " << divInfo.name() << ", " << divInfo();;
```

The examples in this section were simple and meant to show the essence of the property pattern. In the next section we shall see how to use the concept in classes that contain several properties.

In general, we define a property (and property sets) for a class in the class public area. Then clients can access the property directly. It would be pointless to define them in the private interface area because clients could not access them. It would defeat the intent of the pattern in the first place.

## 13.3   PROPERTY SETS

In general, we would also like to model real-life objects that consist of a number of properties. For example, we model the data in a plain option class by properties whose key is of type string and whose value is a double. Furthermore, we may wish to aggregate all the option's data into a single object that we can subsequently access in our code. To this end, we create a class that consists of a list of key-value pairs. This class was first discussed in Duffy (2004) and in this section we introduce an upgraded version of it. We call the class the *Simple Property Set* because it is meant to model lists of key-value pairs (that are essentially properties) and it came into existence as a useful class for non-nested properties. The class interface has two parameters, one for the key type and the other for the value type:

```
template <class N = string, class V = double> class SimplePropertySet
              : public PropertyThing<N, V>
{
private:
        N nam;         // The name of the PSet
        // The SimplePropertySet list using the STL map
        map<N, V> sl;

        // Include keys as redundant data member
        // (Performance and security)
        Set<N> keys;
Public:
        // public members

};
```

Please note that we use the STL map container to store the data and in this case the property set class is a wrapper class that hides much of the low-level functionality of map from clients. Thus, the property set class (we call it PSet for convenience from now on) can be described as 'an STL map made easy'.

Looking at the private members above we see that PSet has data for:

- The name of the PSet (this is a useful feature)
- The map data container
- A redundant data member that contains the current set of keys in the PSet

We include this last member for efficiency and security reasons; in particular, when adding or removing properties from PSet we do not have to check the key in the map but in a somewhat more lightweight Set object.

We now discuss the property set's service functions.

### 13.3.1   Basic functionality

It must be possible to create PSet instances based on various input arguments. Thus, the main constructors are:

```
// Constructors and destructor
SimplePropertySet();                    // Default constructor
SimplePropertySet(const N& name);       // Named property set
SimplePropertySet(const SimplePropertySet<N,V>& source);
SimplePropertySet(const N& name, const Set<N>& keySet);
```

The last constructor is interesting because it allows us to create a PSet based on a name and a set of keys. The property values in the PSet will get default values. This constructor can be used when we configure a PSet with keys that reside in some unique *repository*. Then we are guaranteed that the keys in the PSet come from a reliable source.

We show the code that actually implements the last-mentioned constructor:

```
template <class N, class V>
      SimplePropertySet<N,V>::SimplePropertySet(const N& name,
            const Set<N>& keySet)
{ // Create a property set from a set of attribute definitions

      nam = name;
      keys = keySet;
      // Now iterate in the keys and do default constructor
      Set<N>::iterator it;
      for (it = keys.Begin(); it != keys.End(); it++)
      {
            add(Property<N,V>(*it, V()));
      }
}
```

### 13.3.2   Addition and removal of properties

We have provided functionality for adding both properties and PSets to a PSet. Thus, you may add a property to a Pset or you may prefer to add the individual components of the property and everything will be taken care of in the code:

```
void add(const Property<N,V>& p);
void add(const N& key, const V& value);
```

For example, we show how to code this latter member function by a simple delegation to map:

```
template <class N, class V>
      void SimplePropertySet<N,V>::add(const N& key, const V& value)
{ // Add a key+value pair to the list

      pair<N,V> tmp;
      tmp.first = key;
      tmp.second = value;
      sl.insert(tmp); // Add el. with name + value
      // Update the key set
      keys.Insert(key);
}
```

Similarly, we can remove properties by either of the following functions:

```
void remove(const N& key);    // Remove elements with "key" O(1)
void remove(const Property<N, V>& prop);
```

The code for the first function is given by:

```
template <class N, class V>
      void SimplePropertySet<N,V>::remove(const N& key)
{ // Remove all elements with "key" O(1)

      sl.erase(key);

      // Also remove the key from the key list
      keys.erase(key);
}
```

### 13.3.3 Navigating in a property set: creating your own iterators

In many applications it may be necessary to create your own templated collection classes and it will be thus necessary to define mechanisms for navigating in these structures. Of course, we implement these mechanisms using user-defined iterators in C++. In the current context we essentially wish to iterate in a PSet in the knowledge that it has an embedded map. We define two iterators, one of which can modify the elements in the PSet while the other is a read-only iterator:

```
typedef typename map<N, V>::iterator iterator;
typedef typename map<N, V>::const_iterator const_iterator;
```

Of course, we need member functions that tell us where the beginning and end of the PSet are:

```
// Iterator functions
iterator Begin();             // Return iterator at begin of composite
const_iterator Begin() const;

iterator End();               // Return iterator after end of composite
const_iterator End() const;
```

Just to show how easy it is to program these functions we give two representative examples:

```
template <class N, class V>
   SimplePropertySet<N,V>::iterator SimplePropertySet<N,V>::Begin()
{
 // Return iterator at begin of composite

   return sl.begin();
}

template <class N, class V>
   SimplePropertySet<N,V>::iterator SimplePropertySet<N,V>::End()
{ // Return iterator after end of composite

   return sl.end();
}
```

This technique can be extended to any user-defined data container.

### 13.3.4 Property sets with heterogeneous data types

We give a brief discussion of how to design property sets in which the data is heterogeneous. For example, we can create a class for a person containing strings, numbers and other data types.

In general, we wish to create property sets in which the individual properties in the set have values belonging to any data type. For example, let's say we wish to model various kinds of instruments such as options, bonds and swaps. Then we can define a property set to achieve this end:

```
SimplePropertySet<string, Instrument*> myPortfolio;
```

We can then add any object of a class derived from `Instrument` to the set. At this stage it is a good idea to give a simple example of how this mechanism is going to *pan out*. We are working on the assumption that we have a class hierarchy where there is an abundance of, or at least some polymorphic behaviour present. In concrete terms, this means the base class in the hierarchy has at least one pure virtual member function. To this end, let us consider the model hierarchy:

```
class Instrument
{ // Base class for all derivative products
public:
            virtual void print() const = 0;
};

class Option: public Instrument
{
public:
        void print() const
        {
                cout << "An option\ n";
        }
};

class Bond: public Instrument
{
public:
        void print() const
        {
                cout << "A bond\ n";
        }
};

class Swap: public Instrument
{
public:
        void print() const
```

```
        {
                cout << "A swap\ n";
        }
};
```

What we now do is to create several concrete instruments, add them to a heterogeneous property set and then iterate over the set while printing each instrument in the set:

```
int main()
{
        SimplePropertySet<string, Instrument*> myPortfolio;

        // Create a number of specific instruments and add to portfolio
        Option myOpt;
        Bond myBond;
        Swap mySwap;

        // Now add components to PSet
        myPortfolio.add(string("O"), &myOpt);
        myPortfolio.add(string("B"), &myBond);
        myPortfolio.add(string("S"), &mySwap);

        // Print out the PSet
        SimplePropertySet<string, Instrument*>::const_iterator it;

        for (it = myPortfolio.Begin(); it != myPortfolio.End(); it++)
        {
                (it->second)->print(); cout << endl;
        }
        return 0;
}
```

Understanding this example means that you can apply the idea to other problems in Quantitative Finance. We mention that this approach is an implementation of the *Collection-Members* relationship that we discuss in section 13.4.2.

What happens if we wish to create heterogeneous property sets containing data from sources that have no a-priori underlying relationships? For example, we might wish to define the following properties having the incompatible data types such as double, DatasimDate and string on the one hand and a variety of financial instruments on the other hand. To this end, we define a new data hierarchy as shown in Figure 13.1. In this case we have an abstract base class (non-templated) that is the root for all concrete data types. We can bring any object or data type into the hierarchy by wrapping it in another class called Wrapper<T>. We discuss a simple version and it is possible to extend the functionality using design patterns. The code for the classes in Figure 13.1 is given by:

```
class AnyType
{ // Base class for all wrapped types
```

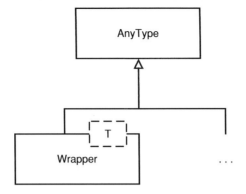

**Figure 13.1**   New data types

```
public:
        AnyType() {}
};


template <class T> class Wrapper : public AnyType
{ // Generic wrapper for any data type
private:
               T obj;
public:
        Wrapper() { obj = T();}
        Wrapper(T wrappedObject) { obj = wrappedObject;}

        // Need to know if current type is same as another type
        // This is a template member function
        template <class T2>
                bool sameType (const T2& t2)
        {
                if (typeid(Wrapper<T>) == typeid(t2))
                {
                        return true;
                }
                return false;

        }
};
```

This code now allows us to create heterogeneous property sets. We take the example of the
C++ class that models a person. We already discussed this example in an earlier chapter. In
this case we now model it as a property set (incidentally, for ease of readability we keep the
original member data in the class). The new structure is given by:

```
class Person
{
```

```
public: // Everything public, for convenience only

            // Data
            Wrapper<string> nam;           // Name of person
            Wrapper<DatasimDate> dob;      // Date of birth
            Wrapper<DatasimDate> createdD; // When object was created
            SimplePropertySet<string, AnyType*> props;
};
```

Fortunately, the external interface specification for the constructor does not change when compared to the first version. The body however, is different because the (new) property set must be initialised. The code is:

```
Person (const string& name, const DatasimDate& DateofBirth)
{
        nam = name;
        dob = DateofBirth;
        createdD = DatasimDate();// default, today REALLY!

        // Now add this stuff into the property set
        props = SimplePropertySet<string, AnyType*>();
        props.add(string("Name"), &nam);
        props.add(string("DOB"), &dob);
        props.add(string("CreatedDate"), &createdD);
}
```

Client software still functions properly because the public interface has not changed with the exception of a new property that we define in the public area.

Now let's say that we would like to print the properties in the class Person. To this end, we iterate but – and this is the crux – we cannot discover what the real value type is without using RTTI and *dynamic casting*. Let us take the sample code to show what we mean:

```
void print() const
{ // Who am I?

        cout << "\ n** Person Data **\ n";

        SimplePropertySet<string, AnyType*>::const_iterator it;

        for (it = props.Begin(); it != props.End(); it++)
        {
                cout << "Key " << it ->first << endl;

                // No value printed because we lack polymorphism
                // MUST USE RTTI AND DYNAMIC CASTING

        }
}
```

The big question is thus: should we try to define a heterogeneous property set on what is essentially incompatible data? Probably not. A more hard-coded approach might be preferable.

## 13.4  PROPERTY SETS AND DATA MODELLING FOR QUANTITATIVE FINANCE

Quantitative Finance is concerned (among other things) with derivatives pricing applications. We usually implement these applications using a combination of algorithms and data. The data may represent input data or output. We distinguish between two kinds of data in QF applications:

- Type 1: configuration data and data that represents properties in a financial problem
- Type 2: data that is needed in algorithms and calculations (typically, vectors and matrices)

In this section we concentrate on Type 1 data and in particular, we show how the property set can be used to model various kinds of data that is needed in Quantitative Finance. To this end, we discuss a number of scenarios that are based on the system patterns in Buschmann (1996). In particular, we focus on the so-called *Whole-Part pattern* that allows us to aggregate objects together in order to form a semantic unit. In this sense the aggregate object (the 'Whole') encapsulates its constituent components, known as the 'Parts'. The Whole organises the collaborations between the parts and provides a common interface to its functionality. In general, direct access to the parts is not possible. This pattern occurs in many application areas, and not just Quantitative Finance:

- Computer Aided Design and Computer Graphics
- Manufacturing
- Tracking and monitoring applications

In this section however we focus on property sets and the various special cases of this pattern.

### 13.4.1  Fixed assemblies (assemblies-parts relationship)

In this case the whole (or product) has a number of tightly integrated parts and we differentiate between the parts and the whole. Some simple examples are:

- A molecule consists of atoms
- A person has a name and a date of birth
- An option has a fixed set of data (usually in the form of hard-wired properties)

In all cases the number and types of the parts are predetermined; once the whole has been created it is not possible to add or delete parts at run-time. An example of how to document this relationship is shown in Figure 13.2(a).

### 13.4.2  Collection-members relationship

In this case the parts are similar, both in structure and type. The collection, or whole provides functionality such as:

- Iterating over the members
- Performing operations on the members

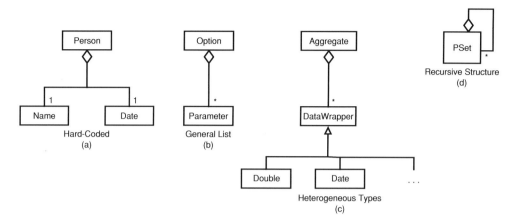

**Figure 13.2**  Stuctures for property sets

Thus, there is no distinction between individual members of a collection because all of them are treated equally; they are all of the same type. Let us take an example of a class that represents entities having PSet instances as member data:

```
template <class Name, class Value> class EntityThing
{
private:

public:
        // ...

        // The defining structure and behaviour of entities. Notice
        // that these are public "objects" and that we can use the
        // member functions of the corresponding template classes.

        Property<Name, Value> name;                    // The ID of the entity
        SimplePropertySet<Name, Value> properties;   // The properties

};
```

This kind of relationship has many applications because it is so flexible. Typical examples are:

- Serialisation of a PSet instance to disk or to a database
- Initialising a PSet instance from some data source
- Adding extra functionality to a PSet instance using the *Visitor* design pattern (Duffy, 2004)

We have the beginnings of a simple Reflection package and RTTI functionality, that is the ability at run-time to query an object as well as the ability to add and remove properties at run-time.

An example of how to document this relationship is shown in Figures 13.2(b) and 13.2(c). In the second figure the whole consists of a number of references to an abstract base class.

### 13.4.3   Container-contents relationship

In this case the whole is nothing more than a container for its parts. Furthermore, the parts are less tightly coupled than with a Collection-Members relationship, for example. The components or parts may even be dynamically added to, or removed from the whole. An example of this relationship is a postal package containing food, wines and chocolate. This relationship is best modelled using sets or multisets. We have already seen some examples in Chapter 12.

### 13.4.4   Recursive and nested property sets

In some applications we may with to create property sets whose values are also property sets. In this case we speak of a nested or recursive data structure. Examples of where these structures can be used are:

- General tree structures (for example, directories and files)
- Nested property data
- Associative arrays and matrices

An example of how to document this relationship is shown in Figure 13.2(d). An associative matrix is a matrix whose rows and columns are accessed, not by using integral types but by strings for example. A good example is a volatility surface.

## 13.5   LATTICE STRUCTURES

Lattice structures are well known in quantitative finance. For example, the binomial and trinomial pricing models are built on lattice data structures. In this section we concentrate on so-called *recombining trees* as seen in Figure 13.3. We wish to model these multinomial structures using C++ classes. There are a number of issues to take care of, such as:

(a) Do we create a separate class for each value of N in Figure 13.3 or can we create a generic class that is able to handle all cases, that is one template class incorporating N as a generic parameter? In the latter case we could then create one template class and instantiate it for any value of N
(b) The lattice node value is generic, that is we can place any data type on the nodes

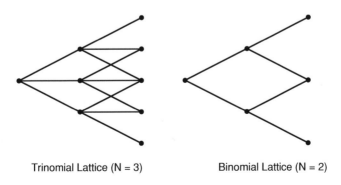

Trinomial Lattice (N = 3)          Binomial Lattice (N = 2)

**Figure 13.3**   Examples of lattices

(c) We iterate in the lattice in the horizontal and vertical directions by using indices of integral type (we could define STL-like iterators but these are less intuitive in this case in my opinion)

To this end, we define a template class that realises the above requirements. The template parameters and member data of the lattice class are:

```
template <class V, class I, int NumberNodes>
                    class Lattice
{ // Generic lattice class


private:
        // Implement as a full nested Vector class
        Array<Vector<V, I>, I > tree;

        // Redundant data
        I nrows;            // Number of rows
        int typ;            // What kind of lattice (number of nodes)
};
```

Thus, we see that the lattice is implemented as an array of vectors; in the horizontal direction we define an array and each element of the array is a vector, thereby giving us the flexibility to choose the size of the vector as we please. Furthermore, we see that the parameter that represents the node type (for example, binomial, trinomial, pentagonal) is one of the template parameters.

The public member functions in this class are declared as follows:

```
public:
        // Constructors & destructor
        Lattice();                          // Default constructor
        Lattice(const I& Nrows);        // Number of rows and branch factor
        Lattice(const I& Nrows, const V& val); // + value at nodes
        Lattice(const Lattice<V, I, NumberNodes>& source);
        virtual ~Lattice();            // Destructor

        // Iterating in a Lattice; we need forward and backward versions
        I MinIndex() const;                // Return the minimum row index
        I MaxIndex() const;                // Return the maximum row index
        I Depth() const;                   // The (depth) number of rows

        // Operators
        Lattice<V, I, NumberNodes>& operator =
                (const Lattice<V, I, NumberNodes>& source);

        // Indexing the "outer" array of lattice
        Vector<V, I>& operator [] (const I& nLevel );
        const Vector<V, I>& operator [] (const I& nLevel ) const;
```

```
// We need the form of the lattice at the "base" of the pyramid.
// This will be needed when we use backward induction
Vector<V, I> BasePyramidVector() const;
I BasePyramidSize() const; // Number of discrete points at end
I numberNodes() const;
```

This functionality is sufficient for many of the applications in this book. In particular, it will be used when we model options by using the binomial method in Chapter 15. We show how we have coded one of the constructors in this interface; this creates a lattice with a given depth and in which each node is initialised to a given value:

```
template <class V, class I, int NumberNodes>
    Lattice< V, I, NumberNodes>::Lattice(const I& Nrows, const V& val)
{ // Number of rows and branch factor

    nrows = Nrows;
    typ = NumberNodes;

    tree = Array<Vector<V, I>, I> (nrows + 1, 1); // Start index == 1

    I currentBranch = 1; // There is always one single root

    // Initialise tree vectors (give sizes of vectors)
    for(int n = tree.MinIndex(); n <= tree.MaxIndex(); n++)
    {
        // Create the appropriate vector (in vertical dir.)
        tree[n] = Vector<V, I>(currentBranch, 1, val);

        // Calculate the next number of columns
        currentBranch += (typ - 1);
    }
}
```

### 13.5.1  Some simple examples

We discuss how to use the lattice class and to this end we show some examples. The first example shows how to create some instances:

```
const int typeB = 2;        // BinomialLatticeType;
const int typeT = 3;        // Trinomial Type
const int typeP = 5;        // Pentagonal Type

int depth = 4;

// Create objects of various
Lattice<double, int, typeB> lattice1(depth, 3.14);
Lattice<double, long, typeT> lattice2(depth, 4.6);
```

```
Lattice<double, long, typeP> lattice3(depth, 2.0);

print(lattice1);
cout << endl << endl;
print(lattice2);
cout << endl << endl;
print(lattice3);
```

The contents of each lattice is:

```
Branch Number 1: [3.14, ]
Branch Number 2: [3.14, 3.14, ]
Branch Number 3: [3.14, 3.14, 3.14, ]
Branch Number 4: [3.14, 3.14, 3.14, 3.14, ]
Branch Number 5: [3.14, 3.14, 3.14, 3.14, 3.14, ]

Branch Number 1: [4.6, ]
Branch Number 2: [4.6, 4.6, 4.6, ]
Branch Number 3: [4.6, 4.6, 4.6, 4.6, 4.6, ]
Branch Number 4: [4.6, 4.6, 4.6, 4.6, 4.6, 4.6, 4.6, ]
Branch Number 5: [4.6, 4.6, 4.6, 4.6, 4.6, 4.6, 4.6, 4.6, 4.6, ]

Branch Number 1: [2, ]
Branch Number 2: [2, 2, 2, 2, 2, ]
Branch Number 3: [2, 2, 2, 2, 2, 2, 2, 2, 2, ]
Branch Number 4: [2, 2, 2, 2, 2, 2, 2, 2, 2, 2, 2, 2, 2, ]
Branch Number 5: [2, 2, 2, 2, 2, 2, 2, 2, 2, 2, 2, 2, 2, 2, 2, 2, 2, ]
```

We now give an example of a lattice structure whose node values have a matrix structure rather than a scalar value. This is very easy to do because we already know that template classes can be nested. We need this kind of data structure for certain kinds of interest rate problems. Let us take an example of a lattice whose node values are matrices.

We first prompt the user for input:

```
cout << "Consistent trinomial tree for short rate\ n";
cout << "How many time divisions: " << endl;
cin >> depth;
```

We then create a lattice with matrix elements:

```
// Trinomial lattice with matrix entries
Matrix<double, int> prototype(4,4,1,1);
Lattice<Matrix<double, int>, int, 3> lattice4(depth, prototype);
```

We now iterate in the lattice and we print each matrix element in the vector of matrices:

```
// Now iterate over the lattice and print the matrix elements
for (int j = lattice4.MinIndex(); j <= lattice4.MaxIndex(); j++)
{ // Each indexed j is a vector of matrices
```

```
cout << "Start Level " << j << endl;
for (int i = lattice4[j].MinIndex();
                    i <= lattice4[j].MaxIndex(); i++)
 {
        print(lattice4[j][i]); // This is a matrix

 }
cout << "End Level " << j << endl;

}
```

We have now laid a basis for further work. In the next section we show how to apply the lattice class to a 'hard-coded' binomial solver in C++.

### 13.5.2   A simple binomial method solver

We give a simple example on how to use the lattice class in a simple solver. To this end, we find the price of an option paying a constant dividend. First, we create two modules for:

- Forward induction: initialising the lattice with 'up' and 'down' data
- Backward induction: iterating in the lattice in order to calculate the price

The code for the first activity is given by:

```
// Code here corresponds to forward induction
Lattice<double, int, 2> createLattice (int N, double rootValue,
                double up, double down)
{

    // This is for the binomial method only!!!

    Lattice<double, int, 2> source(N + 1, 0.0);

    int si = source.MinIndex();
    source[si][source[si].MinIndex()] = rootValue;

    // Loop from the min index to the end index
    for (int j = source.MinIndex() + 1; j <= source.MaxIndex(); j++)
    {
        for (int i = source[j].MinIndex(); i < source[j].MaxIndex();
                                                            i++)
        {
            source[j][i] = down * source[j-1][i];
            source[j][i+1] = up * source[j-1][i];
        }
    }
```

```
        return source;
}
```

The code for the backward induction activity is given by:

```
// Code here corresponds to backward induction
double traverse(Lattice<double, int, 2>& lattice,
      Vector<double, int>& Payoff, double p, double discounting)
{
      int ei = lattice.MaxIndex();
      lattice[ei] = Payoff;

      // Loop from the max index to the start (min) index
      for (int n = lattice.MaxIndex() - 1;
                      n >= lattice.MinIndex(); n--)
      {
          for (int i = lattice[n].MinIndex();
                          i <= lattice[n].MaxIndex(); i++)
          {

          lattice[n][i] = discounting * (p * lattice[n+1][i+1]
          + (1.0-p) * lattice[n+1][i]);
          }
      }

        int si = lattice.MinIndex();
        return lattice[si][lattice[si].MinIndex()];
}
```

This code is a straightforward implementation of well-known formulae (see Hull, 2006) and we do not discuss them here.

We describe the discrete versions of the payoff functions for call and put options. In both cases we return arrays of values at the maturity date. To this end, the code for a call option is given by:

```
template <class V, class I>
      Vector<V,I> CallPayOff(const V& K, const Vector<V,I>& StockArr)
{

      V tmp;
      Vector<V,I> result (StockArr.Size(), StockArr.MinIndex());

      for (I i = StockArr.MinIndex(); i <= StockArr.MaxIndex(); i++)
      {
          result[i] = 0.0;
          tmp = StockArr[i] - K;
          if (tmp > 0.0)
                  result[i] = tmp;
```

```
        }

        return result;
}
```

while the code for a put option is given by:

```
template <class V, class I> Vector<V,I>
        PutPayOff(const V& K, const Vector<V,I>& StockArr)
{
        V tmp;
        Vector<V,I> result (StockArr.Size(), StockArr.MinIndex());

        for (I i = StockArr.MinIndex(); i <= StockArr.MaxIndex(); i++)
        {
                result[i] = 0.0;
                tmp = K - StockArr[i];
                if (tmp > 0.0)
                        result[i] = tmp;
        }
        return result;
}
```

A final remark: we have included source code for these generic lattice structures on the CD.

## 13.6   CONCLUSIONS AND SUMMARY

In this chapter we have designed and implemented a number of advanced template classes that are useful in Quantitative Finance applications. In particular, we introduced the Property Pattern and we went on to show how to model lists of property using the Property Set template class. Furthermore, we showed how to create a data container that is able to store various kinds of data in a binomial, trinomial or multinomial lattice. We designed these classes by using STL and the Vector classes in Duffy (2004) as the workhorse; for example, we have implemented a property set as a map. There are two main advantages to this approach: (a) we hide difficult-to-remember STL code in a wrapper class and (b) we provide a simple interface that the client can use.

Finally, the underlying techniques and patterns in this chapter are generic and you can apply them to your own situation. The exercises and projects discuss these issues in some detail.

## 13.7   EXERCISES AND PROJECTS

1. (Robustness) the current version of the code for the Property Set class does not have any provisions for exception handling in the following sense:
   E1: accessing or removing a property that does not exist
   E2: inserting a property or key that already exists

   In general, it is impossible to prescribe the policy and it is up to the client software to take care of these situations.

Answer the following questions:

(a) Use the techniques from chapter 9 to ensure that exceptions will be thrown if the exceptions E1 and E2 occur. This means that the bodies of member functions add() and remove() will need to be modified

(b) How could you implement a policy-free exception handling mechanism for property sets, that is no exception handling code is included as in case (a) but that each client determines if E1 and E2 are really exceptions? For example, we may wish to do nothing if we add a key to a property set that already exists.

2. (Code Review) Examine the source code for SimplePropertySet. In particular, make sure you understand how this class uses the STL map to which it delegates. Furthermore, investigate how the following code can be optimised:

```
template <class N, class V>
    void SimplePropertySet<N,V>::value(const N& name, const V& value)
{ // Change value of Property, key "name"

    // NO exception handling
    if (hasProperty(name) == false)
        return;

    // (Sledgehammer) we iterate over list until we find value
    map<N,V>::iterator it;
    for (it=sl.begin(); it!=sl.end(); it++)
    {
        if ((*it).first == name)
        {
            (*it).second = value;
        }
    }
}
```

(hint: use the find() algorithm that either returns an iterator that 'points' to the found record or to end()).

3. (Quick question)
In section 13.5.1 we defined a parameter as follows:

```
const int typeB = 2;      // BinomialLatticeType
```

Why must the variable be declared as const?

# 14

## An Introduction to Design Patterns

### 14.1 INTRODUCTION AND OBJECTIVES

In this chapter we give an introduction to the famous Design Patterns of the 'Gang of Four' (GOF, 1995) and their applications to QF. In particular, we give an overview of the *Creational, Structural and Behavioural* pattern categories and the specific patterns in each category. In order to help us implement each pattern we discuss the use of patterns to aid in the development of a flexible library of two-dimensional shapes (the package is called CADObject ) that the current author and colleagues developed in the 1990's. The library is extendible because we needed to use it in many diverse applications. Design patterns came to the rescue. We create a basic C++ class hierarchy for shapes and we show how it can be extended and/or modified by using patterns while ensuring that the software remains stable and maintainable. The source code can be found on the CD.

The advantages of using CADObject as the first application to show the use of patterns are:

- Lines, circles and other two-dimensional shapes are tangible and well defined; there is not much room for misunderstanding
- CADObject has been in existence since 1993 and has been applied to various domains such as mechanical engineering, optical device technology and computer graphics. Since then we have seen which patterns were useful and which were not
- The code for classes in CADObject can be copied and used in new QF applications with minor changes. For example, the Composite pattern can be used to model classes for Collateral Debt Obligation (CDO) products
- Finally, the code has been well written (to the best of our knowledge) and we use this code in courses as an example of good coding practice in C++

Having developed the design patterns for two-dimensional shapes we progress to giving some examples for QF. The examples are small but they show the essence of a particular pattern.

In the following chapters we shall make extensive use of patterns when we discuss lattice methods, finite difference schemes and Monte Carlo method.

Design pattern promote the creation of flexible software systems. For more information on design patters in QF, see Duffy (2004).

### 14.2 THE SOFTWARE LIFECYCLE

This is a book on programming in C++ with applications to Quantitative Finance. However, raw programming skills alone will not help you to create high-quality software. It would seem that efficiency, accuracy and reliability are important requirements when developing QF applications. However, there are a number of steps that we need to take before we start programming. This remark refers to the software lifecycle and the major steps are (see Duffy, 2004):

*(Phase 1) Requirements Analysis*: do we know the customer's 'wants and needs', do we, as developers understand the problem and is the problem documented unambiguously?

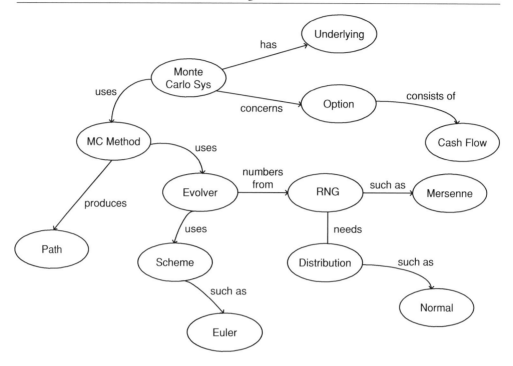

**Figure 14.1**  System decomposition of applications

*(Phase 2) Analysis*: We decompose the problem/system into smaller subsystems. Each subsystem has well-defined responsibilities and does one thing well. The subsystems are loosely coupled and they cooperate in order to satisfy the goals of the system under discussion. We can use the *concept mapping technique* to identify these subsystems and their relationships (Duffy, 1995). For example, a concept map for a Monte Carlo simulation framework is shown in Figure 14.1. We shall map this framework to C++ code in a later chapter.

We sometimes call Phase 2 the *conceptual design phase*.

*(Phase 3) Detailed Design*: This is where we commence with a detailed analysis of the C++ classes that realise the functionality in the system, their member data and the relationships with other classes. We create class diagrams using the Unified Modeling Language (UML). In a later section we shall give an introduction to this language.

During detailed design we need to address a number of software quality requirements such as:

- Interoperability: the ability to customise the software system to work with different external systems such as data sources (databases, XML, real-time data feeds), user interfaces and hardware drivers
- Efficiency and Performance: The algorithms in the system must be fast (good response time) and they must consume as few resources as possible
- Accuracy: the software system must produce accurate results
- Maintainability: it must be easy to correct bugs and it must be easy to add new functionality to the system without causing the system to crash like a pack of cards

Design patterns help us achieve these requirements, as we shall see in this and the following chapters. We document this phase using UML class diagrams. We call them *design blueprints*, a term that is used in mechanical engineering

*(Phase 4) Implementation*: In this phase we map design blueprints to C++. We define rules that map classes and relationships to C++. The later chapters of this book describe the actual mappings.

*(Phase 5) Maintenance and End of Life*: Software products are born, evolve, are modified and eventually die. Once a software system has been delivered to a customer, someone needs to maintain it. A well-documented and elegant design is certainly an asset in this case. Unfortunately, not all software systems are well designed. This topic is outside the scope of this book.

## 14.3   DOCUMENTATION ISSUES

We wish to document our design in a way that is easy to understand and in such a way that we do not have dig into source code in order to discover the intent of a particular design. To this end, we adopt the notation from the Unified Modeling Language (UML), an initiative from the Object Management Group (www.omg.org). UML is the de-facto standard for modelling and documenting object-oriented and component software systems. It has facilities for modelling software systems from multiple perspectives and for the complete software lifecycle, from initial concept to deployment.

In this section we discuss how UML models and documents structural relationships between classes. There are three specific types:

- Generalisation/specialisation
- Aggregation (and composition)
- Association

In general, all software systems are composed from objects and classes. They form a network (directed graph) in which the classes and objects represent the nodes or vertices and the arcs are represented by one of the three relationships above. We shall see many examples and realisations in the following chapters.

### 14.3.1   Generalisation and specialisation

The first relationship is called generalisation/specialisation (see Figure 14.2(a)): a type D1 is a specialisation of type B if it has all the properties of B but it may have functionality that B does not have. Alternatively, we say that B is a generalisation of D1. In the context of C++, this relationship reduces to the well-known *inheritance relationship*. We take the following simple example:

```
class B
{ // Base class
private:
        double* d;
public:
        // Public interface
};
```

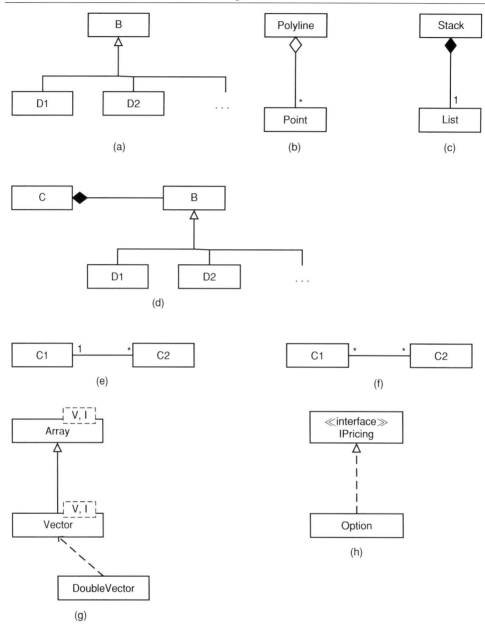

**Figure 14.2** UML class documentation

```
class D1 : public B
{ // Derived class
private:
        int* iarr;
public:
        // Public interface specific to D1
};
```

### 14.3.2   Aggregation and composition

The second kind of relationship is a special case of the *Whole-Part pattern* (see Buschmann, 1996). In this case we are discussing the Aggregation relationship and its special case, Composition. In general, a Whole object consists of zero or more Part objects. With Aggregation, the parts can be added to or removed from the Whole at run time while with Composition the parts must be added to the Whole at initialisation time (that is, in the constructor of the Whole). An example of the former is a polyline consisting of points; in a CAD package it is possible to create a polyline consisting of a variable number of points:

```
class Polyline
{
private:
        list<Point*> elements;
public:
        // Members here

        // Manipulating elements
        void add(Point* pt);
        void remove(Point* pt);
};
```

Thus, we can add and remove points anytime after the polyline has been created and this is depicted in Figure 14.2(b). With Composition on the other hand, the parts must be created in the constructor of the Whole (see Figure 14.2(c)):

```
class Stack
{
private:
        list<double> elements;
public:
        // Default constructor, initialise parts
        Stack() : elements(list<double> ()) {}

        // Manipulating elements
        double pop();
        void push(double value);
};
```

We now discuss how to combine Generalisation and Composition. The arrangement is shown in Figure 14.2(d) and this pattern underpins many of the specific GOF patterns. In general terms we describe the pattern as follows:

*The client is initialised in its constructor by an address of a derived class D(1, 2, . . . ) of the base class B. The client delegates to B because B and each of its derived classes encapsulates functionality that C does not have (nor cares to have!)*

The configuration in Figure 14.2(d) is an example of the *separation of concerns* idea; each class in a network performs one major task and it delegates to other 'acquaintance' classes that implement the services that it needs. We give a simple but representative example of how clients delegate to their servers. First, the base and derived classes are:

```
class B
{ // Base class for Delegation
private:
public:
      B() {}
      virtual double getValue() = 0;
      virtual ~B() { }
};


class D : public B
{ // Derived class
private:
            int* iarr;
            int size;
public:
      D(int N) : B()
      {
            size = N; iarr = new int[size];
            for (int j = 0; j < N; j++)
            {
                  iarr[j] = double(N-j);
            }
      }
      double getValue() {return iarr[0]/double(size);}
      ~D() { delete [] iarr; }
};
```

We now define the client class. It contains a pointer to the base class B and this is the only class it knows. Furthermore, it delegates to its server using polymorphic (virtual) member function (incidentally, this 'trick' is one of the secrets of Design Patterns; if you learn this technique well then you will have few problems):

```
class Client
{
private:
            B* b;
public:
        Client(B& delegate) { b = &delegate; }

        // The function that delegates
        double clientValue() const
        {
                double tmp = b -> getValue();
                // Modify for current situation
```

```
                return tmp * 100.0;
        }
};
```

An example of how to use these classes is:

```
int main()
{
        int arraySize = 10;
        D myDerived(arraySize);

        Client myClient(myDerived);
        cout << "Client value: " << myClient.clientValue() << endl;
        return 0;
}
```

### 14.3.3   Associations

We now discuss the third major relationship, namely association. This represents a more loosely coupled relationship between classes than either Aggregation or Generalisation. We distinguish between one-to-many and many-to-many relationships if only for the reason that the latter are more difficult to implement than the former.

A *one-to-many* (or 1:N) association (see Figure 14.2(e)) is one that associates one object of class C1 with zero or more objects of class C2 while each object of class C2 is associated with one (and only one) object of class C1. We give an example that is a variation of the example in the previous section:

```
Class C1
{ // "Associate" class
private:
                int* iarr;
                int size;
public:
        C1(int N)
        {
                size = N;
                iarr = new int[size];
                for (int j = 0; j < N; j++)
                {
                                iarr[j] = double(N-j);
                }
        }
        double getValue() const {return iarr[0]/double(size);}
        ~C1() { delete [] iarr; }
};
```

The client class has a pointer to its server class and its interface is given by:

```
class C2
{
private:
        C1* ass;
public:
        C2(C1& associate) { ass = &associate; }
        // The function that delegates
        double clientValue() const
        {
                double tmp = ass -> getValue();
                // Modify for current situation
                return tmp * 100.0;

        }
};
```

Finally, we create a program to show how these classes communicate:

```
int main()
{
        int arraySize = 10;
        C1 myAssociate(arraySize);
        C2 myClient(myAssociate);
        cout << "Client value: " << myClient.clientValue() << endl;
        return 0;
}
```

*Many-to-many* relationships are a 'different kettle of fish' because they model sophisticated relationships, see Figure 14.2(f). A full treatment is outside the scope of this chapter but we can implement an N:N relationship in two different ways:

- By breaking the relationship into two 1:N associations
- By creating a class that uses STL multimap<K,V>

We have created a class that models N:N relationships, part of whose interface is given by:

```
template <class D, class R> class Relation
{ // Classes representing mappings from D to R
private:

        // "Control" information
        Set<D> s1;        // Domain Set
        Set<R> s2;        // Range Set

        // Information about the mapping itself. These two
        // multimaps must be kept consistent
        multimap<D, R> f;        // The mapping itself
        multimap<R, D> finv;     // The inverse mapping
```

```
public:
    // Essential members
    Relation();
    Relation (const Set<D>& domainSet, const Set<R>& rangeSet);
    Relation(const Relation<D,R>& r2);

    // Building and breaking the Relation
    // The set element in the relations
    void addDomainElement(const D& d);      // Add d to Domain Set
    void addRangeElement(const R& r);       // Add r to Range Set
    void removeDomainElement(const D& d);     // Remove d +links
    void removeRangeElement(const R& r);      // Remove r +links

    // Define relationship between EXISTING elements
    void addRelation(const D& d, const R& r); /
    void removeRelation(const D& d); // Remove between d and ALL r
    void ClearAll();        // Break all links and sets
    void ClearLinks();      // Break links only, sets remain

    // Iterator functions (going from D direction)
    typedef typename multimap<D, R>::iterator iterator;
    typedef typename multimap<D, R>::const_iterator const_iterator;

    iterator Begin(); // Return iterator at begin of relation
    const_iterator Begin() const; // Return const iterator at begin
    iterator End(); // Return iterator after end of relation
    const_iterator End() const; // Return const iterator at end

    // Iterator functions (going from R direction)
    typedef typename multimap<R, D>::iterator iteratorInv;
    typedef typename multimap<R, D>::const_iterator const_iteratorInv;

    iterator BeginInv(); // Return iterator at begin of relation
    const_iterator BeginInv() const;// Return const iterator at begin
    iterator EndInv(); // Return iterator after end of relation
    const_iterator EndInv() const;// Return const iterator after end

    // Selectors
    const Set<D>& DomainSet();
    const Set<R>& RangeSet();

    Set<R> range(const D& d);       // Set of r for a d
    Set<D> domain(const R& r);      // Set of d for an r

    bool inDomain(const D& d) const;    // Is an element in domain?
    bool inRange(const D& r) const;     // Is an element in range?
```

```
    virtual ~Relation();
    Relation<D,R>& operator = (const Relation<D,R>& r2);

};
```

This is an extremely useful class because it models one of the most powerful data structures that we need in applications. We provide some examples on the CD.

### 14.3.4  Other diagrams

UML supports a number of other techniques to help us model the relationships between classes. First, it has support for *parametrised classes*, that is, classes whose data are parametric or generic. As an example, consider the situation on Figure 14.2(g) in which we derive a class Vector<V,I> from a class Array<V,I>. Of course, V and I are the parametric types that represent value and index types, respectively. When developing applications we usually replace these generic types by concrete types (this is called '*binding*'). We document this binding as shown in Figure 14.2(g) and it is a visual representation of the C++ code:

```
typedef Vector<double, long> DoubleVector;
```

Of course, we can document association, aggregation and composition relationships that involve generic underlying data types.

Finally, UML supports *component technology*. A component (typically a DLL or executable file on disk) is a software entity that implements one or more interfaces, an *interface* being a collection of methods (functions) that have no implementation. In fact, an interface may have no data nor may it have non-abstract methods. In the context of C++, an interface is a collection of pure virtual member functions. However, interfaces are not first-class objects in C++ (there is no keyword 'interface') but we can emulate this mechanism by defining interfaces as structs having pure virtual functions only:

```
// Emulate interfaces C# in C++ for a possible migration
// to languages that support them
#define interface struct

template <class V, class I = int>
interface IOneDimensionalAccess
{
        // Operators
        virtual V& operator [] (I index) = 0;// Subscripting operator
};


template <class V, class I = int>
        interface ITwoDimensionalAccess
{
        // Operators
        virtual V& operator () (I row, I column) = 0;
};
```

We define a similar array class that implements the first interface:

```
class SimpleArray : IOneDimensionalAccess<double> // Index == int
{
private:
        double first;
        double second;
public:
        SimpleArray() { first = 1.0; second = 2.71;}
        double& operator [] (int index)
        {
                if (1 == index) return first;
                if (2 == index) return second;

        }
};
```

A code sample that uses this class is:

```
int main()
{
        SimpleArray myArr;
        cout << myArr[1] << ", " << myArr[2] << endl;
        return 0;
}
```

See Figure 14.2(h); here we see how to document interfaces and components.

## 14.4   AN INTRODUCTION TO DESIGN PATTERNS

Design patterns are officially documented in GOF (1995). The authors distinguish between three main categories of patterns and the specific patterns in each one help the developer to create flexible C++ classes.

### 14.4.1   Creational patterns

The first Creational category consists of patterns that create objects in flexible ways, for example:

- Factory Method: define an interface for creating an object, but let derived classes decide which class to instantiate
- Abstract Factory: provide an interface for creating families of related or dependent objects without specifying their concrete classes
- Prototype: create an object as a clone or copy of another, 'prototypical' object
- Singleton (the over-hyped pattern): ensure that a class has only one instance and provide a global point of access to it

These patterns are discussed in more detail in Duffy (2004) but we shall also see a number of examples of them in this book as well.

We give one example of a creational pattern, in this case the Abstract Factory that creates one-factor option objects. The basic option class is defined as:

```
class Instrument
{
public:


};

class Option : public Instrument
{
public:
        // PUBLIC, PURE FOR PEDAGOGICAL REASONS
        double r;           // Interest rate
        double sig;         // Volatility
        double K;           // Strike price
        double T;           // Expiry date
        double b;           // Cost of carry
        double SMax;        // Far field condition
        char type;          // Call or put

        Option(){}

        // An option uses a polymorphic payoff object
        OneFactorPayoff OptionPayoff;

};
```

The interface for the base class in the current pattern is given by:

```
class InstrumentFactory
{
public:


        virtual Option* CreateOption() const = 0;

};
```

Now, we define a concrete factory class that creates an option based on console input:

```
class ConsoleInstrumentFactory : public InstrumentFactory
{
public:


        Option* CreateOption() const
        {
                double dr;          // Interest rate
                double dsig;        // Volatility
                double dK;          // Strike price
                double dT;          // Expiry date
                double db;          // Cost of carry
                double dSMax;       // Far field boundary
```

```
        cout << "Interest rate: ";
        cin >> dr;

        cout << "Volatility: ";
        cin >> dsig;

        cout << "Strike Price: ";
        cin >> dK;
        dSMax = 4.0 * dK; // Magix Number !!!!

        cout << "Expiry: ";
        cin >> dT;

        // Should ask what kind of option (as in Haug, 1998)
        cout << "Cost of carry: ";
        cin >> db;

        Option* result = new Option;

        cout << "Payoff 1) Call, 2) Put: ";
        int ans;
        cin >> ans;
        if (ans == 1)
        {
                result-> type = "C";
                (*result).OptionPayoff =
                        OneFactorPayoff(dK, MyCallPayoffFN);
        }
        else
        {
                result-> type = "P";
                (*result).OptionPayoff =
                        OneFactorPayoff(dK, MyPutPayoffFN);
        }

        result->r = dr;
        result->sig = dsig;
        result->K = dK;
        result->T = dT;
        result->b = db;
        result->SMax = dSMax;

        return result;

    }
};
```

In order to promote Information Hiding we define a function that gives a pointer to an abstract factory:

```
InstrumentFactory* GetInstrumentFactory()
{
        return new ConsoleInstrumentFactory;

        // Later other specific concrete factories
}
```

We now see how this factory is used in a client program. We notice that the client has no idea of the identity of the specific factory object!

```
int main()
{
        InstrumentFactory* myFactory = GetInstrumentFactory();
        Option* myOption = myFactory ->CreateOption();

        // Further processing with option

        return 0;
}
```

### 14.4.2   Structural patterns

Once an object has been created we place it in some association with other objects. The most important structural patterns are:

- Adapter: Convert the interface of one class into an interface that clients expect. A good example is to adapt the interface of list<T> class to define a stack<T> class.
- Composite: Compose objects into tree structures and recursive aggregates
- Bridge: Decouple a class from its implementation so that the two can vary independently. We shall see an example in Chapter 16 when we discuss the Finite Difference Method
- Façade: Provide a unified interface to a set of interfaces.

More examples of these patterns will be discussed in later chapters.

### 14.4.3   Behavioural patterns

These are patterns that have to do the member functions in classes. There are three sub-categories in this case:

- *Variational patterns*: methods that perform the same tasks but in different ways. Examples are Strategy (flexible algorithms), Command (encapsulation of a request as an object) and Template Method (define an algorithm having variant and invariant parts)
- *Extension patterns*: add new functionality to a class without disrupting the source code of the class. The Visitor is the only pattern in this category.
- *Notification*: these patterns ensure that data remains consistent in a network of objects. Examples are Observer and Mediator.

| 'What' / 'How' | Functionality | Efficiency | Maintainability | Portability |
|---|---|---|---|---|
| Factory Method | △ | ○ | ○ | ○ |
| Abstract Factory | ○ | ○ | ○ | ⊘ |
| Bridge | △ | △ | ⊘ | ⊘ |
| Composite | ○ | △ | ○ | △ |
| Adapter | ○ | ○ | ○ | ○ |
| Property Pattern | ○ | ○ | ○ | △ |
| Visitor | ○ | △ | ○ | ⊘ |
| Strategy | ○ | ⊘ | ○ | ○ |
| Observer | △ | ⊘ | △ | △ |

**Figure 14.3**   Pattern sanity check

## 14.5   ARE WE USING THE WRONG DESIGN? CHOOSING THE APPROPRIATE PATTERN

In the previous section we give an overview of – in my opinion – the most useful patterns for QF applications. The next question is to determine how useful a given design pattern is in a particular context and how much effort it takes to implement it. As developer, you need to evaluate each pattern on its own merits. For every feasible solution there is always an exception? Nonetheless, we propose the general guidelines as shown in Figure 14.3. You can use this matrix in different ways:

- Scenario 1: given a certain desired software requirement that our software system should satisfy, which patterns add to or detract from the realisation of this requirement?
- Scenario 2: We may consider using a certain design pattern. Is its use compatible with the more general requirement?

In Figure 14.3 the symbols have the following significance:

- Solid circle: pattern is a good realisation of the requirement
- Hollow circle: pattern is a reasonable realisation of the requirement
- Triangle: a 'catch-all', in this case the pattern does not add value, is not applicable or its use may even be detrimental to the realisation of the requirement. Another conclusion is that a triangle can imply that the use of a pattern will not add appreciably to the realisation of the relevant requirement

Finally, if you do decide to use design patterns in a project you will need to take the following estimates into account before you send a cost breakdown report to management:

- How long does it take to understand the pattern at a high level?
- How long does it take to create useful code that uses patterns?
- How long does it take to create small, medium-sized (or even large) software projects that use patterns?
- How useful is a design pattern in a given application context?

It is important to take all of these consumers of time and energy into account.

## 14.6    CADObject, A C++ LIBRARY FOR COMPUTER GRAPHICS

We describe a class library that uses design patterns. It began life as an addin for CAD software systems in the 1990's and since then has matured to the stage that it supports many of the GOF patterns. Central to CADObject is the class hierarchy. Some of the classes in the hierarchy are shown in Figure 14.4. The basic functionality is for two-dimensional geometrical manipulations such as:

- Creating basic shapes in different ways
- Geometric properties of shapes
- 'Interactions' between shapes, for example intersections

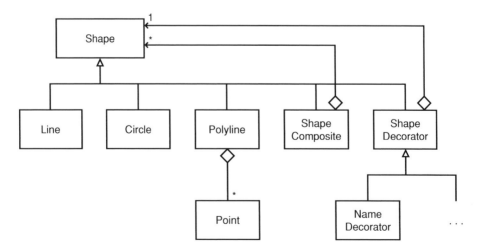

**Figure 14.4**    Class hierarchy

We can already discover a number of patterns in Figure 14.4. First, `Polyline` is an example of a Whole-Part (Collection-Members) pattern because it consists of zero or more `Point` instances. Second, we can create arbitrarily complex shapes by application of the `ShapeComposite` pattern; a Composite is a Shape and it consists of zero or more Shape instances. This implies that composites can contain other composites. Finally, a special case of a composite pattern is a *Decorator* (also known as *Wrapper*) pattern; as its name implies we embed a Shape instance in the Decorator object.

We give some examples of how we have coded the classes in Figure 14.4. We first examine `ShapeComposite`. It is derived from Shape and it is also an aggregation of Shape instances. Thus, it must be possible to add and remove shapes at run-time. The class interface is given by:

```cpp
class ShapeComposite: public Shape
{
private:
        // The shapelist using the STL list
        std::list<Shape*> sl;
public:
        // User can use the STL iterator
        typedef std::list<Shape*>::iterator iterator;
        typedef std::list<Shape*>::const_iterator const_iterator;

        // Constructors and destructor
        ShapeComposite();                        // Default constructor
        virtual ~ShapeComposite();               // Destructor

        // Iterator functions
        iterator Begin();                        // Return iterator at begin
        const_iterator Begin() const;            // const iterator at begin
        iterator End();                          // Return iterator after end
        const_iterator End() const;              // const iterator at end

        // Selectors
        int Count() const;                       // Number of shapes in list

        // Add functions
        void AddFront(Shape* s);                 // Add shape at the beginning
        void AddBack(Shape* s);                  // Add shape at the end

        // Remove functions
        void RemoveFirst();
        // Remove first shape
        void RemoveLast();
        // Remove last shape
        void RemoveAll();        // Remove all shapes from the list

        // Operators
        ShapeComposite& operator = (const ShapeComposite& source);
};
```

We can see that this class uses a list<Shape*> as underlying data structure and the composite class delegates to it. This is a form of reusability. The list<T> class offloads much of the housekeeping chores, thus allowing the composite class to concentrate on application-related issues. We give a number of examples to show how this principle works. For example, the code for removing all the elements from a composite is:

```
void ShapeComposite::RemoveAll()
{ // Remove all shapes from the list

    // Create STL list iterator
    std::list<Shape*>::iterator it;

    for (it=sl.begin(); it!=sl.end(); it++)
    { // Delete every shape in the list
        delete (*it); // Delete shape
    }

    // Remove the shape pointers from the list
    sl.clear();
}
```

Furthermore, the code for adding and removing shapes is very easy and is basically a 'one-liner':

```
void ShapeComposite::AddFront(Shape* s)
{ // Add shape at the beginning of shapelist. No copy is made.

    sl.push_front(s);
}

void ShapeComposite::AddBack(Shape* s)
{ // Add shape at the end of shapelist. No copy is made.

    sl.push_back(s);
}
// Remove functions
void ShapeComposite::RemoveLast()
{ // Remove last shape

    delete sl.back();       // Delete the shape
    sl.pop_back();              // Remove shape pointer from list
}

void ShapeComposite::RemoveFirst()
{ // Remove first shape

    delete sl.front();      // Delete the shape
    sl.pop_front();         // Remove shape pointer from list
}
```

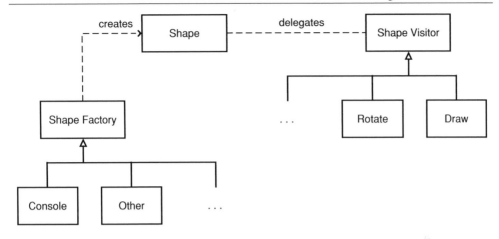

**Figure 14.5**   Input and output for class hierarchy

We have provided the source code for an edited and beautified version of some of the classes in CADObject on the CD. **It is useful to learn how we have set up the software because, once you understand the code you can then apply it to many QF applications.**

## 14.7   USING PATTERNS IN CADObject

We have applied a number of creational and behavioural patterns to CADObject, for example:

- Abstract Factory
- Builder (for creating Composites and other complex objects)
- Visitor pattern (that allows us to extend the functionality of the classes in CADObject)

The UML diagram for two of these patterns is shown in Figure 14.5. The source code for these patterns can be found on the accompanying CD.

## 14.8   CONCLUSIONS AND SUMMARY

We have given an overview of a number of software development techniques that we shall need in later chapters of this book. In particular, we have given an introduction to Design Patterns, some examples of use and applications to QF.

In Figure 14.6 we describe the semantic relationships between the GOF patterns by using concept mapping techniques.

More information on Design patterns can be found in GOF (1995) and in Duffy (2004) where we have provided examples that can be used in QF applications.

## 14.9   EXERCISES AND PROJECTS

1. (Modelling Figure 14.3 in C++) Implement the matrix as shown in Figure 14.3 as an associative matrix with the following data types as arguments:

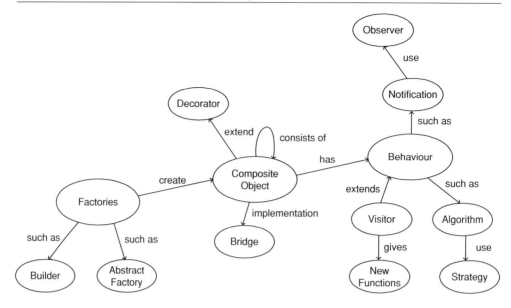

**Figure 14.6**   Concept map for design patterns

```
AssocMatrix<int, string, string>
```

Build the matrix using the member functions in `AssocMatrix`. Furthermore, create functions that realise the following functionality:
(a) Given a pattern, which requirements does it realise? The output is an ordered list
(b) Given a requirement, which patterns are most suitable for its realisation? The output is a list containing the top three patterns.

2. (Creating Concept Maps and UML Class Diagrams) This is a general example and it has no direct relevance to QF. But it is useful to do the exercise because you can use the same techniques in other situations and applications.

3. We describe some semantic relationships in a software system that manages journals, their issues and the articles that are published in those issues. The relationships are:
   - An Issue is an appearance of Journal
   - An Issue consists of Articles
   - A Reader is interested in a Journal
   - An Article refers to an Article
   Answer the following questions:
   (a) Create a concept map for this problem
   (b) Determine which relationships in the concept map are associations, which are aggregations and which are generalisation/specialisation relationships. Based on your answers create an UML class diagram. In this way you will have succeeded in finding the classes in the current problem domain as well as their relationships.
   (c) Implement the resulting UML diagram in C++

# Part III
# QF Applications

# 15
## Programming the Binomial Method
### in C++

## 15.1 INTRODUCTION AND OBJECTIVES

In this chapter we design and implement a set of C++ classes for pricing options and other derivative products with the help of the binomial method. The goal is to produce a small software system that produces accurate results, is easy to maintain and that can be adapted to new requirements. We provide full C++ source code so that you can experiment with the software and extend it (see the exercises) for new kinds of problems. Modelling the binomial method using C++ is useful for a number of reasons. First, most readers know the method and it is documented in many books (see for example, Cox and Rubinstein, 1985; Haug, 1998; Hull, 2006). This means that the reader will be able to appreciate how we designed and implemented the resulting code because we are solving a well-known problem. This will speed up the learning process. Second, we use appropriate design patterns, templates and C++ functionality to create a software system that is maintainable and also easy to understand. Finally, once you have understood the design of the software for the binomial method you can use that knowledge to help you create software for other derivatives products such as interest rate models and real options. Furthermore, we give some guidelines on how to apply and adapt the techniques that we discussed in this chapter.

The core process in this chapter is to calculate the price of an option (and its sensitivities such as delta and gamma) by using binomial lattices as underlying containers. Recall that we have already designed a template class that holds generic node values and that can be instantiated to support binomial, trinomial and multinomial structures:

```
Lattice<V, I, int NumberNodes> etc...
```

This is the data structure that will hold the results of calculations and that will eventually allow us to price the derivative product. To this end, we can implement the core process by three semi-independent activities:

A1: Build the initial lattice structure (allocate memory)
A2: Execute the Forward Induction step
A3: Execute the Backward Induction step

Activity A1 involves allocating memory for the basic lattice structure while activity A2 initialises the node values for the underlying asset in the lattice using well-known strategies such as CRR, JR, modified CRR and others (see Clewlow and Strickland, 1998). Activity A3 performs the backward induction step by calculating the derivative price, starting from the discrete version of the payoff function and working back from the maturity date to the current time where this price is found.

We document the current problem using standard visual techniques, for example using the Unified Modeling Language (UML). Having done that and understood the resulting diagrams we shall see that the corresponding C++ code is easy to create, understand and maintain. In this way we hope to show that it is possible to write good C++ code. The secret is to do a good design up-front before we start coding.

## 15.2   SCOPING THE PROBLEM

In this section we define the financial problem that we then map to C++ code. It is always tempting to implement very general one-factor problems at the outset but we do not do this for two reasons. First, we prefer to explain the *essentials* of the problem and then map these to C++. In this way, we get a clear understanding of the subject matter. Second, the software development process is an iterative one and we prefer to develop our systems in an incremental fashion by adding more functionality to existing and tested code.

We examine the Black Scholes model as is discussed in the literature (Black and Scholes, 1973; Hull, 2006), that is:

- The price of the underlying instrument is a geometric Brownian motion with constant drift and volatility
- It is possible to short sell the underlying stock
- There are no riskless arbitrage opportunities
- Trading in the stock is continuous
- There are no transaction costs
- All securities are perfectly divisible (e.g. it is possible to buy 1/100th of a share)
- The risk free interest rate is constant, and it has the same value for all maturity dates

Furthermore, we assume that no dividends are paid. It is well known that the above assumptions are not always valid. For example, the assumption of constant volatility is not realistic. Nonetheless, we shall adhere to these assumptions in this chapter. Our interest in the binomial method is in showing how to implement a well-known method in C++.

## 15.3   A SHORT OVERVIEW OF THE BINOMIAL METHOD

In this chapter we are mainly interested in pricing one-factor European call and put options based on a single asset S whose values change according to the Stochastic Differential Equation (SDE) given by:

$$dS = \mu S dt + \sigma S dW \tag{15.1}$$

where

$\mu =$ drift (constant)
$\sigma =$ volatility (constant)
$dW =$ Wiener (Brownian motion) process

In other words, the asset price behaviour is determined by a Geometric Brownian Motion (GBM). Thus, equation (15.1) consists of both a deterministic part and a non-deterministic part. In general, asset price takes a random course and we wish to simulate this behaviour in discrete time. To this end, the binomial method assumes that the underlying asset price takes only one of two values, namely it can increase by a certain amount u or it can decrease by a certain amount d. We depict the situation pictorially in Figure 15.1; in a short period of time $\Delta t$ the asset price S can change to uS or to dS where $u > 1$ and $d < 1$. Since the problem is

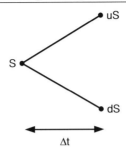

**Figure 15.1** Basic lattice, multiplicative

stochastic there is a certain probability of an up or down movement. Thus, in order to model the asset random walk we must calculate the following terms:

$$u = \text{'up' jump value}$$
$$d = \text{'down' jump value}$$
$$p_u = \text{probability that asset price is } uS$$
$$p_d = \text{probability that asset price is } dS$$
$$(p_d = 1 - p_u) \tag{15.2}$$

In general, we create a so-called binomial tree from some initial point (called time zero or 0 for convenience) to the maturity date T by dividing the interval [0, T] into N equal subintervals. We then extend the random walk on a single interval as in Figure 15.1 to the general case with N intervals. An example in the case N = 3 is shown in Figure 15.2. We call this a *recombining tree* because of the alignment of nodes. We see that the number of nodes increases by one when moving from one time interval to the next one. As we shall see in a later section we shall model the general tree structure (an example of which is given in Figure 15.2).

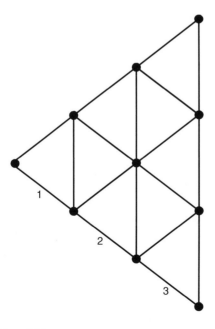

**Figure 15.2** Example of a binomial tree

Before we are able to price an option we must build the binomial tree. This is the so-called forward induction phase. We assume for the moment that we are using the SDE in equation 15.1 and furthermore we must calculate the coefficients in equation 15.2. There are a number of different strategies for doing this, for example:

- CRR: Cox, Ross and Rubinstein (1979)
- And many more . . .

We sometimes work with a variation of equation (15.1) by using a logarithmic transformation:

$$dx = vdt + \sigma dW, \quad (x = log(S))$$
$$\left(v \equiv r - \tfrac{1}{2}\sigma^2\right) \tag{15.3}$$

The CRR method is:

$$u = exp\left(\left(r - \tfrac{1}{2}\sigma^2\right)\Delta t + \sigma\sqrt{\Delta t}\right)$$
$$d = exp\left(\left(r - \tfrac{1}{2}\sigma^2\right)\Delta t - \sigma\sqrt{\Delta t}\right)$$
$$p_u = \tfrac{1}{2}, \quad p_d = 1 - p_u \tag{15.4}$$

The CRR strategy is one of the first methods used to construct the binomial tree. There are other methods, one of which is called the modified CRR. In particular, this method is an improvement over CRR especially at the strike price K because it is here that the payoff function is not smooth and we need some way of suppressing the numerical oscillations that occur there. The JR method is:

$$u = exp\left(\sigma\sqrt{\Delta t}\right)$$
$$d = exp\left(-\sigma\sqrt{\Delta t}\right)$$
$$p_u = \tfrac{1}{2} + \frac{r - \tfrac{1}{2}\sigma^2}{2\sigma}\sqrt{\Delta t}, \quad p_d = 1 - p_u \tag{15.5}$$

Thus, we have a first-order accurate scheme for constructing the binary tree at each time step. Another way to create a binomial tree is to define a new variable called x that is the logarithm of the asset price S as already shown in Equation (15.3).

The modified CRR method is:

$$u = e^{K_N + V_N}$$
$$d = e^{K_N - V_N}$$
$$p_u = (e^{r\Delta t} - d)/(u - d) \tag{15.6}$$

where

$$K_N = log(K/S)/N$$
$$V_N = \sigma\sqrt{\Delta t}$$

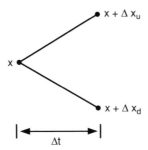

**Figure 15.3**   Basic lattice, additive

In contrast to a multiplicative process we now create the node values in the binomial method by an *additive process* as motivated in Figure 15.3. Again, there are a number of strategies for calculating the increments, for example the EQP method is:

$$a = v\Delta t, \quad b = \tfrac{1}{2}\sqrt{4\sigma^2 \Delta t - 3v^2 \Delta t^2}$$

$$\Delta x_u = \tfrac{1}{2}a + b$$

$$\Delta x_d = \tfrac{3}{2}a - b$$

$$p_u = p_d = \tfrac{1}{2} \tag{15.7}$$

and the TRG method is:

$$\Delta x_u = \Delta x_d = \sqrt{\sigma^2 \Delta t + v^2 \Delta t^2}$$

$$p_u = \tfrac{1}{2} + \tfrac{1}{2}\frac{v\Delta t}{\Delta x} = \tfrac{1}{2}\left(1 + \frac{v\Delta t}{\Delta x}\right) \tag{15.8}$$

We now have five methods for constructing the binomial tree. We now deal with the backward induction process. This process calculates the option price, commencing at t = T using the payoff function there until we arrive at t = 0 where we get the desired option value. To be specific we concentrate on vanilla call and put European options.

## 15.4   SOFTWARE REQUIREMENTS FOR A BINOMIAL SOLVER

Before we jump into the C++ code details we feel that it is important to think about the software prototype that we are about to create. In short, how flexible should our software be? In general, we need to determine those features that must be supported in the system. At the very least, we would like to have the following features:

F1: In general, the system should be implemented, not by one monolithic class but by a set of inter-connected classes with each class having a very specific functionality. There should be as little coupling as possible between these classes in order to promote adaptability

F2: It must be possible to choose between a number of models for generating values for the forward induction process. Many of these models are named after their respective inventors and the methods have short names such as CRR, JR, TRG and modified CRR. It must be possible for the developer to add new models to the system with minor consequences for the stability of the system

F3: It must be possible to define flexible payoff functions; for example, we should be able to create an option as a put or call. This facility has to be done in an object-oriented way by creating a `Payoff` class hierarchy, for example.

These are essential features and must be supported in the first version of the software (in this case the software that is provided on the accompanying CD). It would be nice to have other features, such as:

F4: Improve the stability and accuracy of the binomial scheme by using a trinomial lattice as underlying data type. We need to investigate which classes and interfaces will need to be modified in order to effect this requirement

F5: Binomial methods are used in a number of financial engineering applications, for example to model the short rate and in Real Options. Which pieces of the software need to be modified in order to do this?

F6: In Numerical Analysis, certain problems (such as interpolation and integration) are amenable to a solution using binomial trees. Can we use some of the classes in this chapter to solve these problems? If the answer is yes we will have succeeded in creating highly generic software because it has been applied in at least two problem domains.

In this chapter we concentrate on the design of features F1, F2 and F3.

## 15.5    CLASS DESIGN AND CLASS STRUCTURE

In general, writing one monolithic program in C++ to implement a Binomial Solver leads to code that is unmaintainable, difficult to understand and difficult to extend.

Furthermore, it takes longer to get such code up and properly running than code that has been designed using real software engineering principles. For this reason, we look at the current problem from a design perspective and we develop C++ code that is both maintainable and reliable. The experience gained here can and will be applied in other branches of financial engineering.

The approach in this context is to partition the problem into loosely coupled classes in which each class has a well-defined responsibility (it does one thing well) and having well-defined interfaces to other classes. Furthermore, nasty, changeable and difficult design decisions are hidden as private data and private functions.

### 15.5.1    UML class structure

The main goal of the Binomial Solver is to calculate the price of a stock option. Call and put options are supported as well as European and American exercise styles. Part of the class structure is shown in Figure 15.4 and it contains the following classes:

- `Lattice`: the data structure/data store that holds all data in memory. It is a class that is an instantiation of the `Lattice` template class. It contains functionality for creating a lattice object, initialising its nodes and navigating from node to node and from one time level to the next time level

- `BinomialLatticeStrategy`: the base class for all specific strategies for calculating critical parameters `u`, `d` (up and down values) and `p` (the probability of making a jump). We provide a number of well-known formulae (such as CRR. JR and modified CRR) and the user may add-in his or her own special cases with ease

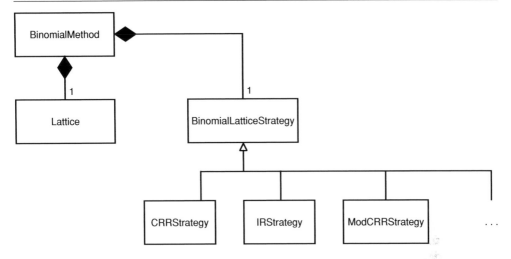

**Figure 15.4**   Models and strategies

Other classes are:

- `Binomia Method`: class that calculates the option price
- `Option` and `Payoff`: two classes containing option-related data and payoff functions, respectively. This is where all source data and algorithms come from
- `Director`: in this version of the software we have modelled this code as a `main()`. It steers the whole process as it were and its responsibilities are:

A1: Get option data and calculate discrete payoff function
A2: Create and initialise an instance of `BinomialMethod`
A3: Build the binomial lattice with a given 'start' value S of the underlying asset
A4: Calculate the discrete payoff function
A5: Calculate the option price

In a future version we could offload some of `Director` functionality to other, more appropriate classes. We use apply the *Builder* design pattern (GOF, 1995) to help us create a more flexible design. For the moment however, we are satisfied with the way the code has been set up.

### 15.5.2   Information flow

We now discuss how work gets done. In particular, we describe the steps to be taken in order to calculate the option price. In general, the participating objects call each other's member functions in order to get the data and information that they need. We identify four phases or states that correspond roughly to the five activities in section 15.5.1. A short summary:

I: The `Director` gets the essential parameters from the `Option` instance and calculates the discounting factor
II: Create a new instance of `BinomialMethod`
III: Modify lattice based on starting stock price S
IV: Calculate the option price

These are the steps that can be retraced in the resulting C++ code. We now discuss the code that realises these steps.

## 15.6  APPLYING DESIGN PATTERNS

The code in this chapter uses a number of structural and behavioural design patterns. First of all, we partitioned the problem into a network of loosely coupled classes and this is a small framework of classes in its own right.

We discuss the most obvious patterns that we have used here. Perhaps the most important pattern in Figure 15.4 is the Strategy because it provides the interface for calculating the essential parameters in the binomial method, namely:

- u: the up variable
- d: down variable
- p: probability of an up movement

In this version of the software we model these parameters as protected data (for convenience). This means that derived classes of the abstract Strategy base class can access this data directly. In fact, each derived class will update this data in its own way, as we have already seen in equations (15.4) to (15.8). The strategy classes support both multiplicative and additive binomial processes. The base class contains the common variables u, d and p and the corresponding public member functions that can access them. Its interface is:

```
class BinomialLatticeStrategy
{ // Based on Clewlow and Strickland 1998
protected:
            double u; double d; double p;
            double s; double r; double k;
            BinomialType bType; // Multiplicative or arithmetical
public:
            // ...
            // Public inline functions for normal clients
            double downValue() const { return d;}
            double upValue() const { return u;}
            double probValue() const { return p;}
            BinomialType binomialType() const { return bType;}
};
```

Each specific strategy for calculating u, d and p is mapped to a class. For example, the CRR strategy is defined as:

```
class CRRStrategy: public BinomialLatticeStrategy
{
public:
      CRRStrategy(double vol, double interest, double delta);
};
```

This simple class has a constructor having parameters that represent the volatility, interest rate and the step size (delta) in the time direction. The code for this class is given by:

```
CRRStrategy::CRRStrategy(double vol, double interest, double delta)
        : BinomialLatticeStrategy(vol, interest, delta)
{
        double R1 = (r - 0.5 * s * s) * k;
        double R2 = s * ::sqrt(k);

        u = ::exp(R1 + R2);
        d = ::exp(R1 - R2);

        double discounting = ::exp(- r*k);
        p = 0.5;
}
```

The code for the other strategies is given as:

```
JRStrategy::JRStrategy(double vol, double interest, double delta)
        : BinomialLatticeStrategy(vol, interest, delta)
{

        double k2 = ::sqrt(k);
        u = ::exp(s * k2);
        d = 1.0/u;
        p = 0.5 + ((r - 0.5 * s * s) * k2 * 0.5) / s;
}
```

```
EQPStrategy::EQPStrategy(double vol, double interest, double delta)
        : BinomialLatticeStrategy(vol, interest, delta)
{

    bType = Additive;

    // For additive method: page 19 Clewlow/Strickland formula 2.17
    // "v" is "nu" here, for "v" see page 18 formula 2.14
    double nu = r - 0.5 * s * s;

    double a = nu * k;
    double b = 0.5 * ::sqrt( (4.0 * s * s * k) -
                                (3.0 * nu * nu * k * k) );

    // EQP parameters: page 19 formula 2.17 Clewlow/Strickland 1998
    u = 0.5 * a + b;
    d = 1.5 * a - b;
    p = 0.5;
}
```

```
TRGStrategy::TRGStrategy(double vol, double interest, double delta)
            : BinomialLatticeStrategy(vol, interest, delta)
```

```
{

        bType = Additive;

        // Needed for additive method: page 19 formula 2.19
        // "v" is "nu" here, for "v" see page 18 formula 2.14
        double nu = r - 0.5 * s * s;

        double nudt = nu * k;
        // TRG parameters: page 19 formula 2.19
        u = ::sqrt( s * s * k + nudt * nudt );
        d = - u;
        p = 0.5 * (1.0 + (nudt/u) );
}


ModCRRStrategy::ModCRRStrategy(double vol, double interest,
                double delta, double S, double K, int N)
                    : BinomialLatticeStrategy(vol, interest, delta)
{

            // s == volatility, k = step size in time
            double KN = ::log(K/S) / double (N);
            double VN = s * ::sqrt(k);

            u = ::exp(KN + VN);
            d = ::exp(KN - VN);
            p = (::exp(r * k) - d) / (u - d);
}
```

Another interesting pattern that is 'embedded' in the base Strategy pattern is the Template Method pattern. Recall that this pattern, as with Strategy models an algorithm and the algorithm consists of an *invariant* part that never changes and a *variant* part that can change. In the current case the invariant part corresponds to the construction of the binomial lattice itself while the variant part corresponds to the different ways (for example, CRR) to calculate the parameters u, d and p. The implementation of the Template Method pattern has to do with the creation of the binomial lattice as is shown as follows:

```
virtual void updateLattice(Lattice<double, int, 2>& source,
                                double rootValue) const;
```

This function builds the lattice data structure based on the parameters u, d, p and a root value. The code is:

```
void BinomialLatticeStrategy::updateLattice
            (Lattice<double, int, 2>& source, double rootValue) const
{ // Find the depth of the lattice; this a Template Method Pattern
        int si = source.MinIndex();
        source[si][source[si].MinIndex()] = rootValue;
```

```
        // Loop from the min index to the end index
        for (int n = source.MinIndex() + 1; n <= source.MaxIndex(); n++)
        {
            for (int i = source[n].MinIndex();
                        i < source[n].MaxIndex(); i++)
            {
                source[n][i] = d * source[n-1][i];
                source[n][i+1] = u * source[n-1][i];
            }
        }
}
```

## 15.7   THE BUILDER AND DIRECTOR CLASSES

We now have a lattice structure to hold data as well as the strategies for actually building the lattice. In order to complete the model, we need more classes and functions:

- BinomialMethod; this is an instance of a Builder pattern (see GOF, 1995) and it carries out a number of duties, such as:
  - Forward induction (build the tree)
  - Backward induction (calculate option price)
  - Other housekeeping chores
  This is a 'workhorse' class. Its interface is given by:

```
class BinomialMethod
{
private:
            // Underlying data structure
            Lattice<double, int, 2> lattice;// Number == 2 binomial
            BinomialLatticeStrategy* str; // Pointer to an algorithm

            double disc;

public:
        // Default constructor
        BinomialMethod();

        // Constructor taking discount factor, strategy (e.g. CRR)
        // and the number of time steps

        BinomialMethod (double discounting,
                BinomialLatticeStrategy& strategy, int N);

        // Initialise lattice data structure
        void buildLattice(int N);
```

```
        // Initialise lattice node values (Forward Induction)
        void modifyLattice(double  U);

        // Calculate derivative price (Backward Induction)
        double getPrice(const Vector<double, int>& RHS);

        // Handy function to give us the size at expiry date
        Vector<double, int> BasePyramidVector() const;

        // Underlying lattice
        const Lattice<double, int, 2>& getLattice() const;

};
```

The source code is on the CD. The code that executes the backward induction process by calculating the option price based on the discrete payoff function is given by:

```
double BinomialMethod::getPrice(const Vector<double, int>& RHS)
{
        double pr = str -> probValue();
        int ei = lattice.MaxIndex();
        lattice[ei] = RHS;

        // Loop from the max index to the start (min) index
        for (int n = lattice.MaxIndex() - 1; n >= lattice.MinIndex(); n--)
        {
                for (int i = lattice[n].MinIndex();
                                        i <= lattice[n].MaxIndex(); i++)
                {
                        lattice[n][i] = disc * (pr * lattice[n+1][i+1]
                                        + (1.0-pr) * lattice[n+1][i]);
                }
        }
        int si = lattice.MinIndex();
        return lattice[si][lattice[si].MinIndex()];
}
```

- Director; this is the class that drives the process. In the current implementation it is the main() program. In a later version it could be upgraded according to the structure of the Builder pattern as described in GOF (1995). The Director communicates with BinomialMethod by means of well-defined member functions. It collaborates with the following classes and functions:
- A simple option class:

```
class Option
{
public:
        double r;        // Interest rate
        double sig;      // Volatility
        double K;        // Strike price
```

```
        double T;              // Expiry date
        int type;              // 1 == Call, 2 ==  Put

        double payoff(double S)const
        { // Hard-coded here!
            if (type == 1)
            {
                if (S > K)
                        return (S - K);
                return 0.0;
            }
            else
            {
                if (S < K)
                        return -(S - K);
                return 0.0;
            }
        }
    };
```

- Determine which Option factory to use:

```
EuropeanOptionFactory* getFactory()
{
        return new ConsoleEuropeanOptionFactory;
}
```

- Determine which strategy to use (for example, CRR):

```
BinomialLatticeStrategy* getStrategy(double sig, double r, double k,
                                     double S, double K, int N)
{
        cout << "\ n1. CRR, 2. JR, 3. TRG, 4. EQP, 5. Modified CRR: ";
        int choice;
        cin >> choice;

        if (choice == 1)
                return new CRRStrategy(sig,r,k);

        if (choice == 2)
                return new JRStrategy(sig,r,k);

        if (choice == 3)
                return new TRGStrategy(sig,r,k);

        if (choice == 4)
                return new EQPStrategy(sig,r,k);

        if (choice == 5)
                return new ModCRRStrategy(sig,r,k, S, K, N);

}
```

• Calculate the discrete payoff function:

```
// This could be made into a member function of Option
Vector<double, int> calcPayoffVector(Vector<double, int> xarr,
                                        const Option& opt)
{
        // We need the form of the lattice at the "base" of the pyramid.
        // This will be needed when we use backward induction

        Vector<double, int> result (xarr);

        for (int j = xarr.MinIndex(); j <= xarr.MaxIndex(); j++)
        {
                result[j] = opt.payoff(xarr[j]);
        }

        return result;
}
```

## 15.8   THE PROCESS AND THE STEPS

We have now described what is needed in order to calculate the option price. The steps are
documented in the code:

```
// Phase I: Create and initialise the option
EuropeanOptionFactory* fac = getFactory();
Option* opt = fac -> create();
delete fac;

// Get the number of time steps and S value
int N = 200;
cout << "Numbers of steps: ";
cin >> N;
double S = 200;
cout << "Give underlying value: ";
cin >> S;

// Time step (deltaT) and discounting factor
double k = opt->T / double (N);
cout << "Step size " << k << endl;
double discounting = ::exp(- opt->r*k);
cout << "Discounting " << discounting << endl;

// Phase II: Create the binomial method
BinomialLatticeStrategy* lf =
                getStrategy(opt->sig, opt->r, k, S, opt->K, N);
BinomialMethod bn(discounting, *lf, N);
```

```
// Phase III: Forward Induction
bn.modifyLattice(S);

// Phase IV: Backward Induction
Vector<double, int> RHS = bn.BasePyramidVector();
if (lf -> binomialType() == Additive)
{
    RHS[RHS.MinIndex()] = S * ::exp(N * lf -> downValue());
    for (int j = RHS.MinIndex() + 1; j <= RHS.MaxIndex(); j++)
    {
        RHS[j] = RHS[j-1]
                    * exp(lf->upValue() - lf->downValue());
    }
}


Vector<double, int> Pay = calcPayoffVector(RHS, *opt);
double pr = bn.getPrice(Pay);
cout << "PriceN: " << pr << endl;
```

This concludes the discussion of the code for the Binomial Method, version 1.

## 15.9   TEST CASES AND EXAMPLES

We give two examples and we present the numerical results based on the C++ code that we have written for the binomial method. The scope is suitably restricted by assuming:

- No dividend
- No early exercise

We compare the results from the five strategies for various values of N, the number of subdivisions of the time interval (0, T).

The first case is a European put with $T = 1$ (1 year), $S = 5$, $K = 10$, $r = 0.12$, $\sigma = 0.5$ with $N = 256$ and $N = 512$. The results are shown in Table 15.1. The exact solution based on the Black Scholes formula is $P = 4.0733$.

The second case is a European call with $T = 0.25$, $S = 60$, $K = 65$, $r = 0.08$, $\sigma = 0.3$. The results are shown in Table 15.2 for the case $N = 256$. The exact solution based on the Black Scholes formula is $C = 2.1334$.

**Table 15.1**   Binomial method European put (exact: 4.0733): $T = 1$, $S = 5$, $K = 10$, $r = 0.12$, $\sigma = 0.5$

|        | N = 256  | N = 512  |
|--------|----------|----------|
| CRR    | 4.07278  | 4.07309  |
| JR     | 4.07248  | 4.07324  |
| TRG    | 4.07248  | 4.07324  |
| EQP    | 4.0726   | 4.07302  |
| ModCRR | 4.07174  | 4.0725   |

**Table 15.2**    Binomial method European call
(exact: 2.1334): T = 0.25, S = 60, K = 65,
r = 0.08, $\sigma$ = 0.30

| | N = 256 |
|---|---|
| CRR | 2.13395 |
| JR | 2.13468 |
| TRG | 2.13471 |
| EQP | 2.12669 |
| ModCRR | 2.12951 |

It is possible to extend the C++ code for the binomial method in a number of directions, for example early exercise and continuous dividend yield. See the exercises.

## 15.10   CONCLUSIONS AND SUMMARY

In this chapter we have designed and implemented a customisable software framework in C++ for pricing one-factor plain options with no early exercise. We have decomposed the system into a network of loosely coupled classes that we design using the famous design patterns as documented in Chapter 14 of the current book as well as in Duffy (2004) and GOF (1995).

In the next section we have a number of exercises and projects that extend the current framework to early exercise features, calculation of option sensitivities (the 'greeks') and problems with continuous dividends.

## 15.11   EXERCISES AND QUESTIONS

1. (Kick-off Questions)

    Here are some general questions concerning the code in this chapter:

    (a) What are the advantages and disadvantages of declaring the member data in the base class `BinomialLatticeStrategy` to be protected?

    (b) Would it be advantageous to implement the lattice structure using the STL `vector<T>` as in:

```
vector<vector <V> > tree
```

    instead of

```
// Implement as a full nested Vector class
Array<Vector<V, I>, I > tree;
```

    Remark: the next set of questions is concerned with extensions to the C++ code that we have programmed for the Binomial method:

    • Support for early exercise features (American options)
    • Approximating option sensitivities (the Greeks)
    • Option on stocks paying continuous dividends

In general, you will need to modify the lattice data structure in the current implementation so that the lattices vertices can store other data structures besides double:

```
// Old underlying data structure
Lattice<double, int, 2> lattice;
```

We will need to modify this container, for example:

```
Lattice<pair<double, double>, int, 2> lattice;
```

The precise structure will depend on the kind of data we need to store at a given vertex.

2. We wish to model both call and put American options. In this case we need to modify the code so that the option price at each time level satisfies the constraint:

$$V_j^n = max \left( e^{-rk} \left( pV_{j+1}^{n+1} + (1 - p)V_j^{n+1} \right), K - S_j^n \right)$$

This is the constraint for a put option and a there is a similar formula for call options.
Answer the following questions:
(a) How must the data structure be modified in order to accommodate this new requirement?
(b) Modify the code for the backward induction process so that it can model American options
(c) How would you model option delta in the model?

$$delta = \frac{\partial C}{\partial S} \approx \frac{\Delta C}{\Delta S} = \frac{C_1^1 - C_0^1}{S_1^1 - S_0^1}$$

3. We wish to model some other option sensitivities, for example:

$$vega = \frac{\partial C}{\partial \sigma} \approx \frac{C(\sigma + \Delta\sigma) - C(\sigma - \Delta\sigma)}{2\Delta\sigma}$$

$$\rho = \frac{\partial C}{\partial r} \approx \frac{C(r + \Delta r) - C(r - \Delta r)}{2\Delta r}$$

How would you do this in C++?

4. We wish to modify the code so that we can model assets paying a continuous dividend yield. The underlying S is now modelled by the stochastic differential equation (SDE):

$$dS = (r - D)Sdt + \sigma SdW$$

This equation allows us to model options on indices, foreign exchange rates and futures contacts, for example. We can just replace the term r in the current model by r − D, where D is the continuous dividend yield. For example, the TRG model now becomes:

$$\Delta x = \sqrt{\sigma^2 \Delta t + \nu^2 \Delta t^2}$$

$$p_u = \frac{1}{2} + \frac{1}{2}\frac{\nu\Delta t}{\Delta x}$$

$$\nu = r - D - \frac{1}{2}\sigma^2$$

Modify the framework so that it works with continuous dividend yields. Test your code using examples from the literature and your own applications.

5. (Improving the Performance of the Binomial Method)
The different strategies for calculating the up and down factors use the exponential function. This is a costly function to evaluate and numerical analysts often use approximations to it, for example *Padé approximants* (see Duffy, 2006 where these are used in a partial differential equation and finite difference context). For example, a common approximation to exp($-z$) is the *Cayley map* given by r(z) = (2 − z)/(2 + z). We can then use this function instead of the exponential function and to this end we have created a modified version of the JR and CRR methods. For example, the modified version of the latter method is:

```
PadeCRRStrategy::PadeCRRStrategy(double vol, double interest,
        double delta) : BinomialLatticeStrategy(vol, interest, delta)


{
                double R1 = (r - 0.5 * s * s) * k;
                double R2 = s * ::sqrt(k);

        //      No expensive exponentials (anymore)
        //      u = ::exp(R1 + R2);
        //      d = ::exp(R1 - R2);

                // Cayley transform
                double z1 = (R1 + R2);
                double z2 = (R1 - R2);

                u = (2.0 + z1) / (2.0 - z1);
                d = (2.0 + z2) / (2.0 - z2);

                double discounting = ::exp(- r*k);
                p = 0.5;
}
```

We have tested the new strategies using the same data as in the test cases in section 15.9 and we get similar results. This is good news but what is more reassuring is that Cayley map calculations are (much) more efficient; we estimate that the efficiency gains are somewhere in the range [9, 13] on average. We have based this estimate on the simple 'stress test' program:

```
int main()
{
        double R1 = 2.0;
        double R2 = 4.44;
        long N = 1000000000;

        for (long j = 1; j <= N; j++)
        {
                double u1 = ::exp(R1 + R2);
                double d1 = ::exp(R1 - R2);
        }
```

```
// Cayley transform
double z1 = (R1 + R2);
double z2 = (R1 - R2);

for (long i = 1; i <= N; i++)
{
        double u2 = (2.0 + z1) / (2.0 - z1);
        double d2 = (2.0 + z2) / (2.0 - z2);
}

return 0;
}
```

We can apply these techniques to more complex lattice models where the exponential function needs to be evaluated at many nodes, for examples, binomial and trinomial methods for the short rate, implied trees and other mesh-based applications.

# 16

# Implementing One-Factor Black Scholes in C++

## 16.1 INTRODUCTION AND OBJECTIVES

In this chapter we design and implement the one-factor Black Scholes equation using finite difference methods (see Duffy, 2004; Duffy, 2006 for a detailed discussion of this technique). We provide the reader with a C++ framework that he or she can use to numerically price an option as well as offering the facility to extend the framework in a non-intrusive way. For example, it is possible to extend the framework as follows:

- Define your own one-factor financial models
- Design and implement new finite-difference schemes

The current software provides support for general PDEs and for the well-known Black Scholes PDE and its accompanying data (such as strike price $K$, expiry $T$ and so on). Furthermore, we have implemented the explicit and implicit Euler schemes (first-order accurate).

The UML class model for the current problem is shown in Figure 16.1 and it is similar in structure and intent to the corresponding diagram that we discussed in Chapter 15. The major difference is the fact that we now have a problem whose functions have two input parameters instead of one parameter. This makes the problem more difficult to program at the function level (lots of 'nitty-gritty' detail) but conceptually the architecture is the same as in Chapter 15. We can even generalise the results of this chapter to n-factor derivatives problems by using the design in Figure 16.1 as a baseline.

We now discuss the details of the proposed solution.

## 16.2 SCOPE AND ASSUMPTIONS

As already stated we focus on one-factor models in this chapter. In other words, we consider initial boundary value problems for second-order parabolic differential equations in one space dimension. The general problem is described as follows:

$$Lu \equiv -\frac{\partial u}{\partial t} + \sigma(x, t)\frac{\partial^2 u}{\partial x^2} + \mu(x, t)\frac{\partial u}{\partial x} + b(x, t)u = f(x, t) \text{ in } D$$

$$u(x, 0) = \varphi(x), \quad x \in \Omega$$

$$u(A, t) = g_0(t), \quad u(B, t) = g_1(t), \quad t \in (0, T) \tag{16.1}$$

where

$$\Omega = (A, B) \text{ and } D = \Omega \times (0, T)$$

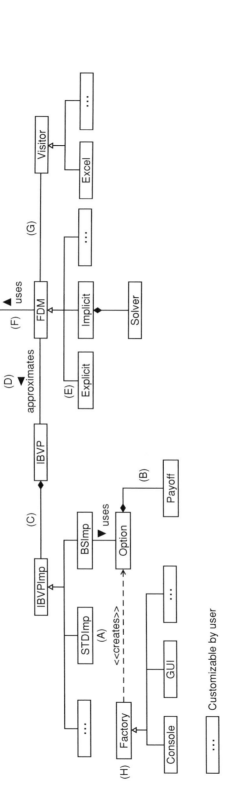

**Figure 16.1** UML class diagram of finite difference solution

We note that this problem subsumes many special cases and in particular it is able to support the original Black Scholes model as discussed in the literature (Hull, 2006; Wilmott, 1998) as well as more general problems, for example problems with non-constant coefficients and inhomogeneous right-hand term in the PDE in system (16.1).

Furthermore, we assume that the boundary conditions are of Dirichlet type, that is the value of the solution $u$ is known at the boundary points. A discussion of Neumann, Robin and the linearity/convexity boundary conditions is outside the scope of this chapter. For a detailed mathematical discussion of these issues, see Duffy (2006).

## 16.3   ASSEMBLING THE C++ BUILDING BLOCKS

Since we take a modular approach in this book, we design and implement the UML class diagram in Figure 16.1 using already developed classes and design patterns (as discussed in previous chapters):

- Template classes for vectors and matrices. These classes have built-in functionality for mathematical operations and we provide a number of libraries for more advanced mathematical computation
- The classes in Figure 16.1 deploy a number of design patterns. First, we apply the *Bridge* pattern in area C to allow us to construct multiple implementations of the class IBVP, the class that models the components of the initial boundary value problem described by system (16.1). For example, we have provided two implementations (as can be seen in areas A and B), namely a standard implementation and an implementation that is a faithful representation of the Black Scholes model. We note from area (H) that the parameters of the Black Scholes model can be generated using an *Abstract Factory* patterns. The code in this book provides specific functionality for entering data using the `iostream` library (using the overloaded operators << and >>).

The second pattern that we use is the *Template Method* pattern as can be seen in area F. Here we create an abstract class called FDM containing default data (for example, generated mesh data from `Mesher` class) as well as the basic algorithmic framework for constructing the approximate solution to the pricing problem. Specific parts of the algorithms are implemented in the derived classes in area (E). The user can add his or her own favourite finite difference schemes by the specialisation process.

Finally, we can use the *Visitor* pattern to present the output from the finite difference schemes in various media. This is shown in area G and in particular we are interested in displaying output in Excel in the form of cell data and line charts, for example. We have not implemented this pattern here, however. We leave it as a student exercise.

## 16.4   MODELLING THE BLACK SCHOLES PDE

The C++ classes in this part of the design are similar to those in Chapter 15 except that we need to model all the components in system (16.1):

- The region in which the IBVP is defined
- The coefficients of the PDE in (16.1)
- The (Dirichlet) boundary conditions
- The initial conditions

The class interface for the class IBVPImp is given by:

```
class IBVPImp
{
public:

        virtual double diffusion(double x, double t) const = 0;
        virtual double convection(double x, double t) const = 0;
        virtual double zeroterm(double x, double t) const = 0;
        virtual double RHS(double x, double t) const = 0;
        virtual double BCL(double t) const = 0;
        virtual double BCR(double t) const = 0;
        virtual double IC(double x) const = 0;
};
```

Realising that this is in fact a template (in the broadest sense of the word) for many kinds of specific problems we can implement it using a *Bridge* pattern. An important case indeed is when we wish to model the original Black Scholes equation and to this end we create a class called BSIBVPImp that actually implements the components in system (16.1). Furthermore, the well-known Black Scholes parameters are modelled in a class called Option and this has an embedded Payoff object (we already have discussed the C++ payoff hierarchy).

The structure of the class BSIBVPImp is defined as follows:

```
class BSIBVPImp : public IBVPImp
{
public:
        Option* opt;
        BSIBVPImp(Option& option) {opt = &option;}
        double diffusion(double x, double t) const
        { // simulates diffusion
        double v = (opt -> sig);
                return 0.5 * v * v * x * x;
        }
        // Define the other coefficients here
};
```

Notice that there is an embedded Option pointer whose interface is given by:

```
class Instrument
{
public: // Abstract Base class for all Derivatives

};
```

```
class Option : public Instrument
{
public: // Data public for convenience only
        double r;        // Interest rate
        double sig;      // Volatility
        double K;        // Strike price
```

```
        double T;        // Expiry date
        double b;        // Cost of carry

        Option() {}

        // An option uses a polymorphic payoff object
        OneFactorPayoff OptionPayoff;
};
```

We are now ready to describe the actual implementations of the coefficients, boundary conditions and initial conditions (payoff) for a call option. First, the coefficients are implemented as follows (N.B. x denotes the underlying!):

```
double diffusion(double x, double t) const
{ // simulates diffusion
    double v = (opt -> sig);
    return 0.5 * v * v * x * x;
}
double convection(double x, double t) const
{ // simulates drift
    return (opt -> r) * x;
}
double zeroterm(double x, double t) const
{
    return - (opt -> r);
}

double RHS(double x, double t) const
{
    return 0.0;
}
```

while the boundary conditions and initial condition corresponding to call options are given by:

```
double BCL(double t) const
{

    return 0.0;
}
double BCR(double t) const
{
    return 3.0 * K;        // Magic number
}
double IC(double x) const // Initial condition
{
    return (*opt).OptionPayoff.payoff(x);
}
```

Here is an example of code:

```
InstrumentFactory* myFactory = GetInstrumentFactory();
Option* myOption = myFactory->CreateOption();

// Derived implementation class
BSIBVPImp bs (*myOption);
bs.opt = myOption;
```

### 16.4.1  Creating your own one-factor financial models

Looking at Figure 16.1 again we see that it is possible to define new derived classes of IBVPImp, thus allowing us to incorporate a number of one-factor models into our framework. For example, initial boundary value problems for barrier options are a good candidate. In this case the boundary conditions are of Dirichlet type and the boundaries can be constant or time-dependent. We can also model rebates in this case. We have already discussed finite difference schemes for barrier option problems in Duffy (2006).

Another extension to the framework lies in the ability to define different kinds of pay-off functions by creating new payoff classes. For example, we can model symmetric and asymmetric power options by defining their respective payoff functions.

## 16.5   FINITE DIFFERENCE SCHEMES

We now discuss areas D, E and F in Figure 16.1. First, the class FDM is the base class for all finite difference schemes that we will use to model one-factor problems. It contains common data and functions that are inherited by all derived classes. In particular, it is a repository (or blackboard data structure) containing the following kinds of data:

- Mesh data (step-sizes, mesh arrays)
- Vectors and matrices to hold the calculations (they hold option prices)
- Other redundant data

The data in the base class is declared as protected because we wish to be able to access this data in derived classes. The data members of the FDM class are given by:

```
protected:
    IBVP* ibvp;            // Pointer to "parent"
    long N;                // Number of t subdivisions of interval
    double k;              // Step length; redundant data

    long J;                // The number of x subdivisions
    double h, h2;          // Step length; redundant data

    double tprev, tnow;
    long currentIndex, maxIndex;
    Mesher m;
```

```
        Vector<double, long> xarr;

        NumericMatrix<double, long> res;   // Contain the results

        // Other data
        long n;                            // Current counter
        Vector<double, long> vecOld;
        Vector<double, long> vecNew;
};
```

We have implemented the *Template Method* pattern by defining invariant and variant parts of an algorithm:

```
class IBVPFDM
{
public:
        // N.B. !!! Resulting output of size N+1 and start index 1
        NumericMatrix<double, long>& result(); // Result of calculation

        // Hook function for Template Method pattern
        virtual void calculateBC() = 0; // Tells calculate sol. at n+1
        virtual void calculate() = 0; // Tells calculate sol. at n+1
};
```

The body of the 'key' invariant algorithm is given by:

```
NumericMatrix<double, long>& IBVPFDM::result()
{ // The result of the calculation

L1:
        tnow = tprev + k;
        // Template Method pattern here
        // Variant part
        calculateBC(); // Calculate the BC at n+1

        // Variant part; pure virtual hook functions
        calculate (); // Calculate the solution at n+1
        if (currentIndex < maxIndex)
        {
            tprev = tnow;
            currentIndex++;
            // Now postprocess
            res.Row(currentIndex, vecNew);
            vecOld = vecNew;
            goto L1;
        }
        return res;
}
```

Here we see that we 'march' in time and calculate the approximate solution at each time level. The derived classes must define the 'hook' functions `calculateBC()` and `calculate()`. It will be the responsibility of each derived class to do this. To this end, we now discuss how to effect this for explicit and implicit Euler schemes.

### 16.5.1  Explicit schemes

We discuss the application of the well-known explicit Euler scheme to the initial boundary value problem (16.1). In other words, we use *Forward Differencing in Time and Centred Differencing in Space (FTCS)*. After some manipulation and arithmetic we can show how to determine the value at time level $n + 1$ in terms of the value at time level $n$:

$$u_j^{n+1} = (A_j^n u_{j-1}^n + B_j^n u_j^n + C_j^n u_{j+1}^n)/h^2 - kf_j^n$$

where

$$\begin{cases} A_j^n = (k\sigma_j^n - \dfrac{kh}{2}\mu_j^n) \\[2mm] B_j^n = (h^2 - 2k\sigma_j^n + kh^2 b_j^n) \\[2mm] C_j^n = (k\sigma_j^n + \dfrac{kh}{2}\mu_j^n) \end{cases} \qquad (16.2)$$

$$1 \le j \le J - 1, \quad n \ge 0$$

Thus, the solution can be calculated without the need to solve a matrix system at each time level. Of course, the boundary conditions must be defined:

```
void calculateBC()
{ // Tells how to calculate sol. at n+1
    vecNew[vecNew.MinIndex()] = ibvp->BCL(tprev);
    vecNew[vecNew.MaxIndex()] = ibvp->BCR(tprev);
}
```

Then, the C++ code implementing algorithm (16.2) is given by:

```
void calculate()
{ // Tells how to calculate sol. at n+1
    // Explicit Euler schemes
    for (long i = vecNew.MinIndex()+1;
        i <= vecNew.MaxIndex()-1; i++)
    {
        tmp1 = k*(ibvp->diffusion(xarr[i], tprev));
        tmp2 = (k*h*0.5 *
          (ibvp->convection(xarr[i], tprev)));

        // Coefficients of the U terms
        alpha = tmp1 - tmp2;
        beta = h2 - (2.0*tmp1) +
            (k*h2*(ibvp->zeroterm(xarr[i], tprev)));
```

```
        gamma = tmp1 + tmp2;
        vecNew[i] = ( (alpha * vecOld[i-1])
                    + (beta * vecOld[i])
                        + (gamma * vecOld[i+1]) ) / h2
                        - (k*(ibvp -> RHS(xarr[i], tprev)));

    }
}
```

An example of using the explicit scheme is:

```
BSIBVPImp bs (*myOption);
```

```
// Now the client class IBVP
IBVPImp* myImp3 = &bs;
IBVP i3(*myImp3, rangeX, rangeT);
ExplicitEulerIBVP fdm3(i3, N, J);
print(fdm3.result());
```

### 16.5.2  Implicit schemes

In this section we take the implicit Euler scheme, sometimes called the *Backward in Time Centred in Space* (*BTCS*) *scheme*. After some manipulation and arithmetic we can show how to determine the value at time level $n + 1$ in terms of the value at time level $n$:

$$A_j^{n+1} u_{j-1}^{n+1} + B_j^{n+1} u_j^{n+1} + C_{j+1}^{n+1} u_{j+1}^{n+1} = h^2(k f_j^{n+1} - u_j^n) \tag{16.3}$$

where

$$\begin{cases} A_j^{n+1} = (k\sigma_j^{n+1} - \dfrac{kh}{2}\mu_j^{n+1}) \\[2mm] B_j^{n+1} = (-h^2 - 2k\sigma_j^{n+1} + kh^2 b_j^{n+1}) \\[2mm] C_j^{n+1} = (k\sigma_j^{n+1} + \dfrac{kh}{2}\mu_j^{n+1}) \end{cases}$$

$$1 \le j \le J - 1, \quad n \ge 0$$

The problem now is that we have three unknown values on the left-hand side of equation (16.3). In order to solve this problem we can employ a number of matrix techniques, for example LU decomposition (Duffy, 2004; Keller, 1992). To this end we write system (16.3) in the vector form:

$$A^{n+1} \underline{U}^{n+1} = \underline{r}^{n+1} \tag{16.4}$$

where

$$\underline{U} = {}^t(u_1, \ldots, u_{J-1})$$

$$\underline{r} = {}^t(r_1, \ldots, r_{J-1})$$

$$A = \begin{pmatrix} B_1 & C_1 & & & \\ A_2 & \ddots & & \ddots & 0 \\ 0 & \ddots & & \ddots & C_{J-2} \\ & & A_{J-1} & B_{j-1} \end{pmatrix}$$

$$r_1^{n+1} = h^2(kf_1^{n+1} - u_1^n) - A_1^{n+1}u_0^{n+1}$$

$$r_j^{n+1} = h^2(kf_j^{n+1} - u_j^n), \quad 2 \le j \le J - 2$$

$$r_{J-1}^{n+1} = h^2(kf_{J-1}^{n+1} - u_{J-1}^n) - C_{J-1}^{n+1}u_J^{n+1}$$

We can solve system (16.4) using the implementation for the LU solver code on the accompanying CD. The complete code for the current derived class is given by:

```
void calculateBC()
{ // Tells how to calculate sol. at n+1
     vecNew[vecNew.MinIndex()] = ibvp->BCL(tnow);
     vecNew[vecNew.MaxIndex()] = ibvp->BCR(tnow);
}


void calculate()
{ // Tells how to calculate sol. at n+1
     // In general we need to solve a tridiagonal system
     double tmp1, tmp2;

     for (long i = 1; i <= J-1; i++)
     {
          tmp1 = (k*ibvp->diffusion(xarr[i],tnow ));
          tmp2 = (0.5 * k * h*
            (ibvp->convection(xarr[i], tnow)));

          // Coefficients of the U terms
          A[i] = tmp1 - tmp2;
          B[i] = -h2 - (2.0*tmp1) +
            (k*h2*(ibvp->zeroterm(xarr[i],tnow)));
          C[i] = tmp1 + tmp2;

          F[i] = h2*(k *
            (ibvp -> RHS(xarr[i], tnow)) - vecOld[i+1]);
     }

     // Correction term for RHS
     F[1]   -= A[1] * vecNew[vecNew.MinIndex()];
     F[J-1] -= C[J-1] * vecNew[vecNew.MaxIndex()] ;

     // Now solve the system of equations
     LUTridiagonalSolver<double, long> mySolver(A, B, C, F);
```

```
Vector <double, long> solution = mySolver.solve();

for (long ii = vecNew.MinIndex()+1;
        ii <= vecNew.MaxIndex()-1; ii++)
{
    vecNew[ii] = solution[ii-1];
}
}
```

### 16.5.3   A note on exception handling

In the case of the implicit Euler method (see system (16.4)) it is important that the solution can be found at each time level. In general, we demand that system (16.4) has a unique solution. A sufficient condition is that the matrix A be *positive definite*. But how does this requirement translate to C++ code? In this case we call the `assert` macro (defined in `<assert.h>`). If the matrix is not diagonally dominant the program will stop executing:

```
// Now solve the system of equations
LUTridiagonalSolver<double, long> mySolver(A, B, C, F);

// The matrix must be diagonally dominant; we call the
// assert macro and the programs stops
assert (mySolver.diagonallyDominant() == true);

Vector <double, long> solution = mySolver.solve();
```

A more elegant solution is to us the exception handling mechanism in C++.

### 16.5.4   Other schemes

In this chapter we have discussed two schemes to approximate the solution of system (16.1). As can be seen from Figure 16.1 we can devise other schemes by creating derived classes from FDM and implementing the appropriate pure virtual 'hook' functions. For example, the following schemes can be programmed:

- Crank-Nicolson scheme (this is gotten by taking the average of the explicit and implicit schemes in equations (16.2) and (16.3))
- Richardson extrapolation: we apply the scheme (16.3) on two meshes of sizes $k$ and $k/2$. Then we use the second-order approximation:

$$W_j^n = 2V_{2j}^{2n} - U_j^n, \quad 1 \le j \le J - 1 \tag{16.5}$$

where $U$ and $V$ are the values corresponding to the finite difference schemes on mesh sizes $k$ and $k/2$, respectively.
- Special schemes, for example schemes for problems with low volatility and/or large convection terms (Duffy, 1980; Duffy, 2004; Duffy, 2006).

We discuss these schemes as exercises at the end of this chapter.

## 16.6   TEST CASES AND PRESENTATION IN EXCEL

The classes in this framework allow us to calculate the price of an option for arrays of stock prices and at a discrete set of time levels up to and including the expiry date $T$. In this chapter we have assembled these values in a NumericMatrix object. We can then present this matrix in Excel using the ExcelDriver class.

### 16.6.1   Creating the user interface dialogue

In the special case of the initial boundary value problem that models the one-factor Black Scholes problem we have employed an *Abstract Factory pattern* to realise the input of the specific parameters (such as the strike price $K$, expiry date $T$ and so on). The main program does not have to worry about the details of how data is created but instead it delegates to a factory object that takes care of such details.

We now discuss how we have implemented the Abstract Factory pattern in the current context and how it is used in the client program. In this chapter we concentrate on inputting data using the iostream library. In fact, you can define your own factory classes (for example, in MFC or Microsoft SDK) to allow you to input data in other ways as well.

The top-level interface for the factory is given by:

```
class InstrumentFactory
{
public:

    virtual Option* CreateOption() const = 0;

};
```

At this moment we have defined an interface for one kind of financial instrument, namely an option. This interface can easily be extended to support other instrument types. The console implementation is given by:

```
class ConsoleInstrumentFactory : public InstrumentFactory
{
public:
    Option* CreateOption() const
    {
        double dr; // Interest rate
        double dsig; // Volatility
        double dK; // Strike price
        double dT; // Expiry date
        double db; // Cost of carry
        cout << "Interest rate: ";
        cin >> dr;
        cout << "Volatility: ";
        cin >> dsig;
        cout << "Strike Price: ";
```

```
    cin >> dK;
    cout << "Expiry: ";
    cin >> dT;
    cout << "Cost of carry: ";
    cin >> db;

    Option* result = new Option;

    cout << "Payoff 1) Call, 2) Put: ";
    int ans;
    cin >> ans;
    if (ans == 1)
    {
        (*result).OptionPayoff
            = OneFactorPayoff(dK, MyCallPayoffFN);
    }
    else
    {
        (*result).OptionPayoff
            OneFactorPayoff(dK, MyPutPayoffFN);
    }

    result->r = dr;
    result->sig = dsig;
    result->K = dK;
    result->T = dT;
    result->b = db;

    cout << "ACK: Press ANY key to continue: ";
    cin >> ans;

    return result;
    }
};
```

Using factory objects is much the same as using 'normal' objects in C++. In general, we prefer to hide the choice of factory in a function:

```
InstrumentFactory* GetInstrumentFactory()
{

    // Only 1 factory in this version, like model T
    return new ConsoleInstrumentFactory;
}
```

Then client code has a pointer to an abstract factory at run-time. To this end, here is an example of use:

```
InstrumentFactory* myFactory = GetInstrumentFactory();
Option* myOption = myFactory->CreateOption();

// Derived implementation class
BSIBVPImp bs (*myOption);
bs.opt = myOption;
```

### 16.6.2   Vector and matrix output

In general, the output from finite difference schemes is some kind of data structure that contains the option price for certain values of the underlying and at certain points in time. We may also be interested in calculating option delta and gamma, in which case we can take divided differences of the option price.

In the current framework we use two `Vector` instances and one `NumericMatrix` instance. The vectors hold the values at the time levels $n$ (previous) and $n + 1$ (current) while the matrix holds the values at all time levels up to $N$ (where $Nk = T$) and all points in $S$ space, including the boundaries. Having calculated the desired values we are then free to decide how we are to display them.

### 16.6.3   Presentation

There are various output display devices to which we can send our calculated values. In this chapter we are interested in displaying vectors and matrices in the following ways:

- To the console (useful for quick debugging)
- In Excel (for extended and sophisticated presentation)

The first option is easy to apply. It displays the results on the console. We have two generic functions for such presentation:

```
template <class V, class I>
    void print(const Array<V,I>& array);

template <class V, class I>
    void print(const Matrix<V,I>& array);
```

The second set of functions presents vectors and matrices in Excel. The main functions are:

- Displaying a vector in Excel
- Displaying a list of vectors in Excel
- Displaying a matrix in Excel

An example of using these functions in Excel is given by:

```
ImplicitIBVP fdm2(i2, N, J);
Mesher m(rangeX, rangeT);
Vector<double, long> XARR = m.xarr(6);
Vector<double, long> vec = fdm.result()[2];
printOneExcel(XARR, vec, string("explicit"));
Vector<double, long> vec2 = fdm2.result()[2];
printOneExcel(XARR, vec2, string("implicit"));
```

## 16.7   SUMMARY

We have shown how to apply design patterns to the creation of a customisable framework in C++ for the one-factor Black Scholes PDE. It is possible to define your own PDE model and it is possible to apply special-purpose finite difference schemes by the specialisation process. The framework represents a stable software environment in which you can develop and test option models.

## 16.8   EXERCISES AND PROJECTS

1. (Improving performance) For the implicit Euler scheme we used the algorithm for LU decomposition to solve a system of equations at each time level. In particular, the arrays in equation (16.4) are copied into the member data of the class LUTridiagonalSolver. Performance can be improved by using pointers instead, as the following code suggests:

```
// Defining arrays (input)
Vector<V,I> * a;    // The lower-diagonal array [1..J]
Vector<V,I> * b;    // The diagonal array [1..J] "baseline array"
Vector<V,I> * c;    // The upper-diagonal array [1..J]
Vector<V,I> * r;    // Right-hand side of equation Au = r [1..J]
```

Client code should still keep functioning but there will be an improvement in performance.

2. (LU Decomposition and Complex Numbers) In some cases and applications we are interested in solving linear systems of equations where the coefficients are complex-valued. We take the example of the time-dependent linear Schrödinger equation in one dimension (Pauling and Bright Wilson, 1963; Press *et al.*, 2002):

$$i\frac{\partial \psi}{\partial t} = -\frac{\partial^2 \psi}{\partial x^2} + V(x)\psi, \quad -\infty < x < \infty \tag{16.6}$$

where

$$\psi = \text{Schrödinger wave function}$$
$$V(x) = \text{one-dimension potential}$$
$$i = \sqrt{-1}$$

This equation describes the scattering of a one-dimensional wave packet by the potential $V(x)$. We have assumed for convenience that Planck's constant $\hbar = 1$ in this example. We rewrite equation (16.6) in the equivalent form:

$$i\frac{\partial \psi}{\partial t} = H\psi \tag{16.7}$$

where

$$H = -\frac{\partial^2}{\partial x^2} + V(x)$$

The operator $H$ is called the *Hamiltonian operator* and it determines the time variation of the system. We are now interested in approximating equation (16.7) using finite difference schemes. To this end, the explicit Euler FTCS scheme is given by:

$$i\frac{\psi^{n+1} - \psi^n}{k} = H\psi^n \tag{16.8}$$

or

$$\psi^{n+1} = (1 - iHk)\psi^n$$

while the implicit Euler BTCS scheme is given by:

$$i\frac{\psi^{n+1} - \psi^n}{k} = H\psi^{n+1} \tag{16.9}$$

or

$$(i - Hk)\psi^{n+1} = i\psi^n$$

or

$$(1 + iHk)\psi^{n+1} = \psi^n$$

Scheme (16.8) is unstable while (16.9) is stable. However, neither scheme is *unitary* in the sense of the original problem, that is, the total probability of finding the particle somewhere is 1:

$$\int_{-\infty}^{\infty} |\psi(x)|^2 dx = 1 \tag{16.10}$$

A remedy for this is to use the so-called *Cayley form* (this is in fact the Crank Nicolson scheme):

$$i\frac{\psi^{n+1} - \psi^n}{k} = \frac{H}{2}(\psi^{n+1} + \psi^n) \tag{16.11}$$

or

$$\left(1 + \frac{i}{2}Hk\right)\psi^{n+1} = \left(1 - \frac{i}{2}Hk\right)\psi^n$$

This scheme is unitary; you can check this by a bit of complex arithmetic. Finally, we must discretise the operator $H$ in the $x$ direction by using a centred scheme, for example. We then get a fully discrete scheme and it can be cast in a form as in system (16.4) except the coefficients are complex-valued.

We have provided a test program to show how the template classes can be used. The objective in this exercise is to show how to program the fully-discrete version of (16.11) using the finite difference method. Here is a simple example of how to use the code in this book. For illustrative purposes we solve a 2 × 2 complex system:

```
J = 2;
Vector<Complex, long> A(J,1,Complex(1.0, 0.0));
Vector<Complex, long> B(J,1,Complex(0.0, 1.0));
Vector<Complex, long> C(J,1,Complex(1.0, 0.0));
Vector<Complex, long> R(J,1,Complex(0.0, 0.0));
R[1] = Complex(0.0, 2.0);
LUTridiagonalSolver<Complex, long> mySolver2(A, B, C, R);
```

```
Vector<Complex, long> result2 = mySolver2.solve();
print(result2);
```

Now you can see the classes that you need to use.

3. (Barrier options) The finite difference schemes in this chapter are suitable for modelling one-factor barrier option problems with continuous monitoring. We can support both single and double barrier problems because Dirichlet boundary conditions are applicable in these cases. Constant, time-dependent and exponential barriers can easily be modelled as well as the ability to include rebates functions into the boundary conditions. We have found that the implicit Euler scheme gives good results, especially near the barrier. Test the code with some examples of barrier options.

   In many cases the boundary conditions may be discontinuous at a finite number of points in S space. For example, rebates are sometimes defined as *step-functions* for given ranges of S and in these cases it may be necessary to average-out or smooth these discontinuous functions in order to avoid inaccuracies in the approximate solution.

   Which classes in the framework would you need to modify if you wish to model barrier options with discrete monitoring? Recall that we must determine the jump conditions at the monitoring dates. An algorithmic approach to approximating this problem is given in Duffy (2006). The major addition to the code is that the marching process in time must be modified.

4. (American options) The code in this chapter is for European options only but the code can easily be extended to American put (and call) options. In this case we must ensure that the constraint for a put option price $P$ satisfies:

$$P(S, t) \geq \max(K - S, 0) \tag{16.12}$$

where $K$ is the strike price and S is the price of the underlying. We wish to satisfy the same constraints in the difference schemes, for example. One possible solution is to check the constraint at time level $n + 1$:

$$u_j^{n+1} = \max(u_j^{n+1}, \max(K - S_j, 0)) \tag{16.13}$$

Where would you incorporate this feature into the framework while at the same time not 'disturbing' the current functionality for European options?

5. (Second-order Accuracy) The implicit Euler BTCS scheme (16.3) is first-order accurate in time. It is possible to achieve second-order accuracy by two applications of BTCS on meshes of size k and k/2. We have coded this in the case of a scalar initial value problem (see Code or CD):

```
void calculate()
{
    // Extrapolated implicit Euler; create two solutions on k/2
    // and k called v(k/2) and v(k), respectively.  Then form
    // the new array 2*v(k/2) - v(k).  Code can be optimised (later)

    // Refined mesh and solution
    Vector<double, long> res2 (2*N + 1, 1);
```

```
double k2 = k * 0.5;
res2[res2.MinIndex()] = (ivp -> startValue());
for (long i = res2.MinIndex() + 1;
     i <= res2.MaxIndex(); i++)
{
    res2[i] = ( res2[i-1] + (k2 * ivp->f(i*k2)) ) /
        ( 1.0 + (k2 * ivp->a(i*k2)) );
}
// Rougher mesh
Vector<double, long> res1 (N + 1, 1);
res1[res1.MinIndex()] = (ivp -> startValue());
for (long ii = res1.MinIndex() + 1;
     ii <= res1.MaxIndex(); ii++)
{
    res1[ii] = ( res1[ii-1] + (k* ivp->f(ii*k)) ) /
        ( 1.0 + (k* ivp->a(ii*k)) );
}

// Extrapolated solution
for (long iii = res1.MinIndex() + 1;
     iii <= res1.MaxIndex(); iii++)
{
    res[iii] = (2.0 * res2[(2*iii)]) - res1[iii];
}
}
```

The objective of this exercise is to generalise this code to the current initial boundary value problem. Create the code for this problem and integrate it into the framework. Test your work by modelling a Black Scholes benchmark example whose solution you know.

6. (Approximating the Greeks) The C++ code in this chapter produces a matrix of values; the rows represent time levels while the columns are discrete values of the underlying. Knowing this fact, we can use divided differences to find approximate values for the delta, gamma and theta of the option price. Implement the code for this problem and integrate it in the framework. What data structure do you intend to use?

7. (*Linear Interpolation*) You may wish to calculate the option price at some point between two given mesh points. You should first determine in which sub-interval of the mesh that this point falls and then use linear interpolation to calculate the option price. Finally, if you decide to use *cubic spline interpolation*, you can use the *LU* solver (Dahlquist and Björck, 1974).

# 17

# Two-Factor Option Pricing: Basket and Other Multi-Asset Options

## 17.1 INTRODUCTION AND OBJECTIVES

In this chapter we apply the finite difference method to the class of so-called *correlation options* (Zhang, 1998). These are options involving two or more underlying assets and these assets can have a positive or negative correlation. In order to reduce the focus and to keep the discussion tractable we discuss basket options. A basket option consists of a number of assets, each one having a certain weight factor in the 'basket'.

We define a basket option model as an initial boundary value problem for the two-factor Black Scholes and we subsequently approximate the solution by an explicit finite difference scheme (the theory of such schemes is discussed in Duffy (2006) as well as their applications to Quantitative Finance). Finally, we implement the scheme in C++ and the solution applies a number of design patterns in order to promote reusability and flexibility.

The results in this chapter could be extended and generalised to other finite difference schemes, for example Splitting methods, ADI and Finite Elements. We refer the interested reader to Duffy (2006) and Topper (2005) for more information. We discuss one specific scheme in this chapter.

## 17.2 MOTIVATION AND BACKGROUND

In general we model correlation options on multiple underlyings by a partial differential equation:

$$\frac{\partial u}{\partial t} + Lu = 0 \tag{17.1}$$

where

$$Lu \equiv \frac{1}{2} \sum_{i,j=1}^{n} \sigma_i \sigma_j \rho_{ij} S_i S_j \frac{\partial^2 u}{\partial S_i \partial S_j} + r \sum_{i=1}^{n} S_i \frac{\partial u}{\partial S_i} - ru$$

in which   $\rho_{ij}$ = asset correlations
         $r$ = risk-free interest rate
         $\sigma_j$ = volatility of asset $j$.

This is a second-order parabolic differential equation of the convection-diffusion type; the diffusion terms correspond to the volatility while the convection terms correspond to drift. In order to define a unique solution we need to define some auxiliary conditions. First, we define an initial condition (the *payoff function*) that gives the solution of equation (17.1) at t = 0. Furthermore, we need to give boundary conditions on the boundaries of the domain in which equation (17.1) is defined. We will discuss this issue in the next section when we discuss two-factor (put) basket options. A full treatment in the general case is outside the scope of this chapter and a discussion is given in the author's book on PDE and FDM for Quantitative Finance (Duffy, 2006).

In the context of multi-asset options the PDE (17.1) does not change but the difference lies in the payoff condition (and possibly the boundary conditions). In particular, the payoff determines the specific kinds of option. Some types are:

- Exchange options
- Rainbow options
- Basket options
- Best/worst options
- Quotient options
- Foreign exchange options
- Spread options
- Dual-strike options
- Out-performance options

Even though many of these option problems have analytical solutions (as discussed in Zhang, 1998) we wish to approximate them using the finite difference method. This is discussed in detail in Duffy (2006) where the focus is on the maths while in this chapter we discuss the same problem from the C++ viewpoint. To this end, we provide C++ code in the form of a class hierarchy for all the above payoff types. The base class has one pure virtual member function that is an interface specification for calculating the payoff function:

```cpp
class MultiAssetPayoffStrategy
{
public:
    virtual double payoff(double S1, double S2) const = 0;
};
```

Specific option types are modelled as derived classes of this class. The code for a quanto option, for example is given by:

```cpp
class QuantoStrategy : public MultiAssetPayoffStrategy
{
private:
        double Kf; // Strike in foreign currency
        double fer; // Fixed exchange rate
        double w; // +1 call, -1 put
public:    // All code is inline
        QuantoStrategy(double foreignStrike, double cp,
                                        double forExchangRate)
        {
            Kf = foreignStrike; w = cp;
            fer = forExchangRate;
        }

        double payoff(double S1, double S2) const
        {
            return fer * DMax ( w * S1 - w*Kf, 0.0);
        }
};
```

while the code for a basket option is given by:

```
class BasketStrategy : public MultiAssetPayoffStrategy
{ // 2-asset basket option payoff

private:
        double K;              // Strike
        double w;              // +1 call, -1 put
        double w1, w2;         // w1 + w2 = 1
public:
        // All classes need default constructor
        BasketStrategy()
        {
            K = 95.0; w = +1; w1 = 0.5; w2 = 0.5;
        }
        BasketStrategy(double strike, double cp, double weight1,
                                                double weight2)
        {
            K = strike; w = cp; w1 = weight1; w2 = weight2;
        }
        double payoff(double S1, double S2) const
        {
            double sum = w1*S1 + w2*S2;
            return DMax(w* (sum - K), 0.0); // Use a max function
        }
};
```

We shall use this class (in the next section) as a data member of a class that models the data in a basket option. For the C++ code for the other option types please see the CD.

A final remark: the code for these classes is default inline, as can also be seen from the two examples just given. In a production environment, we would suggest creating separate header and code files.

## 17.3   SCOPING THE PROBLEM: PDEs FOR BASKET OPTIONS

Most of the two-factor option models result in the same PDE. It is possible to set up a general framework but we decide to focus on some specific problem in order to keep the material understandable. In particular, we examine a two-factor basket put option on a rectangle. The PDE is given by equation (17.1) and the payoff function has already been given in section 17.2. As far as boundary conditions are concerned the PDE (17.1) degenerates to one-factor PDEs on the lower boundaries and in this case we need to solve these PDEs either exactly or numerically. We choose for the former option because there is an exact solution for the one-factor Black Scholes equation (see Haug, 1998) and we provide the corresponding C++ source code on the CD. As far as boundary conditions are concerned, we define the value of the put to be zero at the far-field boundary.

We now specify the mathematical model for the two-factor basket put option problem. The PDE is given by:

$$\frac{1}{2}\sigma_1^2 S_1^2 \frac{\partial^2 f}{\partial S_1^2} + \frac{1}{2}\sigma_2^2 S_2^2 \frac{\partial^2 f}{\partial S_2^2} + \rho\sigma_1\sigma_2 S_1 S_2 \frac{\partial^2 f}{\partial S_1 \partial S_2}$$

$$+ (r - q_1)S_1 \frac{\partial f}{\partial S_1} + (r - q_2)S_2 \frac{\partial f}{\partial S_2} = rf - \frac{\partial f}{\partial t} \qquad (17.2)$$

where $f$ is the option variable and D is the two-dimensional region $(0,100) \times (0,100)$ (this is the same as the test problem in Topper 2005). The payoff function is given by:

$$f(S_1, S_2, T) = \max[0, K - (w_1 S_1 + w_2 S_2)] \text{ in } D \qquad (17.3)$$

while the boundary conditions at $S_1 = 0$ and $S_2 = 0$ are:

$$f(S_1, 0, t) = g\left(S_1, \frac{K}{w_2}, t\right) \qquad (17.4)$$

and

$$f(0, S_2, t) = g\left(S_2, \frac{K}{w_1}, t\right) \qquad (17.5)$$

respectively. Finally, the far-field boundary conditions correspond to a zero value, namely:

$$f(100, S_2, t) = 0 \quad \text{and} \quad f(S_1, 100, t) = 0 \qquad (17.6)$$

The equations (17.2) to (17.6) constitute an unambiguous specification of the problem that we wish to solve using the finite difference method and its subsequent realisation in C++.

## 17.4   MODELLING BASKET OPTION PDE IN UML AND C++

We now discuss how to model problems (17.2) to (17.6) using object-oriented techniques and C++. We take a pragmatic approach and we do not attempt to design the most generic model for solving the current problem but we take the 'middle road' in the sense that some parts of the program will use design patterns while other parts will use hard-coded procedural and modular code. To this end, we map the system (17.2) to (17.6) to an object model that we subsequently document in UML. First of all, we model the data in the system using C++ classes and we provide factory classes (using the Abstract Factory pattern) that create instances of these classes. See Figure 17.1. This is the visual representation of the C++ code and we use such diagrams when we wish to discuss a design problem without getting bogged down in detail. Of course, we can 'zoom' in to specific areas in the diagram by examining the corresponding C++ code and this is what we now do.

### 17.4.1   Data classes for instruments

The base class for all instruments is empty at the moment but it may receive functionality in a later version:

```
class TwoFactorInstrument
{
public:
};
```

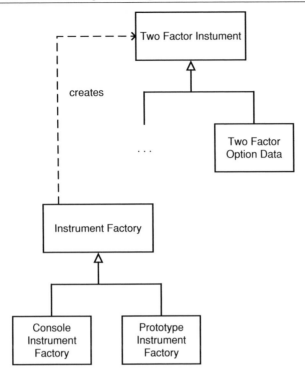

**Figure 17.1**  Data and factories

The derived class that we are interested in is in fact an encapsulation of the data that we need in order to define a basket option:

```
class TwoFactorOptionData : public TwoFactorInstrument
{
//private:
public: // For convenience only
        // An option uses a polymorphic payoff object
        BasketStrategy pay;
public:
        // PUBLIC, PURE FOR PEDAGOGICAL REASONS, 13 parameters
        double r;                        // Interest rate
        double D1, D2;                   // Dividends
        double sig1, sig2;               // Volatility
        double rho;                      // Cross correlation
        double K;                        // Strike price, now place in IC
        double T;                        // Expiry date
        double SMax1, SMax2;             // Far field condition
        double w1, w2;
        int type;                        // Call +1 or put -1
```

```
TwoFactorOptionData()
{
        // Initialise all data and the payoff

        // Use Topper's data as the default, Table 7.1

        r = 0.01;
        D1 = D2 = 0.0;
        sig1 = 0.1; sig2 = 0.2;
        rho = 0.5;

        K = 40.0;
        T = 0.5;

        w1 = 1.0;
        w2 = 20.0;

        type = -1;

        // Now create the payoff Strategy object

        pay = BasketStrategy(K, type, w1, w2);

        // In general 1) we need a Factory object as we have
        // done in the one-dimensional case and 2) work with
        // pointers to base classes
}

double payoff(double x, double y) const
{
        return pay.payoff(x, y);
}

};
```

Please note that the member data are public for convenience only. In real applications we would use private member data or property sets. Furthermore, this class has an embedded payoff function this is specific to basket options.

Having defined the data class, we would like to create instances of it. At the moment we have two factories as can be seen in Figure 17.1:

- *Console Factory*: creates the data by allowing the user to interactively enter values for the appropriate member data
- *Prototype Factory*: creates default data; client software can then use a 'prototypical' object without having to enter the data each time. This option is useful when testing Proof-of-Concept (POC) examples where the emphasis is on getting the code up and running

The base class for all factories is:

```
class InstrumentFactory
{
public:
      virtual TwoFactorOptionData* CreateOption() const = 0;
};
```

The factory class (some code has been removed) for console input is:

```
class ConsoleInstrumentFactory : public InstrumentFactory
{
public:

        TwoFactorOptionData* CreateOption() const
        {

            double dr;          // Interest rate
            double dsig1, dsig2;    // Volatility
            double div1, div2;      // Dividends
            double drho;
            double dK;          // Strike price
            double dT;          // Expiry date
            double dSMax1, dSMax2; // Far field boundary

            double dw1, dw2; // Weights of each asset
            int dtype;          // C +1, P -1
L1:
            cout << "Type Call +1, Put -1: ";
            cin >> dtype;
            dtype = -1;         // !!! for the moment

            cout << "Interest rate: ";
            cin >> dr;

            cout << "Strike: ";
            cin >> dK;

            cout << "Volatility 1: ";
            cin >> dsig1;

            cout << "Volatility 2: ";
            cin >> dsig2;

            cout << "Dividend 1: ";
            cin >> div1;

            cout << "Dividend 2: ";
            cin >> div2;
```

```
cout << "Correlation: ";
cin >> drho;

cout << "First Far Field: ";
cin >> dSMax1;
cout << "Second Far Field: ";
cin >> dSMax2;

cout << "weight 1: ";
cin >> dw1;

cout << "Weight 2: ";
cin >> dw2;

cout << "Expiry: ";
cin >> dT;

cout << "Is this correct, carry on?";
char c; cin >> c;
if (c != "y" && c != "Y")
{
     goto L1;
}

TwoFactorOptionData* result = new TwoFactorOptionData;

result->r        = dr;
result->sig1     = dsig1;
result->sig2     = dsig2;
result->rho      = drho;

result->D1       = div1;
result->D2       = div2;

result->K        = dK;
result->T        = dT;
result->SMax1    = dSMax1;
result->SMax2    = dSMax2;

result->type     = dtype;

result->w1       = dw1;
result->w2       = dw2;

// Now assign the payoff function
result->pay = BasketStrategy(dK, dtype, dw1, dw2);

return result;

}
};
```

The factory class for the creation of prototypical data is:

```
class PrototypeInstrumentFactory : public InstrumentFactory
{ // Returns a prototype object

public:

        TwoFactorOptionData* CreateOption() const
        {
                TwoFactorOptionData* result = new TwoFactorOptionData;

                // Results take from Topper 2005
                result->r       = 0.1;
                result->sig1    = 0.1;
                result->sig2    = 0.3;
                result->rho     = 0.5;

                result->D1      = 0.0;
                result->D2      = 0.0;

                result->K       = 40.0;
                result->T       = 0.5;
                result->SMax1   = result->K * 2.0;
                result->SMax2   = result->K * 2.0;

                result->type    = -1; // Put, temp

                result->w1      = 1.0; // Topper
                result->w2      = 1.0;

                // Now assign the payoff function
                result->pay = BasketStrategy(result->K, result->type,
                                    result->w1, result->w2);

                return result;
        }
};
```

In applications, we prefer to choose the desired factory object by encapsulating all decisions
in a function, usually dissociated from the main application logic:

```
InstrumentFactory* GetInstrumentFactory()
{
        int choice = 1;
        cout << "Factories: 1) Console 2) Prototype ";
        cin >> choice;

        if (choice == 1)
```

```
        {
                return new ConsoleInstrumentFactory;
        }
        else
        {
                return new PrototypeInstrumentFactory;
        }
}
```

This implies that our application code is unaware of how the data was created. This improves software portability and it makes the code easier to read. It also improves reusability because these factory classes can be used in other applications, and not just the current one.

It is possible to create other factory classes that allow us to input data using dialog boxes (GUIs), disk files and real-time data feeds, for example.

### 17.4.2 Modelling the PDE with C++ classes

The second attention point is to model the PDE itself as a C++ class. What do we need to model?

- The functions that constitute the PDE (17.1) (including mixed derivative terms)
- The functions that represent the boundary conditions
- The payoff function

In this version, we are assuming that Dirichlet (absorbing) boundary conditions are being used (and thus, we do not support Neumann or convexity boundary conditions in this version) and at the near fields we assume that the two-factor PDE is satisfied and hence degenerates into a one-factor PDE.

The UML class diagram for the formulation for the initial boundary value problem is given in Figure 17.2. We define an abstract base class 'IBVP' that defines the interface specifications for general two-factor PDE systems. In our case we model basket options and this implies that we must implement these abstract member functions using the basket option data. Furthermore, this class uses the services of a class 'BasicOption' that gives the exact solution of the one-factor Black Scholes equation for the appropriate parameters such as the strike price, time to expiry and so on. We paraphrase Figure 17.2 as follows:

*We model a two-factor basket option class as a specialisation of an abstract initial boundary value problem. Each basket option is composed of an object containing the relevant option data and two instances of a one-factor Black Scholes class. One instance plays the role of the one-factor Black Scholes equation in the first underlying while the second instance plays the role of the one-factor Black Scholes equation in the second underlying.*

We now discuss the actual C++ code corresponding to Figure 17.2. The specification for the abstract class IBVP consists mainly of pure virtual member functions:

```
class IBVP
{
private:
        Range<double> xaxis;           // Space x = S1 interval
        Range<double> yaxis;           // Space y = S2 interval
        Range<double> taxis;           // Time interval
```

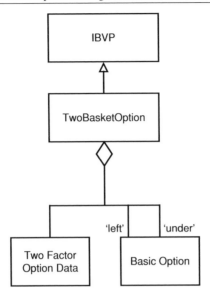

**Figure 17.2**  Structure of basket option problem

```
        // NOT: IBVPImp* imp;              // Bridge implementation
        // In this implementation we use inheritance

public:

        IBVP();
        IBVP (const Range<double>& xrange, const Range<double>& yrange,
                                        const Range<double>& trange);
        // Selector functions
        // Coefficients of parabolic second order operator
        virtual double diffusion1(double x,double y, double t) const = 0;
        virtual double diffusion2(double x,double y, double t) const = 0;
        virtual double convection1(double x,double y,double t) const = 0;
        virtual double convection2(double x,double y,double t) const = 0;
        virtual double crossTerm(double x, double y, double t) const = 0;
        virtual double zeroTerm(double x, double y, double t) const = 0;
        virtual double RHS(double x, double y, double t) const = 0;

        // Boundary and initial conditions
        virtual double BCLeft(double y, double t) = 0;
        virtual double BCRight(double y, double t) = 0;

        virtual double BCUnder(double y, double t) = 0;
        virtual double BCUpper(double y, double t) = 0;
        virtual double IC(double x, double y) const = 0;

        // The domain in which the PDE is "played"
        Range<double>& xrange();
        Range<double>& yrange();
```

```
        Range<double>& trange();
};
```

The class `TwoBasketOption` implements these functions using a combination of analytic functions and option data. The structure of the class mirrors the Composition relationship in Figure 17.2 and is given by:

```
class TwoBasketOption: public IBVP
{
//private:
public:        // For convenience
                TwoFactorOptionData opt; // Nasty parameters hidden in here

                // Two instances on Lower and Down boundaries
                BasicOption leftOption;
                BasicOption downOption;
};
```

Each member function is implemented in this class and the function bodies are direct mappings of the coefficients in the system (17.2) to (17.6), for example:

```
// Coefficients of parabolic second order operator
inline double TwoBasketOption::diffusion1(double S1, double S2,
                                                double t) const
{
        double s = opt.sig1;
        return 0.5 * s * s * S1 * S1;

} // Coefficient of second derivative

inline double TwoBasketOption::diffusion2(double S1, double S2,
                                                double t) const
{

        double s = opt.sig2;
        return 0.5 * s * s * S1 * S2;

} // Coefficient of second derivative

inline double TwoBasketOption::convection1(double S1, double S2,
                                double t) const
{

                return ((opt.r) - (opt.D1)) * S1;
} // Coefficient of first derivative
```

```
inline double TwoBasketOption::convection2(double S1, double S2,
                            double t) const
{

        return ((opt.r) - (opt.D2)) * S2;

}      // Coefficient of first derivative

inline double TwoBasketOption::crossTerm(double S1, double S2,
                            double t) const
{

            return (opt.rho) * (opt.sig1) * (opt.sig2) * S1 * S2;

}      // Mixed derivative term

inline double TwoBasketOption::zeroTerm(double S1, double S2,
                            double t) const
{

        return - (opt.r);

} // Coefficient of zero derivative

inline double TwoBasketOption::RHS(double S1, double S2, double t)
                                    const
{

            return 0.0;
}      // Inhomogeneous forcing term

// Boundary and initial conditions
inline double TwoBasketOption::BCLeft(double S2, double t)
{    // Left hand boundary condition

    // Solution of put Euro g(S2, K/w1, t). This code is on the CD
    // leftOption.T = t;
    leftOption.T = opt.T - t;

    return leftOption.Price(S2);
}

inline double TwoBasketOption::BCRight(double S2, double t)
{      // Right hand boundary condition

    return 0.0; // Put
```

```
    // For a call it will be different
}


inline double TwoBasketOption::BCUnder(double S1, double t)
{ // Lower S2 = 0 boundary condition

    // Solution of put Euro g(S1, K/w2, t)

    //      downOption.T = t;
            downOption.T = opt.T - t;
            return downOption.Price(S1);
}
```

A very important remark here is that the PDE and the exact formula for the one-factor Black Scholes equation use different times scales (one uses t and the other uses $T - t$).

```
inline double TwoBasketOption::BCUpper(double S2, double t)
{ // Upper hand boundary condition

        return 0.0; // Put

        // For a call it will be different
}


inline double TwoBasketOption::IC(double S1, double S2) const
{      // Initial condition

        // Severe information hiding and that's good

        return opt.payoff(S1, S2);
}
```

We now give an example of creating an instance of a basket option class. We first create its data using a factory:

```
TwoFactorOptionData* getOption()
{
        // Choose which factory you want and initialise the data
        InstrumentFactory* myFactory = GetInstrumentFactory();
        TwoFactorOptionData* myOptionData = myFactory ->CreateOption();

        return myOptionData;
}
```

Then we create the basket option by including this data in it and giving the region in which the PDE is defined:

```
// Steps
      // 1. Create option data (via Factory)
      // 2. Create the basket option == IBVP + Data

      TwoFactorOptionData* optData = getOption();

      // Create mesh points in x and y directions (Useful)
      Range<double> rx(0.0, optData->SMax1);
      Range<double> ry(0.0, optData->SMax2);
      Range<double> rt(0.0, optData->T);

      // Step sizes
      long NX = 40; long NY = 80; long NT = 7000;

      Vector<double, long> xMesh = rx.mesh(NX); // NX + 1 elements!!
      Vector<double, long> yMesh = ry.mesh(NY); // NY + 1

      TwoBasketOption opt(rx, ry, rt, *optData);
```

We have now completed the definition of the *continuous problem*. It is now time to approximate this problem using the finite difference method.

## 17.5   THE FINITE DIFFERENCE METHOD FOR TWO-FACTOR PROBLEMS

We approximate the system (17.2) to (17.6) using the finite difference method. This subject is documented in Duffy (2006) for general second-order parabolic partial differential equations and their applications to Quantitative Finance. In particular, the finite difference method can be applied to the current problems. We use standard differencing in the space (underlying) direction while we use *explicit Euler* for time marching. The advantage of using explicit Euler method is that it is easy to understand and to program; the disadvantage is that it is only *conditionally stable* (as with the trinomial method) and this implies that **we need to take small time steps in the discretisation process**. Anyways, it is pedagogically acceptable because we wish to show the feasibility of the project. When applying the finite difference method to system (17.2) to (17.6) we pay attention to the following issues:

- Approximating derivatives by divided differences
- Approximating boundary and initial conditions
- Assembling the discrete system of equations
- Solving the system of equations and producing results

We now discuss each of these in turn. The basic idea is to produce a matrix of results at each time level, starting from time level t = 0. At each time level we solve the discrete system of equations while taking the boundary conditions into consideration at the same time. We make use of the template classes Vector<V,I> and NumericMatrix<V,I> as essential building blocks in the algorithms and procedures.

## 17.6  DISCRETE BOUNDARY AND INITIAL CONDITIONS

Before we can assemble the discrete set of equations we need to define the *auxiliary conditions*. First, we define the discrete initial conditions in the interior of the region (you can see this from the upper and lower bounds of the loops in the code):

```
void DiscreteIC(
                const Vector<double, long>& xMesh,
                const Vector<double, long>& yMesh,
                const TwoBasketOption& option,
                NumericMatrix<double, long>& Solution)
{
    // Initialise the matrix in the interior of the domain
    for (long j = Solution.MinColumnIndex()+1;
                    j <= Solution.MaxColumnIndex() -1 ; j++)
    {
        for (long i = Solution.MinRowIndex()+1;
                    i <= Solution.MaxRowIndex()- 1; i++)
        {

            Solution(i,j) = option.IC(xMesh[i], yMesh[j]);
        }
    }
}
```

A numeric matrix is created and this will be used in subsequent calculations.

Second, boundary conditions corresponding to Dirichlet (absorbing) conditions on the space boundary need to be defined. The boundary is partitioned into top, bottom left and bottom right line segments and the appropriate boundary conditions are defined there:

```
void DiscreteBC(
                const Vector<double, long>& xMesh,
                const Vector<double, long>& yMesh, double t,
                TwoBasketOption& option,
                NumericMatrix<double, long>& Solution)
{
    // Initialise the "extremities" of the solution, that is along
    // the sides of the domain

    long i, j; // Index for looping

    // Bottom
    long index = Solution.MinColumnIndex();
    for (i=Solution.MinRowIndex()+1;i<=Solution.MaxRowIndex(); i++)
    {
        Solution(i, index) = option.BCUnder(xMesh[i], t);
    }
```

```
// Top
index = Solution.MaxColumnIndex();

for (i=Solution.MinRowIndex()+1;i<= Solution.MaxRowIndex(); i++)
{
        Solution(i, index) = option.BCUpper(xMesh[i], t);
}
// Left
index = Solution.MinRowIndex();

for (j=Solution.MinColumnIndex();
                j<= Solution.MaxColumnIndex(); j++)
{
        Solution(index, j) = option.BCLeft(yMesh[j], t);
}

// Right
index = Solution.MaxRowIndex();

for (j = Solution.MinColumnIndex()+1;
                j <= Solution.MaxColumnIndex(); j++)
{
        Solution(index, j) = option.BCRight(yMesh[j], t);
}
}
```

As with initial conditions, a numeric matrix is updated.

## 17.7   ASSEMBLING THE SYSTEM OF EQUATIONS

We use three data structures in the algorithm:

- `MOld`: the solution at time level n
- `MNew`: the solution at time level n+1
- `repository`: an array of `NumericMatrix` that store the solution at all time levels

The last data structure (this is an array of matrices and it could consume a lot of memory) could be removed for performance reasons but we have used it in the code because it can be sent to Excel for visualization (this topic will be discussed in a later chapter). In the test program on the CD we have the option of using it or not.

The updating algorithm that computes a solution at time level n+1 in terms of the solution at time level n has the following form:

1. Create the (continuous) basket option
2. Initialise `MOld`
3. Define the discrete initial conditions
4. Define the algorithm that calculates `MNew` from `MOld`

We do not reproduce the code here as it can be found on the CD. However, we motivate the code for step 4 and to this end we use the notation in Figure 17.3 that define mesh points in a

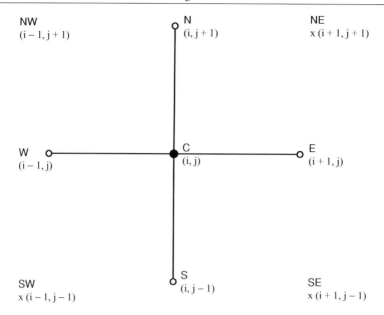

**Figure 17.3**   Naming conventions

neighbourhood of a mesh point C having indices (i,j). Then the code for the algorithm is given by:

```
// Discrete BC for level n+1; We use the points of the Compass so that
// we have 9 points
DiscreteBC(xMesh, yMesh, current, opt, MNew);
for (long j = MinC; j <= MaxC; j++)
{
        for (long i = MinR; i <= MaxR; i++)
        {
        xtmp = xMesh[i];
        ytmp = yMesh[j];
        difftmp1 = opt.diffusion1(xtmp, ytmp, current);
        difftmp2 = opt.diffusion2(xtmp, ytmp, current);
        contmp1 = opt.convection1(xtmp, ytmp, current);
        contmp2 = opt.convection2(xtmp, ytmp, current);

        // Initialise the coefficients
        aW = lambda1* difftmp1 - beta * contmp1;
        aE = lambda1* difftmp1 + beta * contmp1;
        aS = lambda2* difftmp2 - gamma * contmp2;
        aN = lambda2* difftmp2 + gamma * contmp2;

        aSW = alpha * opt.crossTerm(xtmp, ytmp, current);
        aSE = - aSW; aNE = aSW; aNW = -aSW;
```

```
        aC = 1.0 - 2.0 * (lambda1* difftmp1 + lambda2* difftmp2)
                     + k * opt.zeroTerm(xtmp, ytmp, current);

    MNew(i, j) = aW * MOld(i-1,j) + aS * MOld(i,j-1)
                     + aE * MOld(i+1, j) + aN * MOld(i,j+1)
                     + aSW * MOld(i-1,j-1) + aSE * MOld(i+1,j-1)
                     + aNE * MOld(i+1,j+1) + aNW * MOld(i-1,j+1)
                     + aC * MOld(i,j);
    }
}
```

This is the heart of the algorithm as it were. If we have used another finite difference scheme (for example, implicit Euler or Crank Nicolson) the code would look different but the output would be the same, namely the numeric matrix MNew.

## 17.8   POST PROCESSING AND OUTPUT

The values at all time levels and at each (space) mesh point are placed in a *tensor* (a fancy name for an array of matrices):

```
// Now the data structure to hold all values, all start indices
// start at 1.
bool storeData = false;
Tensor<double, long> repository(MOld.Rows(), MOld.Columns(), 1);
long index = 1; // Index for the array of matrices

cout << "Choose a tensor output (Y/y)?";
char choice; cin >> choice;
if (choice == "Y" ||  choice == "y")
{
        repository = Tensor<double, long>(MOld.Rows(),
                                          MOld.Columns(), NT+1);
        storeData = true;
}
```

At each time level $n + 1$ we add the current value of MNew to it:

```
// Postprocessing ...
// Go to next time level
index++;
cout << index << ",";

if (storeData == true)
{
        repository[index] = MNew; // Add matrix to tensor
}
```

When all time levels have been processed, the tensor can be exported to Excel. In this case we call a function from the Visualisation package (to be discussed in a later chapter). We use a try block just in case; we may have given the matrix and array data in the wrong order and the procedures in the package check for this eventuality:

```
try
{
        if (storeData == true)
        {
                cout << "Number of time steps is" << NT << ", Frequency? ";
                int freq; cin >> freq;
                printTensorInExcel(repository, xMesh, yMesh,
                                string("Basket"), freq);
        }
        else
        {
                printMatrixInExcel(MNew, xMesh, yMesh,
                                string("Price at N"));
        }
}
catch (DatasimException& e)
{
        e.print();
        return 0;
}
```

## 17.9   SUMMARY AND CONCLUSIONS

We have designed and implemented a small framework to find an approximate solution to a two-factor basket option PDE model. We have used the explicit Euler method for convenience but we must realise that this scheme is *conditionally stable* and this means that the step size in the t direction must be of the same order as the square of the step size in the space direction(s). A more suitable solution would be to employ implicit schemes (see Duffy, 2006 for a more detailed discussion) but this topic is outside the scope of this chapter.

We have tested the code for a number of cases, in particular the examples in Topper (2005) where the Finite Element Method (FEM) is used to approximate PDEs for multi-asset option problems.

This chapter has only scratched the surface. Hopefully, it will give you insights into FDM.

## 17.10   EXERCISES AND PROJECTS

1. (Payoff Functions) Examine the classes for two-factor payoff functions on the CD. Convince yourself that the code is correct. How would you generalize the code for a basket option class to N underlying assets and N weight factors? (hint: use template class to give full flexibility for value types and dimension value. You may need to instantiate the template class for $N = 2, 3$ and larger values.)

2. (Flexible Payoff Hierarchy, **medium-sized project**) In this chapter we have created payoff classes with hard-coded (and public) member data. In this exercise we wish to redesign these classes so that each one has its data in the form of a property set:

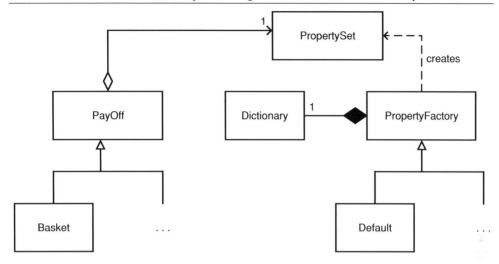

**Figure 17.4**   New payoff hierarchy

```
class BasketOption: public Payoff
{
public:
      SimplePropertySet<string, double> data;
      // ...
};
```

We also wish to apply the Factory Method patterns to create property sets, as shown in Figure 17.4. To this end, we create a factory class:

```
class PropertyFactory
{
protected: // Derived classes can access this data directly
      // keys + set of property names
      map<string, Set<string> dict;
public:
      SimpleProperySet<string, double>* createProperty() = 0;
};
```

```
class DefaultFactory : public PropertyFactory
{
public:
SimpleProperySet<string, double>* createProperty()
{
      // create property with names from dictionary
};
```

Write the code for the class diagram in Figure 17.4. Test your program.

# 18
# Useful C++ Classes for Numerical
# Analysis Applications in Finance

## 18.1 INTRODUCTION AND OBJECTIVES

In this chapter we give an introduction to some techniques in numerical analysis because they are needed in quantitative finance applications. Numerical analysis is a branch of mathematics that is concerned with the discovery of robust and efficient computational methods that approximate the solution of problems in engineering, mathematical physics, economics and other fields. In general, a problem that is defined in a continuum is approximated by another problem defined in a discrete finite domain. Numerical analysts then devise computable algorithms that are subsequently programmed in a computer.

Our interest in numerical analysis in the current context is that we need to approximate certain problems that arise in quantitative finance applications. In particular, we discuss the following topics:

- LU decomposition: decomposing a matrix into the product of a lower triangular and an upper triangular matrix
- Solving tridiagonal matrix systems; this is especially important when we approximate differential equations by finite difference and finite element methods, for example
- Linear and cubic spline interpolation

Of course, there is much more to numerical analysis than the above three techniques but a full discussion of other related and interesting topics is outside the scope of the current book.

## 18.2 SOLVING TRIDIAGONAL SYSTEMS

Tridiagonal matrices are characterised by the fact that their values are zero everywhere except on their main diagonal, super diagonal and sub-diagonal elements, which are in principle non-zero. These matrices are very important in a number of applications and are needed in areas such as:

- Matrix systems in finite difference and finite element methods
- Cubic spline interpolation (solution of a tridiagonal system)
- Solution of boundary value problems

We have discussed the problem of solving matrix problems of the form

$$Ax = b$$

where A is a tridiagonal matrix in Duffy (2004). We include a short discussion of the C++ code that realises the solution of the above problem in this chapter.

### 18.2.1   A tridiagonal solver in C++

In general, the problem

$$Ax = b$$

is solved in two steps:

(a) decompose A into the product of a lower triangular matrix L and an upper triangular matrix U
(b) the problem $Ax = b$ is solved in two simpler steps $Lz = b$ and $Ux = z$

We discuss how we solved this problem from a C++ perspective. First, we created a template class with a generic underlying type. This is because we cannot predict the kinds of specific data types that customers need. Some examples are:

• Tridiagonal matrices whose element are of type `double` or `float`
• Tridiagonal matrices whose element are of type `Complex` (this is the class we discussed in Chapter 5)
• Block tridiagonal matrices (each non-zero element is itself a matrix)

It would be nice if we could write a generic solver that was flexible enough to handle all three of the above scenarios. To this end, we now discuss the code. We have created a class that encapsulates the structure of the diagonals of the tridiagonal matrix as well as the vector r that plays the role of the inhomogeneous term in the system $Ax = b$. Furthermore, we define a number of so-called 'work arrays' that hold the elements of the decomposed matrices L and U as discussed above. The class has three constructors:

• Default constructor
• Copy constructor
• Constructor with four vectors as input (three for the vectors in the matrix, and one for the inhomogeneous vector r above)

We also have a member function that tells us if the matrix is diagonally dominant. If it is then we will have a solution to the matrix problem. If the matrix is not diagonally dominant then we need to perform some kind of pivoting but this is outside the scope of the current problem. Fortunately, many of the boundary value problems we work on lead to diagonally dominant tridiagonal matrix systems.

Finally, the class has a member function that produces a solution (in the form of a vector) to the problem. The mathematical details are given in Duffy (2004).

The full class interface is given by:

```
#ifndef LUSolver_HPP
#define LUSolver_HPP

#include "vector.cpp"           // Arrays with mathematical properties
#include "numericmatrix.cpp"    // Matrices with numerical properties

template <class V, class I> class LUTridiagonalSolver
```

```cpp
{ // Solve tridiagonal matrix equation
private:

        // Defining arrays (input)
        // V2 optimise so to work with pointers
        Vector<V,I> a; // The lower-diagonal array [1..J]
        Vector<V,I> b; // The diagonal array [1..J] "baseline array"
        Vector<V,I> c; // The upper-diagonal array [1..J]
        Vector<V,I> r; // Right-hand side of equation Ax = r [1..J]

        // Work arrays

        // Coefficients of Lower and Upper matrices: A = LU
        // V2 use of Templated static vectors, but we must be careful
        Vector<V,I> beta;       // Range [1..J]
        Vector<V,I> gamma;      // Range [1..J-1]
        // Solutions of temporary and final problems
        Vector<V,I> z; // Range [1..J]
        Vector<V,I> u; // Range [1..J]

        long Size;

        void calculateBetaGamma();   // Calculate beta and gamma
        void calculateZU();          // Calculate z and u

public:
        LUTridiagonalSolver();

        // Initialise all necessary data
        LUTridiagonalSolver(Vector<V,I>& lower_A,
                Vector<V,I>& diagonal_B, Vector<V,I>& upper_C,
                Vector<V,I>& rhs_R);
        LUTridiagonalSolver(const LUTridiagonalSolver<V,I>& source);

        virtual ~LUTridiagonalSolver();

        // Assignment operator
        LUTridiagonalSolver<V,I>& operator
                = (const LUTridiagonalSolver<V,I>& source);

        // Calculate the (final) solution to Ax = r
        Vector<V,I> solve();

        bool diagonallyDominant() const;

};
```

The full source code for this class is given on the CD but it is instructive to look at some of the functions. First, here is the code to calculate the elements of the matrices L and U (please note that these are private members because client code does not need to know this level of detail):

```
template <class V, class I>
        void LUTridiagonalSolver<V,I>::calculateBetaGamma()
{ // Calculate beta and gamma. Beta is the main diagonal elements of
  // L and gamma is the upper diagonal elements of U (detailed in
  // Duffy 2004).

    // Size == J

    // Constructor derived from Array (size, startIndex [,value])
    beta = Vector<V,I> (Size, 1);
    gamma = Vector<V,I> (Size - 1, 1);

    beta[1] = b[1];
    gamma[1] = c[1] / beta[1];

    for (I j = 2; j <= Size-1; j++)
    {
            beta[j] = b[j] - (a[j] * gamma[j-1]);
            gamma[j] = c[j]/beta[j];

    }

    beta[Size] = b[Size] - (a[Size] * gamma[Size-1]);

}


template <class V, class I>
            void LUTridiagonalSolver<V,I>::calculateZU()
{ // Calculate z and u == x in the current case

    z = Vector<V,I> (Size, 1);
    u = Vector<V,I> (Size, 1);

    // Forward direction
    z[1] = r[1] / beta[1];

    for (I j = 2; j <= Size; j++)
    {
            z[j] = (r[j] - (a[j]*z[j-1]) ) / beta[j];

    }
```

```
// Backward direction
u[Size] = z[Size];

for (I i = Size - 1; i >= 1; i--)
{
        u[i] = z[i] - (gamma[i]*u[i+1]);

}

}
```

The most important member function calculates the solution to the tridiagonal system:

```
// Calculate the solution to Au = r (u is same as x in the text!)
template <class V, class I> Vector<V,I>
LUTridiagonalSolver<V,I>::solve()
{

        calculateBetaGamma();          // Calculate beta and gamma
        calculateZU();                 // Calculate z and u

        return u;

}
```

Finally, we have provided a member function to check if the matrix is diagonally dominant:

```
template <class V, class I>
        bool LUTridiagonalSolver<V,I>::diagonallyDominant() const
{
        if (::fabs(b[1]) < ::fabs(c[1]))
                return false;

        if (::fabs(b[Size]) < ::fabs(a[Size]))
                return false;

        for (I j = 2; j <= Size-1; j++)
        {
                if (::fabs(b[j]) < ::fabs(a[j]) + ::fabs(c[j]) )
                        return false;
        }

        return true;
}
```

The CD contains the source code for this problem as well as a number of test cases. This matrix decomposition method was used in Chapter 16 where we applied the finite difference method to the one-factor Black Scholes partial differential equation.

## 18.3   AN INTRODUCTION TO INTERPOLATION

In this section we give an introduction to the problem of finding a function (this could be a polynomial, a rational function or some other computable function) that agrees with the set of discrete values:

$$y_0 = f(x_0), y_1 = f(x_1), \ldots, y_{N-1} = f(x_{N-1}) \tag{18.1}$$

where

$$x_0, x_1, \ldots, x_{N-1} \text{ are given mesh points } (x_i \neq x_j \text{ for } i \neq j)$$

There are different ways of approaching this problem. Some of the techniques are:

- Polynomial interpolation
- Rational function interpolation
- Cubic spline interpolation
- Other methods (a discussion is outside the scope of this chapter)

We give an introduction to the mathematical background to the first three methods. We discuss each one in turn.

### 18.3.1   Polynomial interpolation

Polynomial interpolation entails finding a polynomial $p$ of degree $N - 1$ that agrees with the values in (18.1), that is:

$$p(x_j) = y_j, \quad j = 0, 1, \ldots, N - 1 \tag{18.2}$$

To this end, we discuss *Neville's algorithm*. This entails building the desired polynomial from polynomials of lower degree.

Let $p_0$ be the zero-order polynomial passing through $(x_0, y_0)$, thus $p_0 = y_0$. In a similar fashion we define $p_1, p_2, \ldots, p_{N1}$ to be the zero polynomials passing through $(x_j, y_j)$, for $j = 1, \ldots, N - 1$. Now, we define $p_{01}$ to be the linear polynomial passing through both $(x_0, y_0)$ and $(x_1, y_1)$. Similarly, we define the polynomials $p_{12}, p_{23}, \ldots p_{(N-2)(N-1)}$. Finally, $p_{012\ldots(N-1)}$ is the polynomial of degree $N - 1$ passing through all $N$ points.

We can represent this process as a binomial tree as shown in Figure 18.1. The tree is built up by recursively filling it in from left to right and the relationship between a 'parent' polynomial

$$
\begin{array}{llll}
x_0: & y_0 = p_0 & & \\
 & & p_{01} & \\
x_1: & y_1 = p_1 & & p_{012} \\
 & & p_{12} & \\
x_2: & y_2 = p_2 & & \\
 & & p_{23} & \\
\vdots & \vdots & & \vdots \\
x_{N-1}: & y_{N-1} = p_{N-1} & &
\end{array}
$$

**Figure 18.1**   Tree structure for interpolation

and its 'children' is given by:

$$P_{j(j+1)...(j+m)} = \frac{(x - x_{j+m})P_{j(j+1)...(j+m-1)} + (x_j - x)P_{(j+1)(j+2)...(j+m)}}{x_j - x_{j+m}},$$

$$(m = 1, 2, \ldots, N - 1) \tag{18.3}$$

where x is the value at which we wish to calculate the interpolated value.

### 18.3.2    Rational function interpolation

The problem with polynomials is that they do not approximate some kinds of functions very well and in these cases we can approximate them by rational functions. A rational function is the quotient of two polynomials (a *numerator* and a *denominator*) as follows:

$$r(x) = \frac{P_p(x)}{Q_q(x)} = \frac{\sum\limits_{j=0}^{p} p_j x^j}{\sum\limits_{j=0}^{q} q_j x^j} \tag{18.4}$$

where $p$ is the degree of the numerator polynomial and $q$ is the degree of the denominator polynomial. There are $p + q + 1$ unknown coefficients in equation (18.4) (one is arbitrary) and since the rational function will pass through $N$ points we must have

$$N = p + q + 1$$

In general, we must specify the desired order of both the numerator and the denominator when using rational functions as interpolators. The advantage of rational functions is that they can model *poles*. A pole in this case is a zero of the denominator in equation (18.4).

We construct a tree that is similar to the one in Figure 18.1. The end-result is the interpolated value as well as an error estimate. We discuss the *diagonal rational functions* where the degrees of the numerator and denominator are equal if N is odd and the degree of the denominator is larger by one if N is even.

The algorithm in the current case is similar to the algorithm in equation (18.3):

$$R_{j(j+1)...(j+m)} = \alpha + \frac{\alpha - \beta}{\left(\dfrac{x - x_j}{x - x_{j+m}}\right)\left(1 - \dfrac{\alpha - \beta}{\alpha - \gamma}\right) - 1} \tag{18.5}$$

where

$\alpha = R_{(j+1)...(j+m)}$
$\beta = R_{j...(j+m-1)}$
$\gamma = R_{(j+1)...(j+m-1)}$  $(m = N - 1)$

The algorithm is started as follows:

$$R_j = y_j \tag{18.6}$$

and

$$R = R_{j(j+1)...(j+m)} = 0 \text{ for } m = -1$$

### 18.3.3 Cubic spline interpolation

Another method for interpolating data is to use spline functions. These are more suitable than polynomials because they are less likely to exhibit large oscillations that characterise high-degree polynomials. In this section we introduce *cubic spline functions*. They have been used in a variety of disciplines such as Computer Aided Design (CAD), computer graphics and the numerical solution of ordinary and partial differential equations using the Rayleigh-Ritz-Galerkin method.

We now introduce the method. As before, we work on the interval $(a, b)$ and let us suppose that

$$\delta = \{x_j : j = 0, 1, \ldots, n\}$$

is a partition of $(a, b)$ with

$$a = x_0 < x_1 < \ldots < x_n = b$$

We define the given values as follows:

$$Y = \{y_j : j = 0, 1, \ldots, n\}$$

and we define the quantities

$$h_{j+1} = x_{j+1} - x_j, \, j = 0, 1, \ldots, n - 1$$

We are now ready to define what a cubic spline is. This is a continuous function whose derivatives up to order two are also continuous at the interior mesh points as defined above. Furthermore, the spline is a polynomial of third degree on each subinterval.

In order to uniquely specify the spline $S_\delta$ we must give 'boundary conditions' at $x = a$ and at $x = b$. The relevant mutually exclusive options are as follows:

$$S_\delta''(Y; a) = S_\delta''(Y; b) = 0$$

$$S_\delta'(Y; a) = \alpha, \quad S_\delta'(Y; b) = \beta \quad (\alpha, \beta \text{ given}) \tag{18.7}$$

In this case, either the second order derivatives of the spline function are zero at $x = a$ and $x = b$ or the first order derivatives of the spline function are given at $x = a$ and at $x = b$ and have values $\alpha$ and $\beta$, respectively. It can be shown (Stoer and Bulirsch, 1980) that the cubic spline can be written in the form:

$$S_\delta(Y; x) = M_j \frac{(x_{j+1} - x)^3}{6h_{j+1}} + M_{j+1} \frac{(x - x_j)^3}{6h_{j+1}} + A_j(x - x_j) + B_j, \quad j = 0, \ldots, n - 1$$

where

$$A_j = \frac{y_{j+1} - y_j}{h_{j+1}} - \frac{h_{j+1}}{6}(M_{j+1} - M_j)$$

$$B_j = y_j - M_j \frac{h_{j+1}^2}{6}$$

All parameters and coefficients are known with the exception of $M_j$ and we can solve for these parameters by writing the problem as a tridiagonal system:

$$A\underline{M} = \underline{d}$$

$$A = \begin{pmatrix} 2 & \boxed{\lambda_0} & & & & & \\ \mu_1 & 2 & \lambda_1 & & & & \\ & \mu_2 & \ddots & \ddots & & 0 & \\ & & \ddots & \ddots & \ddots & & \\ 0 & & & \ddots & \ddots & \lambda_{n-1} \\ & & & & \boxed{\mu_n} & 2 \end{pmatrix}$$

$$\underline{M} = {}^t(M_0, \ldots, M_n)$$

$$\underline{d} = {}^t(d_0 \ldots, d_n) \tag{18.8}$$

where the elements of the matrix depend on the boundary conditions (18.7), namely zero values for the second-order derivatives (case (a)) or given values for the first-order derivatives (case (b)).

Case (a)

$$\lambda_0 = 0, \quad d_0 = 0, \quad \mu_n = 0, \quad d_n = 0$$

Case (b)

$$\lambda_0 = 1, \quad d_0 = \frac{6}{h_1}\left(\frac{y_1 - y_0}{h_1} - \alpha\right)$$

$$\mu_n = 1, \quad d_n = \frac{6}{h_n}\left(\beta - \frac{y_n - y_{n-1}}{h_n}\right)$$

The other coefficients are:

$$\lambda_j = \frac{h_{j+1}}{h_j + h_{j+1}}, \quad \mu_j = 1 - \lambda_j = \frac{h_j}{h_j + h_{j+1}}$$

$$j = 1, 2, \ldots, n-1$$

$$d_j = \frac{6}{h_j + h_{j+1}}\left\{\frac{y_{j+1} - y_j}{h_{j+1}} - \frac{y_j - y_{j-1}}{h_j}\right\}$$

We now have reduced the problem of interpolating data points by cubic splines to a problem of solving a tridiagonal matrix system. We can thus use the results from section 18.2.

We provide the source code and examples for cubic spline interpolation on the CD.

## 18.4  SUMMARY AND CONCLUSIONS

We have given a short introduction to some topics in Numerical Analysis that are useful in Quantitative Finance applications. In particular, we discussed solving tridiagonal matrix systems and one-dimensional interpolation problems using polynomials, rational functions and cubic splines.

The full source code for these algorithms can be found on the CD.

# 19
## Other Numerical Methods
## in Quantitative Finance

## 19.1 INTRODUCTION AND OBJECTIVES

In this chapter we discuss a number of important issues that are related to the pricing of derivatives, notably options and interest rates using the trinomial method. We have included this chapter because the *trinomial method* is popular and most readers will be acquainted with it. We take the viewpoint of the C++ developer: we design and implement the method and working code is provided on the CD. We also pay some attention to improving the performance by approximating the computationally intensive calculation of the exponential function by so-called Padé rational functions.

Another important topic in this chapter is a discussion of generic data structures that are needed in Quantitative Finance. One can create such data structures and subsequently use them in applications. In this way we can concentrate on the algorithm or application at hand without getting embroiled in the low-level details of data access and data storage.

We have included some exercises and projects to help the reader apply the techniques to his or her applications.

## 19.2 THE TRINOMIAL METHOD FOR ASSETS

In Chapter 15 we introduced the binomial method for pricing one-factor options. We assumed that the underlying asset price makes either an upward or downward movement at any moment in time. In this section, however we assume that the asset can move in three possible directions:

- up
- no move
- down

This assumption underlies the trinomial method that we now discuss. We first review some known theory.

The SDE for the risk-neutral geometric Brownian motion (GBM) of an asset price paying a continuous dividend yield is given by:

$$dS = (r - D)Sdt + \sigma S dW \qquad (19.1)$$

where

$r$ = risk free interest rate
$D$ = continuous dividend yield
$S$ = asset price
$\sigma$ = volatility
$dW$ = Wiener (or Brownian motion) process
$dt$ = small interval of time

Equation (19.1) is the starting for many more advanced models. Our main interest in this chapter is in showing how to use this in conjunction with the trinomial method to produce C++ code that calculates the price of an option. It is sometimes convenient to use a logarithmic variable x = log(S) in which the SDE in equation (19.1) becomes:

$$dx = \nu dt + \sigma dW, \quad \nu = r - D - \tfrac{1}{2}\sigma^2 \tag{19.2}$$

Then, the stochastic variable x can move up, down or retain the same value in a small interval of time as shown in Figure 19.1. Each movement has an associated probability and it is well known that the three probabilities have the values:

$$p_u = \tfrac{1}{2}(\alpha + \beta)$$
$$p_m = 1 - \alpha$$
$$p_d = \tfrac{1}{2}(\alpha - \beta) \tag{19.3}$$

where

$$\alpha = \frac{\sigma^2 \Delta t + \nu^2 \Delta t^2}{\Delta x^2}$$

$$\beta = \frac{\nu \Delta t}{\Delta x}$$

The reader can check that the probabilities add up to 1:

$$p_u + p_m + p_d = 1$$

We extend the trinomial process in Figure 19.1 to a trinomial tree in much the same way as in Chapter 15 for the binomial method. In particular, we need to define forward and backward induction processes:

● Forward induction: we create a trinomial tree structure on the time interval [0, T] where T is the maturity date. Since the method is a special case of an explicit finite difference scheme the step lengths in the x and t directions are related by the expression:

$$\Delta x = \sigma \sqrt{3 \Delta t} \tag{19.4}$$

We then build the tree using this expression and the information in Figure 19.1.

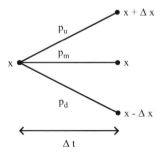

**Figure 19.1**   Trinomial tree model

• Backward Induction: At t = T we define the call or put payoff function. For example, in the case of a call option we have:

$$C_j^N = max(S_j^N - K, 0) \qquad (19.5)$$

We now compute option values as discounted expectations in a risk-neutral world:

$$C_j^n = e^{-r\Delta t}(p_u C_{j+1}^{n+1} + p_m C_j^{n+1} + p_d C_{j-1}^{n+1}) \qquad (19.6)$$

where K is the strike price.

We now discuss how to implement this code in C++. One option would be to design a framework using the results in Chapter 15 as a foundation (this is an exercise, see below). It is also possible to create a meaner version of the framework by assembling classes and procedures that implement the above algorithms and expressions. There are three main activities:

A1: Create and initialise the lattice data structure
A2: Modify the values in the lattice using equation (19.4)
A3: Calculate the option price using algorithm (19.6)

We already created a lattice template class that we can use in the current context. For example, here is some code to create a simple trinomial data structure:

```
const int typeT = 3;      // Trinomial Type
int depth = 5;            // The number of time steps

Lattice<double, int, typeT> lattice2(depth);
```

The forward induction code to modify the mesh points in the data structure is based on the code for the binomial method except there is one extra term:

```
// Up and down values from Figure 19.1
up = deltaX;
down = - deltaX;

// Loop from the min index to the end index
for (int n = lattice.MinIndex() + 1;
                    n <= lattice.MaxIndex(); n++)
{
        for (int i = lattice[n].MinIndex();
                    i < lattice[n].MaxIndex(); i++)
        {
                lattice[n][i-1] = down * lattice[n-1][i];
                lattice[n][i] = lattice[n-1][i]; // New for Tri.
                lattice[n][i+1] = up * lattice[n-1][i];
        }
}
```

Finally, algorithm (19.6) is implemented by the following code:

```
// Loop from the max index to the start (min) index
for (int n = lattice.MaxIndex() - 1; n >= lattice.MinIndex(); n--)
```

```
{
    for (int i = lattice[n].MinIndex();
                i <= lattice[n].MaxIndex(); i++)
    { // Uses the probabilities pu, pm and pd; and discounting
        lattice[n][i] = disc * (pu * lattice[n+1][i+1] +
                    pm * lattice[n+1][i] + pd * lattice[n+1][I-1]);
    }
}
```

The above code represents the frame or skeleton that calculates the price of a plain option using the trinomial method. The complete program can be found on the CD.

## 19.3   LATTICE DATA STRUCTURES

We now give a discussion of some data structures that can be used in advanced lattice models. For plain option problems there is no need to create a lattice but it is needed when we wish to store extra state information at a lattice node or when we are modelling options with early exercise feature. It is easy to handle these new requirements in C++ because the lattice class is generic and we can nest arbitrary data types in it. We discuss some scenarios shortly.

Where can we employ flexible lattice structures? Here are some examples:

- Modelling the short rate: the structure at each node is a matrix with three rows and two columns
- Storing option sensitivity data at each lattice node: for example, storing both the asset price and option price at each node. This is enough information to allow us to calculate the option's delta, gamma and other 'greeks'
- Two-factor binomial and trinomial methods; we can use the lattice template class to model these methods
- Generalised lattice structures where we index the time axis, not by integers but by other types such as string and dates, for example. This approach promotes the maintainability of applications because we work directly with indices that are relevant to the domain in question instead of being forced to use unnatural integer indices

We discuss each of these topics in some detail.

## 19.4   TRINOMIAL TREE FOR THE SHORT RATE

The discussion in this section is based on Clewlow and Strickland (1998). Our objective is to revisit the formulae and algorithms in that book and cast them in a form that can be used in an eventual implementation in C++. Furthermore, we provide source code for the solution on the CD so that the reader can use the code with specific parameters.

We wish to create short-rate trees that are consistent with the process:

$$\begin{cases} dr = \mu(r, t)dt + \sigma dW \\ \mu(r, t) \equiv \theta(t) - \alpha r(t) \end{cases} \tag{19.7}$$

This is a form of the Vasicek model (Ornstein-Uhlenbeck) and it defines an elastic random walk around some trend with a so-called *mean-reverting characteristic*.

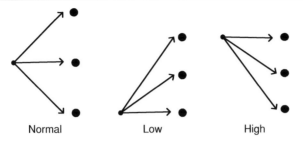

| Normal | Low | High |

**Figure 19.2**   Branching process and short rate

For mean-reverting processes for the short rate we can experience a variety of movements as shown in Figure 19.2. There are three basic scenarios:

- Normal case: here r can move down by an amount $\Delta r$, remain the same or move up by an amount $\Delta r$
- Low: the short rate r is currently low and it can stay the same, move up by value $\Delta r$ or move up by value $2\Delta r$
- High: the short rate r is currently high and it can stay the same, move down by value $\Delta r$ or move down by value $2\Delta r$

These two last branching processes are determined by mean reversion in the short rate to a long-term value. This has consequences for the numerical schemes, because in contrast to the binomial method in Chapter 15 the start and end indices (denoted by j) must be calculated as we build the tree.

As with the 'normal' trinomial method as discussed in section 19.2 we must calculate the jump probabilities from a node at time level n to three nodes at time level n + 1. To this end, we define R(t) as the yield at time zero (0) on a pure discount bond maturing at time t. We construct the value of $\theta(t)$ so that the tree is consistent with the yield on a bond maturing at time (n + 2), that is R((n + 2) $\Delta t$):

$$\theta(n\Delta t) = \frac{1}{\Delta t}(n + 2)R((n + 2)\Delta t) + \frac{\sigma^2 \Delta t}{2} + \frac{1}{\Delta t^2} \log \left( \sum_j Q_j^n e^{-2r_j^n \Delta t + \alpha r_j^n \Delta t^2} \right) \quad (19.8)$$

This formula uses the formula for state prices:

$$Q_j^n = \sum_{j'} Q_{j'}^{n-1} p_{j',j} d_{j'}^{n-1} \text{ where}$$

$p_{j',j}$ = probability of moving from node

$(n - 1, j')$ to node $(n, j)$ \quad (19.9)

We note that $Q_0^0 = 1$

At time t = 0 we get

$$\theta(0) = \frac{2R(2\Delta t)}{\Delta t} + \frac{\sigma^2 \Delta t}{2} + \frac{\alpha r_0^0 \Delta t^2 - 2r_0^0 \Delta t}{\Delta t^2} \quad (19.10)$$

**Table 19.1**   Node structure for short rate model

| | |
|---|---|
| $r_j^n$ | $p_{u,j}^n$ |
| $Q_j^n$ | $p_{m,j}^n$ |
| $\mu_j^n$ | $p_{d,j}^n$ |

Having done this, we can now calculate the discrete drift term:

$$r_j^n = r_0^0 + j\Delta r, \quad \forall j \text{ at time level } n$$
$$d_j^n = e^{-r_j^n \Delta t}$$

$$\text{(Note that } r_0^0 = R(\Delta t)) \tag{19.11}$$

The new nodes are:

- $(n+1, k+1)$ (upper node)
- $(n+1, k)$ (middle node)
- $(n+1, k-1)$ (lower node)

The value of k is chosen so that $r_k^{n+1}$ is as close as possible to the expected value of r. In the Normal case we can put $k = j$, for the Low case we have $k = j+1$ and for the High case we have $k = j - 1$. The jump probabilities are now given by:

$$p_{u,j}^n = \alpha + \frac{\eta}{2\Delta r}$$
$$p_{m,j}^n = 1 - 2\alpha$$
$$p_{d,j}^n = 1 - p_{u,j}^n - p_{m,j}^n \tag{19.12}$$

where

$$\alpha = \frac{\sigma^2 \Delta t^2 + \eta^2}{2\Delta r^2}$$
$$\eta = \mu_j^n + (j-k)\Delta r, \quad k = j+1, j-1$$
$$\mu_j^n = \text{ drift rate of } r \text{ at node } (n, j)$$

We are now in a position to describe the steps in the current algorithm:

1. Create the short-rate and discount factors at time n using equation (19.11)
2. Update the pure security prices at time level n for every node j using formula (19.9)
3. Calculate $\theta(n\Delta t)$ based on formula (19.8) (and (19.10))
4. Determine the drift rate based on formula (19.7)
5. Decide on the branching condition by determining the value of k as discussed above
6. Calculate the probabilities based on the expressions (19.12)

We note that certain data must be stored at each node, as shown in Table 19.1. It is possible to model this as a lattice class in which the values are matrices. We give a simple example of use; in this case we create a lattice with three time steps $N = 3$ whose node values are matrices with three rows and two columns:

```
// Trinomial lattice with matrix entries
int Nrows = 3; int Ncols = 2; int startIndex = 1;
```

```
int N = 3;            // Number of time steps
Matrix<double, int> nodeStructure(Nrows, Ncols,
                          startIndex, startIndex);
Lattice<Matrix<double, int>, int, 3>
                  trinomialLattice(N, nodeStructure);
```

The source code for the steps in this chapter can be found on the CD.

## 19.5   THE MULTIDIMENSIONAL BINOMIAL METHOD

We give a short introduction to the problem of pricing an option having two underlying assets by applying the binomial method. Please note that we have solved this problem using the finite difference method in Chapter 17.

The SDEs governing the correlated assets is given by:

$$dS_1 = (r - D_1)S_1 dt + \sigma_1 S_1 dW_1$$

$$dS_2 = (r - D_2)S_2 dt + \sigma_2 S_2 dW_2 \tag{19.13}$$

These assets are correlated:

$$dW_1 dW_2 = \rho dt, \quad \rho = \text{correlation} \tag{19.14}$$

As with the one-factor binomial method we transform the SDEs to give new SDEs:

$$\begin{cases} dx_j = v_j + \sigma_j dW_j, & x_j = log(S_j) \\ v_j = r - D_j - \frac{1}{2}\sigma_j^2, & j = 1, 2 \end{cases} \tag{19.15}$$

The assumption in the binomial method is that the asset price can go up or down; in this case there are four possibilities as depicted in Figure 19.3. The calculation of, and the values of the four probabilities are well known and we refer the reader to Clewlow and Strickland (1998). We then use the notation

$$C_{ij}^n \text{ or } P_{ij}^n$$

to denote the price of a call or put option at time level n and mesh point (i,j). Then the essence of the backward induction process is:

$$C_{ij}^n = p_{dd}C_{i-1,j-1}^{n+1} + p_{ud}C_{i+1,j-1}^{n+1} + p_{du}C_{i-1,j+1}^{n+1} + p_{uu}C_{i+1,j+1}^{n+1} \tag{19.16}$$

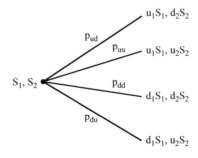

**Figure 19.3**   Two-factor binomial process

As usual, we need to define the payoff function, for example a *call spread option*:

$$max(S_1 - S_2 - K, 0) \tag{19.17}$$

Since the binomial method is a special case of an explicit finite difference scheme we cannot prescribe the mesh size at will and we thus have the following constraints:

$$\Delta x_1 = \sigma_1 \sqrt{\Delta t}$$
$$\Delta x_2 = \sigma_2 \sqrt{\Delta t} \tag{19.18}$$

# 19.6   GENERIC LATTICE STRUCTURES

Template classes can be customised to a variety of situations by using a number of techniques, for example:

- Nesting of template classes
- Full and partial template specialisation
- Combining these two techniques

We give three examples of the above techniques. The first example is concerned with a data structure in *technical analysis* in futures markets (candlestick figures). The second example is a generalised lattice class in which the horizontal axis' type is generic (for example, dates) and not just of integer type.

## 19.6.1   Candlestick charts

A candlestick chart is an array of data in time. Each node in the array consists of four prices:

- The opening price
- The closing price
- Daily high price
- Daily low price

Each node is associated with a date because we wish to know what the node information is for each day of trading. Furthermore, we access node information using a date as key. In this case the STL vector<T> is not sufficient and we need to use a map<K, V>, AssocArray<K,V> or SimplePropertySet<K,V>. We use property sets in the current example.
    The main data structure is declared as follows:

```
typedef SimplePropertySet<string, double> CandleStickNode;
SimplePropertySet<DatasimDate, CandleStickNode> timeSeries;
```

We have used an alias for readability reasons. Thus, this structure consists of a set of nodes whose key is a date and whose data is another set containing candlestick information. We create a prototypical candlestick object as follows:

```
CandleStickNode candlestickPrototype;         // Bullish
candlestickPrototype.add("DH", 100.0);        // Daily High
candlestickPrototype.add("DL", 70.0);         // Daily Low
candlestickPrototype.add("CP", 90.0);         // Closing Price
candlestickPrototype.add("OP", 80.0);         // Opening Price
```

The next step is to create an array of dates that we subsequently use as the keys for candlestick information:

```
int nYears = 2; int nPeriodsperYear = 4;
Vector<DatasimDate, int> result =
            createDateArray(today, nYears, nPeriodsperYear);
```

The code for this function is on the CD and the body of the function is:

```
Vector<DatasimDate, int> createDateArray(const DatasimDate& start,
                                    int numYears, int npy)
{
    // For each year find the dates in it and add to result
    // In fact, a Strategy pattern

    // Initialise the array
    Vector<DatasimDate, int> result (numYears*npy + 1, 1);

    // Calculate number of months per period
    int nMonths = 12/npy;

    result[result.MinIndex()] = start;

    for (int i = result.MinIndex() + 1; i <= result.MaxIndex(); i++)
    {
            result[i] = result[i-1].add_months(nMonths);
    }
    return result;
}
```

Having constructed the array of dates we then construct the 'outer' property set by creating a copy of the prototypical candlestick object:

```
// Now populate the Time series at each date with the prototype
for (int j = result.MinIndex(); j <= result.MaxIndex(); j++)
{
        timeSeries.add(result[j], candlestickPrototype);
}
printTS(timeSeries);
```

The output from this program is:

```
Printing a time series
23/April/2006 -> CP, 90::DH, 100::DL, 70::OP, 80::
23/July/2006 -> CP, 90::DH, 100::DL, 70::OP, 80::
23/October/2006 -> CP, 90::DH, 100::DL, 70::OP, 80::
23/January/2007 -> CP, 90::DH, 100::DL, 70::OP, 80::
23/April/2007 -> CP, 90::DH, 100::DL, 70::OP, 80::
23/July/2007 -> CP, 90::DH, 100::DL, 70::OP, 80::
23/October/2007 -> CP, 90::DH, 100::DL, 70::OP, 80::
```

```
23/January/2008 -> CP, 90::DH, 100::DL, 70::OP, 80::
23/April/2008 -> CP, 90::DH, 100::DL, 70::OP, 80::
```

Of course, we need to provide functionality to modify candlestick information for each date. We use the interface of the property set class to effect this.

Now let us suppose that we wish to define a new property that models the volume or amount of trading on a particular day. We then define a property and add it to the time series object:

```
// Now add new information/property to the candlestick and insert into
// time series. Shows the flexibility of our data structure.
    candlestickPrototype.add("Volume", 1000); // Trading Volume

    for (j = result.MinIndex(); j <= result.MaxIndex(); j++)
    {
        timeSeries.value(result[j], candlestickPrototype);
    }
    printTS(timeSeries);
```

The output from this modified program is now:

```
Printing a time series
23/April/2006 -> CP, 90::DH, 100::DL, 70::OP, 80::Volume, 1000::
23/July/2006 -> CP, 90::DH, 100::DL, 70::OP, 80::Volume, 1000::
23/October/2006 -> CP, 90::DH, 100::DL, 70::OP, 80::Volume, 1000::
23/January/2007 -> CP, 90::DH, 100::DL, 70::OP, 80::Volume, 1000::
23/April/2007 -> CP, 90::DH, 100::DL, 70::OP, 80::Volume, 1000::
23/July/2007 -> CP, 90::DH, 100::DL, 70::OP, 80::Volume, 1000::
23/October/2007 -> CP, 90::DH, 100::DL, 70::OP, 80::Volume, 1000::
23/January/2008 -> CP, 90::DH, 100::DL, 70::OP, 80::Volume, 1000::
23/April/2008 -> CP, 90::DH, 100::DL, 70::OP, 80::Volume, 1000::
```

### 19.6.2  (Highly) generic lattice structures

We generalise the lattice class to accommodate requirements where the horizontal axis is modelled as a generic type. Then the new lattice class is declared as follows:

```
template <class K1=string, class K2=string,class V=double, class I=int>
                class GenericLattice

{ // K1 = horizontal type, V = vertical type, K2 = key of V
  // I = indexing at a given x axis value

private:
public:
    SimplePropertySet<K1, Array<SimplePropertySet<K2, V>, I > > lat;
    // ...
};
```

There are four generic types:

- K1: the outer key
- K2: the inner key
- V: the node data type
- I: index type to access the elements of a node

In fact, this data structure is a nested associative array. An example of use is:

```
int main()
{
    SimplePropertySet<string, double> candlestickPrototype;
    candlestickPrototype.add("DH", 100.0); // Daily High
    candlestickPrototype.add("DL", 70.0);  // Daily Low
    candlestickPrototype.add("CP", 90.0);  // Closing Price
    candlestickPrototype.add("OP", 80.0);  // Opening Price

    // Create the x array of Dates
    int nYears = 2; int nPeriodsperYear = 4;
    DatasimDate today;

    Vector<DatasimDate, int> xarr =
        createDateArray(today, nYears, nPeriodsperYear);

    GenericLattice<DatasimDate, string, double, int>
            deltaLattice(xarr, candlestickPrototype);

    print(deltaLattice);

    cout << "Finish";

    return 0;
}
```

In this case we have created a simple function to print instances of the generic lattice structure:

```
template <class K2, class V, class I>
    void print(const GenericLattice<DatasimDate, K2, V, I>& source)
{

SimplePropertySet<DatasimDate, Array<SimplePropertySet<K2, V>, I > >
                                    ::const_iterator it;

    for (it= source.lat.Begin(); it!=source.lat.End(); it++)
    {
        DatasimDate tmp = (*it).first;
        print(tmp, STD, "/");
        cout << endl;
    }
        cout << "]";
}
```

This data structure is useful in fixed income applications, for example.

## 19.7    APPROXIMATING EXPONENTIAL FUNCTIONS

Many numeric algorithms use exponential functions. The exponential function is expensive to compute and a common technique is to approximate it using rational functions (a rational function is the quotient of two polynomials and we have already discussed it in some detail in Chapters 15 and 18). In particular, we employ *Padé rational approximations* whose numerators and denominators are polynomials of degree q and p respectively. We use the notation R(p, q) to denote such functions. Some common and practical approximations to the exponential function are:

$$r(z) = 1/(1+z) \quad (R(1,0))$$

$$r(z) = (2-z)/(2+z) \quad (R(1,1))$$

$$r(z) = (12 - 6z + z^2)/(12 + 6z + z^2) \quad (R(2,2)) \tag{19.19}$$

The Padé approximation $R(1, 1)$ is sometimes called the *Cayley map* and we have already discussed it in the exercises in Chapters 15 and 16. We have carried out some experiments and have found it to be an accurate approximation to the exponential function and results in a twelve-fold speed up when compared to the time it takes to use the exponential function from the C library `<math.h>`.

## 19.8    SUMMARY AND CONCLUSIONS

We have given an overview of the trinomial method and its applications to option pricing and tree building for the short rate. The approach is algorithmic in nature and it is important that we write the formulae in such a way that they can be easily mapped to C++. In this way we hope that the reader can apply the technique to other problems in quantitative finance.

Finally, we have introduced a number of template classes that realise generic data structures and that can be used in several kinds of relevant applications.

## 19.9    EXERCISES

1. (Creating a Trinomial Framework)
   Copy the source code from Chapter 15 (the binomial method) into a new directory. Then 'morph' the code in such a way that it becomes suitable for application of the trinomial method.

2. (Trinomial Tree using the Functional Programming Model)
   Implement the steps 1–6 in section 19.4 using C-like procedures. Compare your answers with those found from exercise 1.

3. (Two-Factor Binomial Method, Project)
   Implement the algorithms and formulae in section 19.5 using C++. As in exercises 1 and 2, you either copy and modify the original framework or use a functional programming model. Your code should support:
   • Call and put options
   • Early exercise features
   • Different kinds of correlation options
   In the last case we are referring to different payoff functions for multi-asset options such as exchange, rainbow, basket and best/work, for example (see Duffy, 2006; Zhang, 1998).

# 20

# The Monte Carlo Method Theory
## and C++ Frameworks

Dr. Joerg Kieritz and Daniel J. Duffy

## 20.1 INTRODUCTION AND OBJECTIVES

In this chapter we introduce the Monte Carlo simulation method and its application to the pricing of financial derivatives. It was first applied to Quantitative Finance in Boyle (1977) and it has become an important tool to price a range of one-factor and multi-factor options. In general, we perform a numerical simulation by approximating the stochastic differential equation that models the underlying asset corresponding to the derivative product. In this sense we construct a game or experiment.

We have written this chapter for a number of reasons. First, we think it is important to discuss the theory of this method and its implementation in C++ because of its popularity in Quantitative Finance; in a sense the current book would not be complete without some treatment of the method. Second, the Monte Carlo method is very robust (if slow) and it always gives a reasonably good answer to pricing problems. Finally, it can be used to check if other methods (such as the finite difference and lattice methods) are performing.

The structure of this chapter is based on three main themes:

- The theory of the Monte Carlo Method and its numerical approximation
- A software architecture and framework for MC
- Implementation in C++

We provide source code on the accompanying CD that you can use and adapt to your own problems and applications.

## 20.2 A SHORT HISTORY OF THE MONTE CARLO (MC) METHOD

The Monte Carlo method gets its name from the Monaco principality presumably because of the casinos and roulette tables in the city. A roulette table is a kind of random number generator. The name 'Monte Carlo method' and the systematic development of the corresponding theory dates from around 1944. Serious research into the method originates from work on the atomic bomb during the Second World War. This work involved a direct simulation of the probabilistic problems concerned with random neutron diffusion in fissile material. A leading light in this period was John von Neumann.

## 20.3 EXAMPLES OF THE APPLICATION OF THE MONTE CARLO METHOD

We refer to a number of examples and application areas where the Monte Carlo method has been used with great success. It is useful to know that it can be used in domains other than that of Quantitative Finance. Some application areas are:

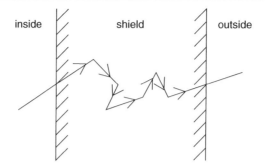

**Figure 20.1**   Neutron transport

- Reactor and particle physics, for example the movement of neutrons in a slab of shielding material as shown in Figure 20.1. Neutrons enter the shield area and they collide with other particles and are thus forced to make a random journey and they may actually pass through the shielding material
- Traffic problems (telecommunications, traffic flow, all kinds of networks)
- Models of conflicts
- Queueing problems
- Calculations of multiple integrals
- Numerical Analysis: solution of large linear systems of equations, solution of partial differential equations and stochastic optimisation

### 20.3.1   Calculation of definite integrals

One very important application of the Monte Carlo method involves the approximation of integrals in $n$ dimensions. In order to motivate what is to come we examine some 'classical' (non-Monte Carlo based) numerical integration schemes for the case $n = 1$. In this case we wish to approximate the definite integral of the function $f(x)$ on the interval $(a, b)$ and to this end we partition $(a, b)$ into $M + 1$ equally sized subintervals. See Figure 20.2. On each

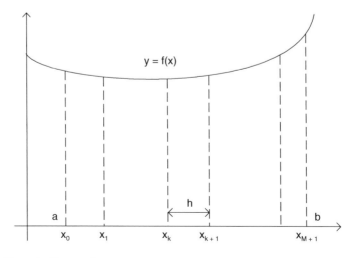

**Figure 20.2**   Numerical integration

subinterval we approximate the integral as follows:

$$\int_{x_k}^{x_{k+1}} f(t)dt \sim \frac{h}{2}(f(x_k) + f(x_{k+1})) \tag{20.1}$$

Then, on the full interval $(a, b)$ we get the approximate rule:

$$\int_a^b f(t)dt = h \left( \tfrac{1}{2} f_0 + \sum_{j=1}^M f_j + \tfrac{1}{2} f_{M+1} \right) \tag{20.2}$$

where

$$f_j \equiv f(x_j), \quad j = 0, \ldots, M+1$$

Looking at the problem from a more general perspective we can write all schemes in the generic form:

$$\int_a^b f(t)dt \approx h \sum_{j=0}^{M+1} w_j f_j \tag{20.3}$$

where $w_j$ are called the weights.

This approach generalizes to $n$ dimensions in which case we propose a numerical integration scheme on the unit cube:

$$\int_{I^n} f(t)dt \approx h^n \sum_{k_1=0}^{M+1} \cdots \sum_{k_n=0}^{M+1} w_{k_1} \ldots w_{k_n} f(k_1, \ldots, k_n) \tag{20.4}$$

where

$I^n = $ unit cube $= [0, 1]^n$
$w_{k_j} = $ weights $j = 1, \ldots, n$
$(k_1, \ldots, k_n)$ is some point in $I^n$

The Monte Carlo approach will have the same general form as in equation (20.3) except that the weights are all equal to 1 and the points in $n$-space (where the function is evaluated) are all randomly chosen. In general we take random samples and then determine the average of all the calculations. Let us take the case $n = 1$ again. Then we have:

$$\int_a^b f(t)dt \sim \frac{b-a}{M} \sum_{k=1}^M f(x_k) \tag{20.5}$$

where $x_k$ is a random number in $(a, b)$.

In the $n$-dimensional case we wish to approximate the integral of a vector function on a set $B \subseteq \mathbb{R}^n$ and we assume that the Lebesgue measure or volume on this set is finite, that is $0 < \lambda_n(B) < \infty$. We transform $B$ into a probability space with probability measure defined by $d\mu = dt/\lambda_n(B)$. Then for any function $f \epsilon L^1(\mu)$ we get:

$$\int_B f(t)dt = \lambda_n(B) \int_B f d\mu = \lambda_n(B) E_\mu(f) \tag{20.6}$$

where $E_\mu(f)$ is the expected value of $f$ in the measure $\mu$

Now the essence of the Monte Carlo method in this context is that we approximate the expected value by taking $M$ independent $\mu$-distributed random samples $x_1, \ldots, x_M$ and then using the approximation:

$$E_\mu(f) \sim \frac{1}{M} \sum_{k=1}^{M} f(x_k) \tag{20.7}$$

Using the strong law of large numbers we know that this procedure converges almost surely, abbreviated, a.s. Thus, the final formula is given by:

$$\int_B f(t)dt \sim \frac{\lambda_n(B)}{M} \sum_{k=1}^{M} f(x_k) \tag{20.8}$$

This formula may need to be modified because there is a possibility of choosing non-uniformly distributed numbers in the region of integration. The only way to ensure a good distribution of the random numbers is to generate many of them. This makes the Monte Carlo an expensive method to use and we can reduce the error in the method if we can generate a sequence of numbers that are uniformly distributed. These are called *quasi-random sequences* and lead us to define the so-called *Quasi-Monte Carlo (QMC)* method; in the current context the formula (20.8) is still valid but the function arguments are now deterministic. They are chosen in such a way so as to improve the performance of the algorithm.

### 20.3.2   Device reliability

We take an example from Sobol (2004). But before we discuss this example we need to introduce some background material. A *random variable* is said to be discrete if it can assume any of a set of discrete values $x_1, \ldots, x_n$. Associated with each value is its probability of occurring. We say that each random variable has a probability of occurring and we write this fact as follows:

$$p\{\xi = x_i\} = p_j, \quad j = 1, \ldots, n$$

We can thus write the so-called distribution of the random variable $\xi$ as a table:

$$\xi \sim \begin{pmatrix} x_1 & x_2 & \cdots & x_n \\ p_1 & p_2 & \cdots & p_n \end{pmatrix}$$

There are two constraints that we must place on the probabilities, namely:

$$p_j > 0, \quad j = 1, \ldots, n$$

$$\sum_{j=1}^{n} p_j = 1$$

The latter condition demands that the random variable $\xi$ must assume one of the listed probability values in each trial. We define the *mathematical expectation*, or the *expected value* of the random variable $\xi$ by the expression:

$$M\xi = \sum_{j=1}^{n} x_j p_j \quad (\text{or } E\,\xi \equiv M\,\xi)$$

We now define the *variance* of the random variable $\xi$ by the expression:

$$D\xi = M([\xi - M\xi]^2) = M(\xi^2) - (M\xi)^2$$

The expected value and the variance are the two most important numerical characteristics of a random variable and we shall need them for the example in a moment. We now introduce a very important concept called the *law of large numbers*. In general terms the law states that the average of a random sample from a large population is likely to be close to the mean of the whole population. There are two forms of this law:

- The *weak law*: if $X_1, X_2, \ldots$ is an infinite sequence of uncorrelated random variables where all the random variables have the same expected value $\mu$ and variance $\sigma^2$ then the sampled average $\overline{X}_n = (X_1 + \ldots + X_n)/n$ converges in probability to $\mu$
- The *strong law*: If $X_1, X_2, \ldots$ is an infinite sequence of random variables that are independent and identically distributed (with $M(|X_j|) < \infty$ and where each $X_j$ has mean $\mu$) then

$$P(\lim_{n \to \infty} \overline{X}_n = \mu) = 1$$

The law states that the sample average converges almost surely to $\mu$.

The law of large numbers justifies our intuition: the expected value of a random variable is the long-term average when sampling repeatedly.

We now introduce the promised example. Consider a device or some piece of equipment that consists of a network of components and we assume that the quality of the device is determined by the value of an output parameter $U$ that we compute as a (non-linear) function of all the components in the network:

$$U = f(c_1, c_2, \ldots)$$

where $c_j$ is a component in the network $j = 1, 2, \ldots$

The main problem in real life is that the parameters of the components are not known exactly; in other words, their real values differ from the values 'on the box' as it were. We model all the component parameters as well as the output as random variables. However, we must overcome a number of problems; first, it may not be clear which parameters are the most inaccurate and second for large networks the computed parameter limits can be overestimated for the simple reason that not all parameters are simultaneously functioning at their worst. Thus, we use the above theory to calculate the estimated value of the output variable and its corresponding variance. The main steps are:

1. Estimate the probability characteristics of the individual components. We do this experimentally by examining a large batch of such elements. In many cases their distributions tend to be normal.
2. We need to know the form of the function $f()$ above.

We compute a random value of the parameters for each component and we then compute U using the formula:

$$U = f(c_1, c_2, \ldots)$$

where $c_j$ is a component in the network $j = 1, 2, \ldots$

We repeat this experiment N times (the number of simulations) with different random numbers to obtain values

$$U_1, U_2, \ldots U_N$$

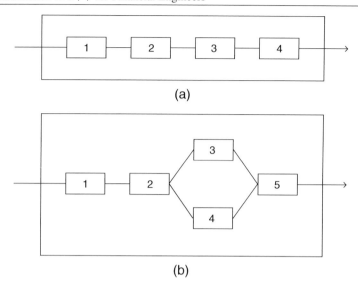

**Figure 20.3**   Devices and components

We then apply the formula for the expected value above to give:

$$MU \sim \frac{1}{N} \sum_{j=1}^{N} U_j$$

With the variance having the value:

$$DU \sim \frac{1}{N-1} \left( \sum_{j=1}^{N} U_j^2 - \frac{1}{N} \left( \sum_{n=1}^{N} U_j \right)^2 \right)$$

We have now finished our discussion of the example. A special case is when we wish to estimate how long (on average) a device will function before it breaks down. In this case each component in a network has a breakdown time and this is the specific parameter of interest in this case. Let us consider the two component networks in Figure 20.3. For case (a) the function becomes:

$$t = min(t_1, t_2, t_3, t_4)$$

While in case (b) the function is:

$$t = min(t_1, t_2, max(t_3, t_4), t_5)$$

As before, we measure *breakdown times* for the components and we finally get an estimate for the breakdown time for the networks as follows:

$$M\theta = \frac{1}{N} \sum_{j=1}^{N} t_j$$

where $t_j$ = value of $t$ in the *jth* numerical experiment

## 20.4   THE MONTE CARLO METHOD IN QUANTITATIVE FINANCE

The first paper on the application of the Monte Carlo method to option pricing was Boyle (1977). He took the example of a plain call option and calculated its price using MC. We briefly discuss how he did it. First, we need to define some notation:

- $S_t$ = current stock price at time $t$
- $r$ = risk free rate (paid quarterly)
- $\sigma^2$ = variance rate (per quarter)
- $D_t$ = dividend payable at time t (paid quarterly)
- $K$ = strike price
- $T$ = Expiry date
- $C$ = code option price

We assume that the ratio of successive stock prices follows a lognormal process with mean $\exp(r)$. Thus, the ratio $S_{t+1}/S_t$ has a density function of the form $e^{\sigma \tilde{x}}$ where $\tilde{x}$ is a normally distributed random variable with mean 0

$$E(S_{s+1}/S_t) = \int_{-\infty}^{\infty} e^{\sigma \tilde{x}} e^{-\tilde{x}2/2} = e^{\sigma^2/2} \tag{20.9}$$

We write the distribution of the stock price by the vital formula:

$$S_{t+1} = S_t e^{(r - \sigma^2/2 + \sigma \tilde{x})} \tag{20.10}$$

Thus, this formula allows us to generate the stock price at any time level $t$. We generate $S_1$ in the first time period from $S_0$ (which is the stock price at $t = 0$). If $S_1 > D_1$ then $S_1 - D_1$ is used as the initial value for the second period. In general, the value $S_{t+1}$ is generated at period $t$. If $S_{t+1} > D_{t+1}$ then the value $(S_{t+1} - D_{t+1})$ is used to initiate the stock price in the next period. If $S_{t+1} < D_{t+1}$ we stop the process and start a new simulation. We repeat the process to produce $S_T$ that we subsequently substitute in the payoff function $C = \max(S_T - K, 0)$.

We then discount this value at the risk-free rate to obtain an estimate of the desired option price, namely:

$$\hat{C} = \frac{1}{N} \sum_{j=1}^{N} e^{-r(T-t)} \max\left( S_T^{(j)} - K, 0 \right) \tag{20.11}$$

where $N$ = number of simulations and $S_T^{(j)}$ = stock price corresponding to the $j$th simulation at time $T$.

### 20.4.1   An overview of stochastic differential equations (SDE)

We give a short overview of the theory of Stochastic Differential Equations (SDE) and how to approximate them using the finite difference method (FDM). It is not intended as a detailed exposition in any way but we do wish to introduce enough material to help us understand why it is useful in Monte Carlo simulation. In short, an SDE models the underlying asset in general. We need to be able to find the solution of the SDE in order to be able to generate paths. In some cases it may be possible to find an exact solution but in general we must resort to numerical approximations. Let us consider the scalar SDE:

$$dX_t = a(t, X_t)dt + b(t, X_t)dW_t \tag{20.12}$$

We call $a(t, X_t)$ the *drift* coefficicent and $b(t, X_t)$ the *diffusion* coefficeint. Furthermore, $X_t$ is often referred to as an *Itô diffusion process*. In this work we focus on three types of SDE's in particular:

- The geometric process
- The square root process
- The mean reverting process

We now discuss each of these processes. Each specific process is a specialization of the generic SDE (20.12). In the *geometric process* we have $a(t, X_t) = A(t)X_t$ and $b(t, X_t) = B(t)X_t$ and hence we get the SDE:

$$dX_t = A(t)X_t dt + B(t)X_t dW_t \tag{20.13}$$

The *square root process* is similar to the geometric process but in this case we have $b(t, X_t) = b\sqrt{X_t}$ and hence:

$$dX_t = aX_t dt + b\sqrt{X_t}dW_t \tag{20.14}$$

Finally, the *mean-reverting process* is described by the SDE:

$$dX_t = A(t)(C(t) - X_t)dt + B(t)X_t dW_t \tag{20.15}$$

In this case the process will revert to the value $C(t)$ with the period of reversion being determined by $A(t)$.

We now give a brief summary of the finite difference schemes to approximate SDEs. A more complete treatment, including C++ source code can be found in Duffy (2004). We construct one generic FDM scheme for the SDE (20.12) ($a = A, b = B$). The scheme depends on a number of constant parameters whose values will be different depending on the FDM scheme. As usual, we partition the interval $[0, T]$ and we define approximations at mesh points as follows:

$$Y_{n+1} = Y_n + \{\alpha\bar{a}_\eta(\tau_{n+1}, Y_{n+1}) + (1 - \alpha)\bar{a}_\eta(\tau_n, Y_n)\}\Delta_n$$
$$+ \{\eta b(\tau n + 1, Y_{n+1}) + (1 - \eta)b(\tau_n, Y_n)\}\Delta W_n \tag{20.16}$$

with

$$\bar{a}_\eta = a - \eta b \frac{db}{dX_t}$$

And where

$\Delta_n = \text{step size} = \dfrac{t_n - t_0}{n}$

$\Delta W_n = $ standard Wiener process that has a normal distribution over $\Delta_n$ with mean $= 0$ and variance $= \Delta n$

$\alpha = $ drift variable (implicit or explicit), $\alpha \in [0, 1]$

$\eta = $ diffusion variable (similar to $\alpha$), $\eta \in [0, 1]$

We need to define some more notation.

The coefficients $a(t, X_t)$ and $b(t, X_t)$ are considered to be of the form

$$a(t, X_t) = A(t)X_t^Q$$

and

$$b(t, X_t) = B(t)X_t^W$$

Therefore, $b(t, X_t)\dfrac{db}{dX_t}$ in (20.16) now becomes

$$b(t, X_t)\frac{db}{dX_t} = B(t)^2 W X_t^{2W-1}$$

From now on, the drift coefficient $a(\tau_n, X_{\tau_n})$ and the diffusion coefficient $b(\tau_n, X_{\tau_n})$ will be referred to respectively as $a_n$ and $b_n$ (and $c(r_n, X_{taun})$ as $C_n$). The time-step $\Delta_n$ will be $k$. Furthermore, a factor

$$\xi a_{n+1}c_{n+1}k + (1+\xi)a_n c_n k$$

is added to (20.16) to facilitate the simulation of the mean reverting process. For the geometric and square root process this factor is removed by simply setting $C_n = 0$. Also the fitting factors are added. Taking all of the above into account, the genereal form of equation (20.16) now becomes:

$$\begin{aligned} &Y_{n+1} - \alpha\frac{p1(\tau_{n+1})}{\sigma_{drift(\tau_{n+1})}}Y_{n+1}^Q + \alpha p2(\tau_{n+1})Y_{n+1}^{2W-1} - \eta\frac{p^3(\tau_{n+1})}{\sigma_{diff(\tau_{n+1})}}Y_{n+1}^Q \\ &= Y_n + (1-\alpha)\frac{p1(r_n)}{\sigma_{drift(\tau_n)}}Y_n^Q - (1-\alpha)p2(\tau_N)y_N^{2W-1} \\ &+(1-\eta)\frac{p^3(\tau_n)}{\sigma_{diff(\tau_n)}}Y_n^Q + \xi a_{n+1}c_{n+1}k + (1-\xi)a_n c_n k(18) \end{aligned} \qquad (20.17)$$

with

$$\begin{aligned} p1(\tau_n) &= a_n k \\ p2(\tau_n) &= \eta B(t)^2 W k \\ p3(\tau_n) &= B(t)\Delta W_n \end{aligned}$$

Note that any scheme with $\alpha > 0$ or $\eta > 0$ can only be solved in the linear case, meaning $Q = W = 1$. If $Q$ and $W$ are anything but 1 only fully explicit schems (Euler, Predictor-Corrector and Richardson) are capable of approximating the solution.

We give special examples of scheme (20.17) in Figure 20.4.

| | $\alpha$ | $\eta$ | $\xi$ | Q | W |
|---|---|---|---|---|---|
| Euler | 0 | 0 | 0 | - | - |
| Implicit Euler | 1 | 1 | 1 | - | - |
| Crank Nicolson | $\frac{1}{2}$ | $\frac{1}{2}$ | $\frac{1}{2}$ | 1 | 1 |

**Figure 20.4** Special parameter values

Finally, we mention the Richardson extrapolation method for improving accuracy, the Milstein method that is an improvement on the explicit Euler method and the Predictor-Corrector method. First, the Richardson scheme is based on the Euler scheme applied on meshes of size $k$ and $k/2$. To this end, we know that the exact and approximate solutions are related by the expression:

$$Y_N(k) = X_t + e(T)k + O(k^2)$$

for a partition with $N$ subdivisions. Now, if we take twice as many subdivisions, that is $2N$ we get an analogous expression for the error:

$$Y_{2N}(k/2) = X_t + \tfrac{1}{2}e(T)k + O(k^2)$$

We eliminate the first-order term from these expressions to give us:

$$Z_N(k) = 2Y_{2N}(k/2) - Y_N(k)$$

This discrete function $Z$ is now a second-order approximation to the exact solution of the SDE. In the Milstein method we add a special term to the Euler scheme, namely:

$$\tfrac{1}{2}b(t, X_t)\frac{db(t, X_t)}{dX_t}\{(\Delta W)^2 - k\}$$

This additional term should reduce the negative effect of noise on convergence. Finally, the Predictor-Corrector method uses a predictor value and then a corrector value to calculate an approximate solution to the SDE.

Some conclusions on the methods are:

- *Euler*: robust and easy to program but it does not converge fast to the exact solution. In general, it is one of the worst schemes around
- *Implicit Euler*: It has more or less the same characteristics as the Euler method although it performs less well. It is not suitable for non-linear problems
- *Crank-Nicolson*: Good to excellent convergence in most cases. It would seem that it is one of the best methods for mean-reverting processes. It is not suitable for non-linear problems
- *Predictor-Corrector method*: Converges fast (and consistently). It is better than the Crank Nicolson method. It can also deal with non-linear problems
- *Richardson*: This is a very robust and accurate scheme and is similar in this respect to the Predictor-Corrector method

## 20.4.2   Other background information

On the CD we have delivered two pdf files that discuss a number of topics related to the Monte Carlo method. We refer to them here and the interested reader should consult the CD for more detailed information:

- Probability theory and confidence intervals
- Path generation
- Distributions and random number generation
- Pseudo random numbers
- The Quasi Monte Carlo method

## 20.5  SOFTWARE ARCHITECTURE FOR THE MONTE CARLO METHOD

The Monte Carlo method is a popular method that is widely used to price a range of derivative products (see Boyle, 1977). There are a number of good references on the method, for example Glassermann (2004) and Jaeckel (2002). For a more generic treatment of numerical solutions to stochastic differential equations see Kloeden *et al.* (1994). In this chapter we wish to describe how we have applied this body of knowledge of the Monte Carlo method to produce a software system that is able to price a range of one-factor and multi-factor option pricing problems. In order to reduce the scope of this chapter, we examine only one-factor models.

We are interested in producing a software product that is robust, flexible and that performs well at run-time. In particular, we quantify these general requirements by listing a number of features that the software should have:

- *Suitability*: the MC solver is able to model a wide range of one-factor and multi-factor option types. In fact, it would be nice if the solver knew as little as possible of the derivative products that it is modeling because it allows different kinds of users to 'plug' their models into the solver without having to write new code
- *Accuracy*: it is well known that the MC method gives us a convergent solution in general, albeit slowly. The solver that we write in C++ must reflect this accuracy
- *Performance*: the response time should be as good as possible, given the fact that we are using the Monte Carlo method. To this end, we could consider efficient random number generators, clever C++ data structures and using Halton and Sobol sequences, for example. Furthermore, we would expect the performance to be a hundred times better than a corresponding application written in VBA, for example.

Having defined a number of objectives that we would like to achieve, we now turn our attention to describing how we realized them using software design techniques.

We have produced a software architecture and it has been applied to option pricing models using both the binomial and finite difference methods. The architectures are based on the generic design principles in Duffy (2004). In this article we adopt the same approach by partitioning the problem into a network of loosely coupled subsystems and classes. In general, we use a number of small-grained patterns and we connect them to form a larger configuration. In particular, we have implemented the following patterns:

- *Whole/Part* and *Aggregation Structures*: in general, we partition large, complex objects ('whole') into smaller and specialized objects ('parts'). This approach promotes reusability and maintainability of the software.
- *Mediator*: objects that act as intermediaries between a number of other objects. These communicating objects have no direct knowledge of each other. Instead, they must interface with the mediator which in this case plays the role of a façade.
- *Delegation Mechanism*: Classes operate on a client-server basis: the client class calls a member function in a server class. Server classes are specialised to carry out certain tasks such as random number generation and calculation of the mean and variance of statistical distribution functions.

Please see the documentation on the CD where we explain the design and the implementation of the framework in more detail.

## 20.6   EXAMPLES AND TEST CASES

We take some examples. These results are based on the article Duffy (2005).

### 20.6.1   Plain options

To illustrate the applicability of our design we study some well-known options namely a simple plain vanilla call. A European plain vanilla call has payoff $max(S_T - K, 0)$ at maturity $T$. We give the convergence table calculated via our setup with parameters Spot = 100, Strike = 100, Maturity = 1 year, Volatility = 25%, $r = 3\%$.

The results are shown in Figures 20.5 and 20.6.

| Number of Paths | Value | St. Error | Rel. Difference To BS |
|---|---|---|---|
| 262144 | 11.3480 | 0.04 | 0.00 % |
| 253952 | 11.3483 | 0.04 | 0.00 % |
| ... | | | |
| 16384 | 11.3433 | 0.14 | 0.05 % |
| 8192 | 11.3400 | 0.20 | 0.07 % |

**Figure 20.5**   Plain vanilla price

### 20.6.2   Barrier options

As a first exotic option we consider a standard Up-and-Out call. This is quite common in the equity derivatives market. This option has the same payoff as a plain vanilla call but only if the

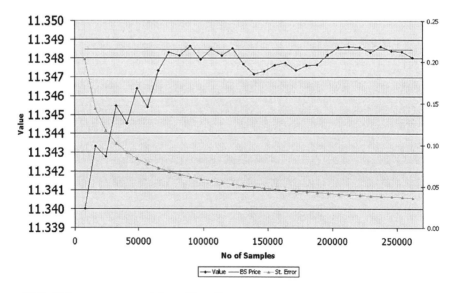

**Figure 20.6**   Value convergence plain vanilla call

| Number of Paths | Value | St. Error |
|---|---|---|
| 262144 | 0.5042 | 0.0035 |
| 253952 | 0.5047 | 0.0036 |
| ... | | |
| 16384 | 0.0142 | |
| 8192 | 0.4954 | 0.0202 |

**Figure 20.7**   Up and out: Error

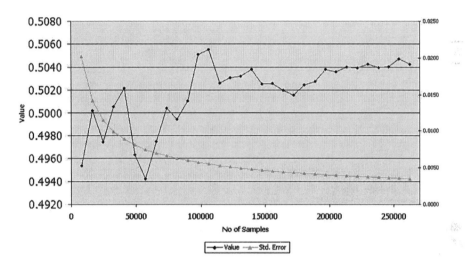

**Figure 20.8**   Value convergence up and out call

asset price stays below a barrier level at certain discretely chosen times up to its maturity. Here we consider the parameters Spot = 150, Strike = 136, Maturity = 4.5 year, Volatility = 15 %, riskless rate r = 2 % and Barrier = 164. To evolve the assets path we use the congruential generator Ran1 again with 32 batches of 8,192 samples. The results are shown in Figures 20.7 and 20.8.

### 20.6.3   Asian options

The final example is the case of an Arithmetic Asian call. In contrast to a geometric Asian option a closed form pricing formula is not available. The payoff is given by $\max\left(\frac{1}{N}\sum_{i=1}^{N} S_{t_i} - K, 0\right)$. The parameters are chosen to be Spot = 100, Strike = 95, Maturity = 2 year, Volatility = 42,5 %, riskless rate r = 3 %. Now, the random number generator is the Mersenne Twister, see Matsumoto (1998) again with 32 batches of 8,192 samples. The results are shown in Figures 20.9 and 20.10.

| Number of Paths | Value | St. Error |
|:---:|:---:|:---:|
| 262144 | 17.6714 | 0.0611 |
| 253952 | 17.6847 | 0.0621 |
| ... | | |
| 16384 | 17.5318 | 0.2432 |
| 8192 | 17.2734 | 0.3415 |

**Figure 20.9**    Asian: Error

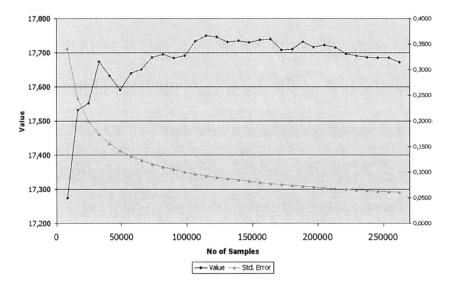

**Figure 20.10**    Value convergence arithmetic Asian call

## 20.7   SUMMARY AND CONCLUSIONS

We have given an introduction to the theory of the Monte Carlo method and its application to option pricing. The main focus however was to show how to design and implement a software architecture that can be used in a number of application areas and that can also be extended to new pricing models.

We give some examples to show how the method works; first, we price a plain call option and second we price arithmetic Asian call options with discrete monitoring dates. Finally, we have modelled barrier options using the method. We implemented a flexible and easily extendable Monte Carlo backbone. Using our framework the generalisation to $d$ dimension is straightforward. Then, we would be able to price path-dependent multi-asset options or asset allocation problems. There is a significant speed-up when using a C++ implementation. The generation of certain quasi random numbers like Halton or Sobol numbers is a hundred times faster than using the same algorithm in a VBA setting.

Further applications of *variance reduction methods* such as antithetics, control variates or stratifications will further speed up computations. The implementation allows for further applications, e.g. credit modelling or asset allocation since the generator and the probability distributions are flexible.

## 20.8   APPENDIX: COMPARING MONTE CARLO WITH OTHER NUMERICAL METHODS

In this book we have discussed three main methods for derivatives pricing, namely:

- Lattice methods (for example, binomial and trinomial methods)
- The Finite Difference Method (FDM)
- The Monte Carlo (MC) method (the topic of this Chapter)

We now pose the question: which of the above three methods should we choose in a particular context and for a particular application? Without being trite, the answer depends on your point of view. In particular, we examine the methods from the perspective of ISO 9126 (that we discussed in Chapter 1):

- Accuracy: how good is the numerical solution and how close is it to the exact solution? MC is most accurate because it always converges to the true solution, albeit at a slow pace. FDM schemes can also be accurate in low dimensions while lattice methods are bad performers (they are special cases of explicit finite difference schemes)
- Performance: this is basically the time it takes to calculate the option price. FDM wins hands-down. Furthermore, as we have seen that it costs little extra effort to calculate option sensitivities using FDM (as we have shown in Chapter 17). With MC on the other hand, we must approximate the greeks using finite differences and *path recycling*. This obviously results in a performance penalty

    At the moment of writing we can price a two-factor basket option with $NX = NY = 200$ and $NT = 100$ in about 9 seconds on an average PC
- Applicability/Suitability: The Monte Carlo method can be applied to very many kinds of one-factor and multi-factor derivatives problems while FDM is suitable for problems with at most three factors, after which time we get an exponential increase in complexity with the current finite difference theory. Lattice methods are the least resilient of the three methods
- Fault tolerance: MC is very robust and it tends to plod along to an approximate solution. With FDM, we have to be very careful how we program the schemes and a certain amount of Numerical Analysis expertise (and intuition) is needed to create a reliable scheme, especially for nonlinear problems and problems with 'nasty' boundary conditions.

We summarise these conclusions in Figure 20.11 where the numbers have the following *g* meanings:

|  | FDM | MC | Lattice |
|---|---|---|---|
| Accuracy | 2 | 1 | 3 |
| Performance | 1 | 3 | 2 |
| Applicability | 2 | 1 | 3 |
| Fault Tolerance | 3 | 1 | 2 |
| Maintainability | 2 | 1 | 3 |
| Extendibility | 2 | 1 | 3 height |

**Figure 20.11**   Method comparison

1. The 'Best' method to satisfy the given requirement
2. The second best
3. Least suitable candidate of the three

## 20.9   EXERCISES AND PROJECTS

1. (Numerical Integration) Use the Monte Carlo method to find an approximate value for the two-dimensional integral

$$\int_0^1 \int_0^2 xy\,dx\,dy$$

2. (Testing the Software) We take the following example (see Clewlow and Strickland (1998). p. 84): Price an at-the-money European call option with:
   - $T = 1$ (1 year maturity)
   - $S = 100$ (current price)
   - $K = 100$ (strike price)
   - Volatility $= 0.2$
   - Interest rate $r = 0.06$
   - Dividend yield $= 0.03$
   - $N = 10$ (number of time steps)
   - $M = 100$ (number of simulations)

   You should get the value 9.3846 as an estimate for the price of the call option. The standard deviation is 12.2246 and the standard error is 1.22246. Experiment with larger values of M in order to improve accuracy.

3. (Project: Modelling of Swing Options in Energy Markets) We examine some models that are used in commodity markets, in particular energy markets that are among the most complex commodity markets. Some difficulties are:
   - The local nature of the markets
   - Severe inelasticity in supply and demand
   - Volume constraints on transfer and storage

   The processes that model the spot price of energy commodities are not lognormal. They are strongly mean-reverting and they depend on several time scales. Thus, the standard formulae that we used for option pricing are no longer applicable. There are a number of mean reverting models in use in this sector:
   - *One-factor models*: this is an SDE involving the spot price $S$ as unknown variable:

$$dS_t = \alpha(L - S_t)d_t + \sigma S_t^\partial dW_t$$

   where

$$\partial = 0, \text{ or } 1$$
$$\alpha > 0, \sigma > 0 \text{ and } L \text{ are constants}$$

   and

$$\alpha(L - S_t) \text{ is called the drift term}$$

   The constant $L$ is the equilibrium of the SDE. In general, the mean value of the spot price reverts to $L$ in the long term. It plays the role of an attractor that means that when the spot price $S$ is greater than $L$ the drift term becomes negative thus forcing the spot price to decrease. We can employ a similar argument when the spot price is less than $L$

- *Two-factor models*: These models allow the long run mean $L$ or the volatility to be stochastic. This leads to two distinct models. We take the former case in this exercise. In this case the systems of SDEs is given by:

$$\begin{cases} dS_t = \alpha(L_t - S_t)d_t + \sigma S_t^\gamma dW_t^{(1)} \\ dL_t = \mu L_t dt + \xi L_t^\delta dW_t^{(2)} \end{cases}$$

where

$dW_t^{(1)}$ and $dW_t^{(2)}$ are uncorrelated Brownian motions
$S_t$ = spot price
$L_t$ = long-term equilibrium price
$\alpha$ = rate of mean reversion
$\gamma = 0$ or $1$
$\delta = 0$ or $1$
$\sigma$ = spot price volatility
$\mu$ = equilibrium price drift
$\xi$ = equilibrium price volatility

We thus assume that $\alpha, \sigma, \mu$ and $\xi$ are constant but in general they could be time-dependent in order to capture seasonal effects. Finally, the noise terms are called *additive* if $\gamma$ and $\delta$ are equal to 0 and they are called *proportional* if $\gamma$ and $\delta$ are equal to one.

- *Three-factor models*: these allow us to model spikes in electricity prices. The governing system of SDEs is given by:

$$dS_t = \alpha(L_t - S_t)dt + \sigma S_t^\gamma dW_t^{(1)}$$
$$dL_t = \mu(M_t - L_t)dt + \xi L_t^\gamma dW_t^{(2)}$$
$$dM_t = \beta M_t dt + \lambda M_t^\gamma dW_t^{(3)}$$
$$(\gamma = 0 \text{ or } 1)$$

where $M_t$ is a second level of stochastic mean reversion that introduces higher local shocks to $S_t$ via $L_t$. Local shocks to the spot price are triggered by the combined nonlinear effects of

$$L_t \text{ and } M_t$$

Answer the following questions:
(a) Apply the Predictor-Corrector method as discussed in section 20.4 to the two-factor model with the following values for the parameters:

$$\alpha = 10$$
$$\sigma = 0.4$$
$$\gamma = 1$$
$$\mu = 0$$
$$\xi = 0.05$$
$$\delta = 1$$

(b) Implement the algorithm in C++ on the interval $[0, 10]$ (hence $T = 10$) and with 50 subdivisions: Display the arrays for spot price and equilibrium using the Excel Visualisation package that accompanies this book (see the code on the CD).

(c) Having found sample values of the spot price and equilibrium calculate the price of a call option using the Monte Carlo method using 100,000 samples.

(d) Compare and contrast the explicit Euler and Milstein methods for the two-factor model. Display both sets of results in Excel.

(e) Analyse the approximation error using the central limit theorem and consult the literature on the term standard error.

# 21
# Skills Development: from White Belt to Black Belt

*'Get it working, then get it right, then get it optimised'* Anonymous

## 21.1 INTRODUCTION AND OBJECTIVES

In this chapter we summarise a number of issues pertaining to the design and implementation of libraries, algorithms and applications for use in Quantitative Finance. The programming language is C++ and this is the de-facto standard in this domain. Based on history and the evolution of the software industry in general it is our humble opinion that C++ will remain a dominant force for many years to come. Of course, one must not exclude the fact that other software tools and languages may gain in popularity at the cost of C++.

This chapter summarises the first 20 chapters of the current book and we define a process so that the reader can learn C++ at his or her own pace. In particular, we measure skills by analogy with the Japanese sport of judo; everyone on the judo mat has a colour that tells others his or her level of expertise. The colours are white, yellow, orange, green, blue, brown and black (incidentally, there are ten grades of black). In judo, it takes between two and three years before one can become a black belt. In this book we concentrate on three critical levels:

- Green belt
- Brown belt
- Black belt

We define what the attainment of each of these grades entails and we also devise a plan to help the readers get their desired grades.

## 21.2 REVIEW OF BOOK

This is a book on the C++ and its applications to Quantitative Finance. No previous knowledge of C++ or C is assumed because all the necessary background information is contained in the book and we introduce and elaborate each new topic with as little reference to other sources as possible. The book is partitioned into four major sections with each section devoted to one major attention point. We now discuss each part in some detail.

## 21.3 PART I: C++ ESSENTIAL SKILLS

This part consists of ten chapters and it is here that we introduce and elaborate on the basic syntax of the C++ language. We also give some simple examples, some of which are generic in nature and some of which have direct relevance to Quantitative Finance.

The main attention points are:

- Introduction to classes: creating a class and objects
- Creating robust classes
- Operator overloading
- Memory management in C++
- Introduction to inheritance; advanced inheritance
- Run-time behaviour in C++ (casting, exception handling)
- Introduction to generic programming and templates

A good understanding of the chapters in this part is essential if you wish to progress to more advanced topics. In particular, it is essential that you know the difference between stack and heap memory, how to create objects on the stack and on the heap and what the significance of the operators `new` and `delete` is. We advise the reader to study Chapters 22 and 23 as background to the current section because it is in these chapters that we discuss essential C syntax that is needed if you wish to understand the syntax of C++.

After having read, studied and done the exercises in this part you should have gained a good knowledge of the syntax of C++.

## 21.4  PART II: DATA STRUCTURES, TEMPLATES AND PATTERNS

This section discusses how to create and use reusable data containers and algorithms in C++. Many C++ books tend to focus on the object-oriented aspects of the language but we must realise that C++ is a *multi-paradigm language* in the sense that the developer is not forced to work in an object-oriented fashion but may choose to create generic software (using the C++ template mechanism). A developer may even choose to use the C++ compiler to develop programs based on a functional model, as we see with the C language. Furthermore, we can even combine the object-oriented, generic and functional programming models in real-life application development. Not everything is, or should be modelled as an object.

The main focal points in this part are:

- Introduction to Complexity Analysis and Data Structures
- Introduction to the Standard Template Library (STL)
- Using the STL in Quantitative Finance applications
- Introduction to Design Patterns

The chapters in this section are very important if you wish to make the transition from the green-belt grade of Part I to brown-belt level. We discuss a number of important issues such as an overview of important data structures in Computer Science, which specific data structure to choose for a particular application (based on Complexity Analysis) and whether to write your own data structure or use one from the STL. Finally, we give an overview of the famous Design Patterns and we give some guidelines on how to use them in Quantitative Finance. Design Patterns pervade much of the C++ code that implements the applications in Part III of the book.

After having read, studied and done the exercises in this part you should have gained a good knowledge of templates, libraries and design patterns. In short, we lay the foundation for application development by designing and implementing building blocks that we shall assemble to produce non-trivial applications.

## 21.5   PART III: APPLICATIONS IN QUANTITATIVE FINANCE

This is the section in the book where C++ 'comes to life' as it were. We apply the syntax, data structures and design patterns from the first two parts of the book to create frameworks that will allow us to create applications for pricing derivatives. In general there are three major activities in any application:

- Input
- Processing
- Output

In this book we use the console medium for input and output. We have resisted discussing specific graphics libraries (such as MFC, OWL and WinForms) because they are not part of the C++ language. However, we do provide mechanisms for displaying the results of calculations (for example, array and matrix data) in Excel. This is the subject of Chapter 24 and it augments the results in Duffy (2004) where we discuss creating Excel Addins in C++.

The main points are:

- Binomial and Trinomial methods in C++
- One-factor and two-factor models with the finite difference method
- The Monte Carlo method
- Some useful methods in Numerical Analysis

After having read, studied and done the exercises in this part you should have gained a good knowledge of how to design and implement useful applications in C++. There are different approaches to help the reader achieve this end. Some suggestions are:

- Read the chapters and study how we designed the system in C++
- Examine and run the code on the CD; study the code to see how the system was developed
- If you have time, it is advisable to do the exercises and projects at the end of each chapter

## 21.6   PART IV: BACKGROUND INFORMATION

We have included this part in order to keep the book as self-contained as possible. In particular, we have included two chapters on the C programming language because it is (still) a subset of C++ and there are a number of issues in the language whose understanding will enhance your confidence with C++. Second, we give an introduction to the Component Object Model (COM) and C++ interfacing to Excel.

The main points are:

- A self-contained summary of the C language
- A visualisation package for data presentation in Excel
- An introduction to the Component Object Model (COM)

After having read, studied and done the exercises in this part you should have gained a good knowledge of a number of software techniques that may be of indirect and direct use when you develop applications in C++ under the Windows operating system(s).

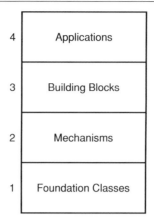

**Figure 21.1**    Software layering

## 21.7    CHOOSING A PROGRAMMING PARADIGM

In this section we give a very brief summary of how we have designed and developed the software in this book. On the one hand, we have developed libraries, modules and other reusable artefacts that we can use in various kinds of applications while on the other hand we employ higher-level design patterns and frameworks to create working applications. In other words, we adopt both a *bottom-up* and a *top-down* approach. There are two main advantages in using this tactic: first, by creating low-level modules (for example, useful data structures and algorithms) we know that we are creating software that *will* be used later in an application while adopting a top-down approach ensures that the scope of the problem at hand is specified in the initial stages of the software development lifecycle and that our software system will converge to a solution that the customer envisaged.

We develop software as a series of *conceptual layers*. This is the so-called 'uses' hierarchy that was developed in the 1960's. We adopt a four-layer regime as shown in Figure 21.1. The software entities in layer n use the functionality of the software entities in layer n-1. This process takes place by using aggregation, inheritance or association relationships, for example. On the other hand, the software entities in layer n-1 have no knowledge of the software entities in layer n.

The main layers and their responsibilities are now introduced.

### 21.7.1    Layer 1: foundation classes

These are typically the application-independent data structures and algorithms that are needed by the other levels. In this case we are referring to the STL and the data structures in this book, for example `Vector`, `NumericMatrix`, `AsssocMatrix` and `SimplePropertySet`.

The object-oriented and generic paradigms are well represented in this layer.

### 21.7.2    Layer 2: mechanisms

A mechanism is a group of related modules that perform actions on the data structures in layer 1. The modules could be logically associated into namespaces so as to avoid possible function name collisions.

We have provided a number of mechanisms on the CD for vectors, matrices, lattices and dates. It is possible to create your own mechanisms on top of other data structures.

The functional and generic paradigms are well represented in this layer. Normally, objects play the role of input arguments and return types of functions.

### 21.7.3   Layer 3: building blocks

Here we build 'solvers' consisting of a network of objects that cooperate in order to carry out one specific duty. They are self-contained units but they do not have input or output functionality. Instead, they accept input in the form of data structures, for example while the output can be a built-in type or a data structure. An example of a building block is an LU solver for tridiagonal matrix systems.

The object-oriented and generic paradigms are well represented in this layer. The functions in the mechanisms are used in the member functions of the classes in layer 3.

### 21.7.4   Layer 4: application level

This is the layer in which we develop applications including the integration of input, processing and output. A number of typical examples are discussed in Part III of the book. An example of an application is the binomial solver that we introduced in Chapter 15.

## 21.8   SUMMARY AND CONCLUSIONS

This chapter was written with the objective of giving a global overview of the contents of this book. It provides the reader with a roadmap and guide on possible approaches to learning this complex and wonderful language that is called C++.

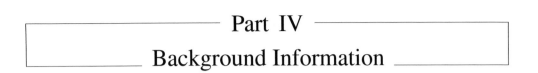

# Part IV
## Background Information

# Basic C Survival Guide

## 22.1 INTRODUCTION AND OBJECTIVES

We have written two chapters that give an overview of the most important features of the C language that you will need to understand if you wish to create robust C++ applications. Some people tend to criticise C++ because it is too low-level and difficult to understand but in my experience if you get the basics right then you will have few problems. To this end, this chapter concentrates on the basics of C and it may be skipped if you are a proficient C programmer. We recommend that you read chapter 23 because it discusses some C syntax that we use in our C++ code and applications.

We discuss built-in data types in C, memory allocation issues, including the dreaded 'pointer' mechanism. Furthermore, we introduce a number of issues relating to the structure of C programs, code and header files and other practical issues. Finally, we give a list of features in C that we tend to avoid because on the one hand, their use makes our code difficult to understand or to maintain and on the other hand, these features have been superseded by better constructs in C++.

One of the reasons for the emergence of C++ was to produce a language that would be a 'better C'. Of course, another reason was to support the object-oriented paradigm. In short, C++ allows us to combine the functional and object-oriented paradigms and we make use of them in this book. We adopt a multi-paradigm approach in this book (by the way, the third paradigm is generic programming as realised by the C++ template mechanism.)

The standard reference on the C language is Kernighan and Ritchie (1988) (also known as K & R). In particular, you should understand most of the chapters (especially chapters two, five and six) in K & R if you wish to be a good C++ programmer. A good knowledge of C means that you will waste less time testing and debugging your C++ applications.

Summarising, we discuss the following syntax in this chapter:

- Built-in data types in C
- Structure of a C program
- What are pointers and references?
- Stack-based and heap-based memory allocation
- Why C++ is a 'better C'
- Test case: numerical integration in one dimension

After having read and understood this chapter you will have a good basic understanding of the C language.

## 22.2 BASIC DATA TYPES

C has support for the numeric and alphanumeric data types that you would expect in a high-level programming language. The basic C types are:

- `char`: holds a single character (usually a byte)
- `int`: an integer
- `float`: single-precision floating point
- `double`: double-precision floating point

There are also a number of qualifiers to these data types but we will not have any need for them in this book. The above four basic types suffice in nearly all cases. In fact, we hardly ever use the char types (and the dreaded character pointer `char*`) in financial engineering application. If we need to use data types based on characters we tend to use the STL (Standard Template Library) `string` class.

The number of bits in each data type in C is compiler and hardware dependent. The maximum and minimum allowed sizes for the different data types are defined in the header file `<limits.h>` for integral types and `<float.h>` for floating-point types.

## 22.3   THE C PREPROCESSOR

The *C preprocessor* is not part of the C language and in general terms we can see it as a macro language. Its main functions are:

- Macro definitions and substitution
- Conditional compilation and file inclusions
- Source file inclusion

With the exception of the last feature we try to minimise the amount of preprocessor code in our applications because it does not compile the code that it processes and unexpected results can occur. However, in some cases it is needed.

In general the preprocessor works with so-called *directives* that we place in the source code files. Using directives allows us to communicate with the preprocessor. Each directive must begin with the character '#'. For example, to include a file we use the `include` directive as follows:

```
#include <limits.h>
```

This is the standard syntax for system header files. When you wish to include your own files, you should use the following notation (double quotes), for example:

```
#include "MonteCarlo.h"
#include "Option.hpp"
```

These directives have the effect that the preprocessor searches for the given file in a set of standard directory locations.

Another feature is the `macro`. This is a useful way to define 'magic numbers' so that if you have to change their value you only have to do it in one place. Some examples are:

```
#define MAX 256
```

This statement defines a constant called `MAX` with a value 256. When you compile a source file that uses this constant, every occurrence of it will be replaced by the given value. It is also possible to define macros that use arguments as the following example shows:

```
#define sqr(x) ((x) * (x))
```

Note that this expression is not a function; it is pure symbol substitution technique. We advise against this extended use of the macro directive.

We now come to an essential macro feature that you will need in large C and C++ applications. In this case we usually partition our code into multiple files. Of course, we do not want to include the same file twice, so to this end we use the so-called *conditional compilation directives*:

```
#ifdef, #ifndef      // if defined, if not defined
#elsif               // else if
#else                // else
#endif               // end of block
```

For example, here is preprocessor code that includes a given file depending on the operating system in use:

```
#ifdef __WINDOWS
      #include <winio.h>
#else
      #include <stdio.h>
#endif
```

Another common application of this feature is when we partition our C or C++ code into two files; first, the header file that contains the function headers only and the code file that contains the bodies of these functions. We mostly include the header file from the code file and of course we want it to be included only once. The conditional compilation directive is one way of achieving this, for example:

```
// This is the header file
#ifndef SOME_VARIABLE
#define SOME_VARIABLE

      // C declarations here

#endif
```

The effect of this directive is that the C code will only be included once, thus avoiding multiple includes and the ensuing compiler errors. This is especially important for us when we create our own classes.

## 22.4   POINTERS AND REFERENCES

We now come to one of the features in C that is the major stumbling block for novice (and some experienced!) C++ programmers. I refer to the dreaded pointer mechanism. Before we are able to tell what a pointer is we must define the concept of an *address*. In general, data is stored in memory, storage location or some other destination of data. We must be able to access the data and to this end we introduce the concept of an address. This is identified by a name, tag or some other label (we shall show in a moment how to do this in C).

Now, we define a *pointer* as a variable that contains the address of some storage. Thus, a pointer is not data as such but is the address of the data. When working with pointers, we have to take the following activities into consideration:

A1: Declaring a variable as a pointer

A2: Ensuring that the address of the pointer actually contains data

A3: Cleaning up memory when the variable is no longer needed.

We first discuss activity A1. We declare a pointer variable to any built-in or user-type by using '*', for example:

```
int* myVar;       // Pointer to an integer
float* myVar2;    // Pointer to a float
Option* myOption; // Pointer to an instance of class Option
```

After having declared the pointer variable in this way we remark that its address is defined but randomly generated. Thus the contents of the address are not defined.**The contents will contain rubbish and junk**. If we wish to initialise the pointer, in effect stating that the pointer address is really 'empty' as it were, we explicitly give it the value zero:

```
myVar = 0;
myVar2 = 0;
myOption = 0;
```

This *initialisation technique* may be useful in applications because we know that the pointer has been initialised.

We can now populate the address with data by use of the '&' operator. This operator calculates the address of a 'normal' variable as the following example shows. First we define two 'normal' variables

```
int i2;
Option opt1;       // Default, prototypical Option instance
```

Then we can now assign the already defined pointers as follows:

```
myVar = &i2;
myVar2 = &i2;
myOption = &opt1;
```

The conclusion is that these three pointers point to data in memory. In order to get at the data itself we must use so-called *dereferencing* using the operator '*', for example:

```
*myVar;
*myVar2;
*myOption;
```

These *dereferenced variables* are just instances of the respective data types. For example, *myVar is a normal int that can be printed, used in expressions and so on:

```
*myVar = 19;
cout << myVar;
```

Finally, pointer cleanup is automatically taken care of by the compiler in the above examples, because pointers live on the stack. This is not the case when the programmer allocates memory on the heap (using `malloc()` or new operators). We shall come back to this issue at a later stage.

## 22.5   OTHER USEFUL BITS AND PIECES

We discuss several other features of C syntax that we use throughout this book. First, the type specifier enum is used to create numeration types. An enumeration is a list of named constants that a variable of that type may have. For example, we define a list of colours as follows:

```
enum Colours {Red, Green, Blue, Indigo, Violet};
```

We can now define some variables of this type as follows:

```
Colours myCol;     // Undefined value
Colours myCol2 = Green;
```

The values associated with named constants are integer values.

Another useful piece of syntax is the keyword 'typedef'. For example, the declaration

```
typedef int Int32;
```

means that Int32 is a synonym for int. The new variable name can be used in code as follows:

```
Int32 myVar = 8;
```

We note that the typedef declaration does not introduce or create a new data type. All it does is to add a new name for an existing type. In fact, this feature is similar to a #define in the sense that nothing new is added to the type. It's just a different name for the same thing.

We make extensive use of the typedef facility with templates in C++, for example:

```
typedef Vector<double, int> DoubleVector;
```

Finally, it is possible to define pointers to functions in C. This feature can be very useful in applications. In C a function is not a variable but we can define so-called *function pointers* (that 'point' to functions). These pointers can be assigned, placed in arrays, passed to functions and returned by functions (Kernighan and Ritchie, 1988).

## 22.6   WHAT TO AVOID IN C

C is a low-level language (this does not mean that this is necessarily bad) and it has much functionality for device-driver and hardware interfacing. It can lend itself to unreadable code, thus making it difficult to maintain. In general, some of the C syntax has been improved upon by C++ and second, some features that work in C but are difficult to understand should be redesigned. We give a short list of features that I feel are not needed in real object-oriented applications:

- void*, these are pointers that can point to any kind of data
- double pointers and multi-dimensional arrays, for example:

```
double** matrix;
int myArray[200][30];
```

- Structs and unions are hardly ever needed; they correspond to record structures
- The C standard input and output; we use the C++ iostream library when needed (mostly for debugging only)

- We use the C++ operators `new` and `delete` for memory allocation and deallocation rather than `malloc()` and `free()`. We certainly do not mix these allocation and deallocation mechanisms.

In short, we like to hide nasty details (this is called *Information Hiding*) in classes and reuse these classes in various applications.

## 22.7   TEST CASE: NUMERICAL INTEGRATION IN ONE DIMENSION

We now develop some C code to integrate real-valued functions of a singe variable by two different numerical integration routines, namely the well-known mid-point rule and the so-called Tanh integration rule. The code is in fact a reverse-engineering of the corresponding C++ code in conjunction with design patterns as described in Duffy (2004).

The main points are:

- Define a global function that accepts a function pointer as input parameter
- Assign the function pointer to a user-defined function and call the numerical integration routine

We concentrate on the midpoint rule to show what we mean. First, in order to write code that works with any real-valued function of a single variable we define a so-called function pointer as follows:

```
double (*f)(double x);
```

This is unusual-looking code but it is just the declaration of a pointer to a function. The name 'f' that we use for the function pointer is just a convenient notation and you could have used any expressive name; for example, the following names are also allowed:

```
double (*func)(double x);
double (*myFunc)(double x);
double (*AnyFuncName)(double x);
```

In applications, we must use concrete functions and to this end we define functions that we will integrate using the midpoint rule:

```
double myFunc (double x) { return x*x*x; }
double myFunc2 (double x) { return log(x) / (1.0 - x); }
```

Continuing, we define the code that numerically integrates a real-valued function of a single variable using the midpoint rule:

```
double MidpointRuleValue(double (*f)(double x), double A, double B,
                                     int N)
{ // Integrate f on the interval [A, B] using the midpoint rule
        double res = 0.0;
        double h = (B - A)/ double (N);
        for (double x = A + (0.5 * h); x < B; x += h)
        {
                res += f(x); // N.B. call the function
        }
        return res*h;
}
```

We now call this function by supplying the above two concrete functions:

```
int main()
{
        int N = 200;        // Number of subdivisions

        double A = 0.0;
        double B = 1.0;

        double d = MidpointRuleValue(myFunc, A, B, N);
        cout << "Approximate integral Midpoint rule is: " << d << endl;

        double d2 = MidpointRuleValue(myFunc2, A, B, N);
        cout << "Approximate integral is: " << d2
                << ", Exact: " << - (3.1415)*(3.1415)/6.0 << endl;
        return 0;
}
```

We can extend the function pointer idea to real-valued functions of several variables (see the exercises).

These ideas can be applied to other branches of Numerical Analysis where we work with functions for interpolation and extrapolation, curve fitting and smoothing. Of course, these topics have numerous applications in Quantitative Finance, for each yield curve calculations.

## 22.8   CONCLUSIONS AND SUMMARY

We have given a review of what we would call essential C knowledge. It is surprising that some C++ programmers go through life without grasping the essentials of pointers, memory allocation and general C *savoir faire*. Hopefully, this and the next chapter will help the reader to appreciate the most important features in C that we need to understand when we design and implement real object-oriented applications in C++.

## 22.9   EXERCISES

1. Test the midpoint rule for the following functions:

| Integral | Exact Answer |
| --- | --- |
| $\int_0^1 \dfrac{\log x}{1 - x^2}\, dx$ | $-\pi^2/8$ |
| $\int_0^1 \log\left(\dfrac{1 + x}{1 - x}\right) \dfrac{dx}{x}$ | $\pi^2/4$ |
| $\int_0^\pi \dfrac{dx}{a + b \cos x}$ | $\dfrac{\pi}{(a^2 - b^2)^{\frac{1}{2}}} \quad a > b > 0$ |

(22.1)

Compare your answers with the exact answers. Experiment with the step size. What is the order of accuracy of the midpoint rule?

2. We show the code for the Tanh Rule:

```
double TanhRuleValue(double (*f)(double x), double A, double B, int N)
{ // Integrate f on the interval [A, B] using the Tanh rule

    double res = 0.0;
    double h = (B - A)/ double (N);
    for (double x = A + (0.5 * h); x < B; x += h)
    {
        res += tanh( (*f)(x) * 0.5 * h);
    }
    return 2.0 * res;
}
```

Test this algorithm using the functions from exercise 1. The type of functions used have absolute value less than 1 (for example, probability density functions).

3. We wish to numerically integrate real-valued functions of two variables:

$$f = f(x, y) \tag{22.2}$$

by modelling them in C as follows:

```
double (*f) (double x, double y);
```

Consider the two-dimensional variant of the midpoint rule on a 'small' box:

$$\int_a^b \int_c^d f(x, y)dxdy \approx h_1 h_2 f(m_1, m_2)$$

where

$$h_1 = b - a$$
$$h_2 = d - c$$
$$m_1 = \frac{(b + a)}{2}, \quad m_2 = \frac{(d + c)}{2} \tag{22.3}$$

Now write a function:

```
double TwoDMidpointRuleValue(double (*f)(double x, double y),
            double A, double B,double C, double D, int N, int M);
```

where N and M are the number of subdivisions in the x and y directions, respectively. Test your code on the unit rectangle $(0,1) \times (0,1)$ for the following functions:

$$\frac{1}{(x - y)^\alpha} \quad \text{for various values of } \alpha$$

$$\frac{1}{\sqrt{x - y}}, \quad \frac{1}{1 - xy}$$

$$\frac{1}{r}, \quad \text{where } r = \sqrt{x^2 + y^2} \tag{22.4}$$

4. Checklist Questions

Make sure that you understand the following concepts, syntax and standards (hint: do some *focused research* in Stroustrup (1997), for example. Consult the index there for starters)

- Integral and floating points types and how to convert/cast from one type to another type. You also need to know about data types, their sizes, declaring them and assigning values to them.
- What is the bool type? What are its values? How can you use it in your C++ code?
- What is an enumeration type?
- We shall need a number of C preprocessor directives when creating C++ classes, in particular when creating header and code files.
- You should know what the following terms mean: declaring a pointer type, initialising a pointer, assigning a pointer to an address, dereferencing

# Advanced C Syntax

*'Back to the Future'*

## 23.1 INTRODUCTION AND OBJECTIVES

In this chapter we continue from Chapter 22 with a more in-depth discussion of C syntax. In particular, we describe the lifecycle of one-dimensional and multi-dimensional arrays, namely creating arrays, accessing and modifying the elements in an array and finally removing an array from memory. These features make extensive use of pointer arithmetic and understanding the code here will improve your general knowledge of C. In practice however, you do not need to get down to this level of detail because STL (Standard Template Library) provides the array classes `vector` and `valarray` and this book provides a number of vector, matrix and tensor classes that you can use in your applications.

We then move on to introduce the concept of *struct*. This is a logical grouping of a collection of one or more variables, possibly of different types. The struct can be accessed as a single entity and in fact it is similar to a class in C++, except in the case of a struct all members are public.

We conclude this chapter with an overview of some of the functionality in the C standard library and it is useful to know what's in the library and how to use it. A particularly important library is `<math.h>` as it contains functionality for many of the common mathematical functions that we need in our financial engineering applications.

Summarising, we discuss the following syntax in this chapter:

- More on pointers
- Pointers to functions
- One-dimensional and multi-dimensional arrays
- The struct concept in C and how to use it
- The C standard library
- Input and output
- A test case (linear regression)

After having read and understood this chapter you will have a good understanding of a number of features of the C language that can give you problems if you do not learn them well.

The topics in this chapter are important for several reasons. First, they are used in C++ applications instead of 'pure' object-oriented constructions and you will need to be familiar with them. In the past, many C++ applications evolved or even degraded into C applications due the fact that C code is easier and quicker to write than C++ code and developers are always under pressure to produce results for management. Second, many potential employers may ask you questions on C syntax during interviews.

## 23.2   FIXED-SIZE AND DYNAMIC ARRAYS

It is possible to create fixed-size arrays on the stack or dynamic arrays on the heap. In order to reduce the scope we concentrate on one-dimensional arrays for the moment. We first look at fixed-size arrays by taking an example of an array of integers of length 4. The declaration is as follows:

```
int myArray[4]; // Fixed array size 4, undefined values
```

To initialise the values we can either do it in a hard-coded way or using a loop, for example:

```
myArray[4] = {2, 3, 4, 5};
```

or

```
For (int j = 0; j < 4; j++) // Looping starts at 0 in C!
{
      MyArray[j] = (2 + j);
}
```

## 23.3   MULTI-DIMENSIONAL ARRAYS

We discuss stack-based multi-dimensional arrays in this section. In general, it is our feeling that writing these arrays yourself is a waste of time, error-prone (especially if you are working on the heap) and a lot of what you need may already be in STL or on the CD accompanying this book.

To take a simple example, let us suppose that we wish to create a matrix (rows and columns) structure with two rows and three columns and to initialise the values identically to 0. The code for doing this is:

```
// Avoid magic numbers
#define ROWS 2
#define COLUMNS 3

// Declare the matrix
double myMatrix[ROWS][COLUMNS];

// Now initialise the values in the matrix
for (int j = 0; j < ROWS; j++)
{
      for (int k = 0; k < COLUMNS; k++)
      {
            myMatrix[j][k] = 0.0;
      }
}
```

We do not discuss creating multidimensional arrays on the heap. There are other ways as we see in the chapters on C++ in this book.

## 23.4   INTRODUCTION TO STRUCTURES

A structure is a collection of one or more variables, possibly of different types under a single name for convenient handling (Kernighan and Ritchie, 1988). It is similar to a record structure in languages such as COBOL and the table structures in relational database theory. These structures also correspond to the member data in a C++ class declaration. However, all data in a structure are public by default. In order to define a structure we use the 'struct' keyword in C. For example, here is how you define a structure for two-dimensional points:

```
struct Point              // Start of a structure declaration
{
        double x;    // x coordinate
        double y;    // y coordinate
};
```

The variables in the struct are called its members. Note that structures can be assigned to, copied and passed to functions and returned by functions. A structure may even contain other nested structures. Lets take some examples to show what we mean. We can declare an instance of a structure and assign its individual elements using the dot notation:

```
struct Point pt;

pt.x = 1.0;
pt.y = 2.0;
```

We now give an example of structure nesting. Consider a LineSegment structure consisting of two points:

```
struct LineSegment
{
        struct Point p1;
        struct Point p2;
};
```

We can then assign the members in this structure as follows:

```
struct LineSegment linSeg;
linSeg.p1 = pt;
linSeg.p2 = pt;
```

Another example from option pricing is to group all the data that belong to an option into a structure:

```
struct OptionData
{
        double r;        // Interest rate
        double sig;      // Volatility
        double K;        // Strike price
        double T;        // Expiry date
        double U;        // Current underlying price
        double b;        // Cost of carry
};
```

We can initialise the data in this structure as follows:

```
struct OptionData myOpt = {0.06, 0.20, 120.0, 1.0, 110.0, 0.0};
```

Summarising, structures can be useful as placeholders for groups of related data (note the members do not necessarily have to be of the same type) and they could be an alternative to classes. For example, structures and functions can be combined to simulate member functions in classes, as the following code shows:

```
double Price(struct OptionData optdata)
{
      // Calculate Black Scholes price in here
}
```

Finally, arrays of structures are also possible for example:

```
struct OptionData portfolio[10];
```

## 23.5  UNIONS

A union, like the structure is a data aggregate. However, a union is a variable that may hold at different times objects of different types and sizes. It gives us a means for manipulating different kinds of data in a single area of storage. A standard example is a the union that can contain either integer or floating point values:

```
union Tag
{
      int ival;
      double dval;
};
```

We can initialise the values in the union using the usual notation, for example:

```
union Tag myTag;
myTag.ival = 7;
myTag.dval = 3.1415;
```

Please note that the original value in `ival` is undefined after the second assignment. Only one variable has the correct value at any given time.

You probably will have little occasion to use unions, but you never know.

## 23.6  USEFUL C LIBRARIES

There are several libraries that we can use without C code. They are documented in Kernighan and Ritchie (1988). Most of them are not used in this book, but there are a number of useful libraries:

### <math.h>

Mathematical functions. It consists of the usual trigonometric functions (in radians) as well as the hyperbolic trigonometric functions, for example:

`tanh(x)` == hyperbolic tangent of x

Other useful functions are:

- `modf(x, double *ip)`: this function splits x into integral and fractional parts, each with the same sign as x. It stores the integral part in `*ip` and return the fractional part
- `fmod(x, y)` floating point remainder of x/y, with the same sign as x. If y is zero, the result is implementation-defined
- `ceil(x)`: smallest integer not less than x, expressed as a double. For example `ceil(2.8)` is 3.0 and `ceil(-2.8)` is -2.0.
- `floor(x)`: largest integer not greater than x, expressed as a double. For example `floor(2.8)` is 2.0 and `floor(-2.8)` is -3.0.

Note that we should call these functions using the *global namespace operator* `'::'`, for example in the example `::sqrt(2.0)`.

**<time.h>**
Date and time types and functions for manipulating date and time.

**<limits.h> and <float.h>**
Contain implementation-defined limits for integral and floating types, respectively.

## 23.7   TEST CASE: LINEAR REGRESSION

Curve fitting is very important in financial engineering. We show how to write C code to find the least squares straight line for N points

$$(x_j, y_j), \quad j = 1, \ldots, N$$

and we wish to find the straight line of the form

$$y = a + bx \tag{23.1}$$

that is the best-fitting line to these points in the least-squares sense. In fact we must calculate the constants a and b in equation (23.1). This entails solving the following equations for a and b. We give the necessary coefficients:

$$
\begin{cases}
a = \dfrac{\sum y \sum x^2 - \sum x \sum xy}{N \sum x^2 - \left(\sum x\right)^2} \\[4mm]
b = \dfrac{N \sum xy - \left(\sum x\right)\left(\sum y\right)}{N \sum x^2 - \left(\sum x\right)^2} \\[4mm]
\text{where we use the shorthand notation} \\[2mm]
\sum x \equiv \sum_{j=1}^{N} x_j \ \ \text{etc}
\end{cases}
\tag{23.2}
$$

Having found the general equation for the least-squares line we can find the y value on the line for any given value of x (or vice versa).

We now discuss how to create code for linear regression. We now must think about mapping this mathematical formulation into C code. We have already programmed this problem using

C++ in Duffy (2004). To this end, we first create two classes that represent points in (x,y) space and a structure that models the (infinite) line as defined in equation (23.1):

```
struct Point
{
      double x;
      double y;
};

struct Line
{ // a + bx

      double a;
      double b;

      void print() const { cout << "a + bx: a = " << a
                          << ", b = " << b << endl; }
      double value(double xval) const { return a + b*xval; }
};
```

We now implement the coefficients of a line's parameters a and b by using the formulae in equation (23.2). To this end, we define some auxiliary 'help' functions. The code should be easy to follow:

```
double sum(double* x, int n)
{ // Sum of elements
      double ans = x[0];
      for (int j = 1; j < n; j++)
      {
            ans += x[j];
      }
      return ans;
}
double sumSquares(double* x, int n)
{ // Sum of squares

      double ans = x[0] * x[0];
      for (int j = 1; j < n; j++)
      {
            ans += (x[j] * x[j]);
      }
      return ans;
}

double innerProduct(double* x, double* y, int n)
{ // Inner product

double ans = x[0] * y[0];
```

```
    for (int j = 1; j < n; j++)
    {
        ans += (x[j] * y[j]);
    }
    return ans;
}
```

Finally, we assemble the above functions into one main function that actually implements formula (23.2):

```
Line LinearRegressionLine (double* xarr, double* yarr, int N)
{ // Find the regression line for a set of input data

    // Now the parameters for the linear regression line
    double sumx = sum(xarr, N);
    double sumy = sum(yarr, N);

    double sumSx = sumSquares(xarr, N);
    double sumSy = sumSquares(yarr, N);

    double ip = innerProduct(xarr, yarr, N);

    double denominator = double(N)*sumSx - (sumx*sumx);
    double A = (sumy*sumSx - (sumx*ip))/denominator;
    double B = (double(N)*ip - (sumx*sumy))/denominator;
    Line lin;
    lin.a = A;
    lin.b = B;
    return lin;
}
```

We now give an example of how to use the code; we create two arrays and we used them as input for the linear regression function:

```
double Xarr[] = {65, 63, 67, 64, 68, 62, 70, 66, 68, 67, 69, 71};
double Yarr[] = {68, 66, 68, 65, 69, 66, 68, 65, 71, 67, 68, 70};

int n = 12;
lin = LinearRegressionLine (Xarr, Yarr, n);
lin.print();
cout << "Give x value: ";
cin >> xval;
cout << "Y value is: " << lin.value(xval);
```

Another example using heap memory is:

```
const int N = 4;
struct Point polyline[N];
```

```
for (int j = 0; j < N; j++)
{
     polyline[j] = createPoint(j, j);

     cout << polyline[j].x << ", " << polyline[j].y << endl;
}

// Now extract the x and y arrays
double* xarr = new double[N];
double* yarr = new double[N];

for (int i = 0; i < N; i++)
{
     xarr[i] = polyline[i].x;
     yarr[i] = polyline[i].y;
     cout << xarr[i] << ", " << yarr[i] << endl;
}

double xval;
cout << "Give x value: ";
cin >> xval;

Line lin = LinearRegressionLine (xarr, yarr, N);
lin.print();
cout << "Y value is: " << lin.value(xval);
```

Of course, the arrays must be cleaned up:

```
delete [] xarr; delete [] yarr;
```

Please see the code on the CD for the full details.

## 23.8   CONCLUSIONS AND SUMMARY

We have given a quick overview of some advanced features in C that are of use when creating C++ code and classes. In particular, we introduce a number of features that allow us to create one-dimensional and two-dimensional arrays. Furthermore, we have introduced the struct and union record data types.

## 23.9   EXERCISES

1. Write code that calculates the standard error in linear regression:

$$s_{y,x}^2 = \frac{\sum y^2 - a \sum y - b \sum xy}{N} \qquad (23.3)$$

2. Section 7 discusses the code for the regression line of y on x. Modify and extend the code in section 7 to find the regression line of x on y:

$$x = a + by \qquad (23.4)$$

where

$$a = \frac{\sum x \sum y^2 - \sum y \sum xy}{N \sum y^2 - \left(\sum y\right)^2}$$

$$b = \frac{N \sum xy - \left(\sum x\right)\left(\sum y\right)}{N \sum y^2 - \left(\sum y\right)^2}$$

(23.5)

# 24

# Datasim Visualisation Package in Excel: Drivers and Mechanisms

## 24.1 INTRODUCTION AND OBJECTIVES

In this chapter we describe and document a small library of C++ classes and functions that present the results of a numerical scheme in a form that is easily understood and comprehended. In this book we are particularly interested in displaying the output from finite difference schemes and lattices methods. For example, we can use the functions in the visualisation package to display the price of a contingent claim and its corresponding sensitivity values (the 'Greeks') in a variety of formats.

The focus in this chapter is on 'exporting' data to Excel. Thus, we are discussing display and visualisation effects and we exclude any discussion of two-way communication between Excel and external applications. The package could be used for a variety of applications, not all of which are discussed here:

- Exporting cell data to Excel for further processing using Addins and VBA code, for example
- Display results from different branches of Numerical Analysis, for example interpolation and yield curve data
- Using Excel as a simple database

The visualisation package uses the containers `Vector`, `NumericMatrix` and `Tensor`. In general, the numerical schemes in this book produce output in one of the above forms and to this end we have created functions to display their values in cellular or graphical format.

## 24.2 FUNDAMENTAL FUNCTIONALITY IN THE PACKAGE

The package consists of two main entities:

- `ExcelDriver`: this is a C++ class that is an adapter or wrapper for the COM interface to Excel
- `ExcelMechanisms`: a suite of generic functions that display one, two- and three-dimensional data in a variety of formats

We now discuss the package from a number of perspectives.

## 24.3 BASIC DRIVER FUNCTIONALITY

We have designed the software for a number of reasons. First, the author developed numerical methods for option pricing models and he wished to display the results of calculations in a form that is easy to visualise and to quickly determine if the results were correct. In particular, we wish to display option prices and their sensitivities for problems having one or more underlyings. Furthermore, we have included functionality as follows:

- Single line graphs in one sheet
- Multiple line graphs in one sheet
- Displaying vectors and matrices as cell data
- Displaying tensors (arrays of matrices) in line graph and cell formats

Finally, we have also included some extra functionality for 'odds and ends':

- Displaying a real-valued functions as a graph in Excel
- Displaying error messages in a new Excel sheet

It is possible to create your own functions by adding them to the ExcelMechanisms header and code files. To this end, you need to determine what the desired functionality is and then implement it in C++ by defining the declaration in ExcelMechanisms.hpp and the body of the function in ExcelMechanisms.cpp. You may need to include code that handles exceptions due to the fact that clients have called the function using incorrect parameters or possibly using correct parameters but used in the incorrect order in the function parameter list.

The interface of ExcelDriver is given by:

```cpp
class ExcelDriver
{
private:
        // Private member data and member functions

public:
        // Constructor. Starts Excel in invisible mode.
        ExcelDriver();

        // Destructor.
        virtual ~ExcelDriver();

        // Access to single, shared instance of ExcelDriver (singleton).
        static ExcelDriver& Instance();

        // Create a chart with MULTIPLE line charts
        void CreateChart(
                const Vector<double, long> & x, X values
                const list<string> & labels,
                const list<Vector<double, long> > & vectorList, const
                std::string& chartTitle, const std::string& xTitle = "X",
                const std::string& yTitle = "Y");

        // Create a chart with SINGLE line charts
        void CreateChart(const Vector<double, long> & x,
                const Vector<double, long> & y,
                const std::string& chartTitle,
                const std::string& xTitle = "X",
                const std::string& yTitle = "Y");
```

```
// Add Matrix to the spreadsheet with row and column labels.
void AddMatrix(const std::string& sheetName,
               const NumericMatrix<double, long>& matrix,
               const list<std::string>& rowLabels,
               const list<std::string>& columnLabels);

// Add Matrix with little overhead
void AddMatrix(const NumericMatrix<double, long>& matrix,
               const std::string& SheetName = "Matrix" );

// Default Excel is NOT displayed on screen
void MakeVisible( bool b);

// For debugging, for example; strings at a row + column
void printStringInExcel(const string& s, long rowNumber,
                        long colNumber, const string& sheetName);
void printStringInExcel(const list<string>& s,
                        long rowNumber, long colNumber,
                        const string& sheetName);
};
```

We see that this class has a special member function that allows us to create a single unique instance of Excel (this is an example of the *Singleton pattern*, see for example Duffy, 2004 and GOF, 1995). This unique object is created using *Lazy Initialisation* and the code that realizes this is given by:

```
// Access to single, shared instance of ExcelDriver (singleton).
ExcelDriver& ExcelDriver::Instance()
{
        static ExcelDriver singleton;
        return singleton;
}
```

We thus see that we can only have one instance of Excel at any one time using the package. If you wish to start several instances of Excel you should then use the default constructor from the driver class.

An example of use is the following: the objective is to create a matrix, annotate its rows and columns and then send the information to Excel. The code to do this is given by:

```
Long N = 20; long M = 30;
NumericMatrix<double, long> matrix(N+1, M+1);

Vector<double, long> xarr(N+1);
Vector<double, long> yarr(N+1);

// Create the x and y arrays
double h1 = 0.1;
xarr[xarr.MinIndex()] = 0.0;
```

```
for (long i = xarr.MinIndex()+1; i <= xarr.MaxIndex(); i++)
{
      xarr[i] = xarr[i-1] + h1;
}


double h2 = 0.2;
yarr[yarr.MinIndex()] = 0.0;
for (long j = yarr.MinIndex()+1; j <= yarr.MaxIndex(); j++)
{
      yarr[j] = yarr[j-1] + h2;
}


// Create textual information
list<std::string> rowlabels = convertToString(xarr);
list<std::string> columnlabels = convertToString(yarr);
std::string sheetName("First");


// Start Excel and make it visible
ExcelDriver& excel = ExcelDriver::Instance();
excel.MakeVisible(true);                 // Default is INVISIBLE!


// Send the matrix to Excel
excel.AddMatrix(sheetName, matrix, rowlabels, columnlabels);
```

See the code on the CD for more examples. In general, we prefer to use the Excel mechanism functions as discussed in the following section. They can be seen as a façade to the low-level functionality in `ExcelDriver`.

## 24.4   EXCEL MECHANISMS

The basic driver class encapsulates some low-level functionality on C++ to Excel interoperability and clients access the class only through its public interface. But the functionality is not extensive enough for larger applications. To this end, we have created a number of procedures (no classes involved) that display vectors, matrices and tensors as line graphs or in cell and range formats. We use these functions in Quantitative Finance applications (see Duffy, 2006), for example.

The header file in this case is given by:

```
// Print one line graph
void printOneExcel(const Vector<double, long>& x,
               const Vector<double, long>& functionResult,
               const std::string& title = string("Title"),
               const std::string& horizontal = string("X"),
               const std::string& vertical = string("Y"),
               const std::string& legend = string("*"));


// Print multiple lines on one graph
void printInExcel(const Vector<double, long>& x,
```

```
                const list<std::string>& labels,
                const list<Vector<double, long> >& functionResult,
                const std::string& title = string("Title"),
                const std::string& horizontal = string("X"),
                const std::string& vertical = string("Y"));

// Print a matrix as cell
void printMatrixInExcel(const NumericMatrix<double, long>& matrix,
                const Vector<double, long>& xarr,
                const Vector<double, long>& yarr,
                const std::string& SheetName =
                                string("Matrix"));
// Print a matrix's rows as line graphs
void printMatrixChartsInExcel(int freq,
                const NumericMatrix<double, long>& matrix,
                const Vector<double, long>& rowAarr,
                const Vector<double, long>& colArr,
                const std::string& SheetName =
                                string("Matrix"));

// Print an array of matrices
void printTensorInExcel(const Tensor<double, long>& tensor,
                long freq = 1);

// Print each matrix in tensor with associated row/column labels
void printTensorInExcel(const Tensor<double, long>& tensor,
                const Vector<double, long>& xarr,
                const Vector<double, long>& yarr,
                const std::string& SheetName =
                                string("Tensor"), long freq = 1);

// Print the vector that is the difference of two vectors
void printDifferenceInExcel(const Vector<double, long>& x,
                const Vector<double, long>& y1,
                const Vector<double, long>& y2,
                const std::string& title =
                        string("Difference"),
                const std::string& horizontal =
                        string("X Values"),
                const std::string& vertical =
                        string("Y Values"),
                const std::string& legend =
                        string("*"), long freq = 1);

// Differences of two matrices
void printMatrixDifferenceInExcel(
                const NumericMatrix<double, long>& matrix1,
                const NumericMatrix<double, long>& matrix2,
```

```
                                const Vector<double, long>& xarr,
                                const Vector<double, long>& yarr,
                                const std::string& SheetName =
                                        string("Matrix"));

// Print discrete values of a continuous function on interval [A,B]
void printDiscreteFunctionValues(double (*f) (double x),
                            double A, double B, long nSteps,
                            const std::string& title,
                            const std::string& horizontal,
                            const std::string& vertical,
                            const std::string& legend);
```

These functions display n-dimensional data (n = 1, 2 and 3) in a variety of formats. Further-more, it is also possible to define so-called *context information* such as:

- The title of the sheet (sheet names must be unique)
- The title of the chart
- The title of the legend
- The title of the horizontal and vertical axes

Of course, we must be careful to define unique sheet names, otherwise Excel will experience a run-time error.

We take a simple example. To this end, we send a tensor to Excel. For convenience we take default values.

```
long nRows = 4;
long nColumns = 3;
long nThird = 12;

// Create three-dimensional structure
Tensor<double, long> t5(nRows, nColumns, nThird);

long startIndex = 1;
Vector<double, long> xarr(nRows, startIndex, 1.0);
Vector<double, long> yarr(nColumns, startIndex, 2.0);
string name("Ten ");

try
{
        printTensorInExcel(t5, xarr, yarr, name);
}
catch (DatasimException& e)
{
            e.print();
            return 0;
}
```

In this case we use the mechanism function to display the tensor. We place it in a try block to ensure that the parameters are given in the correct order. The actual server code checks the dimensions of the parameters as follows:

```
void printTensorInExcel(const Tensor<double, long>& tensor,
                        const Vector<double, long>& xarr,
                        const Vector<double, long>& yarr,
                        const std::string& SheetName, long freq)
{
        // PRECONDITION: Type II, III
        if (xarr.Size() != tensor.Rows() ||
                        yarr.Size() != tensor.Columns())
        {
                string tmp = string("Vectors X, Y, tensor M: ") +
                                getString(xarr.Size()) + comma +
                                getString(yarr.Size()) + bracketL +
                                getString(tensor.Rows()) + comma +
                                getString(tensor.Columns()) + bracketR;

                throw DatasimException(
                        string("Size mismatch of vector(s) and tensor"),
                        string("PrintTensorInExcel"), tmp);
        }

        list<std::string> rowlabels = convertToString(xarr);
        list<std::string> columnlabels = convertToString(yarr);

        ExcelDriver& excel = ExcelDriver::Instance();
        excel.MakeVisible(true);

        std::string tmp;

        for (long i = tensor.MinThirdIndex();
                        i <= tensor.MaxThirdIndex(); i++)
        {
                tmp = SheetName + getString(i);

                if ((i/freq)*freq == i || i == tensor.MinThirdIndex())
                {
                        excel.AddMatrix(tmp, tensor[i], rowlabels,
                                                columnlabels);
                }
        }
}
```

We conclude this section by showing how to display real-valued functions of a scalar variable in Excel. Let us take two functions:

```
double func(double x)
{
        return ::exp((x-0.5)*(x-0.5));
}
```

```
double func2(double x)
{
      return exp(-x*x*0.5);
}
```

We now display them in the intervals [0, 1] and [−5,5], respectively:

```
printDiscreteFunctionValues(
        func, 0.0, 1.0, 20, "Exp", "H", "V", "L");      // 20 discrete steps
printDiscreteFunctionValues(
        func2, -5.0, 5.0, 50, "Gauss", "H", "V", "L"); // 50 discrete steps
```

In this way we can transform a continuous function to a discrete function.

## 24.5   OPTION VALUES AND SENSITIVITIES IN EXCEL

We now give an application of the visualisation package. In this case we display the price of call and put options as well as their sensitivities in Excel. In particular, each graph will be displayed in its own sheet. To this end, we have created some classes and functionality. First, we create a class that implements option pricing functionality and its sensitivities (see Haug, 1998 for the formulae):

```
class Option
{ // Abstract base class for the options
public:

      virtual double Price(double U) const = 0;

};


class ExtendedOption : public Option
{
private:
      // Private member data and functions
public:     // Public property section

      // OPTION PARAMETERS PUBLIC PURELY FOR CONVENIENCE
      double r;           // Interest rate
      double sig;         // Volatility
      double K;           // Strike price
      double T;           // Expiry date
      double U;           // Current underlying price
      double b;           // Cost of carry
      string otyp;        // Option name (call, put)

public:     // Public functions
      ExtendedOption();
      ExtendedOption(const ExtendedOption& option2);
```

```
        ExtendedOption (const string& optionType);
        ExtendedOption (const string& optionType,
                                        const string& underlying);
        virtual ~ExtendedOption();

        ExtendedOption& operator = (const ExtendedOption& option2);

        // Functions that calculate option price and sensitivities
        double Price(double U) const;
        double Delta(double U) const;
        double Gamma(double U) const;
        double Vega(double U) const;
        double Theta(double U) const;
        double Rho(double U) const;
        double Coc(double U) const;
        double Elasticity(double percentageMovement, double U ) const;

        // Modifier functions
        void toggle();            // Change option type (C/P, P/C)
};
enum OptionValueType
        {Value, Delta, Gamma, Vega, Theta, Rho, Coc, Elasticity};
```

The class that presents information in Excel is given by:

```
class ExtendedOptionPresentation
{
private:
            ExtendedOption* curr;
            Range<double> r;          // Extent of x axis
            long nSteps;              // Number of subdivisions

            // Abscissa values
            Vector<double, long> XARR;
public:
    ExtendedOptionPresentation(ExtendedOption& option,
            const Range<double>& extent, long NumberSteps)
{
            r = extent;
            nSteps = NumberSteps;
            curr = &option;

            XARR = r.mesh(nSteps);
}

Vector<double, long> calculate(OptionValueType yval)
```

```cpp
{

    // Contains value at end-points
    Vector<double, long> result (nSteps+1, 1);

    if (yval == Value)
    {
        for (int j=XARR.MinIndex(); j<=XARR.MaxIndex(); j++)
        {

            result[j] = curr -> Price(XARR[j]);
        }

    }

    if (yval == Delta)
    {
        for (int j=XARR.MinIndex(); j<=XARR.MaxIndex(); j++)
        {

            result[j] = curr -> Delta(XARR[j]);
        }

    }

    if (yval == Gamma)
    {
        for (int j=XARR.MinIndex(); j<=XARR.MaxIndex(); j++)
        {

            result[j] = curr -> Gamma(XARR[j]);
        }
    }

    // MORE CODE HERE FOR OTHER GREEKS, SEE CD
}

void displayinExcel( OptionValueType yval)
{

        string text("Value");
        if (yval == Delta)
        {
                text = string("Delta");
        }
        if (yval == Gamma)
```

```
            {
                    text = string("Gamma");
            }

            // MORE CODE HERE FOR OTHER GREEKS, SEE CD

            Vector<double, long> yarr = calculate(yval);
            printOneExcel(XARR, yarr, text);
    }

};
```

This class has inline code and it is responsible for displaying option data in Excel. Here is a program to show how to use it:

```
int main()
{

        // Put option on a stock index
        ExtendedOption indexOption;
        indexOption.otyp = "P";
        indexOption.K = 95.0;
        indexOption.T = 0.5;
        indexOption.r = 0.06;
        indexOption.sig = 0.20;

        double q = 0.0; // 0.05;                     // Dividend yield
        //indexOption.b = indexOption.r - q;
        indexOption.b = indexOption.r; // stock

        // Sub-division of "underlying" interval
        Range<double> extent (0.00, 210.0);
        long NumberSteps = 210;

        ExtendedOptionPresentation myPresent(indexOption,
                                             extent, NumberSteps);
        OptionValueType val = Value;
        myPresent.displayinExcel(val);

        val = Delta;
        myPresent.displayinExcel(val);

        val = Gamma;
        myPresent.displayinExcel(val);

        val = Vega;
        myPresent.displayinExcel(val);
```

```
        val = Theta;
        myPresent.displayinExcel(val);

        val = Rho;
        myPresent.displayinExcel(val);

        val = Coc;
        myPresent.displayinExcel(val);

        return 0;
}
```

You can create a C++ project using the source files from the CD. Then you build and run the project, Excel will start and display the relevant data in line chart form.

## 24.6   FINITE DIFFERENCE METHOD

We have used the visualization package when approximating the Black Scholes partial differential equation using the Finite Difference Method (FDM). We have discussed this issue in some detail in Chapter 16 where we designed and implemented the problem using design patterns (see Duffy, 2004). In this section we discuss a second and improved version of Chapter 19 of Duffy (2004) in which we used exponentially fitted finite difference methods to approximate one-factor plain option problems. Again, source code is provided on the CD.

We summarise the steps that we execute in order to produce data from the finite difference scheme and display it in Excel:

1. Define the continuous problem (the Initial Boundary Value Problem)
2. Define the discrete problem (the Finite Difference Scheme)
3. Calculate option price
4. Calculate option sensitivities
5. Display results in Excel

We now walkthrough the C++ code that realises these steps. We repeat the descriptions of the steps in order to make the code more readable:

- Define the continuous problem (the Initial Boundary Value Problem)

```
// Set all ranges
Range<double> X(Xfrom,Xto);
Range<double> T(Yfrom,Yto);

// Declare all TwoVarDFunctions
TwoVarDFunction<double,double,double> Sigma(*sigma);
TwoVarDFunction<double,double,double> Mu(*mu);
TwoVarDFunction<double,double,double> Forcing(*forcing);
TwoVarDFunction<double,double,double> B(*b);

// Declare all AtomicDFunctions
AtomicDFunction<double,double> Ic(*IC); // Change from Call<->Put
```

```
AtomicDFunction<double,double> Bcr(*BCR);
AtomicDFunction<double,double> Bcl(*BCL);

// Declare the PDE
ParabolicPDE<double,double,double>
                pde(X,T,Sigma,Mu,B,Forcing,Ic,Bcl,Bcr);
```

- Define the discrete problem (the Finite Difference Scheme)

```
// Declare the finite difference scheme
int choice = 3;
cout << "1) Explicit Euler 2) Implicit Euler 3) Crank Nicolson ";
cin >> choice;

OptionType type = EuropeanCallType;

ParabolicFDM<double,double,double>
                FDM(pde,XINTERVALS,YINTERVALS,choice, type);
```

- Calculate option price

```
// Compute option prices
FDM.start();

// Retrieve and store option prices
Vector <double,long> result = FDM.line(); // Does include ENDS!!
```

- Calculate option sensitivities

```
Vector<double, long> xArr = FDM.xarr();
Vector<double, long> tArr = FDM.tarr();

double h = xArr[2] - xArr[1];
double k = tArr[2] - tArr[1];

// Create and fill Delta vector
Vector <double,long> DeltaMesh(xArr.Size()-2, xArr.MinIndex());
for (long kk=DeltaMesh.MinIndex();kk<=DeltaMesh.MaxIndex(); kk++)
{
      DeltaMesh[kk] = xArr[kk+1];
}

Vector <double,long> Delta(result.Size()-2,result.MinIndex());
for (long i = Delta.MinIndex(); i <= Delta.MaxIndex(); i++)
{
      Delta[i] = (result[i+1] - result[i])/(h);
}

// Create and fill Gamma vector
Vector <double,long>
```

```
            GammaMesh(DeltaMesh.Size()-2, DeltaMesh.MinIndex());
    for (long p=GammaMesh.MinIndex(); p<=GammaMesh.MaxIndex(); p++)
    {
        GammaMesh[p] = DeltaMesh[p+1];
    }


    Vector <double,long> Gamma(Delta.Size()-2, Delta.MinIndex());
    for (long n = Gamma.MinIndex(); n <= Gamma.MaxIndex(); n++)
    {
        Gamma[n] = (Delta[n+1] - Delta[n])/(h);
    }


    long NP1 = FDM.result().MaxRowIndex();
    long NP = FDM.result().MaxRowIndex() -1;


    Vector <double,long> Theta(result.Size(), result.MinIndex());
    for (long ii = Theta.MinIndex(); ii <= Theta.MaxIndex(); ii++)
    {
        Theta[ii] =
                -(FDM.result()(NP1, ii) -FDM.result()(NP, ii) )/k;
    }
```

- Display results in Excel

```
    try
    {
                printOneExcel(FDM.xarr(), result, string("Price"));
                printOneExcel(DeltaMesh, Delta, string("Delta"));
                printOneExcel(GammaMesh, Gamma, string("Gamma"));
                printOneExcel(FDM.xarr(), Theta, string("Theta"));

    }
    catch(DatasimException& e)
    {
                e.print();
                ExcelDriver& excel = ExcelDriver::Instance();
                excel.MakeVisible(true);
                long y = 1;
                excel.printStringInExcel(e.Message(), y, y, string("Err"));

                list<string> dump;
                dump.push_back(e.MessageDump()[0]);
                dump.push_back(e.MessageDump()[1]);
                dump.push_back(e.MessageDump()[2]);

                excel.printStringInExcel(dump, 1, 1, string("Err"));
```

```
            return 0;
    }

    return 0;
}
```

Again, you can run the program to produce output in Excel. You should experiment with the source code on the CD.

## 24.7  SUMMARY AND CONCLUSIONS

We have given an overview of C++ functionality for displaying structured data in Excel. In other words, we have produced functions to export vectors, matrices and tensors to Excel where they can be displayed in cellular or line graph form.

The visualisation package in this chapter is useful for a number of reasons. First, the package can be used in conjunction with numerical methods (for example, finite difference or finite element methods) by displaying the computational results in numerical or graphical form. Second, we can use Excel as a simple database by using it to persistently store data in sheets.

## 24.8  EXERCISES AND PROJECTS

1. Create a new suite of template functions that allow us to display STL data containers in Excel. The functions should be generic so that we can support as many specific data types as possible. You should start with the following container types:
   - Lists
   - Vectors
   - Maps

   In general the input that we need to generate a given chart is a list of pairs of elements where for each pair the first element is the name of a variable and the second element is its value. For example, for a call option we might wish to display the following values in a separate Excel sheet:
   - T 1.0
   - K 95.0
   - r 0.06
   - volatility 0.20
   - dividend 0.0

   as well as the data for the finite difference scheme:
   - Number of S steps 200
   - Number of time steps 100
   - Scheme Crank Nicolson

   Write a function that realises this requirement. The pairs will be written from top to bottom starting from a given position with the elements of each pair being written horizontally. You should be able to support the following input:

   ```
   map<string, string>
   ```

The advantage of this input possibility is that we can export many data types to Excel by first converting them to a string, for example Date objects.

The usefulness of this function lies in the fact that it is a record of the input data that you used in order to produce charts and cell data in Excel.

The objective of this exercise is to display the density, cumulative density and hazard functions for various values of $\alpha$ and $\beta$.

2. One of the features of the ExcelMechanisms functionality is that we must give context information in the form of function parameters. Instead of this approach, the objective of this exercise is to encapsulate this information in a class:

```
// ChartStructure.hpp
//
// Simple class to store essential information about a
// two d chart for Excel:
//
//
//           Actual data: Vector
//           Chart title
//           Horizontal and vertical texts
//           Legend text (describes the meaning of the chart line)
//
// NB: All code is inline and we use struct (all public members).
// It is more like a record than a class.
//
// (C) Datasim Education BV 2005
//

#ifndef ChartStructure_HPP
#define ChartStructure_HPP

#include <string>
#include <list>
#include <iostream>
using namespace std;
struct ChartStructure
{
            // Optimise later to work with pointers (get it right)
            Vector<double, long> xdata;
            Vector<double, long> ydata;

            string title;
            string horizontal;
            string vertical;
            string legend;

            // Default constructor, default text only
            ChartStructure()
```

```
        {

                title = string("Title");
                horizontal = string("X axis");
                vertical = string("Y axis");
                legend = string("Legend");
        }

        void print() const
        {
                cout << title << ", " << horizontal << ", "
                        << vertical << ", " << legend << endl;
        }

};

typedef list<ChartStructure> ChartStructureList;

#endif
```

Then we can use instances of this class as input to the mechanisms functionality.

Use the C++ code on the CD. Compile the code and create a test program.

What are the advantages of this approach when compared with the more procedural and less object-oriented approach as used in the Visualisation package?

# Motivating COM and Emulation in C++

## 25.1 INTRODUCTION AND OBJECTIVES

In this chapter we discuss a number of techniques in C++ that are useful to know if we are to understand *interface programming* in general and COM (component object model) in particular. The transition to COM for C++ programmers can be difficult and we hope to make this transition as easy as possible by showing both the similarities and differences between the two paradigms. To this end, we introduce the concept of multiple inheritance and we show how this mechanism is used as a foundation for COM. Furthermore, we create code that simulates COM interfaces. The code is not real COM but it gives us a feeling for what is to come. Finally, we discuss how to simulate interfaces using namespaces in combination with function pointers.

To conclude the chapter, we discuss some of the differences between object-oriented and component technologies. They are not the same, even though they have similar characteristics and can complement each other.

## 25.2 A SHORT HISTORY OF COM

COM grew out of earlier software developments within the Microsoft organisation. Microsoft developed OLE (Object Linking and Embedding) and the first version allowed clients and servers to communicate using DDE (Dynamic Data Exchange). DDE was built on top of the message-passing architecture of Windows. DDE had a number of weaknesses such as lack of robustness, response problems and it was hard to write DDE code that works properly. The solution to this problem was COM. COM was designed to resolve the problems with DDE and OLE.

Some of the early objectives of COM were:

- Transparent cross-platform interoperability: how can developers write components to run in-process or cross-process (and even cross-network) applications using a single programming model?
- Versioning: how to upgrade a component without having to upgrade other components?
- Language independence: how can components written in different languages interoperate?
- Binary-level reusability: how to create a component and how to ensure that these components will work with components from other developers?

## 25.3 AN INTRODUCTION TO MULTIPLE INHERITANCE (MI)

C++ is one of the few object-oriented languages that offers the developer the opportunity to derive a class from two or more base classes. The simplest and most obvious use of MI is to glue two otherwise unrelated classes together as part of the implementation of a third class (Stroustrup, 1997). In this case we call this the *Orthogonal Base Class* scenario. In the sequel

we shall give examples showing the essence of multiple inheritance and how it will be used
as an important concept in COM.

We take the case of a class D1 that is derived from two independent classes B1 and B2. The
interfaces for the base classes are:

```
class B1
{ // Base class
public:
        B1() { cout << "B1 instantiated\ n"; }
        virtual ~B1() { cout << "arrivederci B1\ n";}
};

class B2
{ // Base class
public:
        B2() { cout << "B2 instantiated\ n"; }
        virtual ~B2() { cout << "arrivederci B2\ n";}
};
```

We now create a new class by deriving it from B1 and B2:

```
class D1 : public B1, public B2
{ // Derived class
public:
        D1() : B2(), B1()
        {
                cout << "D1 instantiated\ n";
        }
        virtual ~D1() { cout << "arrivederci D1\ n";}
};
```

In other words, D1 inherits publicly from B1 and B2 and its instances are initialised in this
order even though we call the base class constructors in a different order. We now create an
instance as follows:

```
        D1 d1;
```

The output from this statement is given as follows (notice the calling order of constructors):

```
B1 instantiated
B2 instantiated
D1 instantiated
```

We now turn our attention to the case where the base classes have implemented the same
member function (that is, the signature is the same in each class but the definition of the
function is implemented differently of course). We could call this the *Semi-Orthogonal Base
Class* scenario. The interfaces are defined by:

```
class Base1
{ // Base class
public:
        Base1() { cout << "Base1 instantiated\ n"; }
        virtual ~Base1() { cout << "arrivederci Base1\ n"; }

        virtual void print() const {cout << "Print a Base1\ n"; }
};

class Base2
{ // Base class
public:
        Base2() { cout << "Base2 instantiated\ n"; }
        virtual ~Base2() { cout << "arrivederci Base2\ n"; }

        virtual void print() const {cout << "Print a Base2\ n"; }

};
```

In this case we see that both classes implement the same function. We now derive from these classes but we do not re-implement this common member function. The interface is much the same as before:

```
class Derived1 : public Base1, public Base2
{ // Derived class
public:
        Derived1() : Base2(), Base1()
        {
                cout << "Derived1 instantiated\ n";
        }

        virtual ~Derived1() { cout << "arrivederci Derived1\ n"; }
};
```

Since we are still using inheritance we might have a problem in the following sense; if we create an instance of the derived class and we call the print() function, the question is which one will it call? The answer is that the call is ambiguous. To this end, the following code will not compile:

```
Derived1 d2;
// d2.print(); AMBIGUOUS
```

In order to resolve the ambiguity we must explicitly specify the base class whose function we wish to call. To this end, we use the scope resolution operator as follows:

```
d2.Base1::print();
d2.Base2::print();
```

This code works now but we must decide which route to take as it were. The choice is not difficult in this case but it might become difficult for more complex cases.

We now discuss the following new case that we call the *Common Base Class* scenario. In this case our two original base classes are both derived from a single base class containing member data (we have made it public purely for convenience). The interface of this new class is:

```
class BigBase
{
public:

        // Common data member for all children
        int val;

        BigBase()
        { cout << "BigBase instantiated\ n";
          val = 10;
        }
        virtual ~BigBase() { cout << "arrivederci BigBase\ n";}
};
```

The two 'intermediate' classes are defined as follows:

```
class Base11 : public BigBase
{ // Base class
public:
        Base11() { cout << "Base11 instantiated\ n"; }
        virtual ~Base11() { cout << "arrivederci Base11\ n";}

};
```

```
class Base12 : public BigBase
{ // Base class
public:
        Base12() { cout << "Base12 instantiated\ n"; }
        virtual ~Base12() { cout << "arrivederci Base12\ n";}

};
```

The interface of the derived class is given by:

```
class Derived11: public Base11, public Base12
{ // Derived class
public:
        Derived11() : Base12(), Base11()
        {
                cout << "Derived11 instantiated\ n";
        }

        virtual ~Derived11() { cout << "arrivederci Derived11\ n";}
};
```

We can conclude (correctly) that `Derived11` inherits the member data from `BigBase` but a problem is that this data can be accessed in two different ways. To this end, the following code will not compile:

```
Derived11 d11;
//d11.val = 3; // Ambiguous
```

Instead, we must explicitly specify which path to take as it were\. In this case the following is correct:

```
d11.Base11::val = 1;
d11.Base12::val = 2;
```

The problem just mentioned can be resolved by defining so-called *virtual base classes*. As before, we define the base class:

```
// Group IV: Resolving problems with Common Base Class
class BigBaseA
{
public:

        // Common data member for all children
        int val;

        BigBaseA()
        { cout << "BigBaseA instantiated\ n";
          val = 10;
        }
        virtual ~BigBaseA() { cout << "arrivederci BigBaseA\ n";}
};
```

But we now define new derived classes as follows:

```
class Base11A : virtual public BigBaseA
{ // Base class
public:
        Base11A() { cout << "Base11A instantiated\ n"; }
        virtual ~Base11A() { cout << "arrivederci Base11A\ n";}

};

class Base12A : virtual public BigBaseA
{ // Base class
public:
        Base12A() { cout << "Base12A instantiated\ n"; }
        virtual ~Base12A() { cout << "arrivederci Base12A\ n";}


};
```

Finally, the derived class is defined as:

```
class Derived11A: public Base11A, public Base12A
{ // Derived class
public:
      Derived11A() : Base12A(), Base11A()
      {
            cout << "Derived11A instantiated\ n";
      }

      virtual ~Derived11A() { cout << "arrivederci Derived11A\ n";}
};
```

Having done this work, there is no longer any ambiguity when accessing member data, as the following code shows:

```
Derived11A d11A;
d11A.val = 3; // No Ambiguity
```

Of course, it is still possible to access the member data as follows:

```
d11A.Base11A::val = 1;
d11A.Base12A::val = 2;
```

This now completes our discussion of multiple inheritance. We use this knowledge in the next section.

## 25.4   INTERFACES AND MULTIPLE INHERITANCE

In this section we introduce the concept of an *interface* and its analogies with multiple inheritance in C++. In particular, we are only interested in a special subset of problems, namely:

- Base classes having no member data
- Base classes having only pure virtual member functions

These kinds of classes form the ingredients that allow us to define interfaces in COM. To this end, Microsoft uses the keyword `interface` that is in reality a synonym:

```
#define interface struct
```

Recall that a struct is a class in which all members are public by default. In general, a struct is useful for classes all of whose data is public.

We now discuss a feature in COM called the *Pascal Calling Convention*. To this end, Microsoft has defined the extension `_stdcall`. Functions using this convention remove parameters from the stack before they return to the caller. Pascal functions handle stack cleanup in the same way. With C and C++, on the other hand, the caller cleans up the stack instead of the function. Virtually all functions offered by COM interfaces using the so-called *standard naming convention*.

We now give our first examples of simulated interfaces. To this end, we define interfaces that have some relevance to Quantitative Finance. We define our first interfaces as follows:

```
interface IInstrument
{ // Interface for all derivative products

        virtual double _stdcall price(double S) = 0;
};

interface IHedge
{ // Functions for SimpleOption option sensitivities


        virtual double _stdcall delta(double S) = 0;
        virtual double _stdcall gamma(double S) = 0;
};
```

These two interfaces are specifications for option pricing and hedging functionality, respectively. In general, they define functions that return a value based on some given value of the underlying price. We see that the interfaces have no member data and all functions are *pure*.

We now wish to create a fictitious class that implements the above two interfaces. To this end, we use multiple inheritance:

```
class SimpleOption : public IInstrument, public IHedge
{ // Simple class to show how interfaces work. Phoney
  // output, just for convenience

public:

        // Implement interface IInstrument
        virtual double _stdcall price(double S) { return S; }

        // Implement interface IHedge
        virtual double _stdcall delta(double S) { return 0.5; };
        virtual double _stdcall gamma(double S) { return 0.02; };
};
```

Here we see that this class must implement all three functions if we wish to create its instances. Of course, we can create other classes that implement these interface functions, for example:

```
class SimpleOption2 : public IInstrument, public IHedge
{ // Simple class to show how interfaces work. Phoney
  // output, just for convenience

public:

        // Implement interface IInstrument
        virtual double _stdcall price(double S) { return S* ::exp(-0.1);}
        // Implement interface IHedge
```

```
        virtual double __stdcall delta(double S) { return 1.0 / S; };
        virtual double __stdcall gamma(double S) { return 0.0; };
};
```

The next question is: what is the added advantage of using interfaces? One answer is *standardisation*; the interface defines (in an unambiguous way) what clients should expect. The consequence is that we can write reusable functions that work under all circumstances. We take the following simple example:

```
void print(interface IInstrument* i1, interface IHedge* i2, double S)
{
        cout << i1 -> price(S) << endl;
        cout << i2 -> delta(S) << endl;
        cout << i2 -> gamma(S) << endl;
        cout << endl << endl;
}
```

We can then call function for any class that implements the interfaces IInstrument and IHedge.

Here is code to show how to use these interfaces in applications. An understanding of it will prepare us for COM in the next chapter.

```
int main()
{
        SimpleOption* option = new SimpleOption;
        SimpleOption2* option2 = new SimpleOption2;

        // Get an IInstrument pointer.
        IInstrument* instrument = option;

        double value = option->price(95.0);

        // Get an IHedge pointer.
        IHedge* hedge = option;

        double value2 = hedge->delta(95.0);
        double value3 = hedge->gamma(95.0);

        double val = 15.0;
        print(option, option, val);

        double val2 = 20.0;
        print(option2, option2, val2);

        delete option;
        delete option2;

        return 0 ;
}
```

## 25.5   VIRTUAL FUNCTION TABLES

We now look under the bonnet in order to describe the mechanics of how C++ pure abstract base classes implement COM interfaces.

When defining an abstract base class we are in fact defining the layout of a block of memory. For example, the interface:

```
interface IHedge
{ // Functions for SimpleOption option sensitivities

        virtual double __stdcall delta(double S) = 0;
        virtual double __stdcall gamma(double S) = 0;
};
```

has two parts. The first part, called the *Virtual Function Table* (or vtbl for short) is an array of pointers to the implementations of the virtual functions. The second part is a pointer to the vtbl, also called the vtbl pointer. In a sense we have a double pointer; the vtbl pointer points to the vtbl which in its turn points to a function pointers (in the next chapter we shall see how this feature is implemented as a void** type).

In general, the memory layout for a COM interface is the same as the memory layout that the C++ compiler generates for an abstract base class. The memory layout of a COM interface follows the COM specification.

We shall discuss virtual function tables in more detail in the next chapter. In particular, we shall remark that only one vtbl is created for a class that implements several interfaces. Finally, we remark that multiple instances of a class share the same vtbl.

## 25.6   SUMMARY

We have given an introduction to a number of advanced topics in C++ that are used in COM. Among these is multiple inheritance (MI) and how COM uses it to define interfaces. We also discussed memory layout of abstract base classes and interfaces because COM adopts the C++ specification for this.

We also gave a number of examples in C++ to show how to implement interfaces. In particular, we concentrated on a number of issues:

- We implement COM interfaces in C++ as pure abstract base classes
- A single COM component can implement multiple interfaces
- A C++ class can use multiple inheritance to implement a component that supports multiple interfaces

In the next chapter we shall discuss interfaces in relation to COM.

# COM Fundamentals

## 26.1 INTRODUCTION AND OBJECTIVES

In this chapter we introduce COM. In particular, we discuss interfaces in COM, how to define them and how to use them in simple applications. We also give an overview of the famous IUnknown interface. This is the interface that must be implemented by all COM components and it has three methods defined in it. First, it has a method that allows us to determine if a component supports a given interface. This feature allows us to navigate in a component. Second, COM uses the concept of *reference counting* to determine if a component is being used by a client. If a component is not being used then it can be released. In short, IUnknown provides methods for these features.

## 26.2 INTERFACES IN COM

Interfaces are central to COM. One advantage of using interfaces is that they can be standardised. In other words, a developer can define an interface once and use it after that. Furthermore, other developers know what to expect because they know that the interface will not change.

COM has defined standard interfaces for many aspects of the software development process. In particular, many common activities can be described as interfaces:

- Marshalling and unmarshalling of data between processes
- Persistence and storage of data
- Manipulating properties (name/value pairs)
- IDispatch and Dispinterfaces in Visual Basic
- Interfaces to Excel
- and many more

In general, you do not have to worry about these interfaces but we thought it a good idea to at least mention their existence.

## 26.3 THE IUnknown INTERFACE

Interfaces are sacred in COM. Of course, once we have created a component it would be useful if we could use it in applications. But how do we know what a component has to offer? How do we get an entry point as it were to a component? The answer lies in the fact that every component must implement the IUnknown interface defined as follows:

```
interface IUnknown
{
        virtual HRESULT _stdcall QueryInterface (const IID& iid,
                void** ppv) = 0;
```

```
        virtual ULONG _stdcall Addref() = 0;
        virtual ULONG _stdcall Release() = 0;
};
```

Let us now look at this interface in some detail. We first examine the data types that are used in the interface:

- ULONG: this is a synonym for the unsigned long type
- HRESULT: this is a 32-bit number that specifies the success, warning or error condition of some method. In this particular case we use it when we query for a particular interface. We shall discuss this in more detail later
- IID: this is a so-called interface identifier structure and it is a unique way of identifying interfaces.

Having discussed the data types we now describe what each function in IUnknown does. To commence, QueryInterface() has two input parameters. The first parameter is the interface that we wish to access. The second parameter is the address of the actual interface and is in fact a pointer to a virtual function table, whence the double pointer. Finally, the return value is of type HRESULT. Some possible return values are:

- S_OK: the function succeeded
- S_FAIL: unspecified failure
- E_NOINTERFACE: component does not support the requested interface

There are several other possible return values but we do not discuss them here. In general, we are only interested in whether the function has succeeded or not. To this end, we use the macros SUCCEEDED() and FAILED(), each taking a HRESULT value as input and returning a Boolean.

We now discuss the functions in IUnknown that have to do with *reference counting*. In general, we wish to control the lifetime of a component. We create a component in much the same way as in the previous chapter. But when do we delete it and how? Well, instead of deleting components directly we inform the component when we need to use an interface and also when we are finished using that interface. Basically, we do some counting to keep tabs on a component using a counter:

- Increment the counter by one when a client uses a component
- Decrement the counter by one when we are finished with an interface

When the counter is equal to zero then we know that no more clients are using the interface.

## 26.4  USING IUnknown

We now give a working example of how to implement IUnknown in COM. We use the interfaces and classes from the previous chapter.

```
////////////////
// Interfaces
interface IInstrument: IUnknown
{
        virtual double _stdcall price(double S) = 0 ;
};
```

```
interface IHedge : IUnknown
{
     virtual double _stdcall delta(double S) = 0 ;
};

// A different interface that the current components do not implement
interface IDraw : IUnknown
{
     virtual void _stdcall draw() = 0 ;
} ;

// Forward references for GUIDs
extern const IID IID_IInstrument;
extern const IID IID_IHedge;
extern const IID IID_IDraw;

// IIDs
//
static const IID IID_IInstrument=
     {0x32bb8320, 0xb41b, 0x11cf,
     {0xa6, 0xbb, 0x0, 0x80, 0xc7, 0xb2, 0xd6, 0x82}} ;

static const IID IID_IHedge =
     {0x32bb8321, 0xb41b, 0x11cf,
     {0xa6, 0xbb, 0x0, 0x80, 0xc7, 0xb2, 0xd6, 0x82}} ;

static const IID IID_IDraw =
     {0x32bb8322, 0xb41b, 0x11cf,
     {0xa6, 0xbb, 0x0, 0x80, 0xc7, 0xb2, 0xd6, 0x82}} ;

// Component
//
class SimpleOption : public IInstrument,
          public IHedge
{
     //IUnknown implementation
     virtual HRESULT _stdcall QueryInterface(const IID& iid, void**
ppv) ;
     virtual ULONG _stdcall AddRef() { return 0 ;}
     virtual ULONG _stdcall Release() { return 0 ;}

     // Interface IInstrument implementation
     virtual double _stdcall price(double S)
     {
          cout << "Price: " << S << endl;
          return S;
     }
```

```
    // Interface IHedge implementation
    virtual double __stdcall delta(double S)
    {
        cout << "Delta: " << S * 0.1 << endl ;
        return S * 0.1;
    }
};


HRESULT __stdcall SimpleOption::QueryInterface(const IID& iid,
                                                    void** ppv)
{

    if (iid == IID_IUnknown)
    {
        cout << endl <<
                    "QueryInterface: Return pointer to IUnknown.";
        *ppv = static_cast<IInstrument*>(this) ;
    }
    else if (iid == IID_IInstrument)
    {
        cout << endl <<
            "QueryInterface: Return pointer to IInstrument";
        *ppv = static_cast<IInstrument*>(this) ;
    }
    else if (iid == IID_IHedge)
    {
        cout << endl << "QueryInterface: Return pointer to IHedge";
        *ppv = static_cast<IHedge*>(this) ;
    }
    else
    {
        cout << endl << "QueryInterface: Interface not supported";
        *ppv = 0 ;
        return E_NOINTERFACE ;
    }

    reinterpret_cast<IUnknown*>(*ppv)->AddRef() ;

    return S_OK ;
}


//
// Creation function
//
IUnknown* CreateInstance()
```

```
{
    IUnknown* pI = static_cast<IInstrument*>(new SimpleOption) ;
    pI->AddRef() ;
    return pI ;
}
```

### 26.4.1   Testing the interface

We now give an example using COM interfaces and COM objects.

```
HRESULT hr ;

IUnknown* pIUnknown = CreateInstance() ;

cout << endl << "Client: Get interface IInstrument.";

IInstrument* p1= 0 ;
hr = pIUnknown->QueryInterface(IID_IInstrument, (void**)&p1) ;
if (SUCCEEDED(hr))
{
    cout << endl << "Client: Succeeded getting IInstrument";
    double S = 95.0;
    p1->price(S);
}

cout << endl << "Client: Get interface IHedge";

IHedge* p2 = 0;
hr = pIUnknown->QueryInterface(IID_IHedge, (void**)&p2) ;
if (SUCCEEDED(hr))
{
    cout << endl << "Client: Succeeded getting IHedge";
    p2->delta(15.0) ;
}

cout << endl << "Client: Ask for an unsupported interface.";

IDraw* p3 = 0;
hr = pIUnknown->QueryInterface(IID_IDraw, (void**)&p3) ;
if (SUCCEEDED(hr))
{
    cout << endl
        << "Client: Succeeded in getting interface IDraw";
    p3->draw() ;
}
else
{
    cout << endl << "No inteface IDraw supported:";
}
```

```
cout << endl
    << "Client:Get IHedge from interface IInstrument";

IHedge* p4 = 0 ;
hr = p1->QueryInterface(IID_IHedge, (void**)&p4);
if (SUCCEEDED(hr))
{

    cout << endl << "Client: Succeeded getting IHedge";
    p4->delta(15.0);
}
```

## 26.5   DEFINING NEW VERSIONS OF COMPONENTS

At some stage during a software project you may need to change an interface in some way. Some examples are:

- Add a function to, or remove a function from an interface
- Change the order of functions in an interface
- Modify a function's parameters in some way
- Modify the return type of a function

A golden rule in COM is that you should never change an interface. This is because COM is a binary standard and all information is stored at fixed addresses. If you wish to modify an interface, for example IHedge, then you should create a new version of it called IHedge2, for example.

## 26.6   SUMMARY

We have given a compact introduction to a number of key features of COM. The most important concern was determining if a component has implemented a given interface. In other words, we can query a component at run-time. To this end, we note that each component must implement the IUnknown interface. This interface describes the lifecycle of a component:

- Create a component and increment its reference count
- Query a component to determine which interfaces it supports
- Decrement the reference count to a component when a client releases a reference to it

Using COM and Active Template Library (ATL) for Excel projects is given in Duffy (2004).

# References

Black, F. and Scholes, M. (1973) The Pricing of Options and Corporate Liabilities, *Journal of Political Economy*, **81**, 637–654.

Boyle, P. (1977) Options: A Monte Carlo Approach, *Journal of Financial Economics*, **4**, 323–338.

Buschmann, F., Meunier, R., Rohnert, H., Sommerlad, P. and Stal, M. (1996) *Pattern-Oriented Software Architecture: A System of Patterns*, John Wiley & Sons Ltd, Chichester.

Carr, P. and Madan, D. B. (1999) Option valuation using the fast Fourier transform, *Journal of Computational Finance* Volume 2, Number 4, Summer.

Clewlow, L. and Strickland, C. (1998) *Implementing Derivatives Models*, John Wiley and Sons Ltd, Chichester.

Cox, J. and Rubinstein, M. (1985) *Options Markets*, Prentice-Hall, New York.

Cox, J., Ross, S. and Rubinstein, M. (1979) Option Pricing: A Simplified Approach, *Journal of Financial Economics* 7, 229–263.

Dahlquist, G. and Björck, Å. (1974) *Numerical Methods*, Prentice-Hall, Englewood Cliffs NJ.

Duffy, D. J. (1980) *Uniformly convergent difference schemes for problems with a small parameter in the leading derivative*. PhD Thesis, Trinity College, Dublin, Ireland.

Duffy, D. (1995) *From Chaos to Classes*, McGraw-Hill, London.

Duffy, D. J. (2004) *Financial Instrument Pricing in C++*, John Wiley and Sons Ltd, Chichester.

Duffy, D. J. (2006) *Finite Difference Methods in Financial Engineering, a Partial Differential Equation Approach*, John Wiley and Sons Ltd, Chichester.

Eysenck, M. W. and Keane, M. T. (2000) *Cognitive Psychology*, Psychology Press.

Fabozzi, F. (1993) *Bond Markets, Analysis and Strategies*, Prentice Hall, Englewood Cliffs NJ.

Foley, J. D., van Dam, A., Feiner, S. K. and Hughes, J. F. (1990) *Computer Graphics*, Addison-Wesley, Reading MA.

Frege, G. (1952) On sense and reference. In P. Geach and M. Black (Eds), *Translations from the philosophical writings of Gottlieb Frege*, Basic Blackwell, Oxford.

Glassermann, P. (2004) *Monte Carlo Methods in Financial Engineering*, Springer, New York.

GOF: Gamma, E., Helm, R., Johnson, R. and Vlissides, J. (1995) *Design Patterns, Elements of Reusable Object-Oriented Software*, Addison-Wesley, Reading MA.

Haug, E. G. (1998) *The Complete Guide to Option Pricing Formulas*, McGraw-Hill New York.

Heston, S. L. (1993) A Closed-Form Solution for Options with Stochastic Volatility with Applications to Bond and Currency Options *The Review of Financial Studies* Volume 6, Number 2, 327–343.

Hull, J. (2006) *Options, Futures and other Derivative Securities*, Prentice-Hall, Englewood Cliffs NJ.

Jaeckel, P. (2002) *Monte Carlo Methods in Finance*, John Wiley and Sons Ltd, Chichester.

Keiler, H. B. (1992) *Numerical Methods for Two-Point Boundary Value Problems*, Dover, New York.

Kernighan, B. and Ritchie, D.M. (1988) (K & R 1988) *The C Programming Language*, Prentice-Hall, Englewood Cliffs NJ.

Kloeden, P., Platen, E. and Schurz, H. (1994) *Numerical Solution of SDE Through Computer Experiments*, Springer, Berlin.

Landin, J. (1969) *An Introduction to Algebraic Structures*, Dover, New York.

Moore, R. E. (1966) *Interval Analysis*, Prentice-Hall, Englewood Cliffs NJ.

Moore, R. E. (1979) *Methods and Analysis of Interval, Analysis*, SIAM, Philadelphia.

Pauling, L. and Bright Wilson, E. Jr. (1963) *Introduction to Quantum Mechanics with Applications to Chemistry*, McGraw-Hill, New York.

Press, W. H., Teukolsky, S. A., Vetterling, W. T. and Flannery, B. P (2002) *Numerical Recipes in C++*, Cambridge University Press, Cambridge.

Rudin, W. (1970) *Real and Complex Analysis*, McGraw-Hill, New London.

Scheid, F. (1968) *Numerical Analysis*, Schaum's Outline Series, New York.

Sobol, I. M. (2004) *A Primer for the Monte Carlo Method*, CRC Press, Boca Raton.

Spiegel, M. (1999) *Complex Variables*, Schaum's Outline Series, New York.

Stoer, J. and Bulirsch, R. (1980) *Introduction to Numerical Analysis*, Springer-Verlag, New York.

Stroustrup, B. (1997) *The C++ Programming Language* (3rd Edition), Addison-Wesley, Reading MA.

Topper, J. (2005) *Financial Engineering with Finite Elements*, John Wiley and Sons Ltd, Chichester.

Volkovyskii, L. I., Lunts, G. L. and Aramanovich, I. G. (1965) *A Collection of Problems on Complex Analysis*, Dover, New York.

Wilmott, P. (1998) *Derivatives: The Theory and Practice of Financial Engineering*, John Wiley and Sons Ltd, Chichester.

Zhang, P. G. (1998) *Exotic Options: A Guide to Second-Generation Options* (2nd Edition), World Scientific, New York.

# Index

*Index compiled by Terry Halliday*

Printed and bound by CPI Group (UK) Ltd, Croydon, CR0 4YY

28/10/2024

14581367-0001